MW00377534

SUBVERSION

THE DEFINITIVE HISTORY OF UNDERGROUND CINEMA

SUBVERSION

THE DEFINITIVE HISTORY OF UNDERGROUND CINEMA

DUNCAN REEKIE

WALLFLOWER PRESS
LONDON & NEW YORK

First published in Great Britain in 2007 by
Wallflower Press
6 Market Place, London W1W 8AF
www.wallflowerpress.co.uk

Copyright © Duncan Reekie 2007

The moral right of Duncan Reekie to be identified as the author of this work has
been asserted in accordance with the Copyright, Designs and Patents Act of 1988.

All rights reserved. No part of this publication may be reproduced, stored in a retrieval system,
or transported in any form or by any means, electronic, mechanical, photocopying, recording
or otherwise, without the prior permission of both the copyright owners and the above publisher
of this book.

A catalogue record for this book is available from the British Library.

ISBN 978-1-905674-21-3 (pbk)
ISBN 978-1-905674-22-0 (hbk)

Book design by Elsa Mathern

Printed and bound in Poland; produced by Polskabook

CONTENT

LIST OF ILLUSTRATIONS

FOREWORD

In the West the desire for popular access to professional filmmaking technology has been realised. The advent of cheap digital video cameras along with simplified editing and animation software means that practically anyone with enough time and initiative, and a meagre budget, can now produce broadcast-quality moving images with sync-sound. As an integrated element of broader digital media innovations, the development of web-based video, DVD technology and cheap video projection, there is now the potential for a radically new type of cinema. No longer the mass productions of a centralised transnational industry but a free anarchic international network of local low-/no-budget producers; no longer the consensual epics of corporate capitalism but a fabulous explosion of deviant subjectivities; a free democratic cinema. But the idea of a free cinema is not new; it has been a hope anticipated in a historical conflict almost as old as cinema itself. This complex struggle is cut with repression, paradox and irony, and it is not over. Although access to technology has been a key factor it is by no means the only or even the central one; the fight for a free cinema is cultural, social and political. My purpose in unravelling this history is to define Underground Cinema and expose this discord.

Since the turn of the twenty-first century there has been an increasing range of critical writing which has attempted to document Underground Cinema, but almost all of it has mistaken the Underground for a vague film genre, indistinct from an intersecting cluster of categories including cult features, exploitation movies, art-house cinema, avant-garde films and so on.[1] However, Underground Cinema is not a glamorous catch-all, but a distinct and continuous cultural movement in the history of cinema; it is that movement which has sought to liberate and develop a revolutionary popular cinema.

The focus and context of the history that follows is London between the late 1980s and 2007, since that is the site of my engagement; it is where I have been active as an Underground filmmaker and cinema organiser. But the signifigance and utility of this work is cosmopolitan and allegorical.

This book is a direct extension of 15 years of work as an activist and filmmaker in the London Underground Cinema movement. Although my argument is informed by academic study, its core was formed in practice, participation and experience: making films, live performance, organising cinema events, teaching digital media production, academic research and writing, and producing graphic and propaganda material for the Underground Cinema movement. This is not a list of discrete and autonomous activities, but rather aspects of an interlocking holistic praxis, every component of which overlaps, informs and influences every other. My praxis is subjective and chaotic; it is implicated in a complex system of political contingencies; there is no cool objective vantage point outside the system – there is no alternative, no independence, there is only agency. I am writing as an agent from inside the Underground. However, this should not be taken as a transgression of established experimental film and video history since many of the key texts of British and American experimental film were written by activists and filmmakers, including Jonas Mekas, David Curtis, Malcolm Le Grice, Stephen Dwoskin, Amos Vogel, Peter Gidal and Peter Wollen. The subversion of my method is not my agency, it is my declaration of agency against the phoney objectivity and hidden agency of established experimental film and video history.

Duncan Reekie
London
September 2007

Thanks to everyone who helped in the writing of this book, friends and foes alike

For Mary B.

Introduction

THE DECEPTIVE TYPOLOGY OF EXPERIMENTAL FILM AND VIDEO

The structure of the history that follows is complex and oblique. Rather than a progressive and discrete separation of subject areas, the chapters follow the formation and historical trajectory of a cluster of interrelated cultural currents and tendencies. Rather than a linear chronology of cause and effect or the mapping of decisive historical divisions, this history charts a spiral of similarities, continuities and transitions which advance around and towards the resurgence of the new Underground.

(Re)defining the Underground involves a complicated unlocking and historical recontextualisation of terms. It requires not only a comprehensive investigation and reformulation of accepted academic critical typology, but also the exploration of cultural forms which would traditionally be considered inappropriate to the study of experimental film and video. The breadth and density of my argument ranges from the history of popular theatre and literature, to nineteenth-century French Utopian Socialism, William Morris and the Folklore movement, the function of avant-garde art, the amateur ciné movement, the origins of state art funding, bohemian cabaret and the student revolutions of 1968. This fluidity in turn requires certain critical terms to remain relatively fixed. 'Experimental' is deployed in this book as a broad inclusive expression to designate all the film and video makers, movements, work and practices which have consciously sought diversification against or within established film culture. By diversification I mean not only innovation but also opposition, alternativity, decentralisation, autonomy, hybridisation, transgression or reaction. Experimental is the term which covers the broadest range of work. It refers to both process and product, adapts easily as a noun and an adjective, and it has been accepted by a significant number of divergent film movements and theorists as a transcendent historical term.[1] Experimental in this context would not be limited to formal experimentation but would include experiments in narrative, acting technique, sound, *mise-en-scène*, technology, working practices, distribution, exhibition and every and any aspect of film/video. Moreover, whereas institutionally the avant-garde and the independent film and video sector have defined themselves against or outside the mainstream of dominant commercial popular cinema and television, this definition of experimental film/video would not automatically preclude such work within popular cinema, or subcultural forms which have historically been misinterpreted or omitted from histories of avant-garde and independent film/video, crucially Underground cinema, but also amateur filmmaking, cult cinema, club visuals, pornography and surf movies. Further, this definition of experimental should not enforce connotations of scientific objectivity but should allow practices of irrationality, playfulness, instinct, leisure and subjectivity. Finally, whilst many experimental film/video makers and movements have been involved in political struggle and whilst many have claimed that their practice is a radical political activity, there can be no automatic equivalence between experimental film and a significant struggle for the democratisation of film culture. Experimental film/video can have no essential moral or political value, since, as I intend to demonstrate, experimental filmmakers have frequently advocated radical politics whilst actually pioneering new methods to maintain and modernise bourgeois authority.

Against a transcendental definition of experimental film and video, other key contemporary terms must be understood as relative and specific. The first British 'Underground Cinema' lasted less than a decade as both a movement and a cultural category. It blossomed in the counter-culture of the early 1960s, but by the early 1970s it had been forsaken by its own activists. By the late 1970s it was dismissed as an adolescent phase of the avant-garde movement which emerged from the London Film-makers' Co-operative, and/or the Independent Film movement which developed from the federation of the avant-garde and the radical Agit-prop collectives of the late 1960s. Throughout the 1970s various activists and theorists used the terms 'avant-garde' and 'independent' as interchangeable, but by the end of the decade a clear terminological distinction had developed; 'avant-garde film and video' had come to mean specifically film and video made by artists, whilst 'independent film and video' identified the development of a broader movement which included the avant-garde, but also diverse makers, practices and genres conceived as independent of the ideological and industrial structures of both commercial cinema and television, and the state broadcasting network of the British Broadcasting Corporation (BBC).[2] This independent movement came to include a range of sub-movements and radical interest groups including regional media workshops, community video makers, leftist film collectives, women filmmakers, black filmmakers, gay and lesbian filmmakers, radical documentary makers, artists and animators. During the late 1970s and early 1980s the independent movement secured an extensive infrastructure of both regional and national state funding and distribution and participated in the development of Channel 4, cable television and the reform of the television and cinematic trade unions. But as the independent movement expanded the avant-garde became increasingly isolated, arcane and bitter.[3] By the late 1980s British avant-garde film and video had become a historical term used only in a contemporary sense by the most die-hard adepts. It was consigned to history along with the terms 'abstract film', 'expanded cinema', 'alternative cinema', 'parallel cinema', 'non-narrative film', 'absolute film', 'non-objective film', 'formal film' and 'Structural-Materialist film'. The eventual adoption of the term 'artists' film and video' by the key state agencies in the 1990s finally accomplished and recognised the process begun with the shift from underground to avant-garde; the legitimisation of a new art.

Meanwhile the broader independent movement lost its identity in the industrial, technological and organisational transformations of the 1980s. With the emergence of Channel 4 and the British Film Institute (BFI) as major independent feature-film producers and the massive expansion of independent production companies commissioned to make programmes for Channel 4, cable, satellite and eventually the BBC, the concept of independence from a commercial mainstream became ever more difficult to rationalise. To be an independent film/video maker was no longer an act of conscious political autonomy or radical opposition; it was to be a freelancer in the deregulated media industry.[4] By the mid-1990s leading independent activists and agencies were questioning the contemporary relevance of the concept of independence and beginning to historicise the movement.[5] Nevertheless, although the movement has lost its ideological integrity there remains a complex national network of independent film/video agencies and institutions which is now so dependent on state funding that it can be identified as a sector of the state. It is the 'independent sector' but it is not independent.

This book will also address the claims and strategies of radical film/cultural theory. By radical I mean that cluster of Marxist, Marxian, Socialist and libertarian ideologies that seek a revolutionary egalitarian and democratic transformation of society. Nowadays academic libraries and bookshops are loaded with books and journals of radical film/cultural theory: Marxist analysis, post-Marxist analysis, structuralist analysis, poststructural deconstruction, psychoanalytical film theory, feminist film theory, queer film theory, black film theory, postcolonial film theory, cultural studies, postmodern analysis, white studies, post-theory and so on. As a genre, this literature legitimises its radicalism through the dispassionate authority of academic objectivity. Against this conventional and often bogus objectivity I choose engagement and indiscretion.

I studied film theory at college and university in the 1980s because I loved cinema and I wanted to make radical experimental films. I thought that if I learnt how to theoretically deconstruct film I could use these techniques to construct new films of my own. But the radical film theory I encountered was composed of arcane jargon and intensely complex linguistic, psychoanalytic and philosophical references, and it seemed to me that it was riddled with inconsistencies and fundamental paradoxes. I could not understand how these analytic models related to radical filmmaking and I was constantly frustrated by the ever-shifting fashions and terrain of contemporary theory. After university I gave up theory and started to make short no-budget films and to apply for state production funding, only to discover that the state-funded independent sector was legitimised and structured by the very theoretical discourses I had struggled with as a student. I began to understand that the independent sector was actually the audio/visual element of a broader state project engaged in the integrated production, distribution and exhibition of a legitimate film/video culture. With this revelation I began to make films which were designed to subvert and implode the independent arena and its theoretical base. Eventually this subversive project forced me to investigate and engage with the academic institutions I loathed. I became a participant observer in the realm of theory: an underground agent in the academy. I returned to discover why, in spite of row upon row of sexy shiny books, in spite of the scores of dedicated professionals with their complex theories and scientific language, in spite of the debates and the courses and the endless articles in respected journals, British radical filmmaking and the independent film and video sector had become politically, culturally and industrially wretched.

My argument in this book is prodigiously broad but it still contains many significant omissions and exclusions including, for instance, Third Cinema theory, the contemporary German underground film scene, the history of Australian underground cinema, a history of amateur video and so on. The absence of most of these elements can be justified in the name of the dynamic and coherence of the argument. But there are two crucial omissions that need at least a brief explanation: the first is the absence of an integrated historical assessment of Soviet experimental film 1917–30; the second is the lack of an analysis of the formal qualities of Underground film. In the first case, I will make reference to Soviet experimental cinema, and later, I will even develop a reinterpretation of Eisenstein's theory of montage. However, a functional investigation of the complexity and specificity of Soviet experimental cinema lies beyond the scope of this book. Moreover, whilst it is true that Soviet cinema was invoked as a radical model by the nascent British avant-garde and independent sector, it must also be understood that their social and industrial contexts were irreconcilable; the avant-garde constituted itself as an alternative within capitalism, whilst Soviet experimental film was for a brief season the cinematic vanguard of a revolutionary communist society. In the second case, the focus of this book is Underground cinema not Underground film; the critical axis of this work is cultural, not aesthetic. This does not preclude intermittent analysis of specific films or makers, but this will always be in the context of the industrial and political culture of experimental cinema.

THE LUX

On 19 September 1997 the new Lux Centre for Film, Video and New Media opened in Hoxton Square, Shoreditch, in the East End of London, north of the financial district. In former times Hoxton had been a ramshackle working-class area of small manufacturing workshops, disused warehouses and council estates. Around the early 1990s young artists and art students began to move into the area, attracted by the cheap rent for studio space, the proximity to the city centre and the gritty urban ambience. Following the artists and encouraged by local council initiatives, art galleries, trendy bars, clubs and coffee shops opened in the district and web design companies, graphic designers, magazines and other creative agencies rented offices. By the late 1990s the area had become known as 'Shoho', the Shoreditch Soho. The hub of this gentrification was Hoxton Square, home to the Blue Note night club and the influential 'Brit Art' White Cube 2 gallery. But the square was dominated by the imposing glass and steel facade of the Lux Centre.

The Lux was purpose-built as a joint initiative to house two interlinked experimental media organisations: London Electronic Arts (LEA, established as London

Figure 1: The Lux Centre for Film, Video and New Media

Video Arts in 1976) and the London Film-makers' Co-Operative (LFMC, founded in 1966). The LFMC was one of the last surviving radical media collectives that emerged from the 1960s' counter-culture. Initially it was a screening/distribution group for Underground cinema but as the 1960s progressed it developed into a voluntary, non-profit making, open-access democratic collective committed to the alternative production, distribution and exhibition of experimental film. From the mid-1970s both the LFMC and its filmmaking practice became increasingly dependent on direct and indirect state subsidy. After working out of various temporary premises it moved in 1977 to a rambling factory space in Gloucester Avenue in Camden, but by the late 1980s the building was becoming increasingly dilapidated, the lease had run out and so the LFMC began negotiations with the key state funding agencies to find a new permanent home. The eventual move to the Lux had an initial cost of £4.5 million raised mostly from National Lottery funding administrated by the Arts Council of England but with contributions and support from other organisations including the BFI, the London Film and Video Development Agency (LFVDA), Channel 4 and the European Regional Development Fund. The Lux comprised a cinema, an art gallery, production and post-production facilities, extensive offices and distribution library/storage space. The activities of both the LFMC and LEA were substantially increased in the new centre. The LFMC almost trebled its staff and the cinema launched a comprehensive programme of regular daily screenings and events. In style and ambience it was somewhere between a prestigious public museum and an affluent commercial media facilities house. At the most successful festivals and gallery openings the square was packed with celebrating artists, students and media liggers, and often there would be installations and projections from the gallery – blue pixilated windows in the dark night.

On 1 January 1999 the LFMC proudly announced its merger with the LEA to form the combined Lux Centre for Film, Video and Digital Arts, a unification which was enthusiastically supported by the state funding agencies. In its inaugural programme the Lux reaffirmed its commitment to artists' film and video and independent cinema, and declared:

> The unification brings together our two international collections of artists' film and video in distribution, with work ranging from Maya Deren to John Maybury creating an unparalleled resource for exhibitors world-wide. Production and education facilities are also centralised, enabling clients and members of each organisation to benefit from expertise across technologies, and facilitating the increasingly varied use of moving image technologies by artists.[6]

What the programme did not announce was that since its inception the Lux cinema and the LFMC had consistently failed to generate the turnover to meet their running costs and that they were forced into the merger as a condition of the funding organisations saving them from financial ruin.[7] Neither did the programme admit that the merger was only really extinguishing the final vestige of the LFMC: its name. The London Film-makers' Co-operative had not actually operated as such since 1995, when as a condition of the move to the new building receiving finance it was required that the LFMC abolish its open-access democratic constitution and adopt a normalised hierarchical industrial structure. Nevertheless, between the abolition of the collective arrangement and the unification of the Lux the 'co-op' continued to charge an annual membership fee and to accept new members who probably never realised that there were no members of the co-operative since there was no co-operative. The last vestige of democracy was erased at the final meeting of the LFMC in December 1998 when the vote for unification was passed by an insufficient majority of a managerial group who had no quorum and who had not adequately informed the remaining membership of the meeting.[8]

Despite the merger and a 'recovery plan' administered by the Arts Council the unified organisation sank further into debt and eventually the funders decided to cut their losses. On 2 October 2001 the Lux closed in mid-operation, the staff and clients were removed from the building and the locks were changed.

The fall of the Lux was the failure of the most ambitious project in the history of British experimental film and video. From the early consultations to the final desperate subsidies the state funding of the project must have been considerably over £4.5 million.[9] It ruined the LFMC and LEA and it provided all future potential funders of experimental media distribution and exhibition with a shameful precedent. In a sector in which lone filmmakers and small groups constantly struggle to make self-financed films/videos with budgets on average under £500 the relative loss is unforgivable. From the wreckage only the distribution collection survived, reconstituted and rehoused by the Arts Council as a new vestigial Lux plc.[10]

The causes of the Lux's downfall have been variously attributed to managerial incompetence, internecine schisms, debts accrued by the LFMC before the unification, reckless National Lottery funding policy and political intervention. The final and most debilitating factor was that the Lux building was never actually purchased, but only rented by the BFI from the property developers. As Hoxton became ever more fashionable and gentrified the developers increased the rent and although the BFI was initially committed to supporting these payments, it finally reneged on the deal.[11]

But the underlying cause of the fall of the Lux is far more complex than high rent and incompetence; it must be discovered in the history of avant-garde film and the decline of the British independent film and video movement. The inevitable question is: how did a radical voluntary collective organisation get fatally involved in a commercially incompetent public/private partnership predominantly financed by the gambling losses of ordinary people who had no need or desire for film, video and digital art?

HISTORY

Three months after the unification of the Lux, the BFI published *A History of Experimental Film and Video* by A. L. Rees, 'the first major history of avant-garde film and video to be published in more than twenty years'.[12] Rees's book is roughly half general overview of the avant-garde canon and half a chronology of specifically British avant-garde film and video 1966–98. In December 1998 the Lux staged a three-day retrospective of 'expanded cinema' to celebrate the forthcoming publication.

Rees himself was a crucial and active agent in the British avant-garde, yet his *History* is written supposedly objectively, and he never really acknowledges his own involvement in the events he documents. His activities span over twenty years, and when his book was published he linked three of the most influential agencies in the sector, first as a Senior Research Fellow at the Royal College of Art, second as chairman of the selection panel for Visual Arts Artists' Film and Video at the Arts Council of England and last as a theorist published by the BFI. As chairman of the Artists' Film and Video sub-committee Rees was working with fellow panel members including the artists George Barber, Tacita Dean and William Raban and most interestingly for my alternative history, the theorist and filmmaker Laura Mulvey, author of the highly influential article 'Visual Pleasure and Narrative Cinema' (1975), and co-maker, with her then husband Peter Wollen, of the films *Pentheselea* (1974) and *Riddles of the Sphinx* (1977).[13] Rees also served on the Artists' Film sub-committee of the Arts Council from 1978 to 1985, and so he was responsible, with his fellow eight to ten panel members, for selecting the fifty to sixty filmmakers who were awarded production funding out of the many hundreds of applications received by the Arts Council in that eight-year period. These selected filmmakers would include practically every British film/video maker that is cited in Rees's history from the mid-1970s to the late 1980s. Rees therefore actually had an executive role in the production of the work he historicises. In other words, the work and the makers that Rees cites as historically significant are the work and the makers that he helped select for production. Rees's history is thus not a representative objective overview of a culture subjected to either intense public interest or commercial competition; it is the subjective account of a participant in a closed system of reciprocal justification.[14] Rees writes from a nexus of institutional power and yet he affects the mythical disinterest of independence; I now explicitly oppose this independence.

THE RETURN OF THE UNDERGROUND

Something happened in the early 1990s which did not fit into Rees' chronology, although in his book he does give it brief consideration.[15] Actually, it did not fit into any official chronology.

In the late 1980s and early 1990s, parallel to the final state co-option of the independent sector, a new British Underground Cinema movement emerged from the activities of a cluster of popular unfunded experimental cinema clubs and radical protest video collectives. This rapid and widespread renovation was arguably the most exciting development in British experimental media since the Underground movement of the 1960s; in fact the new British Underground has been far more significant than its predecessor in terms of audience attendance, active participants and film/video production. It has screened the work of hundreds of film/video makers which would otherwise have remained unseen and it has fostered a substantial heterogeneous and loyal new popular audience for experimental film. Yet within the cultural descendants of the original 1960s Underground (the independent sector and artists' film and video), and within the institutions of film/cultural theory (educational establishments, magazine and book publishing, conferences and so on), the new Underground Cinema has been both industrially and theoretically non-existent. There has been no acknowledgement of the Underground in any of the independent sector's journals (such as *Screen*, *Sight and Sound*, *Coil* and *Vertigo*); there has been negligible contact from any of its institutions (such as the BFI, the Arts Council, the Arts and Humanities Research Council (AHRB) British Artists' Film and Video Study Collection); and no attempt has been made to represent it at any of its festivals (the ICA Biennial, Pandaemonium and so on). This total absence cannot be attributed to the obscurity or hostility of the new Underground scene since its activists have developed spectacular and populist publicity strategies: interventions at debates and festivals, an internationally acclaimed network of websites, interviews on national television and radio, and articles in both the national press and popular or cultural magazines.[16] Neither can it be blamed on a lack of resources or initiative in the independent sector, which has a comprehensive network of highly educated professional researchers and theoreticians; moreover, since the advent of the new Underground the independent sector responded by producing a series of television programmes and events which attempted to fabricate the trendy subcultural style of the Underground whilst actually showcasing their own state-funded institutional products amongst now safe Underground classics from the 1960s.[17] The institutional invisibility of the new Underground is not due to inefficiency or the result of an elaborate conspiracy. It is because the independent sector cannot recognise the Underground without acknowledging that it has become more repressive than the mainstream cinema it claims to oppose.

Reader, be careful in what follows and do not conflate people and agencies with their names or their declarations of intent. Eventually we will consider what independence and autonomy actually mean. For now remember that although the LFMC ceased to exist in 1995, its name lived on for four more years.

This book is prescriptive. Its purpose is to discover the strategies and processes mobilised by the bourgeois state to enervate and finally appropriate the radical film movements of the 1960s, and having revealed these strategies to then propose a compendium of subversive and counteractive theoretical and industrial techniques designed for the use of the new international Underground movement. Without an understanding of its history, without a means to subvert appropriation, the new Underground will be co-opted like its earlier incarnations. Of course history never really repeats itself; the radical project of the new Underground is comparable and contiguous to the movement of the 1960s but also essentially historically different. In the realm of theory, the political struggle facing the new Underground is far more daunting than that faced by the radical film activists of the 1960s. Whilst they had only to devise an oppositional praxis against their perception of a monolithic mainstream cinema, the new Underground is forced to confront not only the mainstream but the theory and theorists of the recuperated independent sector.

ART/NOT ART

Chapter 1

A HISTORICAL OUTLINE OF THE ILLEGITIMATE POPULAR TRADITION: CONTINUITY AND RESISTANCE

The decisive agency in the development of contemporary British culture was a conflict between the legitimate and official institution of bourgeois art and the illegitimate and unofficial popular culture. This historical conflict is a complex political struggle which has been fought consciously and unconsciously across a broad range of cultural agents, institutions, industries and communities. It has been fought by ordinary people, by the ruling elite, by artists, amateurs, entertainers, anti-artists, bohemians, educators, industrialists, state bureaucrats and academics. It has been fought with legislation, money, ideology, cunning and violence. What is at stake in this struggle is the hierarchy by which the bourgeoisie strive to maintain their control of culture. And this historical conflict continues, even though the latest strategy mobilised by the bourgeoisie is to negate this history and simulate an affinity between the two cultures.[1]

CARNIVAL

In his highly influential study *Rabelais and His World* (1965) the indomitable Russian literary theorist Mikhail Bakhtin identifies European mediaeval popular culture as an unofficial culture of carnival which had developed out of thousands of years of ancient ritual and festival.[2]

In mediaeval Europe culture was divided into two distinct modes: the official culture of the Catholic Church and the feudal state, and the unofficial popular culture of the carnival, the marketplace and the tavern. Official culture was rigidly hierarchical and served to demonstrate and maintain the divine prestige of God, the monarchy, the Church and the nobility. The unofficial popular culture existed outside and alternative to its opposite and its defining character was the comic/festive ritual of the carnival. Before the development of modern social class and state structure, this ritual was an integral element of the unified culture of the people. As class and state developed so the comic/festive elements were excluded from official culture and became the alternative popular culture of carnival, which took on an oppositional role with feasts, festivals, games, masks, theatre, fools, jugglers, profanity, trained animals, monsters, laughter and parody. Sharing the feast days and Holy Days of the mediaeval year, carnival mimicked and mocked sacred feudal rituals and protocols with comic ones; it became a second world, a second life which existed outside official life. For its duration it was a different way of living, a realm of community, freedom, equality and abundance. Further, although mediaeval culture

Figure 2: *The Land of Cockaigne* (Pieter Brueghel the Elder, 1567)

functioned in two distinct modes they were not discrete or mutually exclusive. The official culture served to integrate every citizen into the great feudal hierarchy but citizens of every rank, both clerical and secular, celebrated the temporary freedom of the carnival.

The characteristic carnival form is grotesque realism, the popular humour which degrades all that is high, spiritual, ideal and abstract, which brings life back to the material, to the people and to the body.[3] The grotesque bodily principle is both positive and negative, it is the womb and the grave, shit and birth, piss and wine, the corpse and the seed, the old and the young. It is the abundance and fertility of the body even in the grotesque degradation of death and deformity; it is the body of the people; of all the people. The most complex theme of carnival is the mask, which enables a play of identity, transgression, the joy of change and reincarnation; it rejects conformity to oneself.[4] The mask reveals the essence of the grotesque: parody, caricature, grimaces, eccentric postures and comic gestures. The laughter of the carnival is ambivalent, nothing is sacred, no one is exempt, the boundaries of life are transgressed.

The carnival is:

Alternative – it lies outside and opposes the official and serious culture of both the Church and the nobility.
Participatory – there is no border between the audience and the performance, everyone and anyone can be the carnival.
Ambivalent – it contains both the positive and the negative, a diversity of

elements in combination but it does not end this diversity by imposing authority, it celebrates ambivalence, it mutates and transforms.

Material – it degrades the abstract and the ideal and celebrates the body and the life of the people.

Utopian – the carnival is a temporary realm of liberty, equality, abundance and happiness; it frees the imagination from the orthodox and the conventional and reveals the possibility of change and the relativity of existence.

Anarchic – there can be no central or single control over the carnival since it is the sum and diversity of its participants.

Transgressive – it transposes, inverts and subverts; the carnival plays with social and sexual identity.

Unfinished – the carnival is always in process.

Bakhtin celebrates the mediaeval culture of the carnival, but he does this in the context of its relevance to the development of the classic literature of the Renaissance: Rabelais, Shakespeare, Cervantes, Dante, Boccaccio and so on. Moreover, he asserts that there would have been no Renaissance without the carnival, for in the carnival tradition the key figures of the Renaissance found the freedom to escape the rigid orthodoxy of feudal Christianity and so to reinterpret ancient humanist classics.[5] But this consummation in turn marked its decline. After the Renaissance the carnival was suppressed and domesticated, although the tradition survived in a residual form and grotesque carnival imagery reappeared transformed in Romanticism.

However, Bakhtin's perception of the death of carnival must be understood as limited by the context of Soviet academic literary studies of the 1940s. From a contemporary context it is clear that there was no discrete end to the carnival, that in fact carnival was syncretically integrated and modified as the defining tradition of a continuous, mercurial and rejuvenating popular culture which can be mapped out of the mediaeval into the present. The Renaissance marks not the end of carnival but the decline of its legitimate status and the beginning of a divided European culture.

Carnival was sanctioned by the official culture and locked into the calendar of the feudal hierarchy but it would be wrong to suppose that it was only the spectacle of freedom, a cultural safety valve, a means by which the Church and the nobility contained and enervated all subversive social energy.[6] The Church may have exploited the carnival as a means to contain subversion, but the carnival exploited the Church as means to celebrate subversion. And carnival was too unstable and anarchic for the official culture to control and would frequently result in violent social clashes or even insurrection.[7] Moreover, to consider mediaeval carnival as a cultural form separate from political action is a misconception based on a post-eighteenth-century perception of politics as a discrete social activity.[8] Carnival was political, as religion was political; carnival could explode into revolt and revolt could release the carnival. Neither can carnival be contained under the categories 'entertainment' or 'leisure', because whilst the carnival was temporary it could also become a subversive means and a political end; it held within it the demand for the carnivalisation of the world. This popular utopian tendency can be tracked through Western history from the millennial wandering mystics of the thirteenth century through to the Ranters and Diggers of the English Revolution in the seventeenth century and the spectacular festivals of the French Revolution of the late eighteenth century.[9] Paradoxically it can be discovered as a crucial element in both the development of industrial mass popular culture and avant-garde art in the nineteenth century. It flourished in the counter-culture of the 1960s and it runs into the free festival movement of the 1970s, punk rock, the Poll Tax riots of 1990, the Road Protest movement and it is currently being celebrated by the international Anti-capitalist movement.[10]

THE RIFT IN CULTURE

Whilst both the common people and the upper classes participated in European mediaeval popular culture, from the sixteenth century onwards the division between popular culture and the official culture of the upper classes increasingly widened.[11] The critical determinant of this separation was the waning of the feudal order, the emergence of the bourgeoisie and the development of the technologies of capitalism.[12] The historical development of popular culture after the Renaissance was determined by a tension between its commodification in the emergence of bourgeois capitalism and by the attempts of the ascendant bourgeoisie to prohibit, exclude and control it. As bourgeois culture defined itself in the suppression of the popular, so popular culture developed in resistance to that suppression. The carnival tradition, though syncretic, underground and often invisible, runs unbroken into contemporary popular culture. It has developed, diverged and mutated, but its historical development is contiguous and material.

As their economic power grew the Renaissance bourgeoisie increased their social status from below and above since not only did they marry into the nobility but they also recruited them into the bourgeois professions. Far from levelling the social order this mobility increased the significance of class difference as an indicator of social value. The emergent bourgeoisie did not want to dismantle the feudal hierarchy, they wanted to ascend it. The feudal nobility who had lived in confidence of their ancient divine right to rule now turned increasingly to culture as proof of their superiority. A process of gradual and regional cultural separation was initiated which had two essential elements: firstly, the historical formation of a discrete and autonomous ruling-class culture; and secondly attempts to reform and suppress popular culture. The formation of a ruling-class culture began with a Renaissance reformation of manners; the ruling classes increasingly withdrew themselves both culturally and materially from the company of 'the people', a category they now cast off. They no longer dined in great halls with their retainers but withdrew into private dining rooms; they no longer sported at the carnival or danced in the marketplace; popular ritual and remedy were dismissed as error, ignorance and folly. In imitation of the Royal courts they began to develop a refined and codified way of behaving and communicating; a polite and courteous society. Through improved technologies of travel and communication and the expansion of formal and classical education this elite culture became standardised. They cultivated a separate polite form of speech or dialect from the common people and sometimes even a different language altogether.[13] In England the upper classes gradually developed a dialect and accent which, in a twentieth-century form, eventually became the official state idiolect enforced by the national state broadcasting corporation, the BBC.

The suppression and proscription of popular culture in England was initially attempted as an element of the successive phases of the Protestant Reformation.[14] The Protestant ethic was essentially bourgeois: godliness, order, reason, discipline, industry, modesty, thrift, restraint and temperance. The Reformation attitude towards popular culture was that the divide between the sacred and the profane should be absolute; there should be no ambivalence. Whereas the Catholic Church had previously tolerated or even encouraged carnival and festive ritual, the puritans of the Reformation considered it to be lewd, shameless, idle, obscene and intoxicated; moreover they denounced certain popular practices as blasphemy and devil worship. Churches were stripped of all ungodly decoration, ornament and ritual. Sermons which drew on the comedy, myth and technique of carnival were discouraged and uneducated popular parish priests were often replaced by university-educated upper-class Protestants. Mediaeval religious drama was effectively eliminated and key festive rituals were prohibited. However, the crucial effect of the Reformation was not to eliminate popular culture or even impede its 'popularity' but to transform it into a secular and illegitimate culture and to widen the divide between the popular and the official culture of the emergent bourgeoisie.[15]

Whilst the emergent bourgeoisie were initiating the suppression of popular culture the expansion of the capitalist economy and advancements in technology were paradoxically expanding, innovating and diversifying the popular. Carnival was always a festival of the marketplace but from around the eleventh century onwards the great mediaeval annual fairs developed as hybrid combinations of carnival, Holy Days, festive ritual and international trade. The leading English fairs at Stourbridge, Nottingham, Colchester, Norwich, Kings Lynn and St. Bartholomew in London became major trading centres for both local and travelling merchants from across continental Europe.[16] With the initial suppression of carnival in the Reformation the fairs became the secular, illegitimate and commercial hubs of the popular tradition. The key characteristics of this popular tradition were conviviality, variety and montage. The two predominant and interactive modes of the tradition were popular performance and popular literature.

The official ruling-class culture which began to develop with the Renaissance was a classicism which consecrated the creative values of authority, order, unity, purity and perfection and opposed the vulgarity, chaos and carnal pleasures of the people. The concept of the citizen that eventually emerged from this culture was the private and domestic individual of bourgeois society. The classical body was conceived as perfect, hermetic and autonomous, neither young nor old, its apertures sealed, its bodily functions hidden.[17] On the contrary the illegitimate popular culture was driven by the creative force of difference and combination. The fair developed as a chaotic, vulgar and heterodox intersection of carnival and commerce which although regionally diverse and localised was also a transient tradition of shifting forms and variations which moved across regional boundaries. Crucial agents in this cultural migration were the bands of itinerant professional performers, show-people and pedlars who roamed from fair to fair visiting the towns and villages along the route. These nomads travelled both individually and as troupes; many travelled far from the countries and cultures of their birth and many were gypsies. The fair developed into a temporary cosmopolitan city of booths, boards and painted banners where commodities were traded, plays were performed, jugglers, acrobats, conjurers, ballad singers, puppet shows and other entertainers hawked for custom, teeth were pulled, charlatans peddled medicine, bears danced, freaks were exhibited, animals performed tricks and amongst the crowd moved every class of humanity from the inquisitive nobility to the lowest peasants, punks, pimps, bawds, thieves, quacks, mountebanks and beggars.

The first great technological innovation to transform popular culture was the development of a popular literature made possible in England by the advent of printing in the mid-fifteenth century.[18] By the mid-seventeenth century popular literature had become a thriving culture of single-sheet broadsides, paper-covered books and pamphlets sold by the thousands on street stalls and hawked by itinerant vendors and ballad mongers. This unofficial literature dealt in songs and stories of love and romance, sensational tales of outlaws, adultery, violent crime, murder, witchcraft, devil worship, monsters, human freaks, miraculous events and bizarre intrigues. Like the contemporary tabloid press and true crime magazines these ballads and tales were a mixture of fact, fiction and myth.[19] In addition to sensational tales, handbills and almanacs, there were also autobiographies by popular writers and personalities, and political and religious tracts, amongst which were those of the Diggers and the Ranters of the English Revolution.[20] The advent of mass printing also expanded popular visual culture; broadsides and pamphlets were frequently illustrated with woodcuts, and text could also be graphically composed. By the end of the seventeenth century there were broadsides which had developed all the essential formal techniques of the comic strip; a narrative would be told by a series of discreet framed images, the temporal action of the narrative was constructed as a montage from frame to frame and the words of characters in the narrative were indicated by banners, speech clouds or bubbles issuing from their mouths.[21] The ballad-seller was often both a hawker of broadsides and a performer, the selling of ballads was a show. To attract an audience the hawkers used a comic sales patter: they would sing and play their ballads, and sometimes they would have a set of illustrations depicting the subject of the ballad, which they would indicate with a wooden pointer.[22] In 1695 the state allowed legislation limiting the number of trading printers to lapse, and so there was a vast increase in the establishment of printers throughout the country and in the production and distribution of popular material. By the early eighteenth century the popularity of the unwieldy broadside had declined to be replaced by the dominance of the chapbook, a small paper-covered book which contained ballads, narrative strips, folk tales, romances, prophecy, political propaganda, sensational crimes and so forth. These were sold by travelling vendors known as Chapmen who would hawk their stock at public gatherings in the cities, at fairs, public executions, alehouses and coffee houses or would travel to market towns and more remote rural communities.[23]

The permanent and professional theatres of Renaissance London developed from the temporary carnival theatres of the Holy Day and the market place during a period of sustained attack upon popular culture by both the state and by Puritan reformers. In an age where a new social mobility began to threaten the feudal hierarchy and the country was riven with religious conflict and civil insurrection the theatre was viewed by the ruling class as a potential threat to the social order. The power of this threat was attributed to the anarchic chaos of the carnival.[24] For its duration the drama of the carnival drops out of the hierarchy of the feudal state, the common players take on the guises and regalia of nobility or even divinity, and yet they also ambivalently remain themselves, free to shift their identity between the real and the dramatic world; this is the 'play'. The play also drops out of time, it resists the feudal time of productive labour and threatens the authority of history for it brings the past and the mythical into the present. There is no unified authority which controls the meaning or the language of the play; the carnival play is improvised, ephemeral and unfinished, it is created by the diverse performances of the players and the shared culture of the audience. As the carnival theatre became established in permanent playhouses so its subversive potential intensified for it was no longer contained by the official sanction of the feudal calender or the social authority of the mediaeval guilds. The playhouse became the site of a utopian collective and promiscuous transgression and hybridisation of culture, a temporary zone in which classical learning, the grotesque, poetry, slapstick, tragedy, comedy, mime and the real interacted and hybridised.[25] Harassed by attack and repression but driven by the ascendant power of capitalism, the playhouses of the early seventeenth century began to negotiate a new legitimacy by adopting the conditions of literature. A process was initiated in which the anonymous improvisational collectivity of carnival theatre was replaced by the individual author and the authority of a text corresponding to the educational and moral status of official literature. With an authoritative text the author becomes accountable to the state and subject to the law, but they also become the individual master and owner of the text and so able to sell it as a commodity; the author is the individual creator of the play and the players are mere servants who act out the text. This process of authorisation became a crucial strategy in the bourgeois suppression and appropriation of popular culture. Exemplary in this process is the historical trajectory of Shakespearean drama, which emerged from the convivial popular theatre of the Renaissance but became by the nineteenth century a strategic site for the bourgeois authorisation of theatre.[26]

The tradition of popular theatre which developed from the carnival was constituted on dramatic convention. Drama depends upon a system of conventions understood and maintained by both the audience and the performers.[27] This mutually-agreed fundamental convention is to frame the drama; to begin it, to sustain it and to end it. The audience must understand where the world ends and the performance begins. The framing conventions developed by carnival theatre and incorporated into Renaissance theatre, pantomime, melodrama and later forms of popular drama are complex, flexible and interactive. The crucial reason for this flexibility is that carnival theatre depends entirely upon convention to construct its frame. The naturalist drama of the late nineteenth and twentieth centuries replaced the necessity for an agreed conventional framing between audience and performance with a set of institutional, technological and mimetic strategies (the proscenium stage, temporal continuity and so on). The carnival play on the other hand depended almost entirely on convention; it had to negotiate its frame with a recognised audience; it was interactive and communal. Without institutional, technological or mimetic devices the carnival play integrated its frame into the performance; the audience was directly addressed and told by the players/characters that a play would be performed, that it was beginning and that it was ending. In Renaissance theatre this direct address became conventionalised as the prologue, the induction and the epilogue. It is the explicit conventionality of framing in Renaissance and later forms of popular theatre that allows the players to shift in and out of the frame without disrupting its integrity; when the players call attention to the frame they do not expose an illusion, they construct a performance.[28] A narrative drama can be divided into three distinct modes: the real-time material theatrical reality of the performers and the audience; the performance of the players; and the narrative world of imagination, history and myth. Corresponding to these modes the player's identity can be either that of actor, of performer playing the character, or the character itself. Naturalist theatre is unified and monistic, its conventions are designed to eliminate theatrical reality and to unite performance and narrative as a mimetic diegesis: the real world. Carnival and Renaissance theatre had neither the means nor the design to do this. Moreover, the narratives of these kinds of drama were constructed from a culture of collective and un/authorised myth, history and popular tales which negated a simple mimetic unification of performance and narrative since the narrative was always a story retold. The conventional framing of the Renaissance theatre allowed the creation of complex ironic structures of interlocking dramatic modes or planes of performance, and within and between these planes the players could shift their dramatic identity. During the narrative the actors could address the audience directly using conventional techniques, crucially the aside in which a character can converse privately with the audience without being heard by anyone else on stage. The aside enables a player/character to narrate to the audience information not manifest in the action, or to make comic comments about the action or to reveal their true thoughts and emotions whilst dissembling within the narrative. To these conventionalised and authorised announcements must be added the unauthorised improvisations and interventions of the players both as performers and characters. The naturalist mimetic demands that the audience suspends their disbelief, their agency, their corporality and accept the drama as real. Popular theatre, rather than constructing a mimetic reality, negotiates its conventions to construct a complex multiform play of narrative, symbolism and spectacle; disbelief is not suspended – play is engaged. Integrating elements of improvisation, myth and the anarchic subversion of the carnival, popular theatre invokes another order of reality – the marvellous.

THE WORLD UPSIDE DOWN

With the triumph of the Puritan Parliament in 1649 popular festive culture was effectively outlawed: fairs were prohibited, the theatres and alehouses were closed, gaming and gambling were banned and even Christmas was suppressed. But rather than eliminating the popular, the Puritan Protectorate drove it underground. Moreover, the revolution brought to the common people hope of a new age of liberty and equality, it turned the world upside down, it transposed and invoked the ambivalent power of the forbidden carnival. Amongst the forces unleashed in the brief revolutionary chaos between the outbreak of the civil war and establishment of the Puritan Protectorate were a cluster of proto-anarchist sects on the fringes of the puritan movement, most significantly Gerrard Winstanley and the Diggers who founded utopian communes on squatted land, and the Ranters who proclaimed the total subversion of feudal society and all its values.[29] In the Ranters' pamphlets and in the ballads and tracts of the Diggers, it is possible to glimpse the counter-culture of the seventeenth century, the possibility of an alternative English society. As Christopher Hill observes in *The World Turned Upside Down*:

> There had been moments when it seemed as though from the ferment of radical ideas a culture might emerge which would be different both from the traditional aristocratic culture and from the bourgeois culture of the Protestant ethic which replaced it. We can discern shadows of what this counter-culture might have been like. Rejecting private property for communism, religion for a rationalistic and materialistic pantheism, the mechanical philosophy for dialectical science, asceticism for unashamed enjoyment of the good things of the flesh, it might have achieved unity through a federation of communities, each based on the fullest respect for the individual. Its ideal would have been economic self-sufficiency, not world trade or world domination. The economically significant consequence of Puritan emphasis on sin was the compulsion to labour, to save, to accumulate, which contributed so much to making possible the Industrial Revolution in England. Ranters simply rejected this: Quakers ultimately came to accept it. Only Winstanley put forward an alternative. Exploitation, not labour, was the curse of fallen (i.e. covetous) man. Abolish exploitation with the wage relationship, and labour in itself, to

contribute to the beauty of the commonwealth, would become a pleasure. Coolly regarded, we must agree that this was never more than a dream: the counteracting forces in society were too strong. It came nearest to realisation in the Digger communities, which might have given the counter-culture an economic base. Their easy dispersal, and the transition from unorganised Ranter individualism to the organised Society of Friends, registers the fading of the dream into the half-light of common day.[30]

With the establishment of the military Protectorate in 1651 the Digger communes were crushed and the key leaders and writers of the Ranter movement were arrested and forced to recant. Crucially, whilst the French Revolution established uprising as a tradition at the core of French politics, the English Revolution culminated in an infinitely flexible social compromise between the bourgeoisie and the nobility.

Ironically, although the revolutionary populism of the Diggers and the Ranters sought to overturn the feudal hierarchy it is with the restoration of the feudal order in 1660 that the popular culture of carnival resurfaces. With the Restoration, the state attempted to exploit popular culture as a celebration of the return of the hereditary monarchic order; the law against theatre was abolished, music was revived in church, old festivals were restored, new festivals were established and the fairs were reinstated and extended. But if the popular was to be permitted, it was also to be controlled and appropriated. The Restoration court monopolised the theatre by granting Royal Patents to only two London theatre companies and increasing the legislative power of the Lord Chamberlain to censor both dramatic and printed material.[31] The Patent theatres became the only legitimate stages, all other theatres were forced to operate outside the law. However, by the early eighteenth century the power of the state to suppress the illegitimate theatres had manifestly failed and so control was revised and consolidated by the Licensing Act of 1737 which amended the laws against rogues and vagabonds, not only to eliminate the illegitimate theatres but also to censor and prohibit subversive work at the Patent theatres.[32]

Yet, in spite of this, the popular theatre found ways to abide and even vanquish suppression. The crucial loophole in the Licensing Act, and in subsequent legislation, was the supposition that theatre was essentially a spoken form. This effectively meant that to perform drama based on spoken dialogue a theatre had to be legitimate and it had to submit its playscripts to state censorship. In response to this repression the illegitimate popular theatres developed spectacular visual and musical forms which evaded prohibition and censorship by minimising spoken dialogue. This process is most discernible in the development of pantomime in the early eighteenth century and in the rise of melodrama and the music halls in the nineteenth century.

The decisive influence on the development of pantomime was the *Theatre de la Foire* ('Theatre of the Fair'), a non-speaking version of the *Commedia Dell'arte* which was imported from the fair booths and travelling theatres of France.[33] In the late seventeenth century the popularity of the Forains ('fair actors') provoked the French state to enact repressive legislation similar to the establishment of the English Patent Houses; by Royal Decree the Forains were forbidden to speak. In response they resisted by devising a mimed version of the *Commedia* which deployed imaginative alternatives to dialogue: hand-held speech banners, placards which descended from the roof, and leaflets and song sheets which were handed to the audience.[34] In the early eighteenth century English pantomime developed from the *Theatre de la Foire* as a hybrid combination of mime, music, comedy, classical allusion, pagan mythology, fairground attraction and topical satire; a spectacle of ambivalence and allegory. As pantomime developed from the eighteenth to the twentieth century it changed and renewed itself within a flexible but constant form. It was a collective creation; the performers would devise their own material, the technicians would create stunts and effects in collaboration with the performers, popular songs would be integrated into the action and the narrative would be a variant of a traditional popular tale.[35] The scriptwriter's role was essentially to integrate the diversity of performance; the authority of the script was provisional.

In the nineteenth century the mute element of pantomime was phased out, classical and pagan allusion were replaced by standardised fairytales and the performance of pantomime became limited to the Christmas season. But within these shifts the form sustained a core of carnival ambivalence, transgression and participation. This mercurial continuity lies in the ironic nature of pantomime as both the universal ancient carnival and the local and contemporary actuality; like the theatre of the carnival, pantomime takes place between dramatic modes, the mythical past and the concrete present. This 'inbetweeness' is conveyed most strikingly by the celebrity performers, the transvestite principal boys and dames and the humans who play animals or 'skin parts'.

MELODRAMA

Melodrama first developed as a popular theatrical form in the illegitimate theatres, travelling companies and fairbooths of the late eighteenth century. Essentially it began as serious pantomime, a form of music-drama (from the Greek *melo* and *drama*), exempt from the state prohibition on spoken dialogue.[36] In a complex interchange between continental and British popular theatre it became by the mid-nineteenth century the unrivalled dramatic entertainment of the English working classes. Moreover, melodrama was not only a theatrical form – it developed as a discourse between the theatre and the rapid expansion of mass popular literature in the mid-nineteenth century. With the supercession of popular theatre by cinema in the early twentieth century, melodrama became the dominant mode of popular film and subsequently television drama.

Formally theatrical melodrama combined and integrated elements of carnival drama (mystery and morality plays), the pantomime and Gothic tragedy. It was a sensual entertainment, a montage of mime, music, dialogue, thrilling spectacle, amazing attractions and visceral shocks. But melodrama also fostered the current of popular realism which runs from the grotesque realism of the carnival to the outlaw tales of the chapbooks. Combining both these aspects, melodrama is a form of fabulous materialism.

The melodramatic narrative is driven by moral conflict at the polarities of good and evil; it is constructed from conspiracy, coincidence, plot twists, reversals of fortune, confessions, revelations, discoveries, extravagant irony, hopeless degradation, catastrophe, redemption and astonishing climaxes of justice, triumph and joy. At the core of the melodramatic narrative is the irrepressible desire for justice in the face of oppression. The moral conflict of the narrative is not played out psychologically in the development of complex personalities but takes the form of a sublime conflict between characters who embody discrete moral archetypes drawn from a traditional repertoire; the innocent heroine, the evil villain, the honest hero, the loyal friend, the fallen woman, the mute child, the comic servant and so forth. Initially derived from mime, the acting style of melodrama is excessive, gestural and symbolic. As in carnival drama and pantomime, the actors are not being their characters, they are playing their characters. Melodrama is not mimetic, it does not seek to fascinate an unseen audience by its verisimilitude; it is designed to produce in its audience a state of heightened affectation, to involve the participant audience in a marvellous parable.

The popular theatre of the nineteenth century formed a vast illegitimate industry active in all the key urban centres which had numerous extensive and prestigious theatres but at its base comprised small saloon theatres, travelling companies, fair-booth theatres and local penny theatres or 'penny gaffs'. In mid-nineteenth-century London, whilst the established theatres dominated the West End, it is estimated that more than half the theatre seats in the city were located in working-class districts, and that taking into account multiple screenings, the penny gaffs had a nightly attendance of around 24,000, and this is probably an underestimation.[37] Typically the gaffs were makeshift venues improvised in disused buildings, warehouses, shacks, cellars and empty shops.[38] Although adults did attend, the overwhelming majority of the audience were working-class youth. Between the early nineteenth century and the Theatres Act of 1843, the gaff programmes were characterised by the variety of the show, which could include a melodrama, comedy, optical illusions, dancing, ballads and pantomime accompanied by live music. The gaff melodramas were appropriated or improvised from popular novels, legitimate melodramas, serial fiction, the latest ballads and frequently from current events and sensational crimes. The young audience would crowd the gaff in close proximity to the action and would often interact with the performance. Both at the gaffs and at the established theatres the audience was convivial and festive. In the cheap seats of the larger theatres parents would bring children and babies, bottles of drink would be passed around, food would be eaten and pipes smoked.

As an integrated narrative mode in the development of nineteenth-century urban popular culture, the critical axis of melodrama was between the theatres and the

Figure 3: A 'penny gaff' theatre by Gustave Dore, 1870

phenomenal boom in popular literature in the first half of the nineteenth century. The development of cheap fiction for the working-class market in the first half of the nineteenth century can be ascribed to a number of factors, chief amongst which were the rapid expansion of working-class education, popular literacy and the development of cheap printing and paper-making technologies in the 1820s. The diversity of the unstamped and popular press of the 1830s included radical newspapers, serial fiction, free-thinking and atheist periodicals, magazines of working-class 'self improvement', historical and scientific knowledge, comedy and satire, theatrical scandal sheets, sports journalism and pornography. The decisive innovation in nineteenth-century popular fiction was the development of narratives written specifically to be read in regular serial instalments. Serial fiction first developed in France, but the thriving English popular magazine industry developed its own characteristic fiction of melodramatic sensation, the weekly serials known as 'penny bloods'. The integration of stage melodrama and penny magazine was both industrial and formal. Many popular writers wrote fiction and melodrama, and adaptations were made from stage to serial, and from serial to stage. Formally the most significant feature of this interaction was the theatricality of the narrative conventions and style of serial fiction and its woodcut illustrations. Narrative devices which had developed in the restrictions of illegitimate non-dialogue melodrama such as mute characters, animal heroes and spectacular visual events often appeared in serial fiction. Moreover, theatrical conventions appeared in the penny bloods transposed into literary form; the narrative would switch between a distinct series of scenes, descriptive sections read like stage directions, there would be long passages of unmediated dialogue and characters would often use rhetorical speech or dramatic monologue.[39] A definitive formal device of stage melodrama was the tableau which conventionally occurred at the end of each act. At a moment of extreme narrative tension, moral significance or emotional affect the actors would strike and hold a group composition in which each character would be momentarily frozen in a gesture or attitude which condensed their dramatic significance into a visual icon. Penny blood woodcuts were frequently composed as tableaux from the theatre, some even including theatrical curtains as frames or footlights running along the base of the frame.[40] This interaction was reciprocal since melodramas adapted from serial fiction would attempt to reproduce the illustrations of the serial fiction as theatrical tableaux. In contemporary popular culture the most immediate continuity of the melodramatic tableau is the freeze frame or 'stop shot' used at the end of an episode of television serial drama. This device is often counterpart to the narrative convention of ending an episode at a moment of unresolved tension: the 'cliffhanger', a device which was routinely used in stage melodrama and serial fiction.

From the 1860s onwards there developed a form of weekly penny serial magazine specifically targeted at working-class youth, which was labelled by its bourgeois detractors, the 'penny dreadful'.[41] The rise of the dreadful can be attributed in part to the rapid expansion of adolescent waged labour in the mid-nineteenth century. The dreadfuls took up the themes and style of the earlier penny bloods but also developed narratives of domestic melodrama and contemporary low-life London based on the adventures of juvenile and child heroes. The dreadful format was not limited to Britain; there were equivalent forms in Europe, and in America the format developed as the dime novel. In the first half of the twentieth century the dimes were superseded by cheap fiction magazines specialising in crime, sport, adventure and science fiction; they had glossy covers and inside pages printed on cheap wood pulp paper – hence 'pulp fiction'. The hard-boiled pulp prose style developed by the multiple authors of the dime novels and later by writers such as Dashiell Hammett and David Goodis was essentially a hybrid of the melodramatic mime tradition which pared down popular narrative to plot, action and dialogue and minimised psychological exposure and interpretation; it is an audio-visual style which parallels the development of cinematic narrative.[42]

The development of the popular and industrial mass culture of melodrama subverted and problematised the concepts of originality and authorship established in legitimate theatre and literature in the Renaissance.[43] Many of the authors of serial fiction wrote anonymously and many serials had more than one author. In the absence of effective copyright law, writers, theatre companies and publishers routinely pirated and plagiarised plots, scenes or entire works from British, European and American authors. Combined with the popular theatre tradition of improvisation and audience interaction, the anonymous, collective and montaged production of nineteenth-century melodrama effectively denied the authority of the playwright. When the standard modern academic canons of great nineteenth-century British literature were compiled in the first half of the twentieth century they listed virtually no authors of drama until the naturalist revival of the 1890s. Consequently the most popular dramatic form in British history was theoretically absent until the late twentieth century.

SUPPRESSION, SEDATION AND GENTRIFICATION

From the second half of the eighteenth century and increasingly into the nineteenth, industrialisation, urbanisation, the decline of the agrarian economy, the rise of evangelical Christianity and bourgeois anxiety about the unlicensed culture of the vulgar classes combined to produce a systematic onslaught of state suppression and legislation against popular culture.[44] The new age of industry and commerce required from its workforce order, moral discipline, thrift and sobriety. As revolution raged abroad and riot raged at home, the state sought to prevent the dangerous public gathering of the common people and to force popular culture from the streets. Regional authorities attempted to suppress unlicensed holiday pleasure fairs and wakes. Fairs which began on a Sunday or which celebrated Christian holy days were especially censured since the mirth and drunkenness of the revellers was viewed as irreverent. In 1839 the Metropolitan Police Act prohibited many popular recreations including sledging and kite-flying on the public highway, and it also granted the police increased powers to raid and close illegitimate theatres. Most of the traditional popular bloodsports were all but eliminated by genteel opposition before the Cruelty to Animals Act of 1835 made them illegal. The only bloodsports which effectively survived were those in which the ruling classes participated (for example, hunting with hounds).[45] Opposition to street football and especially to the large-scale holiday games intensified; the Highways Act of 1835 made it possible to prosecute players, and many of the games which survived were forbidden and forcibly eliminated in the late nineteenth century.[46] In 1855 the great and ancient London Bartholomew Fair was prohibited, and in the decade following the passing of the Fairs Act of 1871 over seven hundred fairs and wakes were banned in England.[47] In 1853 an act was passed to suppress gambling by prohibiting betting shops, but the bookies went underground and continued to operate in pubs and music halls.[48] In 1868 public executions were discontinued, not because the death penalty was considered barbaric, but because the public festivity and the sale of broadside confessions, ballads, food and alcohol was considered profane and bestial; moreover, the gruesome galas disrupted working hours; executions were continued in private. This onslaught of litigation and genteel contempt often met with opposition and resistance. Like earlier suppression it did not eliminate the popular tradition, the culture simply adapted to the new conditions; state suppression was a critical determinant in the development of a hybrid industrialised urban popular culture.

The rift between popular and ruling-class cultures emerged at the beginning of the nineteenth century complicated by the increasing commercialisation of popular culture and by the success of these commercialised popular forms in the sphere of official culture. This intensive urban commercial popular culture was integrated across its range of forms from theatre to fairbooth, circus, tavern, pleasure garden, racetrack, boxing ring, cricket field and so forth. It shared audiences and venues, and many of its practitioners worked across the cultural range.[49] The popular audience was not exclusively working class or urban but the significant absence was the ascendant bourgeoisie. However, as the nineteenth century progressed the bourgeoisie consolidated their economic and social power and began to engage in the pursuit of rational and respectable leisure. Whereas previously the disparate ruling classes had sought to simply prohibit and censor popular culture the rising bourgeoisie now developed a process of suppression, appropriation and gentrification which had three key strategies.[50] Firstly, they infiltrated and colonised the elite culture of the aristocracy; secondly, they developed new specifically bourgeois leisure activities such as public art galleries, museums, promenade concerts, golf and tennis and so on; and thirdly they appropriated certain crucial popular activities, gentrified them, prevented the lower classes from taking part and finally historicised them as inventions of their own. The clearest examples of this are sporting: cricket, rowing and athletics. The institutional base for the appropriation of these sports was education, specifically the new elite public schools founded in the 1840s, where popular sports were standardised, regulated and promoted as a system of social control.[51] But the appropriation of the popular was not restricted to sport – another critical target was theatre.

British theatre was effectively dominated for most of the nineteenth century by popular forms and lower-class audiences. Nevertheless the bourgeois state fought a ruthless war of attrition against the illegitimate theatres, especially against the unlicensed penny gaffs which were frequently raided by the police and the actors arrested and imprisoned.[52] The particular suppression of the gaffs was motivated by successive waves of bourgeois moral panic fixed on the culture of working-class youth.[53] In the institutions and literature of the Victorian establishment a debate raged over the causal relationship between popular culture and juvenile delinquency. The two key terrors were the penny gaffs and the penny dreadfuls; the gaffs were considered to be lawless dens of vice where wild young criminals could fraternise, and the outlaw narratives of the melodramas and dreadfuls were deemed to incite and glorify criminality. Accordingly the bourgeois state embarked on the cyclical project of moral panic, legislation and repression which came to characterise its relationship with popular youth culture in the twentieth century.

Meanwhile, parallel to the campaign of suppression against popular theatre the bourgeoisie developed a tradition of elite theatre based both on the authorisation and gentrification of traditional popular drama, crucially Shakespeare, and on the constitution of a new specifically bourgeois dramatic form: Naturalism.

As the capitalist economy expanded the bourgeois state was torn between the conflicting tensions for the suppression and industrialisation of urban popular culture, between prohibition and commodification. The resolution to this conflict was a process of licensing and sedation.[54] A critical instance of the way that this was implemented, and of the way that popular culture diverged, diversified and adapted to avoid this suppression, can be found in the development of the music hall.

MUSIC HALL

Tavern entertainment in the late eighteenth century was typically convivial, participant and amateur. In the first decades of the nineteenth century the number of urban pubs expanded rapidly, driven by population increase and the relative rise of working-class income. In 1828 the urban pubs were brought under the provision of the Disorderly Houses Act and required to apply for a music and dancing licence; in response many pubs built or adapted separate rooms or buildings as Song Saloons which could now charge an admission fee specifically for the entertainment. The Song Saloons had small stages for the performers, and tables and chairs where the audience could eat and drink; their speciality was participatory singing and most of the performers were amateurs. After years of popular protest and resistance the monopoly of the Patent Houses was broken by the Theatres Act of 1843 which granted licences for dialogue drama to many of the larger illegitimate theatres in London. But the conditions of the licences, which prohibited eating, smoking and the sale of alcohol, essentially forced a cultural polarisation on popular entertainment. Either the venues could go legitimate and target a polite audience, or they could renounce dialogue drama and apply for a music and dancing licence. This stark choice was further enforced upon the gaffs, saloons and the smaller theatres by increased pressure from the police and local authorities against unlicensed venues. From the success of saloon entertainment and the licensing enforcement of 1843, the music halls developed in the second half of the nineteenth century. The predominate centre of music hall culture was the East End of London, drawing on the talent and tradition of Bartholomew Fair and the illegitimate theatres, but Lancashire was also a major centre and halls were established throughout Britain, each region developing its own characteristic forms and performers.

From its roots as an amateur and participatory pub entertainment the music hall developed as essentially convivial and uninhibited; it did not restrain the life of the audience. The music hall programme did not require the rapt attention of a theatre narrative, since it was composed of a variety of discrete turns or acts. The basic small hall or saloon had movable seating allowing the audience mobility throughout the show. They were free to circulate and to enter or leave at any time; they could eat, drink and smoke whilst they watched the show, and at the back of the pit there would be a bar serving drink where they could gather to talk, or promenade. The early music hall performers came from the pub and saloon circuit or were former fairground, gaff or street entertainers and ballad-sellers. The variety programme of the halls integrated music and theatre, fairground and circus acts, and current events, education and technological novelty.[55] The essential entertainment was the comic song with a commentary of witty patter or characterisation, but there were many types of song and many types of singer. At the core of the music hall song was the everyday life of working people: love, sex, marriage, family conflict, housing problems, poverty, politics, leisure and so on. If in certain instances the subject of a song was exotic, eccentric or elite, the ironic context was always the shared experience of the audience. If a song dealt with complex or abstract issues it did so by identifying those issues with clearly defined and understood personalities. In the song the audience recognised their affinity, shared their desires and turned their trouble into pleasure. Apart from the singers there were dancers, musicians, jugglers, acrobats, magicians, ventriloquists, stand-up comedians, eccentric comedians, impressionists, melodramatic and comic sketches, performing animals and a host of astounding novelty acts. The music hall chairman was also a performer who would mediate between the audience and the turns and provide a formal continuity to the diversity of the programme.

The legitimate theatres and the state authorities were ever-vigilant against the encroachment of music hall into dialogue drama; performers often subverted this suppression by striking a dialogue not between actors on stage but between the lone performer and the audience. In doing this they employed the sales-patter tradition of the itinerant ballad-seller, the chapman and the fairground barker. Like Renaissance and popular theatre, music hall performance played between and across the dramatic frame constructing a complicity between audience and performer. They then developed an exclusive popular subculture of shared experience and reference, convention, slang, gesture, accent, intonation, catchphrases, double entendre, parody, pastiche, eccentricity, intertextual reference and irony.[56] This complex and subtle subculture proved very resistant to bourgeois intervention and reform. Bourgeois reformers knew that the vulgar audience found the performers amusing and they were convinced this was because they were transgressing the moral and social order, but they could not prove it because they could not decode the culture; they did not get the jokes. Nevertheless, as it developed in the late nineteenth century, music hall became stratified by class divisions regarding both the types and locations of halls, and seating and ticket prices within.

In London, up until the late 1880s, the range of variety entertainment included pubs, saloons, minor local halls and larger halls in the West End. The saloons on average would hold an audience of around 350, whilst the larger halls held thousands; the Alhambra music hall in Leicester Square could hold 3,500 in 1860.[57] The establishment of the larger halls was accompanied by an institutional shift in audience targeting a broader class mix, decisively towards the more affluent bourgeois audience. This gentrification was accompanied by a deliberate state policy of purging and sedation, implemented by the selective refusal of licences to the smaller halls, saloons and pubs. This sedation was reinforced by the Suitability Act of 1878 which required all music halls to build a proscenium wall dividing the audience from the stage, to install an iron fire curtain and to remove the bar from the body of the hall. This effectively disqualified all but the large affluent buildings; however, it was not strictly applied in London until the late 1880s when the London County Council, guided by a hardheaded ideological mix of radical-liberalism, Fabianism and Temperance evangelism, implemented licensing legislation to deliberately eliminate pub and saloon music hall. This purge was augmented by the tendency after the Suitability Act to build and rebuild music halls with fixed seating, and with the cheap seats up in the gallery; effectively the new music halls were becoming variety theatres. As the grass roots music hall was suppressed, the larger music halls formed and consolidated an industry which was eventually dominated by a few centrally-controlled chains or combines. Finally, under commercial and state pressure the music hall industry of the turn of the century attempted to introduce self-censorship to ban all politically sensitive or vulgar material and to promote an ideology of political conservatism and nationalist jingoism.

The music hall made the bourgeoisie anxious because essentially they suspected that it was a front for something else, a dirty secret that was being kept from them: a temporary zone of convivial and uninhibited pleasure. To the reformers the entertainment on stage seemed to be no more than an excuse for other activities in the hall – drunkenness, prostitution, illegal betting or perhaps even political subversion. The sedation of music hall was a process by which audience participation and vitality was immobilised. The noisy makeshift saloons were replaced by vast and palatial Theatres of Variety, and the popular audience was banished to the cheap seats up in the distant galleries.

CONSOLATION OR SUBVERSION?

It has been argued by Leftist historians of popular culture that the sedation of music hall marked the end of the radical popular tradition and the initiation of a 'culture of consolation'.[58] The argument is that during the revolutionary years of Chartism popular culture was an integral element of radical agitation, but that in the political disillusion of the late nineteenth century, it became a tame depoliticised culture which consoled its working-class audience with cynicism, irony, cheerful stoicism and finally reactionary nationalism. The crucial determinant in this shift would be the state-licensed commodification and industrialisation of popular culture, which following capitalist (Marxist) logic would necessarily serve the interests of the bourgeoisie. In this way the culture of consolation argument is a narrative which explains the origins of mass popular culture as a primary instrument of bourgeois hegemony. But this argument effectively denies creative agency to the participants of popular culture. Fundamentally the argument is flawed because it fails to take the irony and absurdity of music hall seriously; music hall did not console, it opened a marvellous outlaw space in the fabric of everyday life, a space which transformed boredom, poverty and injustice into subversive laughter.

Moreover, the concept of music hall 'depoliticisation' also depends upon the assumption that 'politics' is a specialised activity limited to the legitimate sphere of government, legislation, labour relations, international affairs and so on. However, in the face of hundreds of years of repression and prohibition the continued existence of an illegitimate popular culture became in itself a political act.[59] Most of the cultural workers of music hall came from working-class or lower-middle-class backgrounds; they were subject to exploitative contracts which forced them to work long hours in grim conditions; many died young or ended their lives in poverty. And yet they developed a sublime and subversive comic tradition which can be traced as a core element of twentieth-century British popular culture through critical figures such as Marie Lloyd, Vesta Tilley, Harry Champion, Dan Leno, Kate Karney, George Robey, Charles Coburn, Little Tich, Billy Merson, Fred Karno, Charlie Chaplin, Stan Laurel, Will Hay, Gracie Fields, Jessie Mathews, George Formby, the Crazy Gang, Tommy Handley, Frankie Howerd, Tony Hancock, Morecome and Wise, the Goons and many others. Furthermore, the American Vaudeville tradition, which was essentially a variant of the music hall/variety tradition, became one of the fundamental axes of Hollywood cinema providing not only key figures like Mack Sennett, Buster Keaton, W. C. Fields, Beatrice Lillie, the Marx Brothers, Bob Hope, Judy Garland and countless others, but also the Vaudeville form of variety acts montaged into a compendium feature-film narrative: the comedy sketch, the dance number, the guest star spot and so on.

The industrialisation of popular culture in the short term may have introduced the alienating factory system into the popular and it may have turned the audience for certain types of performance from participants to consumers, but in the long term it ensured that the popular would eventually eclipse the culture of the bourgeoisie. Whilst the reproduction and distribution of cultural commodities has become normalised, the cultural industries have consistently failed to control the means of production: the people. The factory system and its market research division has only ever had limited success in fabricating the popular, and crucially they have historically failed to suppress fundamental popular forms and movements originating outside their professional and legitimate domain; at their most efficient they have only managed to react, market and partially appropriate popular forms such as music hall, jazz, the blues, the counter-culture, underground cinema, science fiction, punk, hip hop and so on. Moreover, it is not as if the industrialised sector of the popular ever was or has become the only sector. The popular is a broad and chaotic diversity of forms and participants: illegitimate, urban, rural, local, regional, temporary, underground, amateur, professional, domestic and public. Moreover, the introduction of industrial management and mass production may have been an innovation of the late nineteenth century, but commercialism was an integral element of the popular as far back as the booths, ballad-sellers and puppet theatres of the mediaeval carnival. The myth of an organic culture exempt from economic transaction is not a tradition of popular culture; it is the bourgeois fantasy of folklore.

The subversive carnival of popular culture winds through cultural history regenerating, transforming, mutating, diverging and combining. Its history is ambivalent; it was loathed and feared by the emergent bourgeois class who sought to suppress and control it, and yet it was also commodified and industrialised by the bourgeoisie and integrated into the mass popular culture of the twentieth century. We can map its regeneration through the sensational outlaw literature of the fairs, the utopian play of Renaissance theatre, the marvellous ambivalence of pantomime, the fabulous materialism of melodrama and the convivial variety of music hall. It is now at the rave, down the pub, in the comic book, the multiplex, the car boot sale, the free festival, the Blackpool illuminations, the football match, the custom car cruise, the re-enactment of the battle of Marston Moor, the bowling alley, the clubs of Ibiza, the *Dr Who* convention, the Exploding Cinema. This is not to mythologise the utopian power of popular culture without acknowledging the history of popular racism, sectarianism, misogyny, homophobia, mob violence and persecution which also lies in the carnival tradition. Neither is it to disregard the hegemonic and colonial exploitation of the mass media by the state or to suggest that critical distinctions should not be made between good and bad popular culture. But it is to contend that popular culture developed as an alternative tradition to the official culture of the state, that it became an unofficial utopian life of the people and that the bourgeois institution of art constituted itself by systematically excluding it.

Chapter 2

THE HISTORY OF ART, THE FUNCTION OF THE AVANT-GARDE AND THE RISE OF MODERNISM

As the bourgeoisie ascended to power in the late eighteenth and early nineteenth centuries they developed a new culture relatively autonomous to both popular culture and the official culture of the ancient feudal hierarchy. It was called Art.[1]

The contemporary meaning of art is complex and contingent; it is specifically the traditional visual arts of painting and sculpture, but it is also a gallery/museum-based cultural institution that includes a range of media and modes (for example performance art, video art) and it is also an ideal of aesthetic perfection that transcends cultural forms and institutions: classical music, legitimate theatre, poetry, literature, ballet, opera and so on. This apparent diversity is unified by its exclusivity. Art excludes the popular tradition: carnival, festive ritual, working-class culture, amateur culture, commercial entertainment and mass media. Moreover, the meaning of art is not essential or eternal; it has radically shifted over Western cultural history. As Victor Burgin notes in *The End of Art Theory*:

> In classical antiquity, the word 'art' (Greek, *tekne*; Latin, *ars*) was the name given to any activity governed by rules; art was that which could be taught and as such did not include activities governed by instinct or intuition. So, for example, music and poetry were not at first numbered amongst the arts as they were considered the products of divine inspiration, beyond mortal accountability. With, however, the elaboration of a mathematics of pitch and harmony (Pythagoras), and of a poetics (Aristotle), music and poetry took their place amongst the 'arts' – alongside, for example, logic and shoemaking.[2]

So in ancient classical culture a definition of the arts would include the sciences of astronomy, geometry and physics. However, there was a distinction between manual arts and intellectual arts and this was taken up in mediaeval Europe as a distinction between the mechanical arts (manual crafts including painting and sculpture) and the liberal arts (intellectual studies such as grammar, arithmetic, astronomy, music, poetry and so on). During the Renaissance, painting and eventually sculpture were recognised as liberal arts. In the late seventeenth and early eighteenth centuries new conception of science developed in the work of Galileo, Kepler, John Ray, Linnaeus, Francis Bacon and others, who began to formulate methods of experimental enquiry and proposition based on mathematical logic and a systematic observation of reality. But the development of science as an experimental method and a type of knowledge did not limit the arts to which science could be applied; science was the theory and art was the practice. The specialised definition of science as the study of

Figure 4: The London South Bank complex of state culture.

the natural world (physics, chemistry and biology), and the exclusion of the arts, did not develop fully until the first half of the nineteenth century. Science then moved from a general meaning of knowledge to a specialised meaning as an experimental and theoretical method concerned with the study of specific verifiable material realities. This science was applied and legitimised in the technological innovations of the industrial revolution. The emergent conception of science and the tendency to specialisation in capitalist production led to an incremental contraction of the arts as they became the seven fine arts; architecture, dance, music, oratory, painting, poetry and sculpture.[3]

In mediaeval Europe the official forms of these seven arts had a primarily sacred/religious social function which in the Renaissance was superseded by a political/courtly social one. The revolutionary accession of the bourgeoisie initiated a radical shift in the purpose of these arts. The development of industrial capitalism created a new consumer economy for the fine arts and so the artist became the producer of a commodity which was sold on the open market to private individuals, collectors and dealers. The established feudal economy of patronage and commission was undermined, the religious function of art was desecrated and artists were alienated from the Royal Court and the nobility. New industrial production methods threatened traditional art practice and new technologies of mechanical reproduction (photography and lithography) depreciated the authenticity and mimetic value of the arts. Concurrently the ascendant bourgeoisie was riven by conflicting impulses to suppress and sedate the vulgar culture of the masses and to exploit the popular with the new techniques of capitalist industry.

These factors combined in a class conflict for the control of the value of good taste. The cultural authority of the Church and the nobility was displaced and art was (re)formulated as the autonomous creation of the beautiful, the perception and study of beauty became the aesthetic, and the appreciation of the beautiful became a question of taste.[4] The unified 'Art' that emerged in the nineteenth century is a product of the development of bourgeois capitalism; it is at once specialised as a visual art and universal as the bourgeois fetish of the aesthetic. There was no singular 'Art' with a capital 'A' before the bourgeois revolution.[5] 'Art' is the autonomous culture of the bourgeoisie and consequently there can be no Renaissance Art, primitive Art or working-class Art. As Roger Taylor observes in *Art, an Enemy of the People*, this is a fact that often eludes both artists and cultural theorists:

> Art is a fetish. As this is so, so mystification becomes part of the concept of art. From outside the form of life, one can say art is nothing over and above what the bourgeoisie classifies as art, that is its meaning, but, from inside the category, such a thought is intolerable because it dismantles the beliefs that go with entering into the activities of the category.[6]

The autonomisation of Art was a process in which the meaning of the official feudal culture was transposed to a new bourgeois purpose. The paradoxical complexity of this process is that this shift was initiated as a revolutionary new social function for the arts (Art), but consolidated as the denial of all social function. The crucible for this process was revolutionary Paris, where the feudal infrastructure that confined the bourgeoisie was transformed by the successive revolutions of 1789, 1830 and 1848. In the revolution of 1789 the break with feudalism was felt to be so absolute that the course of history was suspended and a new history begun; 1789 became the 'First Year of Liberty', the first year of progress. No longer the eternal organic cycle of harvests, generations, festivals, dynasties, death and renewal, bourgeois history became the progress of its own ascendancy, accomplished and recorded by the new technologies of capitalism.[7] The interlocking cultural trajectories that were initiated in this shift were French Romanticism, bohemianism and the avant-garde.[8]

As a concept and as a movement the avant-garde originated in French Utopian Socialism.[9] The word 'utopia', meaning nowhere, was first composed from the Greek by Thomas Moore in his ambivalent speculation *Utopia* (1516). Utopian Socialism developed as the egalitarian gains of the revolution were annulled and it can be traced back to the utopian tradition of the late Renaissance and the eighteenth-century Enlightenment, from Montaigne to Rabelais, Gabriel de Foigny, Fenelon, Morelly, Diderot and Rousseau. The principal theorists of the movement were Henri de Saint Simon (1760–1825) and his rival Charles Fourier (1772–1837). It is from their work that many of the key concepts of Marxism and European anarcho-communism developed in the years between the fall of Napoleon and the revolutions of 1848: the decisive years of the European industrial revolution, as economic power passed from the rural landlords to the urban bourgeoisie. The idea of the artist as vanguard first appears in a fictional dialogue between an artist, a scientist and an industrialist co-written by Saint-Simon in 1825.[10] To Saint-Simon this trinity of bourgeois professionals represents the enlightened hope of a new socialist society, and the lead would be taken by the artists:

> It is we, artists, who will serve you as avant-garde: the power of the arts is in fact most immediate and most rapid: when we wish to spread new ideas among men, we inscribe them on marble or on canvas … and in that way above all we exert an electric and victorious influence. We address ourselves to the imagination and to the sentiments of mankind; we should therefore always exercise the liveliest and most decisive action; and if today our role appears nil or at very least secondary, what is lacking to the arts is that which is essential to their energy and to their success, namely, a common drive and a general idea.[11]

The motor of Saint-Simon's socialism was a scientific rationalism which would sweep away the mystic feudal hierarchy and inaugurate a new united European community, a golden age of prosperity and peace, a meritocracy ruled by scientists, industrialists and artists.[12] Christianity would be replaced by a rational New Christianity and the priests of this new faith would be the artists.

Like Saint-Simon, Charles Fourier and his followers believed that art had a moral and social function in the constitution of a new utopian society. Their model for the new order was a series of autonomous decentralised communes based on a mystical principle of social harmony which could be understood by the harmonic analogies of music and colour.[13] The role of art in the communes would be both integrated and vital. The influence of Utopian Socialism in the 1830s can be traced through French Romanticism and the circle of Victor Hugo to the Art for Art's Sake movement, Symbolism, William Morris, the Garden City movement and the development of Modernism in the twentieth century.

Although the avant-garde developed from this conviction that art should have a moral and social purpose in a utopian society, it must be understood as an opposition to both the feudal order and to the bourgeois economy. It is the denial of both feudal function and commercial utility; it is a demand for total autonomy which culminates in the conviction that art should have no function other than to be art, it should be functionless. This negation of function is the central doctrine of the Art for Art's Sake movement of the mid-nineteenth century and the Aesthetic movement of the late nineteenth century.

As the pioneer of 'l'art pour l'art', the poet and novelist Théophile Gautier pronounced in 1834:

> What is really beautiful can be no other than good for nothing; anything that is useful is ugly because it expresses some need, and those of man are base and disgusting, like his wretched and invalid nature. The most useful part of a house is its latrines ... I am one of those to whom the superfluous is necessary, and I like things and people in inverse proportion to the services they render.[14]

The historical project of the avant-garde, as it developed through the nineteenth century, was the completion of the process of cultural autonomisation initiated in the bourgeois revolution; the avant-garde is the movement which pioneers, implements and maintains the autonomy of bourgeois Art. But this art developed by the bourgeoisie and pioneered by the avant-garde was not functionless. It progressively rendered its social utility and necessity illegible but this was not an absence of function, it was a new function: to be superfluous.

The development of bourgeois capitalism and the accession of the bourgeoisie as the ruling class radically transformed the feudal culture of the Church and nobility; however, it did not replace it. Art was not the advent of a revolutionary new capitalist culture; it was the appropriation and fetishisation of the feudal arts and their sacred and noble function by a new ruling class. As Roger Taylor notes:

> The revolutionary class, through whose activity came about the normalisation of bourgeois social relations (e.g. wage labour, the labour market, the ownership of the means of production) and which contains persons having status on the basis of the older feudal set up, in its aspiration to be the ruling class has the aspiration to take over the life of the ruling class.[15]

The bourgeoisie were brought to power by industrial innovation, and yet they desired the honour and consecration of feudal rule, and so, paradoxically, art became the fetishised ideal of pre-industrial production.[16] Consequently, the fragmentation of the assembly line, the alienation of the worker from the product of their labour, standardisation, automation and the other key innovations of bourgeois capitalism could not be adopted for the production of art.[17] The autonomisation of art is a process of detachment from mass industrial production, to the point where art is defined by its unique authenticity, by its manual creation.

In his celebrated 1936 essay 'The Work of Art in the Age of Mechanical Reproduction', Walter Benjamin proposes that the authenticity of an art object, its unique material history, the viewer's perception of their distance from the work, could be termed the 'aura' of a work.[18] Benjamin locates the origin of the aura in the sacred function of art:

> We know that the earliest art works originated in the service of a ritual – first the magical, then the religious kind. It is significant that the existence of the work of art is never entirely separated from its ritual function. In other words, the unique value of the 'authentic' work of art has its basis in ritual, the location of its original use value. This ritualistic basis, however remote, is still recognisable as secularised ritual even in the most profane forms of the cult of beauty.[19]

For Benjamin, lithography, photography, cinema and the other techniques of mechanical reproduction had the potential to destroy the aura of art and liberate humanity from the oppression of ritual and history. Mechanical reproduction could make art accessible to the masses, and penetrate and reveal a demystified modern reality.

Benjamin's prose is exhilarating but he is betrayed by a fatal misconception of art and by the resiliency and immunity of bourgeois culture to subversion. As the bourgeoisie assumed economic power they developed a commercial market for the sacred and aristocratic arts of the ruling class. But mechanical reproduction could not satisfy the demand of the art market, because the commodity sought by the bourgeoisie is aura. Mechanical reproduction has obviously transformed twentieth-century culture, but it has not destroyed the aura of the work of art, because art was constituted as that which is not mechanically reproducible. Further, there can be no aura until the development of mechanical reproduction; aura is the value of art.

Even Benjamin, in his notes at the end of the essay, acknowledges that without mechanical reproduction authenticity cannot become fetishised as the aura:

> Precisely because authenticity is not reproducible, the intensive penetration of certain (mechanical) processes of reproduction was instrumental in differentiating and grading authenticity. To develop such differentiations was an important function of the trade in the work of art.[20]

This paradox has several irresistible consequences. Since the production of aura is the production of the pre-industrial sacred and aristocratic function of the arts the production process cannot be industrialised. So, whilst the progress of capitalism transformed the social relations and industrial techniques of modern culture, art has remained an autonomous realm of elitism and ritual. John Ruskin, the Victorian pioneer of modern art theory, recognised and celebrated the cult of the aura. In his lecture of 1859, 'The Unity of Art', Ruskin constructs a hierarchy of human pro-duction: 'Manufacture' is production without intelligence; 'Art' is production with intelligence; but 'Fine Art' is the combination of 'the hand, the head and the heart'. (Fine) Art can only be handmade:

> Whatever changes may be made in the customs of society, whatever new machines we may invent, whatever new manufactures we may supply, Fine Art must remain what it was two thousand years ago, in the days of Phidias; two thousand years hence, it will be, in all its principles, and all its great effects upon the mind of man, just the same.[21]

The ever-increasing sophistication and efficiency of mechanical reproduction has not eliminated the aura; it has valorised an auratic hierarchy, at the top of which is the real unique authentic work of art, and below is an ever descending scale of copies each of which has diminishing economic (auratic) value according to its his-torical and material distance from the original. Above all the hierarchy of aura has eternalised art (painting and sculpture) as the paragon of unique authentic objects, for they cannot be reproduced and even to attempt to do so is a crime; forgery. The absence of a unique and authorised object was a crucial factor in the strategies deployed in the development of film and video art; against the ephemeral, sensual and collective experience of popular cinema, avant-garde film and video makers have sought to materialise and objectify the cinematic: selling limited-edition film prints, fetishising unique conditions of exhibition, incorporating film and video into sculpture/installations and so on.

The revolutions which brought the bourgeoisie to power were against the divine authority of the Church and the aristocracy; moreover the scientific rationalism of the nineteenth century increasingly revealed the irrationality of both the Christian God and the hereditary power of the nobility. The bourgeoisie adopted the revo-lutionary demands for democracy and equality in their rise to power, but these demands if taken to their logical conclusion threatened the fundamental ideological legitimacy of social class, without which the bourgeoisie had no right to rule. And so, as it acquired power, the bourgeoisie had to develop the means to legitimise that power. This was the problem addressed by Saint-Simon: who were to be the lords and the priests of the new society?; what was to be the new religion?; who would lead the way? It was to be Art. Since the social hierarchy of the West had been struc-tured by God and the nobility for nearly two thousand years, and since the bour-geoisie actually aspired to this feudal hierarchy, so bourgeois Art syncreticised the hierarchical aristocratic and sacred function of the arts into the capitalist economy. Aura as a commodity is the desire of the bourgeois for aristocratic and theocratic power but it is also their fear that they will never possess it. In the presence of aura the bourgeois contemplates in awe the traditions of divine and hereditary authority. Democracy and equality are antithetical to Art; the value of aura is its scarcity.

The auratic value of ancient art works which actually once had a sacred or courtly function is prodigious, but for the bourgeois, also tainted by their very functionality. The bourgeois artists of the twentieth century removed the taint of function; they discovered how to produce pure aura. The shift from sacred to courtly and finally to bourgeois art is a shift from a collective to a private experience.[22] With the rise of capitalism the traditional social relations of feudalism became irrelevant to the bourgeoisie; the anonymity of the market and the development of waged labour no longer required the cohesive social function of the arts; the bourgeoisie no longer required or desired social contact with the lower classes; and for the late nineteenth-century bourgeoisie the working-class districts of the city were a dreadful and alien abyss. The bourgeois revolutions culminated in an art of individualism and privacy which operated in both the production and reception of the work of art. In production this shift begins during the Renaissance, first with the decline of the mediaeval craft guilds and the collective workshop, and second with the origin of the concept of the genius. In reception this process can be discerned in the rise of art forms which isolated the audience as individuals (the novel, Naturalism), and also in the commodification of the aura.

Before the development of the aura of art, the sacred and courtly artwork had a prestige generated by its social function; the sacred word, the image of God, the King's estate, the music for the pageant and so on. Prestige emanated not from the artwork itself nor from the maker but from the feudal hierarchy of God and the nobility. To use a semiotic model, the prestige of a feudal artwork was the signified not the sign. Moreover, before the Renaissance, art was the work of God and the artist was simply a medium for God's divine creation; it is only with the advent of Renaissance humanism that the work of art begins to become the expression of an individual mortal.[23] The function of courtly art was to represent the glory of the monarch, the nobility and the reign of the court. This prestige emanated from the monarchy and the nobility who also legitimised their authority in the name of God. So, in both sacred and courtly art, prestige is a function of the artwork, in that it is the distance of the viewer from sacred and noble authority. It locates the viewer in the great cosmic feudal hierarchy which begins at its highest with God and then descends by degree through every angel, every human from king to serf, every beast, herb, mineral and finally to the basest elements of existence. With the development of art, the prestige of sacred and courtly art becomes autonomous, it becomes aura; prestige without function. In the presence of great art the modern bourgeoisie are alone, they experience the aura as a fascinating nostalgia, an ineffable exaltation and desire: exaltation that they are at last in the presence of noble and sacred power, and desire for the lost prestige of that power, the prestige which they have commodified.

For this reason the art gallery has become both the church and palace of the aura, and this is also a fundamental reason why art eventually divested itself of even the function of representation.[24]

It is an established doctrine of art theory that non-representational art is a defining development of the avant-garde and that the avant-garde is a defining tendency of Modernism. In semiotic terms, Modernism can be defined as the movement that pursues the rift between the sign and the signified which was revealed by the experiments of Cubism.[25] Before Cubism, realist art was primarily concerned with the representational dynamics between the signified and the real: the referent. Cubism shifts this concern to the dynamic between the sign and the signified, and this shift ultimately facilitates the suppression of the signified, and leads to an art of pure signs: the autonomisation of the content of Art.[26] If the avant-garde is the vanguard of autonomous bourgeois art, so Modernism is the movement that sought to consummate the avant-garde by materialising the autonomy of art as the content of art. This trajectory can be traced from the rise of bourgeois art to its first theoretical articulation, in the Art for Art's Sake movement, as a denial of reference which permits the semiotic shift of Cubism. Modernism is the art of the abstract, the non-objective, the non-representational and the non-narrative. The modernist artist eliminates representation and decoration, and seeks purity of form and material.[27] This compulsion is driven by the fetish of the aura, for as mechanical reproduction becomes ever more mimetically efficient, so aura as a commodity becomes ever more specialised as that which cannot be mechanically reproduced; throughout the nineteenth century new industrial techniques of fabrication undermined art's function as the producer of beautiful objects whilst photography eroded art as the representation of the real. Inevitably the only thing that cannot be mechanically reproduced is aura itself: pure, abstract, superfluous and insignificant.[28] The elimination of representation is a breakthrough in the development of the aesthetic; it is pure aura, the fetish of sacred and courtly authority in its ideal state, beauty without function, insignificant. And this is its function, for this autonomous art can only be appreciated by an autonomous social elite. As French aesthetic sociologist Pierre Bourdieu observed:

> Never perhaps has more been asked of the spectator, who is now required to 're-produce' the primary operation whereby the artist (with the complexity of his whole intellectual field) produced this new fetish. But never perhaps has he been given so much in return. The naïve exhibitionism of 'conspicuous consumption', which seeks distinction in the crude display of ill-mastered luxury, is nothing compared to the unique capacity of the pure gaze, a quasi-creative power which sets the aesthete apart from the common herd by a radical difference which seems to be inscribed in 'persons'.[29]

The function of the superfluousness of autonomous bourgeois art is to articulate the social hierarchy of bourgeois capitalism. Art demonstrates to society that the bourgeoisie now has sacred and noble authority, but to gain this authority the bourgeoisie has abstracted it from its tradition, its function; they have commodified the aura and they have developed a realm of beauty free from human need. This freedom, this life of ease, has become the aesthetic of art.[30] The historical autonomisation of art is a component of the autonomisation of the bourgeois class; the exclusion of necessity, the exclusion of vulgar emotional and sensual pleasure. And it is also the exclusion of those who are chained to necessity, those who display vulgar emotion and sensual pleasure. The nascent bourgeois conception of the body, the classical body, is a body sealed and finished, without growth or death. It is a body without functions, without process, alone. As the bourgeois class liberated itself from the subjection of feudalism, it liberated itself from the base needs and excretions of the body. But the crude and toxic industrial processes which generated the wealth of the bourgeois class turned the cities of the nineteenth century into dark and savage reservoirs of disease and effluent. The very source of their liberation pushed the bourgeoisie ever deeper into privacy, into autonomy, into alienation from the vulgarity of the body, from emotion, from the common people, from the urban squalor of the industrial city, from the source of their own wealth. This alienation is the freedom of the bourgeoisie and it is reproduced in art as the distance of the aesthetic gaze; it transcends the base and carnal pleasures of the body, the vulgar entertainments of the masses, the recklessness of political action, the vulnerability of emotion. In the silent gallery the viewer is never lost, but remains amused with their own perception. Impartiality fixes the superiority of the bourgeois as those who have risen above not only the animal passions of the lower classes but also the superstition of Christianity and the primitive bloodline of the aristocracy. This ascendance is reified in Modernism; function, significance and affection are all purged, the autonomy of art becomes both the form and content of the artwork – pure aura.

Which of course is the terrible irony of Modernism, because the avant-garde is not the spearhead of a radical new future but the means by which the bourgeoisie perpetuate the ancient social hierarchy of feudalism. And Modernism is not modern socially, technologically or industrially but the survival of a feudal handicraft into the age of mechanical reproduction. This is the paradox of autonomisation as a process which eliminates the human from the work of art, for as the human is refused as content, so it becomes the guarantee of aura, as mechanical reproduction becomes ever more efficient so what cannot be reproduced becomes ever more fetishised, which is to say that the humanity of the artist becomes fetishised as the source of the aura.

As the arts became increasingly industrialised and commodified so the artist was thrown into a crisis of function, which is the essential state of the modern artist, caught in an anachronism, a romantic rejection of both the feudal and the bourgeois.[31] Romanticism is the end of feudal prestige and the initiation of the aura. Without the prestige of function the aura of bourgeois art had no signified. Since more than a thousand years of sacred and noble art function could not be eliminated in a revolution, the prestige of art was transferred to the alienated artist genius who became the signified of the aura: noble, sacred, the priest, the King, the saint, the prophet, the witch, the Count, the Princess, the devil, the martyr, the messiah, the god. The autonomisation of art traps the artist in a vestigial feudal ritual, for since aura can only emanate from the divine hierarchy of Christ and his chosen nobility so the artist must shun trade as a proof of their sacred and noble caste. Aura as a commodity can be bought and sold on the capitalist market, but the artist can never enter capitalist industry; to do so would be to lose the gift of aura, to become a designer, a copywriter, an illustrator ... to become an employee. Romanticism opposed capitalism, but this opposition was based on an idealised organic feudalism, a return to a pre-capitalist realm of nature, chivalry and spirituality.[32] The avant-garde as vanguard of art has pioneered this feudalisation, from the mediaeval fantasies of William Morris and the mysticism of the Symbolists to the stigmata and self-immolation of Orlan, Franko B. and Stelarc. The artist becomes for the bourgeois viewer bearer of all sublimated passion, myth and romance. In return they are allowed the freedom of the Year King, the Lord, the human sacrifice, the shamen, the drunk, the taker of drugs, the fool, the overreacher, the prophet, the promiscuous, the impotent. This is why the bourgeois public is fascinated with artist martyrs like Van Gogh, Egon Schiele, Gwen John, Jackson Pollock, Frida Kahlo, Mark Rothko and Jean-Michel Basquiat. The work of the artist martyr is a reliquary; they have become immortal in the new bourgeois chronology. Artists carry the feudal past out of cyclical time into progress; they have been romanticised; they produce aura by repeating the myth of the alienated Messiah King endlessly but always new.

The pure gaze of the bourgeoisie is disinterested. Art turns loneliness, despair, horror and madness into beauty. As capitalism has specialised labour, the artists have become specialised as those who are allowed to express alienation on the condition that it is superfluous. Moreover it has been those artists who expressed their alienation most originally and radically who have pioneered new types of irrelevance.

Painting, sculpture and the other traditional 'arts' are not of themselves repressive, but they are repressive at the points where they enter the cultural institution of art. The Avant-Gardists sought the liberation of the creative spirit. But they did not liberate creativity; on the contrary they initiated a new form of detachment. The function of the avant-garde, as the vanguard of autonomous bourgeois art, is to ensure that all cultural products that penetrate the realm of the bourgeoisie are rendered superfluous.

Chapter 3

FOLKLORE VS. KITSCH: HOW ART THEORISED AGAINST THE POPULAR

The bourgeois institution of Art constituted itself by systematically excluding popular culture; art became the legitimate culture of the bourgeois state and popular culture became the illegitimate non-art. Whereas modern popular culture developed as a chaotic interaction of festive ritual, commerce, technology, prohibition and resistance, producing diverse and divergent cultural forms, the autonomisation of art was a historical process of eliminating, limiting or controlling all interaction that threatened the bourgeois fetishisation of feudal power. Art was initiated as a function of bourgeois society and yet the process of fetishisation in its constitution produced fundamental constraints to its development as the dominant legitimate culture of industrial capitalism. Whilst bourgeois entrepreneurs found they could apply their revolutionary industrial techniques to commodify and mass produce popular cultural forms, they also discovered that applying industrial techniques to art depreciated the aura they coveted; art had to be maintained as an elite pre-industrial handicraft. Consequently, by the late nineteenth century the authority of Art was being challenged by a mass-produced popular culture driven by technological progress, free market competition and democratic social reform. A history of modern art can be mapped by the aesthetic, ideological and institutional strategies deployed to negate this threat. A crucial and integrated element of this negation was the development of theories of culture which sought to historicise, rationalise and maintain the legitimacy of Art and the rift between Art and the popular. This chapter will consider the formative phase of these theories on the understanding that they will later be tracked and contextualised into the development of academic film and cultural theory.

Throughout the twentieth century the study of popular culture has been conceptually fragmented by categories and typologies that have prevented and distorted recognition of its continuous, contiguous and integrated tradition: myth, custom, folklore, folk art, popular art, commercial art, craft, kitsch, mass media, amateurism, outsider art, youth culture, subculture, fan culture and so on. This fragmentation is not a characteristic of Art, which is defined as eternal and unified, transcending all mediums, ethnicities and histories. The reason for this discrepancy is that the history of the academic study of popular culture is a bourgeois history; it was written by an autonomous ruling class observing the alien culture of its subjects. This is not to deny that popular culture is diverse, provisional and ephemeral, but it is to contend that the academic study of popular culture developed from a perception of the popular as an irrational, incoherent and alien wilderness to be mapped and made reasonable; the purpose of art for the bourgeoisie is to identify their culture

Figure 5: Pulp book cover, 1958 (illustrator untraced)

as the apex of a hierarchy which descends through grades of taste into the vulgar and the incoherent. Whilst some radical writers of contemporary cultural studies are currently challenging the fragmentation of the study of the popular there remains a fundamental legacy of separation which is articulated within theory as divisions into various critical typologies and academic disciplines according to perceptions of formal, technological, vocational and historical specificity.[1] A key historical fragmentation in the consideration of film has been between the study of theatre/drama and cinema/film and, as we shall soon discover, this has led to many irrational anomalies. But the fundamental rift in the historical constitution of the academic study of popular culture, the theory industry and the independent film and video sector of the 1970s, is the development of a theoretical practice which is institutionally extraneous and frequently hostile to popular practice; it divides the audience from the academy, education from industry and vocational/professional sectors from theoretical/research sectors. This crucial and complex division is structured by the Art/non-Art model; popular practice is illegitimate non-Art whilst the study of popular culture is a function of legitimate bourgeois culture.

The development of the Art/non-Art binary can be tracked through a series of emblematic theoretical models. One of the earliest and most influential foundations for the system was devised even while Art was consolidating its realm; it is the work of the Victorian poet and critic Matthew Arnold.[2] In his *Culture and Anarchy* of 1869 Arnold (re)defined the nature and purpose of culture in response to the bourgeois anxiety around Chartist demonstrations and radical working-class protest of the preceding years. According to Arnold culture is the study of perfection motivated by the social and moral passion for doing good.[3] It is the best that mankind has produced and its function is to perfect the beauty and intelligence of both the individual and humanity; to bring sweetness and light. Culture is not political or subjective, it is disinterested, harmonious, true and right, it is the will of God. Moreover, culture is the only defence against social anarchy and so it must be cultivated and disseminated by the democratic state. Arnold's definition of culture implicitly and at times explicitly depends on a concept of a relative non-culture: Arnold's culture is Art.

Forty years later the influential art critic Roger Fry integrated the Arnoldian concept of culture into his avant-garde manifesto *Art and Socialism* (1912). Fry was a member of the Bloomsbury Group, a disciple of William Morris, and the founder of the crafts production firm the Omega Workshops.[4] He believed modern life was poisoned by a vulgar commercial pseudo-Art which functioned primarily to symbolise social distinction. Ordinary people had their emotional life drugged by this fake culture and were incapable of seeing beyond its symbolic surface. The artist is a prophet and priest, the articulate soul of mankind. It is the artist who penetrates the sham world and directly apprehends the real; the revelation of ultimate value. Accordingly, the artist cannot be bound by conventional labour relations and must be free from all restraint. Neither capitalism or bureaucratic socialism can liberate Art; the future of Art lies in a society based on the return of manual craft.

In the 1930s Arnold's conception of culture was deployed in the highly influential work of the literary critic Frank Raymond Leavis, his wife Queenie Leavis and their collaborators on the Cambridge University-based journal of literary criticism *Scrutiny* (founded in 1932).[5] Leavis promoted the study of English literature as vital to the social, moral and spiritual life and future of the nation. His critical method was based on the intensive and detailed reading of texts. He rejected theoretical analysis and advocated the personal, vital, intuitive and emotional response of the reader/critic to the text. The ethical value of literature was its capacity to promote the creative, intellectual and emotional growth of the individual. Great literature was defined as that which had a vital and direct relationship with the objective world.[6] But Leavis and his Scrutineers believed that literature was in crisis – it was under attack from all sides by the vulgar mindless pulp and trash of a mass industrial culture which was perverting and dehumanising everyday life.[7] At the core of this belief was a nostalgia for a mythical pre-industrial folk culture, a rural organic community before industry, class and alienated labour. Leavis's solution to the crisis of taste was, as was Arnold's, a programme of national cultural renewal through education. The defining ideological and institutional core of the Leavisite cultural project was the academic study of literature; if the mass culture of cinema, advertising and popular fiction was an abnormal form of 'substitute living' and 'decreation' then the study of literature was the hope of a national culture of tradition, recreation and taste. Through the pages of *Scrutiny* and numerous pamphlets and books, Leavis and his collaborators influenced and inspired a generation of critics, teachers and educationalists, amongst them Richard Hoggart and Raymond Williams, the pioneers of what would become the academic discipline of cultural studies.

Meanwhile, in America, Clement Greenburg formulated perhaps the most celebrated and explicit model for the Art/non-Art binary in 'Avant-Garde and Kitsch' published in the Trotskyist *Partisan Review* in 1939.[8] This essay consolidates the integration of Arnold's concept of culture and the avant-garde developed by Fry. Greenburg divides culture into two opposing factions: the avant-garde which struggles to maintain and develop the tradition of art, and kitsch, the mass commercial popular culture which is a parasitic and fake pseudo-art. According to Greenburg, kitsch was initiated by the industrial revolution which produced a new urban working class alienated from their traditional folk culture. As the working class became literate and relatively affluent they constituted a market for culture and yet they failed to acquire taste. To supply the working-class demand for culture, capitalism produced the commodity of kitsch. What is most innovative in Greenburg's model is the equation of Art and the avant-garde with modernist abstraction and the condemnation of kitsch as realist and narrative; Art is formal, it requires effort to appreciate, it is concerned with cause, whilst kitsch is prefabricated, unequivocal and concerned with effect. This opposition was effectively reproduced in the 1970s as the radical project of British avant-garde film.

A formative influence on Greenburg's essay were ideas developed in German Marxist criticism. However, the classic Marxist attack on popular culture was written in New York a decade later by the German critics of the exiled Frankfurt School: *The Culture Industry: Enlightenment as Mass Deception* (1947) by Theodor Adorno and Max Horkheimer.[9] This compelling denunciation compounds the Art/non-Art binary with Marxist dialectics and elementary Freud to construct a model which anticipates not only the Situationists, British cultural studies and the film theory of the 1970s but also contemporary postmodern theory. For Adorno and Horkheimer commercial popular culture is an industry which rather than man-ufacturing commodities actually produces the subjectivity of its consumers. Art is passionate, serious and transcendent. Mass culture is standardised and industrial, it is a non-culture which negates thought and maintains an obedient working class. It promises freedom in order to enslave, it unifies the worker into the industrial production of life.

> The whole world is made to pass through the filter of the culture industry. The old experience of the movie-goer, who sees the world outside as an extension of the film he has just left (because the latter is intent upon reproducing the world of everyday perceptions), is now the producer's guideline. The more intensely and flawlessly his techniques duplicate empirical objects, the easier it is today for the illusion to prevail that the outside world is the straightforward continuation of that presented on the screen. This purpose has been furthered by mechanical reproduction since the lightning takeover by the sound film. Real life is becoming indistinguishable from the movies.[10]

Further, since popular cinema has eroded the difference between illusion and real life, the divided subjects of bourgeois society no longer struggle for individuality, they merely simulate; the culture industry commodifies life and it is irresistible.

In the 1970s the concept of popular cinema as a repressive industrial appara-tus for the construction of alienated subjects became the legitimising logic for both radical film theory and the independent film and video sector. Drawing from the work of the Frankfurt School, Antonio Gramsci and Louis Althusser, popular cinema was conceived as a crucial agent in the construction and maintenance of bourgeois ideological hegemony, and a core project of both theory and indepen-dent filmmaking became the demystification of hegemonic texts. We will return to demystification towards the end of this book; first we must get to grips with the difference between folklore and popular culture.

The significance of the cultural category of folklore in the context of experi-mental cinema is its potential as a third culture, alternative to both art and popular tradition. The Art/non-Art hierarchy as it appears in the work of Fry, Leavis, Green-burg and Adorno and Horkheimer is predicated on the annihilation of a mythic pre-industrial organic folk culture by the coming of a repressive mass industrial and commercial popular culture. And this assumption was also crucial to the formation of British cultural studies in the mid-1960s. However, in the 1970s a group of radi-cal social historians began to challenge the theoretical foundations of folklore and this historical revision was consolidated in the mid-1990s by Ronald Hutton.[11]

In a series of interconnected works Hutton systematically recontextualised the history of the British ritual year; the calender of folklore, festivals and rites from Christmas through Easter, the May, Corpus Christi, Harvest Home, Halloween to Guy Fawkes night. Although scholars of the aristocracy and the emergent bour-geoisie had studied and anthologised popular cultural forms since the eighteenth century the term 'folklore' was first introduced into the British academic lexicon in the mid-nineteenth century.[12] The folklore movement that developed in the late nineteenth/early twentieth century was ideologically dominated by the work of an elite group of bourgeois intellectuals.[13] The ideological underpinning of folklore was pagan survivalism. This arcane and attractive concept interpreted the popular rites and festivals of Britain as direct survivals of ancient pre-Christian pagan rituals which had persisted over thousands of years, hidden away in the timeless rural wilds and deep forests of England. Inspired by the scientific logic of evolutionism the folklore movement conceived popular festivals as social fossils.[14] So pervasive was this doctrine throughout the twentieth century that it is still widely accepted and propagated by enthusiasts and even by participants in many of the popular rituals. But in the late 1960s cultural historians began to question the fundamental assumptions of survivalism basing their work on exhaustive research of primary historical records. This revision is consolidated by Hutton in great depth and for our purposes it is only necessary to summarise certain critical points.

To begin with, apart from the three specific instances of decking sacred sites with greenery, Christmas presents and midsummer bonfires, there is actually no historical evidence that any other English popular rites or festive rituals are ancient survivals.[15] In fact the history of festive ritual is not a gradual and inevitable linear decline from the ancient sacred but a dynamic process of diverse local creation, renewal and reinvention by the common people. Rather than an inexorable recession from the sacred, the festive tradition has historically waxed and waned. Hutton asserts that far from declining in the late mediaeval period, festive ritual actually diversified and expanded. If the origins of many festive rituals were not ancient and sacred then neither were their functions; Hutton documents the historical development of a complex economy of festive fundraising both as a means of collecting money for the local community and as a form of ritualised begging undertaken by common people in times of unemployment and hardship. The final crucial point is that the tradition of festive ritual cannot be defined as essentially rural since many of the key features of the ritual year developed in urban centres. Festive ritual is not a survival half-remembered and eternally repeated; it is a primary element of a popular culture which is constantly and actively renewed and transformed by the people. The meaning of festive ritual cannot be discovered in a search for origins; it must be grasped in the context of its contemporary celebration. The nineteenth-century narrative of a pre-Christian paganism replaced by the coming of Christianity conceals the essential continuity of the mercurial popular tradition.

The reasons why the bourgeois folklorists of the nineteenth century propagated the doctrine of pagan survivalism are complex and contradictory. The concept of a secret pagan faith abiding in the hidden forests of Albion is essentially a strand of mystical utopian and arcadian Romanticism, whilst the concept of social fossilisation invokes the authority of scientific rationalism. This Enlightenment paradox can be understood if we consider the development of the egalitarianism of the French Revolution. In the years leading up to the revolution of 1789 radical French Enlightenment intellectuals such as Meslier, Morelly, Diderot and Rousseau developed a concept of human equality as a state of nature.[16] During the revolutionary period this egalitarianism was developed and applied by a group of eminent philosophers who were forerunners of both anthropology and the academic study of popular culture.[17] Such egalitarianism was a composite of unreconciled ideology: predominantly Christian millenarianism, classical paganism and rational atheism. Human nature was considered to be universal and perpetual, human beings had developed from a common ancestry, differences between nations and cultures were ascribed to environmental and geographical conditions. All human society was governed by a natural development towards perfection; all men given education and the right circumstances would progress towards self knowledge, happiness and perfection. The highest stage of this perfection was the bourgeois civilisation of Western Europe. According to this logic, the primitive nations of the world could be seen as inhabiting earlier stages of Western development, stages which the West had once passed through.[18] This historical relativity also extended into the internal wilderness of Western Europe; the revolutionary ideologues studied European popular culture as a primitive culture, as a retarded and savage survival of their own past. The revolutionary project was to unite all people in liberty, equality and fraternity by creating a standardised coherent monoculture; by eliminating difference.

However, within the revolutionary ideology there was also a current of utopian primitivism, a hybrid of Christian millenarianism, Neoclassicism and Enlightenment colonialism. Primitive man was also conceived as a noble savage living naturally in an arcadian utopia. In the early writings of the influential Enlightenment philosopher and prophet of Romanticism, Jean-Jacques Rousseau, civilised man's fall from natural liberty and equality is the direct consequence of the development of civilisation; private property, agriculture, industry, law, government.[19] The civilised man has not reached perfection, he has become alienated from his own nature, isolated in a web of civility, illusion and insincerity, unable to trust his fellows or himself.[20] The arts and sciences are merely ornaments to decorate the chains of slaves.

The egalitarianism of the revolution contained the conflicting tendencies of both the Enlightenment confidence in the supremacy of Western civilisation and a utopian primitivism in which Western civilisation was an alienation of human nature. Christian Millenarianism, Arcadia, the concept of the noble savage and the neoclassical emulation of the ancient democratic republics of Greece and Rome, were united in revolutionary egalitarianism as the belief that the revolutionary state was not simply the next phase in linear history, but the triumphant return (revolve) to ancient natural liberty, the end of alienation. This concept of a return to lost liberty, to the state of nature, is fundamental to the work of William Blake, to the formation of Romanticism and to the Utopian Socialism of Charles Fourier.

The decline of the revolutionary Republic, the transition to bourgeois Empire was accompanied by a shift in academic ideology. Revolutionary egalitarianism gave way to academic disciplines of hierarchy and separation legitimated by pseudo-scientific anatomical research, a fundamental concept being race. By the mid-nineteenth century the concept of the noble savage had been replaced in French anthropology by the doctrine of polygenism, a hierarchy of separate and unequal racial origins which legitimated white European supremacy, nationalism and colonial conquest.[21] This new doctrine of natural inequality was a fundamental concept in the bourgeois reconfiguration of society; it was ideologically necessary to suppress the power of utopian egalitarianism unleashed by the revolution. But this suppression was partial and contested; society reconfigured after the ascension of the bourgeoisie was riven with paradox and utopian desire confined and suspended in stratified realms of private and public life. It was this tension which was dramatised and exploited by the romantics and the nineteenth-century bohemians.

In Victorian England the romantic tension between utopian primitivism and racist nationalism found its defining expression in the relocation of a lost Arcadia to the idealised British mediaeval Gothic and Arthurian realms of Walter Scott, John Ruskin, the Pre-Raphaelite Brotherhood and William Morris.[22] This mediaevalism was a component of a wider current of romantic ruralism that developed from the bourgeois experience of industrialisation. In this context there emerged a specifically feudal idealisation of a lost rural organic culture: folklore. In the formation of the cluster of ideology around the Gothic and the mythical folklore, William Morris is both influential and exemplary. Crucially Morris is also the pivotal figure in the development of British avant-garde art, for it is he who synthesised the bourgeois nostalgia for the feudal order with the vision of a socialist utopia structured and validated by art.[23] In his utopian fantasy *News From Nowhere* of 1891 he explicitly locates his project for a revolutionary democratic and egalitarian future as a return to a lost feudal past, a golden age of fellowship, chivalry and craft before the alienation and pollution of the industrial age. But the revolution of *News From Nowhere* does not emancipate the working classes, it gentrifies them. To Morris the urban working classes are a class who have no art; the possibility that they might actually have a different urban popular culture of their own is unthinkable. The only admissible culture for the urban workers is a lost culture, a feudal and rural folk culture which could not challenge the Gothic handicraft fantasy.[24]

Morris is a key figure in the formation of folklore. However, the myth must be understood as a complex ideology which although it became central to the socialist tradition of the Fabian Society and the Labour Party, was also later invoked by the extreme right of the early organic movement, eugenics and British fascism. The invocation of folklore was motivated by the bourgeois desire for historical continuity and unity in an age of revolutionary conflict; it was a denial of class struggle and an appeal to a shared ancestry.

The search for pagan origins was both an attempt to establish a continuity between English culture and the mythology of Victorian classicism, and a strategy to construct a distinctly nationalist English cultural tradition. If the ascendant bourgeoisie desired the sacred and noble power of the aristocracy then they also carried a nostalgic longing for the arcadian days before their ascent, for their lost participation in the popular and the utopia of the revolution. This mystic nostalgia they projected onto the working class as the loss of folklore. The search for folklore was the desire for a popular origin of art, which is to say that aura was inscribed into the rural popular: folklore is the aura of popular culture. The common people could not be the agents of folklore; they could be picturesque savages, they could be objects of crypto-scientific study, like fossils or lost tribes, they could be the primitive mediums of the ancient lost pagan national culture, but they could not be the contemporary creators of an auratic culture; they could not be artists. For if the common people were artists then the hierarchy of taste was meaningless.

The solution to this threat was to objectify the culture of the people as the absent culture of folklore which could be appropriated by the bourgeoisie and then returned to the people as an officially-sanctioned unifying state culture. The ideological project of folklore was not simply a retrospective history but a political programme for a feudal future, and from the late nineteenth century onwards a legion of English intellectuals worked to realise the bourgeois vision of folklore and impose it upon the working class as an official national culture.[25] This official national culture was then deployed against urban popular culture, as the unifying racial/national myth of an ancient feudal Arcadia and as the utopian myth of an aesthetic future.[26] Like the imaginary traces of pagan survivalism, folklore remains as an ancient trace in Modernism, in the post-war rebuilding of Greater London and the new towns of the 1950s and 1960s, where new streets and estates were laid out under the mythic names of Camelot, Avalon and William Morris. Imagine this, 2005, the Brandon Estate, a high-rise council estate in Kennington, South London; nearby is the park where the Chartists met for the Monster Rally of 1848. Above the shabby estate pub, the Canterbury, a modernist mural is fading and flaking. Out on the scrubby lawn amongst the tower blocks is a big concrete plinth, on which is a big abstract sculpture by Henry Moore. On this sculpture the youth of the estate have drawn their names in indecipherable runes.

Folk as a cultural category has now become so paradoxical that it has actually achieved the kind of mysticism that generated its first use. It has no integrity as a description of a rural, oral, pre-industrial or manual popular culture. Moreover the term now maintains a bogus historical rift between pre-industrial rural and post-industrial urban popular culture when actually there was no division, it was a transition. Folklore has become so compromised as to render it absurd, although maybe for this reason it still has ironic and subversive potential. Nevertheless, it must be asked if Bakhtin's carnival is perhaps just another bourgeois feudal fantasy. Certainly Bakhtin's theoretical reading of the carnival is utopian, but it is not a projection of classical harmony and rural sedation, not a mystic realm of aura, not the lost dream of the bourgeoisie. Bakhtin has grasped in carnival the true and enduring hope of the people.

CINEMA AT THE HEART OF THE POP/ART CONFLICT

Chapter 4

MONTAGE CULTURE: CINEMA AS THE POPULAR FUNCTION OF FILM

In 1951 the post-war Labour state held the Festival of Britain on the South Bank of the Thames, where for hundreds of years ballad singers, puppet theatres and itinerant entertainers had set up their booths, and where Philip Astley had built the first circus of the modern tradition in the 1770s.[1] As a contribution to the festival the combined British film industry produced *The Magic Box* (Ronald Neame, 1951), a feature based on the life of the pioneer cinematographer William Friese-Green.[2] The most enchanting scene in this affectionate hokum reclaims the invention of moving-picture technology for Britain: on a dark and rainy night, in his dingy workshop, Friese-Green (Robert Donat) finally stumbles upon the secret of film projection. Having no one to share his discovery with, he invites a neighbourhood police constable into the workshop. The officer is amazed by the eerie supernatural flickering images and his amazement is very convincing since he is played by Laurence Olivier in a star cameo.

It is now widely agreed that cinematography was not discovered like cultural penicillin or invented by a Promethean genius as a gift for innocents. And, contrary to some of the more arcane theoretical speculation there is no reason to suppose that cinema was born into the world as a baby art which then had to pass through the equivalent stages in human psychic development.[3]

The technology of film was developed internationally by diverse agents, in multiple forms, incrementally over very many years. The final desperate race for the complete and integrated technology can be attributed to a number of key technicians working in parallel in the 1890s.[4] But cinema is not primarily a technology; it is a cultural tradition which at its broadest must include technical, formal, economic, industrial, social and historical factors. Moreover, cinema is not and never was an isolated or autonomous culture. Against the standard histories of the technological imperative of film we must now deploy the history of a popular and integrated audio-visual montage, for if it is true that the development of cinema was made possible by advances in technology, it is also inextricably true that the selection and mobilisation of these technological advances was driven by the demands and desires of popular culture. Central to this argument is a conceptual model of (audio-visual) montage as a cultural form distinct and irreducible to either technology or written language/literature. In the first case this is because, although there are obviously medium-specific qualities to every technology, there are, more significantly, audio-visual forms, works, skills, traditions and desires which have transcended technology. In the second case it is because however critically productive the description of audio-visual montage as text may be, it is inescapably a metaphor at a poetic remove

Figure 6: Charlie Chaplin in the cinematic version of the famous Fred Karno 'Mummingbirds sketch': *A Night at the Show* (Charlie Chaplin, 1915)

from a direct investigation of an audio-visual culture. This chapter will return to the history of the illegitimate popular tradition to contextualise the development of popular audio-visual montage. It will also consider and revise three critical models for the historical origins of cinema, devised respectively by Sergei Eisenstein, Tom Gunning and A. Nicholas Vardac. Finally, it will outline the cultural context of the early British film industry and the initiation of the bourgeois sedation of popular cinema.

To (re)define montage we must review the critical conception of the eminent Soviet filmmaker and theorist Sergei Eisenstein. Eisenstein's theory of montage editing is complex, eclectic, provisional and often prescriptive, moreover it changed as it developed and the critical, political and technological context of his work changed. But despite the apparent inconsistencies, it is possible to abstract a set of essential principles. As a filmmaker Eisenstein was above all interested in how to most effectively communicate meaning through film; how to engage the intellect and emotion of the audience. His conception was that cinematic meaning is produced by the combination of discrete elements. In opposition to other contemporary montagists, Eisenstein held that meaning is not assembled by linking frame to frame, shot to shot, rather it is produced by the dialectical conflict between the different elements.[5] Montage is creation by juxtaposition; the meaning produced by the collision of elements cannot be reduced to the sum of the parts, it is a new qualitatively different creation. Moreover, montage is not only located in the juxta-position between shots and frames, it also takes place within the elements of a single frame's composition. In fact montage takes place at every level of film composition from set lighting to acting. The creative act of cinema is the control of montage, through which disparate elements are unified into the compound theme of the film. Whereas it is possible to absolutely minimise the montage composition in a given film, Eisenstein's interest lies in complex audio-visual counterpoint and he makes comparisons between his concept of complex montage and the simultaneity and polyphony of jazz.[6] Montage is movement, and movement is both the condi-tion of montage and a means to engage, analogise and propel the critical conscious-ness of the audience.[7]

A common misconception about Eisenstein is that he considered montage to be the unique principle of film editing, when actually his theoretical framework takes montage to be a transcendent principle of meaning construction applicable to all forms of cultural production from cinema to theatre, music, poetry, painting and so on.[8] This concept of montage as cultural, and not determined by the medium or technology, is consistent throughout his career. Moreover, his first published theorisation of audio-visual montage was not based on his experience or research as a filmmaker, but was concerned with montage in the theatre and it was written when he was a young set designer and theatre director: 'The Montage of Attrac-tions', published in *Lef* magazine in 1923.[9] Eisenstein's concept of the attraction originated from a collaboration with Sergei Yutkevitch on an experimental panto-mime in 1922.[10] Yutkevitch was a member of the Factory of the Eccentric Actor (FEKS), a group of young Soviet Futurists who celebrated the radical power of the popular. During the collaboration with Eisenstein, Yutkevitch visited his favourite fairground attraction, a type of rollercoaster; later whilst he was explaining the in-tense excitement of the ride, Eisenstein came up with the term 'scenic attractions' to describe the techniques they had developed.[11]

'The Montage of Attractions' is an attempt to fuse a psychological model of audience reception with the formal techniques and traditions of popular culture; moreover, combined with accounts of his early work in theatre it becomes clear that Eisenstein formulated his montage theory from his working experience and research into various forms of the popular. In an essay on the origin of his experi-ments with montage written in the 1930s, Eisenstein declared:

I think that first and foremost we must give all credit to the basic principles of the circus and the music hall – for which I have had a passionate love since childhood. Under the influence of the French comedians, and of Chaplin (of whom we had only heard), and the first news of the fox-trot and jazz, this early love thrived. The music hall element was obviously needed at the time for the emergence of a 'montage' form of thought. Harlequin's parti-coloured costume grew and spread, first over the structure of the programme, and fi-nally into the method of the whole production.[12]

From this observation it is possible to (re)define a model of montage to be operative in this history. Whereas Eisenstein considered the agency of montage to be conflict, more accurately and inclusively we could identify the agency as difference. Conceptually difference would include not only conflict between the elements of montage but also a range of relations between elements from contrast to congruence, variation, hybridisation or intervention. Moreover, montage as difference allows us to recognise forms of culture which appear to, or claim to have preceded or surpassed montage and become undifferentiated, pure and absolute, crucially modernist art. Also, rather than defining montage as an essential and universal process of meaning construction, let us specify the use of sophisticated montage as a particular cultural tendency or tradition. Although this tradition would not be exclusive to popular culture, the crucial point is that montage is the definitive form of the popular tradition, and it is the popular which has developed the definitive forms of montage. The historical factors involved in this development are complex. First, many of the conditions of montage are already active in carnival. As Bakhtin observed, the carnival is created by all its participants without hierarchy, it celebrates unity in plurality, it is unfinished and so always connected but fragmented. Carnival is the suspension of authority, it reveals the relativity of order allowing the free change and renewal of elements. As the concept of the human body in Classicism became perfect and closed so the grotesque realist body of carnival is a body of protuberances, holes, components and discharges; a montage body. Further, if we consider the fairground as the definitive and formative site of popular culture then it is possible to apply montage theory to the movement of the fairgoers (audience) around the various booths and attractions of the fair. The fair is an interactive and sensual free montage.

The historical development of the popular theatrical forms so far considered can be recognised as a process of transferring external fairground forms into new internal institutions – for example, the theatre of the Forains into pantomime or the ballad singers into music hall and so on. The key formal transfer from the fair to the new industrial popular culture is variety and conviviality. Further, popular culture has historically developed forms which prioritised sound and image over text, forms which developed complex audio-visual montage to reach audiences with partial literacy and forms developed specifically to subvert more than a century of prohibition of spoken dialogue and the censorship of explicit political expression.

The historical development of cinema as a form of popular audio-visual montage was a gradual and integrated process which developed through a diversity of forms. The first 'peep shows' began as amusements for the wealthy in the early seventeenth century, but by the eighteenth century they had been carried by itinerant showmen throughout Europe.[13] Peep shows were essentially boxes which contained model theatres and the show was a painted landscape, an interior realm glimpsed through an eyehole or lens. In more complex peep shows the scene would be a performed, changing spectacle. Typically night would fall and lights would appear in the windows of a city, an effect produced by perforating the backdrop and lighting it from behind. In some boxes landscape would pass before the eye on a winding roll or the image would be mounted onto a transparent screen which would be transformed by a change in the back lighting. To accompany the peep show and to attract custom the showman or a companion would play music.

Techniques of transparency and perforation to produce lighting effects and transformations were also used on large-scale painted backdrops in the theatre.[14] In the late eighteenth century moving perspective paintings were developed which slowly unfurled on rollers. These 'panoramas' were accompanied by a live commentary or narrative, sound effects, music and song. Meanwhile, in the darkness of the fairbooths there were shadow plays, marionettes, mechanical puppets and magic lantern shows. In the mid-eighteenth century a form of shadow theatre was imported to London from Italy which integrated the black silhouettes of the shadow plays, transparent screens and images projected by magic lantern. The prototype magic lantern dates from a design by Athanasius Kircher around 1646 which projected painted images from glass slides through a lens by means of a candle or lamp. By the early eight-eenth century the showmen and fairbooths were presenting magic lantern shows featuring comic or grotesque images. From the late seventeenth century the magic lantern design was improved by various innovators who increased the brightness and focus of the image. In the eighteenth century various techniques of animating lantern slides were developed involving the movement of two or more slides against each other.[15] In revolutionary Paris, Etienne Gaspard Robert, who worked under the English alias of Robertson, developed a magic lantern show which took the form of a terrifying séance and featured images of ghosts, skeletons and the famous dead projected onto gauze screens or clouds of smoke: the Phantasmagoria.[16] Phantasmagorical techniques were rapidly taken up by other showmen; they were integrated into popular theatre and they became a standard fairbooth entertainment known as the 'ghost show' which persisted into the early twentieth century. In the mid-nineteenth century phantasmagorical effects were used by the celebrated magician and illusionist Robert-Houdin at his theatre in Paris which in 1888 was bought and subsequently managed by the great innovator of film illusion and pantomime cinema Georges Méliès.

A playbill from Richardson's Booth theatre at Bartholomew Fair in 1825 gives an impression of the integration of popular audio-visual montage.[17]

Richardson's Theatre

———

This Day will be performed, an entire New Melo-Drama
called the
WANDERING OUTLAW,
Or, the Hour of Retribution.

Gustavus, Elector of Saxony, Mr. Wright.
Orsina, Baron of Holstein, Mr. Cooper.

Ulric and Albert, Vassals to Orsina, Messrs. Grove and Moore.
St Clair, the Wandering Outlaw, Mr. Smith.
Rinalda, the Accusing Spirit, Mr. Darling.
Monks, Vassals, Hunters, &c.
Rosabella, Wife to the Outlaw, Mrs. Smith.
Nuns and Ladies.
——

The piece concludes with the DEATH OF ORSINA, and
the Appearance of the
ACCUSING SPIRIT

The Entertainments to conclude with a New Comic Harlinquinade,
with New Scenery, Tricks, Dresses, and Decorations, called,
HARLEQUIN FAUSTUS !
OR, THE DEVIL WILL HAVE HIS OWN.

Luciferno, Mr Thomas.

Daemon Amozor, afterwards Pantaloon, Mr. WILKINSON. – Daemon Zio-
kos, afterwards Clown, Mr. HAYWARD. – Violencello Player, Mr. Hartem.
– Baker, Mr. THOMPSON. – Landlord, Mr. WILKINS. – Fisherman, Mr.
RAE. – Doctor Faustus, afterwards Harlequin, Mr. SALTER. – Adelada, afterwards Columbine,

MISS WILMOT.

Attendant Daemons, Sprites, Fairies, Ballad Singers, Flower Girls, &c. &c.
——
The Pantomime will finish with
A SPLENDID PANORAMA,

Painted by the First Artists.

In the early years of the nineteenth century the theatrical set designer Louis Daguerre developed the diorama, a form of three-dimensional panorama show which
used transparent screens, lighting changes and, later, also integrated magic lantern
projection. When, in 1826, Daguerre suggested to Nicéphore Niépce that they collaborate on the invention of a photographic process it was specifically motivated by
the need to improve his diorama business in a competitive market.[18]
  By the mid-nineteenth century magic lantern shows had become an established
and sophisticated popular entertainment incorporating various technical innovations, crucially the development of brighter illumination from limelight, gas and
finally electricity. The increased use of multiple projectors allowed spectacular dis-

solves from image to image and even animated moving sequences. The show would be accompanied by music and a lecturer who would narrate or link the slide sequence, drawing the audience's attention to significant details in the images. Many of the most popular lantern sequences were sensational narratives taken from popular literature and composed as melodramatic tableaux. From the work of Daguerre, Bayard, Fox Talbot and others the photographic lantern slide was developed. Before photography the lantern lecture was dependent on a limited range of hand-painted or printed slides, thus the photographic slide introduced a new element of attraction: the spectacle of reality. Moreover, photographic slides could be industrially reproduced and distributed. An immensely popular form which emerged from the photographic slide lecture was the travelogue, an illustrated narrative journey to exotic lands. The journey or ride is a fundamental fairground attraction which dates back to mediaeval tournaments, horse rides, swings and sledging. Mechanical rides such as wooden roundabouts and wheels powered by people or horses appeared at English fairs in the seventeenth century.[19] In the late sixteenth century there developed in Russia a form of very fast downhill ice sledging which was eventually reproduced in Paris at the end of the eighteenth century by substituting a track of closely-spaced rollers upon which a sled would coast, and from this the rollercoaster developed. The advent of steam power led to the development of mechanised rides such as the carousel, the steam velocipede, the switchback and the big wheel in the late nineteenth century. The Victorian steam carousel was a virtual montage machine designed to engage the diverse senses of both spectators and riders. The commotion of the fair whirls before your eyes as the sky, the mirrors and the gaudy wooden horses lurch and plunge. There is the smell of grease and smoke in the air. This is accompanied by the loud and glittering steam organ with all its various moving components, the automata puppet bandsmen, and around the base and top of the frame a strip of painted tableaux or portraits.[20]

The innovation of moving-image illusion based on the rapid alternation of variant images can be traced to a series of optical experiments and amusements beginning with the spinning disc known as the Thaumotrope (1827). Probably the first device which created continuous animated movement from painted or printed images was Plateau's Phenakistoscope (1833), and as early as 1853 Phenakistoscope techniques were being combined with magic lantern technology to produce projected animated images.[21] The most successful collective entertainment to employ this technology was Emile Reynaud's Pantomimes Lumineuses which he presented at the Musée Grevin in 1892.[22]

In 1894 a parlour opened in Oxford Street, London, displaying Edison's Kinetoscope, a form of peep show which used both photographic and moving-image technology. The first commercial films Edison produced for the Kinetoscope were vaudeville performers doing their acts (famously Annabelle Moore doing her celebrated Butterfly Dance).[23] Incorporating and improving on the Kinetoscope, photographic film projection was developed a year later, most influentially with Lumière's Cinématograph (1895) which was first demonstrated in London in 1896;

however, before it arrived in England Birt Acres had already demonstrated the rival system that he had developed with R.W. Paul.

Although the initial demonstrations of film technology were staged in respectable bourgeois institutes for genteel audiences, cinema is the point where the popular begins to use film technology. Within a year of the Lumière show one-reel films were appearing at fairbooths, music halls and variety theatres, travelling projectionists were touring the country putting on shows in any hall for hire and stage magicians were incorporating film illusion into their programmes. At the music halls the cinematograph was integrated into the programme as a turn amongst the live acts.

In the early years of cinema the larger fairs would often have four or five competing booth cinemas, and the grandest were huge tents with spectacular walk-up façades in which an audience of up to a thousand would watch films accompanied by a majestic mechanical organ.[24] The earliest films were one-shot, static records of events characterised by their astonishing motion: workers leaving a factory, a train leaving a station, a stormy sea, a boat leaving a harbour … The attraction of the first films was not so much their content but the cinematographic process itself; the turn on the music hall bill was not the title of a film, it was the name of the new machine, the Cinematograph or the Bioscope. The projectionist and the projector would be visible or would often stand amongst the audience as a performer, and in the convivial atmosphere of the music hall the audience could shout out requests that certain films or sequences be repeated. As the initial novelty waned and commercial competition increased, filmmaking rapidly expanded into new forms of actuality, travel, sporting events, music hall acts, news, trick films, comedies, ghost stories, animation. These early cinema shows, like the panoramas and magic lantern shows, would be accompanied by music, sound effects and often a lecturer or narrator who would explain the action to the audience and point out details in the film frame that they might otherwise miss.[25] Some films would be shot so that when screened, live actors could lip-sync dialogue or song, like the performers of the shadow theatre.[26]

Around the turn of the twentieth century the culture of the British penny gaff theatres was revitalised by cinema and makeshift gaff cinemas spread rapidly throughout the urban districts. Whilst the gaff theatres had been suppressed by licensing laws and superseded by music hall, cinema gaffs had far lower commercial overheads and they could operate outside of the legal restrictions on theatre and live entertainment. The gaff cinemas flourished until licensing restraints under the Cinematograph Act of 1909 curbed their expansion and encouraged the development of established and purpose-built cinemas. In 1907 the first custom-built cinema was opened in Britain and by 1914 there were between four and five thousand established cinemas. With the move from the fairs, music halls and gaffs of early cinema to the purpose-built and established cinemas there was a concomitant shift in film form from the diversity of the short film programme to longer narrative features. The earliest cinema shows would often use magic lantern slides as the titles between films. Around 1903 intertitles began to be integrated into the films themselves; eventually they became not only titles but carried the dialogue of the characters. By 1906 in both Britain and America many of the basic narrative techniques had been established: spatial and temporal continuity, close-ups, point-of-view shots, through-lines of action and so on. Feature-length films began to be produced around 1910 and around 1915 D. W. Griffith and others initiated the classic Hollywood feature style.

Whilst almost every aspect of the phenomenal cultural generation and expansion of cinema is fascinating, what is really remarkable is that up until relatively recently the early history of the cinema was considered the formation of a spontaneous cause: cinema was suddenly born as a primitive unconstituted infant and then gradually developed into the complex and coherent Seventh Art.[27] However, from the 1980s onwards Tom Gunning challenged this perception in a series of influential articles. In 1993 he conceptualised the theory of an ascendant narrative cinema as 'the continuity model' which is based on three historical assumptions:[28] First, the evolutionary assumption appears in early cinema histories and conceives cinema before 1914 to be a primitive form in which cinema is an unrealised potential. Only through a period of technological and economic research and development does film evolve into its natural and classic narrative form, or what Noël Burch has called the Institutional Mode of Representation.[29] Key writers of this history would be Terry Ramsaye and Lewis Jacobs. Second, the cinematic assumption is based upon the evolutionary assumption, in that it holds that cinema evolved by discovering and exploring its true cinematic essence. To do this cinema had to free itself from the limits of theatre, it had to develop its unique cinematic characteristics, editing, camera mobility, camera angle and so on. Early cinema is primitive precisely because it is theatrical. Key writers influenced by this assumption would be Lewis Jacobs, Georges Sadoul and Jean Mitry. Last, the most subtle and most recent is the narrative assumption articulated by Christian Metz. This is essentially a reworking of the cinematic assumption which defines the true cinematic essence as narrative. Narrative becomes the means and end of the evolution of cinema. These three assumptions interact to explain the continuity from primitive cinema to the classic narrative film form: cinema had to evolve an efficient narrative system; since it did not have the dialogue of theatre it developed its own cinematic language.

Against this continuity model of cinema history, Gunning suggests that early cinema from its inception to around 1906 was not a primitive phase of classic narrative cinema, it was actually a different mode of cinema which developed from the popular variety forms of music hall and fair booth. Borrowing the term from Eisenstein, Gunning names this 'the cinema of attractions'. According to Gunning the cinema of attractions dominated early cinema until about 1906 or 1907 when its dissolution was brought about by the industrial reorganisation of the cinema industry in the wake of the rapid expansion of nickelodeon (penny gaff) exhibition (1907–13). It was during this intersection of economic and social forces that Griffith and other early filmmakers developed the classic narrative form; cinema was narrativised.[30]

Gunning defines the cinema of attractions in contrast to the classic narrative form. Invoking Roland Barthes and the Russian Formalists he asserts that narrative develops in time as a continuous trajectory of cause and effect in a coherent and stable fictional world of characters and locations; a diegesis. The narrative film audience is not acknowledged; rather they are unseen voyeurs. Narrative pleasure is produced by engaging the audience in the pursuit of an enigma and invoking the desire for its resolution, which may be endlessly deferred. In the 1986 article which introduced the concept Gunning proposes that contrary to narrative cinema,

> the cinema of attractions directly solicits spectator attention, inciting visual curiosity, and supplying pleasure through an exciting spectacle, a unique event, whether fictional or documentary, that is of interest in itself. The attraction to be displayed may also be of a cinematic nature, such as the early close-ups … or trick films in which a cinematic manipulation (slow motion, reverse motion, substitution, multiple exposure) provides the film's novelty. Fictional situations tend to be restricted to gags, vaudeville numbers or recreations of shocking or curious incidents (executions, current events). It is the direct address of the audience, in which an attraction is offered to the spectator by a cinema showman, that defines this approach to filmmaking. Theatrical display dominates over narrative absorption, emphasising the direct stimulation of shock or surprise at the expense of unfolding a story or creating a diegetic universe. The cinema of attractions expends little energy creating characters with psychological motivations or individual personality. Making use of both fictional and non-fictional attractions, its energy moves outward towards an acknowledged spectator rather than inward towards the character-based situations essential to classical cinema.[31]

The cinema of attractions is exhibitionist, the audience is acknowledged, the characters look directly into the camera. It astonishes and shocks, it does not develop in time, it is a temporal irruption. The pleasure of the attraction is a conscious fascination and curiosity with visual spectacle, novelty, social taboo and sensational violence. One of the most interesting interactions between the cinema of attractions and narrative form is the apotheosis ending in which early fictional films would culminate in a 'grand finale in which principal members of the cast reappear and strike poses in a timeless allegorical space that sums up the action of the piece.'[32] A tableau.

Gunning's concept of the cinema of attractions is a radical revision of teleological cinema history and the most radical point he makes concerns avant-garde cinema. He asserts that after 1907 the cinema of attractions is superseded by classic narrative film but it is not eliminated, it becomes an integrated component of certain popular genres such as musicals. And it also goes underground into certain avant-garde film practices. Writing in 1986 at the time of the New York Cinema of Transgression movement, Gunning speculated:

Now in a period of American avant-garde cinema in which the tradition of contemplative subjectivity has perhaps run its (often glorious) course, it is possible that this earlier carnival of the cinema, and the methods of popular entertainment, still provide an unexhausted resource – a Coney Island of the avant-garde, whose never dominant but always sensed current can be traced from Méliès through Keaton, through *Un Chien Andalou* (1928), and Jack Smith.[33]

In other words, the cinema of attractions is not only a historical non-narrative alternative to classic narrative cinema, it is a current in the historical avant-garde and a potential new model for the contemporary avant-garde. Gunning is right, but his focus is too narrow and his terminology is misleading. The current he locates is not the avant-garde, it is Underground Cinema. The process of historical narrativisation he describes is only a component of a more fundamental conflict in cinema. The significance of the cinema of attractions is that it provides an alternative model for a radical popular cinema, but Gunning, despite detailed qualifications and protestations to the contrary, is in danger of slipping into the most pervasive and vacuous binary opposition espoused by the 1970s' avant-garde: narrative = hegemony vs. non-narrative = radical. This mantra will be dealt with in some detail later; for now it must suffice to examine Gunning's concept of the narrativisation of early cinema.

Although Gunning subverts the continuity model of cinema history he does not totally negate the assumption that the narrative form of cinema was in some way invented or discovered. However, as far back as 1949 a brilliant study was published which claimed that the essential montage techniques of narrative cinema were actually first developed in the popular theatre. The book was *Stage to Screen: Theatrical Origins of Early Film: David Garrick to D. W. Griffith* by A. Nicholas Vardac, and although it was occasionally cited in various theoretical texts concerning melodrama, its conclusions were neglected by modern film theory.[34] According to Vardac, popular theatre, particularly melodrama, was driven by an aesthetic of mute spectacle to develop cinematic visual narrative techniques decades before the advent of film technology. Late nineteenth-century melodramas would be constructed as pictorial episodes, theatre lights would be faded down at the end of a scene and then back up for a new scene, sound effects and music would cover scene changes, continuous action could proceed from one scene to the next, spectacular effects were used to produce flashbacks, dissolves, transformations, even theatrical tracking shots.[35] Most significantly melodrama developed a form of cross-cutting or parallel montage in which scenes of narrative action taking place simultaneously but in different locations could be dramatically presented to the audience using techniques designed to shift their focus of attention from location to location. These could be different rooms in the same house, different parts of the same city or distant locations such as the narrative linking of the twins in Paris and Corsica in Dion Boucicault's famous version of *The Corsican Brothers* (1852). The most basic method of achieving this parallel action would be rapid scene changing; more sophisticated techniques would break the stage up into sites of action which could be covered and revealed by shutters, or illuminated and blacked out by stage lighting. The introduction of parallel editing in the cinema is traditionally ascribed to D. W. Griffith and certainly he developed many of the narrative montage techniques specific to the cinema, but Griffith's understanding of popular narrative montage techniques was based on years of experience as an actor and writer in theatrical melodrama – he did not so much invent narrative montage techniques as translate them from popular theatre.[36] Vardac goes further. His cinema history is an absolute inversion of both the continuity model and Gunning: he proposes that cinema was not a new cultural or technological medium which gradually developed its own cinematic form, rather it was a necessary migration and culmination of a cultural mode from theatrical to cinematic means. Cinema was invented because popular narrative montage had outgrown the capabilities of the theatre:

> The peak of Victorian aesthetic activity, with its highly pictorial bias in the arts of staging, the drama and the novel, coincided with the final phase in the invention of the motion picture. The relationship suggested by these chronological parallels is significant. It would suggest the well-known adage, 'necessity is the mother of invention'. The motion picture, like the realistic-romantic expression in the arts, was deeply rooted, even during its long period of incubation, in the social needs of the times. The obvious implications would still those untutored critics who maintain that cinema arrived simply when the necessary technical knowledge and equipment were available. Cinema was not born simply with the invention of Eastman's celluloid film nor with the arrival of the motion-picture camera; the need for cinema had been felt as early as 1824, and its conception and early development occurred with analogous advances in the theatre of Realism and romance. Both responded to the same popular 'tension', the same aesthetic preference. The facilities were products of the need, and not the need of the facilities.[37]

Vardac conceives the aesthetic needs which drove the development of narrative cinema as realistic-romantic but he blurs the distinction between the legitimate and the popular theatre precisely during the historic period in which a new legitimate bourgeois art theatre was emerging: Naturalism.

The significance of theatrical Naturalism in cinema history is complex and deceptive. Whereas Naturalism was conceived by its continental pioneers as functional, socially radical and democratic, its trajectory in England is indivisible from the avant-garde autonomisation of art. This would at first appear to be a contradiction in terms since the manifestos of Naturalism above all demand a natural and truthful engagement with contemporary life.[38] Naturalism seeks to apply the objective analytic method of the natural sciences to drama, to dramatise an authentic relationship between action, character and social environment.[39] However, this radical desire for social truth must be seen in the context of the avant-garde as the desire for pure form, the stripping away of all theatrical convention, the elimination of vulgar spectacle and the end of all the demeaning social interaction between the stage and the audience. Central to the naturalist project is the construction of the conventional fourth wall behind which the fictional world, the diegesis, unfolds. Behind the fourth wall the bourgeoisie are private, the trajectory of Naturalism objectifies drama, the conviviality of the popular theatre is replaced by analytic voyeurism. All non-diegetic factors including music are removed, all conventions which might disrupt the diegesis are suppressed. Naturalism should not be confused with the sensational realism of popular theatre – the handling of real contemporary life in melodrama was an issue of content and style rather than a fundamental and overriding formal concern, and realistic effects such as projection, panoramas, live animals, crowd scenes and so on were not used in popular theatre to construct an objective mimetic diegesis, they were spectacular attractions in a fabulous materialism. On the contrary, the demands of naturalist Realism promote the reproduction of contemporary life with the minimum of theatrical convention and effect; the room inevitably becomes the only space it is realistically possible to construct on stage and long scenes in real time become the only authentic temporal realm. The naturalist diegetic has at its core an essential paradox; the pursuit of an objective and natural dramatic reality negates the conventions of spectacular narrative but demands ever-increasing techniques of simulation. The end of the naturalist trajectory is not an ever more authentic representation of contemporary life, it is the recognition that every authentic representation of contemporary life in the theatre is ultimately an illusion; this paradox inevitably becomes the pivotal content of twentieth-century modernist theatre in the work of Pirandello, Beckett, Pinter and so on. This is the autonomy of art theatre, the anxiety that drama can only ever be about itself.

The development of English Naturalism is a complex interplay of industrial and cultural determinants. Its formation can be traced to the mid-nineteenth-century bourgeois pursuit of rational and respectable leisure. Around the 1860s the popular domination of the theatre began to gradually give way to a reconfigured separation between the legitimate and the popular stage.[40] This was partly due to the rise of music hall which annexed the variety/fairground forms of popular theatre, and partly due to the appropriation and gentrification of the legitimate theatre by the ascendant bourgeoisie.[41] Whereas melodrama continued to dominate the popular theatres, the new theatres now began to develop a form of drama based on the bourgeois fascination with and aspirations to genteel society: society drama. The development of this form followed a corresponding shift in stage design, from the apron stage of popular theatre which extended out amongst the audience to the proscenium box set which produced a discrete picture plane or fourth wall. In the 1870s the fully-enclosed proscenium box set was developed which framed the room like a moving painting. Whereas the action of spectacular melodrama required mobile conventional scenery, the society drama developed – and was developed by – the realistic representation of relatively permanent rooms. The natural environment of bourgeois drama became the drawing room. Moreover, the construction of a proscenium wall between audience and stage was one of the principal regulations of the Suitability Act of 1878, which was a key factor in the suppression of pub and saloon music hall.

Gunning and Vardac both locate key shifts in the popular tradition, but they can only be reconciled by a concept of cinema history which is far more complex and pluralistic, a history which identifies and integrates the historical separation of art and popular culture. If the attraction of Realism was a key factor in the development of cinema then this Realism cannot be confused with Naturalism. The bourgeois naturalist tendency of the late nineteenth century is antithetical to the theatrical conventions necessary for the montage techniques identified by Vardac; the process of montage development from theatre to cinema is specifically popular. Whilst popular cinema developed complex and original narrative continuity techniques, this innovation was determined in the context of a sophisticated popular theatrical culture which had developed techniques of audio-visual montage in historical opposition to legitimate culture. The most obvious examples of this are the continuity of mime, music, tableaux and intertitles from melodrama directly into silent cinema. The rapid growth of cinema in the early twentieth century effectively terminated popular theatrical melodrama; the form was transferred to cinema. The cinematification of melodrama in turn accelerated the gentrification of the theatre; the theatrical class conflict of audience riots, police raids and licensing of the nineteenth century ended with the migration of the popular audience from theatre to cinema and the sedation of theatre into art.

The cinema of attractions must be understood not only as a historical phase but as one of the potential and recurrent modes of popular cinema. Gunning's oppositional model of an attractions mode eliminated by the narrative mode of cinema is misleading because they are both forms of an integrated popular montage tradition. Whilst it is true that popular theatre developed a sophisticated narrative montage before cinema it was not the only popular form to do so: serial fiction, magic lantern shows, advertising, wax works and comic strips all developed narrative montage forms before cinema. In particular the modern comic strip developed historically parallel to cinema and the relationship between the two forms has always been interactive. According to M. Thomas Inge many standard cinematic montage techniques appeared in comics before cinema: angle shots, panning, close-ups, cutting, framing and so on.[42] The amazing comic strip illustrator and early animator Winsor McCay graphically produced complex sequences of cinematic montage, perspectives, slow motion and point-of-view shots that were not perfected by cinema until years later. McCay's most celebrated strips were *Dreams of a Rarebit Fiend* (1905) and *Little Nemo in Slumberland*, which ran from 1905 intermittently until 1926. A particularly striking sequence from *Dreams of a Rarebit Fiend* depicts the point-of-view sequence of a man dreaming of his own death, funeral and burial complete with a final shot of earth tumbling down onto his (the reader's) face. A similar sequence was produced cinematically 27 years later by Carl Theodor Dreyer in *Vampyr* (1932).

The diversity of popular culture generated cinema at every level – there are direct continuities from the montage of popular theatre and comic strip, from serial fiction and from the fairground attractions, ghost shows and rides. Gunning is certainly correct in identifying the cinema of attractions as qualitatively different to the later established cinema but the attractions/narrative binary he proposes is not the key to understanding the character of that shift. The key to the development of popular cinema in the long term is that it combined and integrated the diversity of popular culture, and the dominant factor in this integration was the formalisation of popular narrative montage. The cinema of attractions did not disappear in 1907; the model of the classic narrative form deployed by Gunning and many of other theorists is an over simplification. Whilst

Figure 7: The corpse's point-of-view in *Dreams of a Rarebit Fiend* (Winsor McCay, 1905).

it is true that there is a tradition of narrative filmmaking which enforces Gunning's model of classic narrative cinema, it is not the popular; it is far closer to bourgeois Naturalism. This is the crucial point: the concept of classic narrative cinema conflates narrative with bourgeois Naturalism. The form of narrative active in the development of popular cinema was not the naturalist diegetic of mimetic simulation but the complex conventional modes of the popular. Popular cinema operates across the range of the allegorical, playful, convivial, marvellous and materialist strategies of popular culture. Gunning's definition of the cinema of attractions is intrinsic to a far wider range of popular cinema forms than he suggests, including comedy, musicals, horror films, monster films, science fiction, pornography, cartoons, disaster movies, documentaries, nature films, surf movies and so on. Furthermore, many of the popular cinema forms which are dominated by narrative actually use their narrative structure to integrate and display spectacular attractions: the landscape in westerns, the action sequence in crime thrillers or the costume design in romantic drama. Far from being incompatible or mutually exclusive, the montage of popular cinema is actually a synthesis of narrative and attraction – this is the core of Eisenstein's interpretation and even Gunning comes very close to acknowledging it.[43] Popular cinema is a narrative of attractions. Moreover, it must be remembered that the cinema show as a single feature film in a standardised and unadorned auditorium is a relatively recent development. A night at the picture palaces of the 1920s would include a feature film and a full supporting programme of short films, for instance a serial thriller, a cartoon and a newsreel accompanied by live music, collective singing and perhaps music hall entertainers. Up until the 1960s the standard cinema programme was still a double feature or a feature with a supporting short film, and there are still cinema shows such as the children's Saturday morning shows, the drive-in, the all-nighter and the late-night double feature which perpetuate the variety programme. The picture palace synthesised popular spectacular theatre and cinema; the attraction of the show was as much the spectacular design and decor of the venue as the film; the cinematic montage included the total experience from the architecture to the trailers. The cultural significance of cinema in the first decades of the twentieth century cannot be reduced to either a new technology or a new cultural form. The development of cinema was the emergence of an integrated industrial form of the illegitimate popular tradition.

Crucially, the montage of popular cinema must be understood as not simply a formal device but also a culture of multiple and collective production. Popular cinema continued and expanded the techniques of multiple, collective and anonymous production developed in popular theatre. Although popular filmmaking rapidly developed into a hierarchic and stratified industry for the production of a standardised cultural product, there can be no simplistic comparisons to the mass assembly line production of basic or even complex commodities. The collective creative agency active in popular filmmaking must be understood as a sophisticated and chaotic range of overlapping relationships which would include not only the diversity of creative contributions to a film (producer, director, scriptwriter, musical composer, actors, editor, art director and so on), but also the intertextual dynamics of film genre, the star system, the studio system and a range of economic, social and historical factors. As cinema superseded popular theatre and music hall, so it became the crucial site of the border conflict between the popular and bourgeois art, the inevitable target of bourgeois licensing, sedation, gentrification and appropriation. This conflict had two discrete fronts: the first was an initiative within the nascent film industry which was stimulated and guided by state intervention; the second was a movement which sought to appropriate cinema for autonomous art.

The industrial/cultural shift towards bourgeois legitimacy began in the British cinema industry with the consolidation of widespread national distribution and exhibition.[44] From 1905 onwards the bourgeois establishment became increasingly concerned by the social and economic possibilities of cinema and the cinema industry became increasingly interested in the affluent bourgeois audience. The moral panic which had dogged popular culture throughout the late nineteenth century now focused on cinema, specifically the gaffs which polite society viewed with suspicion and disgust; they were considered squalid dens of immorality, the darkness was a veil for criminal activity, the overcrowding encouraged indecent physical contact and the flickering screen caused eye strain and headaches. The films were considered equally vulgar, morbid and unhealthy, especially those which blasphemously depicted religious figures or those which by glamorising robbery and murder seduced the young into a life of crime.

However, the true danger of early cinema was a breakdown in crowd control or fire caused by the explosive nitrate-based film stock and the naked carbon arc flame used for projection. This hazardous technology and the inadequate safety precautions of the early cinemas led to a series of celebrated tragedies. Driven by moral and social concern a series of inquiries were convened to devise and recommend the state control of cinema. Legislation began with licensing under the Cinematographic Act of 1909 which introduced stringent fire regulations and gave local councils power to enforce other regulations such as Sunday closing and the prohibition of particular films deemed offensive. A key requirement of the Act was that the projector should be housed in a room totally separate from the auditorium and the film should be projected through a glazed window.[45] Whilst this measure was ostensibly a fire precaution it had the effect of removing from the audience the presence of the technology of cinematic spectacle; the show became a moving picture, its cause became a mystery. Moreover, since the makeshift gaffs could not comply with the new regulations, their proprietors were forced to rebuild, move to new purpose-built cinemas or go out of business. Just as the Theatres Act of 1843 had forced the penny gaffs to abandon drama and the Suitability Act of 1878 had closed the pub and saloon music halls, so the Cinematographic Act of 1909 suppressed the penny gaff cinemas.

Licensing was followed by sedation. Under pressure from the establishment the cinema industry began to make conspicuous concessions to bourgeois respectability culminating in the development of self-censorship by the industry-convened British Board of Film Censors (BBFC) in 1912. From its inception to around the mid-1930s the Board enforced a strict moral repression which included a prohibition on subjects of sexual, criminal, religious and political controversy. A crucial characteristic of this censorship was that whilst British films rarely attempted to transgress the standards of the BBFC, controversial American films were tolerated partly due to economic pressure and partly because their subject matter was permitted as long as it did not have a British setting. A key instance of this can be seen in the widespread moral panic surrounding gangster films in the late 1920s and 1930s.[46] Eventually the real challenge to the BBFC came not from the established film industry but from the development of sub-standard film systems (16mm/8mm) and from film groups excluded from the national distribution/exhibition circuit. Parallel to the legitimisation of exhibition a shift was taking place in British film production. What is remarkable is that whilst Gunning, writing from an American perspective, can locate the transition from an attractions mode of film production to narrative film production between 1907 and 1913, the same period in Britain is marked by a transition from the attractions mode to the virtual eclipse of British film production by America. Early British filmmakers had at first thrived. London was the centre of the international trade in film, studios were founded in the London suburbs and in the regions, the industry was even exporting to North America. But by 1910 most regional production had ceased and almost all the key early filmmakers had retired.[47] The overriding determinant of this decline was the economic advantage of the American industry in its vast home market and its aggressive export strategy. To reinforce this advantage the American industry extended its vertically-integrated monopoly structure into the British market; between 1912 and 1919 the American industry substantially took control of British cinema distribution and instituted policies of promoting affiliated American films and block- and blind-booking which effectively excluded British film from successful exhibition.[48] However, the strength of American industrial production does not fully explain the degeneration of early British film production, for not only did the industry fail but the films themselves became unpopular with British audiences and exhibitors.[49]

A key factor in the vulnerability of British film was the bourgeois enmity to popular culture. Whereas in America and continental Europe intellectuals and financial investors enthusiastically involved themselves with the development of film production, in Britain investment was principally restricted to exhibition and the bourgeois intelligentsia viewed cinema with contempt. Caught in the tension of bourgeois enmity, relentless competition, lack of investment, legislation and class aspiration, many of the principal British film producers abandoned the early vitality of the attractions mode and sought respectability by producing adaptations of nineteenth-century society drama and classic literature.[50] These moribund epics were essentially records of theatrical performances which reproduced the proscenium arch and fourth wall of the naturalist theatre with a cinema screen and it was estimated in May 1916 that 95 per cent of British production was adapted from theatre and novels.[51] Certainly there were popular films, performers and makers but these were the exceptions. Whilst American and continental European filmmakers were exploring and developing exciting popular narrative montage techniques, British film production stagnated and lost its popular audience.

In the aftermath of the Great War there was a renewed optimism in the future of British production, but by the early 1920s the American domination of the British market was almost total and British production was practically defunct. This crisis was a key element in the development of a new bourgeois intellectual engagement with cinema, mass culture and the potentials of mass communication. In the interwar period a new generation of young university-educated bourgeois activists began first to enter the film industry and second to form a critical culture around organisations such as the London Film Society (founded 1925), the Cambridge Film Guild (founded 1929) and the magazines *Close Up*, *Film Art*, *Cinema Quarterly* and *World Film News*.[52]

The London Film Society was a private cinema club founded by Ivor Montagu and a group of film critics and activists including the director Adrian Brunel and the critic Iris Barry who later became the director of the film department of New York's Museum of Modern Art. It included amongst its earliest members the influential Bloomsbury critic and enemy of pseudo-art Roger Fry and the economist John Maynard Keynes.

The renewed intellectual engagement with pop culture was characterised by conflicting currents of contempt and enthusiasm; the new mass culture was seen as both a barbarous threat and a dynamic discovery. Extreme hostility to mass culture was articulated by significant agents and factions within the London modernist movement. Many established modernist artists and theorists, particularly those associated with the Bloomsbury Group, viewed the masses as little more than irredeemable slaves.[53] Other British Modernists were increasingly disturbed by the American influence on the masses, or like the Vorticist Wyndham Lewis they perceived mass culture as a form of repressive hypnosis; a conceptual precursor of hegemony. Intellectual enthusiasm for cinema and mass culture followed traditional ruling class aesthetic prejudice, negating British popular culture and seeking inspiration in continental Europe and America.[54] America was invoked as both a negative and positive example of the chaotic power of mass culture as Europe was invoked as the pioneer of a new art: avant-garde cinema.

Chapter 5

THE FIRST AVANT-GARDE FILM MOVEMENT: THE VENGEANCE OF ART

'The story of avant-garde films is very simple. It is a direct reaction against the films that have scenarios and stars ... They are the painters' and poets' revenge.'
— Fernand Léger (c. 1924)[1]

In Paris, beginning around 1916, there developed a movement of artists, intellectual cinema clubs, specialist cinemas and independent cinema journals whose avowed purpose was to raise the cinema from the depths of popular entertainment to the sublime heights of art.[2] Within this dynamic pioneer movement there was a diversity of debate about film form and a diverse range of agents were involved: commercial narrative feature filmmakers, abstract animators, Dadaists and Surrealists, artists and anti-artists. There were both groups and individuals who were engaged in radical political activity and who articulated genuine understanding of the popular. Moreover, there were films produced which would influence all subsequent experimental cinema. However, for the limited scope of this history it is necessary to forswear aesthetics and aspirations and to consider the broadest trajectory of the movement. By the early 1920s Paris had become the hub of an international avant-garde movement that sought to spearhead the appropriation of cinema as autonomous art. The fundamental and characteristic modality of this project was the formation of two discrete but integrated and interdependent sectors of activity: theory (literary/academic) and practice (audio-visual).

Prophecies of the nativity of film art appeared early in cinema history, but the most influential oracle was the bohemian poet and critic Ricciotto Canudo.[3] Canudo was Italian but had moved to Paris in 1901 where he worked as a journalist before becoming a professional academic. Around 1908 he began work on a series of theorisations of film as an art.[4] He recognised the subversive power of the popular and the repressive nature of bourgeois culture, and yet he was fatally drawn to the aura of sacred art. He conceived of cinema as a potential new art which would combine all previous arts in a sacred Wagnerian synthesis.[5] The genius of this new art he named the *écraniste* (the screenist): the film artist or author.

According to Richard Abel in his intriguing study *French Cinema: The First Wave 1915–29*, Canudo was one of the group of key founders of the Parisian avant-garde cinema movement which came to include the celebrated writer and music hall entertainer Colette, the theorist/filmmakers Louis Delluc, Marcel L'Herbier, Germaine Dulac, Jean Epstein and Léon Poirier, and critics and organisers such as Léon Moussinac and Jean Tedesco, the theorist who also founded the first specialist art repertory cinema in Paris: the Théâtre Du Vieux-Columbier (1924). Delluc

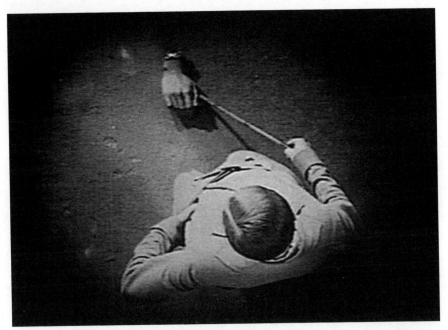

Figure 8: Poking the severed hand in *Un Chien Andalou* (Luis Buñuel and Salvador Dalí, 1929)

and Canudo were the central activists of the formative movement which developed around a network of influential specialist film journals and ciné-clubs.[6] Both had died young by 1924 but the movement continued to thrive, and from the mid-1920s the avant-garde network had consolidated and expanded nationally and internationally. A circuit of independent specialist art cinemas was established in Paris, ciné-clubs were started all over France and links were formed with clubs in Belgium and Switzerland, the London Film Society and the London/Swiss avant-garde journal *Close Up*. In America there was a parallel national ciné-club network known as the Little Cinemas, which was centred around New York but had cinemas in Los Angeles, Chicago, Washington DC, Philadelphia, Boston and Cleveland.[7]

From the diverse and variant writings and activities of this first avant-garde it is possible to formulate the broad elements of a project which would become the basis of all subsequent avant-garde cinema movements, which would be integrated into the development of post-war film theory and which is still recognisable in the contemporary vestiges of the British independent film sector. The avant-garde movement advocated its own centrality and necessity to the future of cinema. The justification for this stems from two interdependent assumptions. First it was proposed that cinema, when perfected, could and must become art, but this could only be achieved through the pioneering work of dedicated artists and intellectuals. Second the creation of cinema art was conceived as not simply a birth but also a redemption; cinema had to be rescued from its vulgar origins.

As Germaine Dulac wrote in 1925:

Among the viewers a few love the cinema for its future possibilities. They will understand. Many others love the cinema in its present state and it is to them that I wish to speak, because it is a terrible mistake to keep this beautiful art prisoner, an art whose future is so much greater than the miserable little stories we make it tell. And I will have finished when I have said it one more time: Our ideal is far beyond our accomplishments; you must help us to liberate the cinema from its shackles and create a pure cinema.[8]

Purity was broadly conceived as cinematic specificity: film should be purged of all aesthetic and formal elements unnecessary, anachronistic or alien to its nature.[9] Within this mystic conception there was a spectrum of experimental practices ranging from rhythmic montage to documentary realism. But the trajectory of the avant-garde inevitably tended towards the modernist extreme of an abstract non-narrative cinema.

The quest for pure cinema which develops in the first avant-garde, particularly in the writing of Dulac and Epstein, can partly be understood as a reaction to vapid naturalistic film adaptations of theatre and literature and partly as a migration of abstraction from modernist art.[10] However, whilst this may be true, it does not take account of the specific cultural context of cinema. If we site the modernist shift to abstraction at the advent of Cubism we could then trace its influence into the various other arts. But the critical point is that cinema was not an art when the avant-garde modernists attempted to assume aesthetic leadership; cinema was a popular culture. The entry of the modernists and the entry of the artists into the field of cinema was simultaneous; the first film artists were avant-garde modernists. Whilst in the traditional arts the modernist revolt was essentially an Oedipal conflict between an elite bourgeois youth and their older generation, in the cinema the avant-garde modernists were opposing not only a tradition of popular culture essentially alien to them but a commercial industry which was structured according to techniques of division of labour, mass reproduction and economics which were totally irreconcilable with the function of art. The demand for cinematic purity is not the trajectory of modernist abstraction or the drive for medium specificity, it is the demand for an autonomous art cinema which will correct a historical aberration; popular cinema. The aberration is that a dynamic creative culture could emerge from outside the legitimate sphere of bourgeois art. As Léger asserted, the avant-garde was a form of artistic vengeance.[11] Popular cinema is conceived as imperfect and impure; popular narrative is an alien imposition that masks and perverts the true form of film art; popular cinema is a falsehood that must be exposed.[12] Avant-garde cinema is not conceived as a break, an end or a transcendence of the art tradition, it is the consecration of the tradition of art as the legitimate authority over cinema; film had to be liberated from trade and from popularity.

The Paris avant-garde realised that to reconfigure cinema as art they would have to reproduce certain crucial elite art institutions. First and foremost they would need a critical/theoretical base which could introduce a hierarchy of aesthetic taste into cinema. From this base they could establish a poetics/theory of cinema, a canon of classic films and a legitimising history of film art. Delluc's early film criticism was essential to the foundation of the film art canon and the conception of an alternative and specifically French cinema.[13] He advocated alternative exhibition and distribution structures; most significantly he campaigned against the variety programmes of popular cinema and proposed separate single-film screenings and repertory screenings of re-released classic films. This tendency can be understood as an attempt to introduce into cinema the equivalent of the separation between popular theatre and legitimate elite bourgeois theatre, and indeed this demand was a founding principle of the first ciné-club.[14] Furthermore, both Delluc and Canudo advocated the introduction of authorship into cinema; against the multiple, collective and industrial creation of popular film they proposed that film should be under the creative control of a single omnipotent writer/director or auteur.[15] As we have already observed in the context of Renaissance theatre, the imposition of a literary author modelled on the moral, educational and legal status of literature proved an effective technique for imposing legitimate authority onto the collective popular.

Once the theoretical base of the avant-garde was established as a network of professional critics/theorists, magazines, specialist journals, lectures and conferences, the key to the implementation of the theory was to construct an alternative art cinema with its own integrated production, distribution and exhibition sectors. This was achieved by the network of dedicated filmmakers, thriving ciné-clubs and fashionable specialist cinemas. Finally the avant-garde sought institutional legitimation from the art establishment and the French state. Institutional recognition was first achieved by Canudo who managed to persuade the prestigious Salon d'Automne to include film screenings from 1921 to 1923.[16] Recognition from the state was another founding demand of the ciné-clubs and it was articulated as a demand for legal and institutional equality with the legitimate theatre and as a recognition of film art as a crucial component of French national culture. Throughout the 1920s the avant-garde movement gained increasing academic and state recognition culminating in the eventual demand for the foundation of a national film archive in the 1930s: the Cinémathèque.

Despite the first avant-garde's pioneering drive to art, and in the context of Underground cinema, it is of crucial significance that, between roughly 1927 and 1930, the economic success of the alternative cinema network encouraged certain key avant-garde activists to engage in projects which sought to transform the movement from an elite bourgeois art into a radical popular industry. The two key areas of activity were attempts to gain a popular audience for avant-garde film and then to industrially integrate avant-garde production, distribution and exhibition. In the former case the outstanding initiative was the Communist ciné-club Les Amis de Spartacus organised by Leon Moussinac, Jean Lods and their friends in 1927.[17] Inspired by the popularity of prohibited Soviet cinema, particularly Eisenstein's *Bronenosets Potyomkin* (*Battleship Potemkin*, 1925), and by the few specialist cinemas which managed to attract working-class audiences, Les Amis de Spartacus was formed as a deliberate attempt to create a popular oppositional cinema movement. So successful were their first programmes at the Casino de Grenelle cinema in March 1928 that they had to hire two more cinemas for simultaneous screenings. The initial programmes included work from the European avant-garde movement and most significantly three banned Soviet features: Eisenstein's *Battleship Potemkin* and Vsevolod Pudovkin's *Mat* (*Mother*, 1926) and *Konets Sankt-Peterburga* (*The End of St. Petersburg*, 1927). Soviet cinema was officially banned but private ciné-club screenings were tolerated. Within three months membership was up to ten thousand, and as the club expanded activity into the suburbs and provinces the membership rose to forty thousand. By September 1928 Les Amis de Spartacus had become a real threat not only to state media control but also to the established French cinema industry. The Paris chief of police summoned Jean Lods and informed him that if the screenings of Soviet film did not cease then undercover police agents would disrupt any further shows. In October Les Amis de Spartacus disbanded and the membership then dispersed.

In the second case the success of the ciné-clubs and the specialist cinemas actually created a demand for avant-garde film which outstripped the production capacity of the disparate and uncoordinated network of avant-garde filmmakers. In response to this several of the specialist cinemas ventured into distribution and production, and the potential for alternative distribution was greatly increased in the mid-1920s by the development of the Pathé sub-standard 9.5mm film system, which radically reduced the cost of cinema technology for clubs and collectors.

The expansion of the avant-garde alternative cinema network throughout the 1920s was dynamic and potentially radical; nevertheless, by the end of the decade it had burned out. The state had suppressed Les Amis de Spartacus, the only real possibility for a mass popular audience, and the coming of synchronised-sound cinema effectively terminated the silent avant-garde. Sound equipment was expensive and difficult to get hold of and most of the filmmakers and the specialist cinemas had no access to the technology. The industry distributors ruthlessly promoted sound film and either refused to rent silent films or allowed their silent prints to become so scratched and shoddy that they were unscreenable. As sound became the acknowledged future of cinema the silent avant-garde's identity as revolutionary pioneers was undermined; their work was suddenly archaic.[18] Many avant-garde filmmakers were forced into the established industry and nearly all the specialist cinemas closed. The ciné-clubs which had once been dedicated to expansion, support and education increasingly turned to preservation and nostalgia. The movement to transform cinema became a campaign to save classics in a national Cinémathèque. But although these factors contributed to the decline of the movement, the essential vulnerability of the avant-garde lay in the ideological contradiction of an art movement that sought to aesthetise a popular and commercial industry.[19]

The critical cause of the fragmentation of the first avant-garde cinema was the failure of its key agents to comprehend the trajectory of their own movement. The aspiration to a mass audience within the avant-garde was a contradiction amounting to the aspiration for a popular art, which would be the realisation of the paradox that makes art obsolete; the sublation of art.[20] That is to say, that the aspiration for a mass avant-garde was at its best naïve and at its worst bogus; either way it was inevitably irrational and doomed. Moreover, the failure of the avant-garde as a mass movement cannot really be deemed a failure since it was never really an element of the avant-garde trajectory. On the contrary, it must be counted a success of the first avant-garde that it appropriated elements of popular cinema and used them to construct an elite and esoteric annex of legitimate art.

In the French avant-garde of the 1920s it is possible to locate not only the advent of avant-garde film but also the seminal variant of Tom Gunning's continuity model of cinema history and the genesis of auteurism and 1970s film theory. And the unresolved instabilities and contradictions of the first avant-garde were perpetuated into the history of avant-garde film.

Chapter 6

BRITISH INDEPENDENT FILM 1925–66: THE RISE OF THE STATE ALTERNATIVE TO POPULAR CINEMA

The British independent film culture which developed in the late 1920s, and into the 1930s, was composed of four distinct but interactive and overlapping sectors: the avant-garde, the Workers' Film movement, the Documentary Film Movement and the Amateur Cine movement. This chapter will track the historical development of the first three of these movements to the Free Cinema group of the mid-1950s and the foundations of the post-war independent film movement. The history of the Amateur Cine movement will be passed over, as it was passed over by the historians of experimental film in the 1970s. However, Amateurism will be redeemed in detail in the next chapter.

The foundation of the London Film Society in 1925 effectively marks the initiation of the first British independent film movement. The national network of film societies which developed from the London society made European avant-garde film and banned Soviet cinema accessible to a generation of artists, bourgeois intellectuals, students, academics and film activists. The overlapping and interactive elements of the independent movement can be most obviously mapped in the transcendence and transit of agents and films across and between the movements. Ivor Montagu, the founder of the London Film Society, is emblematic of this interchange. Born the son of Lord Swaythling and educated at Cambridge, Montagu was active in the avant-garde but in the 1930s he was also a Communist Party activist in the Workers' Film movement and unlike, perhaps, any other member of either movement he was also a successful participant in the popular cinema industry working with Hitchcock as both an editor and a producer.[1] Likewise the independent distribution of Eisenstein's *Battleship Potemkin* played a formative role in the avant-garde, the Workers' Film movement and the documentary movement, however the role played was distinctly different in each context.

The British avant-garde had organisational links with the Paris avant-garde and the international avant-garde ciné-club network, but it was convened and consolidated in a social and economic context divergent to both continental Europe and America. Whereas, in the mid-1920s, France, Germany and several other European nations had industrial film production sectors that were domestically and even internationally competing against the American industry, the British industry was consistently on the verge of total subjection; in 'Black November' 1924 not a single film went into production at any British studio.[2] Consequently the British avant-garde initially perceived its project as specifically an alternative to both the failed British industry and American popular cinema, which was despised but also envied.

Figure 9: *Beyond This Open Door* (B. Vivian Braun, 1934)

As in France the definitive logic of the British avant-garde cinema movement was to (re)construct cinema as an autonomous art; however, the parochial and conservative character of British art was far more resistant to the foundation of a cinematic seventh art and the movement remained isolated from modern art and Modernism.[3] Moreover, with the exception of Kenneth Macpherson's feature film *Borderline* (1930), the films produced by the British avant-garde were short and they had very limited distribution. As in France the axis of early British avant-garde production was formed by the activities of a group of key theorists/filmmakers who organised screenings and wrote for a number of specialist magazines, most significantly the international periodicals *Close Up* (1927–33) and *Film Art* (1933–37).[4] This group would include Oswell Blakeston, B. Vivian Braun, Kenneth Macpherson, Robert Fairthorne and Irene Nicholson. They screened their work at the film societies when they could, but there were also commercial cinemas which were willing to screen avant-garde films and during the mid-1930s there were several specialist cinemas which functioned as venues for both the avant-garde and the film societies.[5] At the end of 1933 *Film Art* proclaimed the foundation of a consecrated avant-garde cinema, the Forum in Villiers Street, London, organised by Braun, Nicholson and M. Hatzfield. But the vitality of the movement was brief and by 1937 *Film Art* had ceased publication and the avant-garde had been subsumed in the amateur film movement and the rise of the documentary movement.

The Workers' Film movement emerged from British Socialist/Communist Party activism around 1929. The movement's origins lie in the development of a national network of Workers' Film societies which were set up initially to screen Soviet cinema and German agit-prop films which had no commercial distribution or had been refused certification by the BBFC. Film societies exempted themselves from prohibition by exploiting loopholes in cinema legislation. The Cinematographic Act of 1909 had been specifically designed to enforce licensing on cinemas projecting flammable film stock to public audiences. The BBFC had no legal power as the actual prohibition of a film screening could only be enforced by local authorities. Further legislation brought in under the Cinematographic Films Act of 1927 required cinemas and film distributors to include a percentage or quota of British films in their programmes. Societies could evade censorship and the quota by using unlicensed halls as venues, by gaining permission for screenings from sympathetic councils, by having society or club membership, and increasingly from the mid-1930s by projecting the new non-flammable 16mm film stock. By 1929 the film society movement had already aroused considerable political controversy by screening imported Soviet cinema and Ivor Montagu had published a polemical pamphlet against film censorship which also included guidelines on how to evade film censorship and exhibit and distribute prohibited films.

By the early 1930s, in spite of concerted state opposition, there were workers' film societies in many regional centres including Cardiff, Manchester, Liverpool and Edinburgh. The societies' programmes were mostly made up of Soviet and continental films but gradually local production groups formed to make their own newsreels and agit-prop documentaries. In 1933 the distribution group Kino formed to distribute Soviet films on 16mm. A year later a filmmakers' organisation, the Workers' Film and Photo League (WFPL) was formed by the production section of Kino. The WFPL declared in its manifesto:

> Workers' Film and Photo League thinks the time has come for workers to produce films and photos of their own. Films and photos showing their own lives, their own problems, their own organised efforts to solve these problems.
>
> For this purpose there must be joint coordinated activity by all working-class film and camera-club organisations, all individual workers, students, artists, writers and technicians interested in film and photography.
>
> Workers' Film and Photo League exists to provide this coordination.
>
> The League will produce its own films giving a true picture of life today, recording the industrial and living conditions of the British workers and the struggle of the employed and unemployed to improve these conditions.
>
> It will produce newsreel magazines of current events of working-class interest.
>
> It will popularise the great Russian films and endeavour to exhibit them to the widest possible audiences.

It will carry on criticism of current commercial films in the Press and in its own literature, and expose films of a militarist, fascist or anti-working-class nature.[6]

At its high point, around the mid-1930s, the Workers' Film movement provided an effective national network of alternative cinemas to a regular mass audience. Screenings were not limited to those organised directly by the societies since many other socialist and labour organisations rented films from the various distribution agencies. Kino had the largest catalogue of films, network of agents and sphere of activity. Their shows could attract audiences of up to a thousand; in 1936 they attracted a total audience of around 250,000; in 1938 it was up to 330,000. In 1935–36 there were 764 Kino shows which rose to 1,372 in 1938.[7] Film production was far more limited and difficult to sustain. The main area of production was 16mm newsreels covering various demonstrations and political events, notably the hunger marches and anti-fascist demonstrations of the mid-1930s. The movement was financially self-sufficient, the societies charged an affordable membership and many groups took money on the door since screenings were often used to raise funds as part of broader campaigns. The shows themselves would often be integrated political events comprising a screening accompanied by music, speakers and a debate. In 1933 the film section of the Workers' Theatre movement (later Kino) even developed mobile street cinema vans with internal projection.[8] From around 1936 onwards the movement began to form a coordinated campaign against the rise of fascism and specifically in support of the Republican cause in the Spanish Civil War. In the last years before World War Two the success of the campaign encouraged the Labour Party, the Co-operative Movement and the British Communist Party to variously initiate major film projects. But the onset of war effectively suppressed the movement since new foreign films could not be imported, wartime restrictions on entertainment and public gatherings made screenings impracticable, film stock for unofficial use was almost unobtainable, many activists were conscripted into the forces and the industrial/political environment was transformed by military production.

Potentially the Workers' Film movement of the 1930s represented a financially viable vertically-integrated democratic alternative cinema, but in practice the success of the movement depended upon the development of a national network of film production groups to replace the movement's dependency on imported foreign films and this was only ever partially achieved. Moreover whilst the war inevitably suppressed the movement there were also a number of ideological and political limits to its duration. The Socialist culture from which the Workers' Film movement developed at the end of the 1920s was an ideological fusion of elementary Soviet Marxist-Leninism and bourgeois Labourism which carried with it the syncretic legacy of William Morris, the temperance movement and Nonconformist Protestantism. The movement essentially theorised capitalist society as a monolithic system historically determined by its oppressive economic base. Popular cinema was conceived as both a product of capitalist oppression and as a means to perpetuate it by diverting the workers from class struggle. Hollywood was a narcotic dream factory that kept workers doped, a foreshadowing of later theories of hegemony. The mission of Communist cinema activists was to screen the films of the Soviet Union, the only country operating outside of capitalist social relations, and then to develop a workers' cinema which would be autonomous/independent to the capitalist film industry and therefore able to reveal the true nature of capitalist society.[9] Film was a weapon in the class war, and the power of this weapon was truth. Reality was objective, natural and apprehensible, and film, unlike all other media, could record and transmit the actuality of real life. In opposition to capitalist deception, social-ist film would confront the worker with the unconstructed truth; education and enlightenment. In its extreme form this agit-prop realism was not only hostile to popular cinema but also to experiments in technique, form and style which were considered bourgeois affectations which would mask or confuse the actuality of class struggle.[10]

Whilst the activists of the Workers' Film movement developed a radical partici-patory alternative to commercial cinema which contributed to a valiant struggle against poverty, unemployment, injustice and fascism, it must also be acknowledged that their political naivety allied them to deeply oppressive cultural and political forces. The movement's agit-prop realism was founded on a contempt for popu-lar cinema which betrayed a profound ignorance of both the history and subver-sive potential of popular culture. Worse still, the concept of the working class as doped and manipulated by the popular was inherently elitist since it cast movement activists as enlightened and the unenlightened masses as manipulated dopes. The movement recognised the unique documentary power of film but mistook the relationship between film and actuality for transparency; they believed film could be exempt from connotation.[11] Ultimately, their faith in a non-ideological access to reality was a bitter irony since at the height of the movement, as the makeshift screens flickered with heroic images of revolutionary triumph, the Stalinist purges were erasing millions of people from the real world and the experimental culture of the revolution was being replaced by Stalinist Socialist Realism.

After the war there was no equivalent socialist/workers' cinema movement, al-though there were a number of fragmented initiatives, notably from the Co-op movement, the Campaign for Nuclear Disarmament (CND) and the Association of Cine-Technicians (ACT, the film workers' trade union founded in 1933, which numbered amongst its leadership Ivor Montagu and the activist Ralph Bond).[12] The fragmentation of the movement was caused by multiple factors, but most signifi-cantly a shift in left politics from an ideology of autonomy and opposition to the expectation of state intervention by the post-war Labour government.[13] Critically, the demand for the nationalisation of the film industry became the pivotal post-war strategy of leftist film activists and the essential imperative of the post-war Indepen-dent Film and Video movement.

Whilst the avant-garde and the Workers' movement passed into obscurity, the crucial precedent for post-war independent cinema was the documentary move-ment founded by John Grierson in the late 1920s. This movement can be assessed as an industrial formation, a coalition of filmmakers and a series of influential films produced between 1929 and the early 1950s. The films were commissioned as advertising, publicity or propaganda by a series of state and commercial corporations. They ranged from poetic documentary such as Basil Wright's *Song of Ceylon* (1934) to lecture/journalistic documentary such as Edgar Anstey's *Housing Problems* (1935); from experimental animation such as Len Lye's *Trade Tattoo* (1936) to wartime propaganda such as Humphrey Jennings' and Harry Watt's *London Can Take It* (1942). They were screened in commercial cinemas but more significantly they were distributed through an alternative exhibition network of film societies, schools, YMCAs, women's organisations, trade unions and mobile cinema vans. The key makers associated with the movement would include Edgar Anstey, Alberto Cavalcanti, Arthur Elton, Humphrey Jennings, Stuart Legg, Len Lye, Norman McLaren, Paul Rotha, Evelyn Spice, Harry Watt and Basil Wright. Several of these filmmakers were also theorists and activists who wrote for *Film Art, Cinema Quarterly* (1932–35, the journal of the Independent Filmmakers Association (IFA)) and its successor *World Film News* (1936–38).[14] Most of the documentary movement's filmmakers eventually had successful careers in various state-funded or commercial organisations and a few founded their own documentary production companies, but they all began by working for Grierson.

Grierson was both an ideologue and a filmmaker. He came from a devout Scottish Protestant background, studied at Glasgow University and travelled to the United States in 1924 as a Rockefeller Research Fellow in social science.[15] In the US he became fascinated by the role of popular culture and specifically cinema in forming public opinion. He studied audience statistics, wrote film criticism, saw jazz bands and visited Hollywood where he met Charlie Chaplin, Harry Langdon and King Vidor.[16] Through his research and writing he became respected by the American film industry as an expert in audience sensibilities. But although he developed a great affection and respect for popular cinema he ultimately considered it a deception and a drug and he became passionately convinced that the modern democratic state had to actively educate its citizens for democracy and that a new alternative cinema was essential to this process. When he returned to Britain in 1927 he approached the Empire Marketing Board and was hired to develop their newly-formed film unit. Whilst executive at the Empire Marketing Board Film Unit (1928–33) and the Post Office Film Unit (1933–41) he recruited and trained most of the central figures in documentary filmmaking, and was the producer of most of the key films.

Grierson and his colleagues developed their conception and practice of the documentary around the same ideological precepts as the avant-garde which they superseded. But they also integrated into the ideology of the avant-garde complex British moral and political tendencies. Whereas the avant-garde had contextualised itself as a progression in the ascendance of art, the documentary movement conceived its project as transcending both the vulgarity and commercialism of popular cinema and the decadence and privilege of the avant-garde.[17] The movement legitimised its practice not by commerce or art patronage but by function; the documentary had a national, moral and civic purpose, it educated and informed the public, it would be the new cinema of the nation. Grierson's decisive and paradoxical innovation was to combine the avant-garde demand for autonomy with a concept of public service which justified state funding. Beginning at the Empire Marketing Board in 1929 he developed an alternative integrated production and distribution industry within the institutions of the state.

To understand the significance of this innovation it must be contextualised within the historical separation and conflict between art and the popular. The ascendance of the bourgeoisie embedded a paradox in the formation of the modern capitalist state; in their rise to power the bourgeoisie invoked liberty but to consummate their rule they appropriated the power and function of the feudal state. The industrial systems which consolidated the bourgeois ascension depended upon a hierarchical division of labour controlled by a class of professional managers and administrators. To rule in the name of freedom and equity the bourgeoisie were increasingly obliged to introduce limited representative democracy and this in turn led to the increasing demand and provision of institutionalised education and social welfare. Both industrialisation and the increasing introduction of representative democracy led to the constitution and comprehensive expansion of a bourgeois civil bureaucracy. Consequently the rise of liberal capitalism and the formation of a centralised interventionist bureaucratic state was a parallel process implemented by the same class and often the same people. Ideologically the bourgeoisie was committed to liberalism and yet to maintain their social hierarchy they employed a centralised state bureaucracy which increasingly penetrated industry and social life at every level. The modern bourgeois bureaucratic state is a hierarchy of trained professional experts; they are the realisation of Saint-Simon's prophecy – a government of scientists, industrialists and artists. The ideological dynamic of this hierarchy developed out of the Protestant ethic and is the myth of representative meritocracy: the rule of those who with effort and ability have acquired power through equality of opportunity. A crucial function of this myth is to cast a moral shadow upon the powerless: if you have no authority it is because you have no ability and you have made no effort. By deploying the myth of the meritocracy as a contemporary condition, an incentive and an aspiration for the future the bourgeoisie have effectively suppressed the radical desires unleashed by successive waves of bourgeois revolution. The bourgeoisie may believe or protest that the meritocracy is historically inevitable but they also understand that it is in their interest to prolong its negotiation for as long as possible, since whilst democratic political debate is dominated by issues of representation and equality of opportunity questions of actual social equality are effectively suppressed. However, with every move towards meritocracy the bourgeoisie are further caught in the tension between an ideological commitment to the meritocratic state and the imperative of power; they are committed to increasing equality of opportunity for the lower classes and yet they have to preserve their elite class identity. As this tension increased in the twentieth century so it became clear that since art was constituted as a fetish specifically to demonstrate and maintain bourgeois cultural dominance, equality of opportunity in the cultural realm would have the tendency to anachronise or even desecrate art. Moreover, the contradiction facing the bourgeoisie was that in their rise to power they invoked free trade and the free market and yet in their aspiration to sacred and noble power they were committed to an elite minority handicraft art culture which increasingly could not compete against the new dynamic industrial forms of popular culture. The complexity of this problem is only matched by the complexity of the solution and we have already glimpsed elements of this in the fabrication of folklore, the ideas of William Morris and the work of Leavis and his Scrutineers. The fundamental resolution was to reconfigure art as classless and to nationalise it as the state culture administrated and distributed by the state bureaucracy and financed by universal taxation. The earliest theoretical foundation for this reconfiguration was devised in the mid-nineteenth century by Matthew Arnold who believed that his beloved 'culture' (art) was threatened by the inevitable ascendance of representational democracy; the bourgeoisie would depose the aristocracy and in doing so they would depose the traditional authority of culture and bring anarchy.[18] The resolution to the crisis would be state education; the state as the nation in its collective and corporate character must become the centre and authority of cultural perfection, which as we know is art. In Arnold's model art does not belong to a particular social class. On the contrary the majority of all the social classes cannot recognise it, but in every class there will be a few individuals with talent; geniuses who recognise and seek perfection. Arnold calls these geniuses aliens because their love of human perfection enables them to transcend class identity.[19] From Arnold we can trace the development of a model of art as a national culture, which can be formulated as a series of interdependent propositions. First, art as the perfection of national culture is central to the health of the nation-state and must therefore be maintained by the state. Second, art and aesthetic taste transcends class and therefore art education and provision should be universal. And last, that if the lower classes receive art education they will be spiritually improved and a precious few may even discover and pursue a talent of genius.

The two crucial areas of cultural nationalisation in the nineteenth century were the development of state art galleries and museums and the introduction of the state education system in the 1870s. State education radically increased popular literacy but it also initiated the development of a unified and centralised curriculum designed to indoctrinate working-class children with bourgeois culture.[20]

The first radical modern innovations in the direct funding of cultural production appeared as a cluster of initiatives in the 1920s, and they were not directed at art institutions but at the new industrial popular culture. By the mid-1920s British commercial cinema was totally dominated by American imports and British film production was in crisis. The imminent collapse of the industry forced the bourgeois establishment to engage in a comprehensive revaluation of the cinema as a cultural and industrial power. American film, it was argued, sold American products and

American culture; Britain was being Americanised and the prestige of the Empire was being undermined in the colonies. To counteract this damage it was argued that the state must intervene and support a strong national cinema which could promote British trade and British colonial values. The key initiatives which developed from this revaluation were the development of the Empire Marketing Board Film Unit; the Cinematograph Film Act of 1927 which was designed to break the American hold on the exhibition circuit by requiring cinemas to screen a fixed percentage or quota of British films; and the foundation of the state-funded BFI in 1933.

Parallel to the initiatives for a national cinema, the British state developed an agency to control and maintain an exclusive monopoly on radio broadcasting: the BBC. A founding imperative of the state monopoly was that it was necessary to regulate the use of the vital and limited radio frequencies, but this was in fact a myth fabricated to contain and control the political potential of broadcasting at a time of great social instability and industrial conflict. In the early years of radio there were many diverse local stations scattered throughout the regions and operated by enthusiasts and amateurs experimenting with the medium. The key strategies deployed in the formation of the BBC were control, unification and centralisation, and the pivotal figure in this development was the first Director-General John Reith. Reith's career has many striking parallels with Grierson. Reith also came from a devout Scottish Protestant background, he studied engineering in Glasgow and as a young man he travelled in the US, where, like Grierson, he was profoundly influenced by the dynamism of American culture. At the core of the model of broadcasting developed by Reith and his colleagues was a commitment to the nineteenth-century bourgeois concept of public service; the moral and civic duty of the privileged to serve the well-being of the community; the redemption and reformation of the less fortunate. Public Service Broadcasting was conceived as a powerful force for the improvement of education, aesthetic taste and social conduct. It would provide impartial information about the world and so produce an enlightened and informed electorate able to participate in modern democracy. It would not follow public desire, but guide public taste by providing the highest quality of programming, and shunning the harmful and the vulgar. It would be a voice for the nation, a culture shared by everyone, wherever they lived and whatever their class. This consensus required a consolidation and standardisation of delivery that led to the gradual elimination of local radio, experiment, audience participation, amateurism and informality.[21] The shared culture of the BBC became predominantly the culture of the educated bourgeoisie of the South-East of England and their accent became BBC-standard English. Although there was an increasing amount of popular entertainment on the BBC in the early years, it was carefully controlled and sedated. Dance music was the dominant form of music transmitted, but it was sedate hotel orchestra jazz and not improvised hot jazz which was excluded as immoral.[22] Moreover, the programming strategy of the BBC conceived popular culture as essentially a form of bait to hook the masses into cultural uplift. The development of Public Service Broadcasting was a response to a broader modernist anxiety around the masses and the Americanisation of British culture.[23] It was both a reaction against mass popular culture and a means to protect and maintain bourgeois culture. Emblematic of this process was the support given to classical music: by 1930 the BBC had founded its own symphony orchestra and by the mid-1930s it was the most powerful patron of classical music in the country, the largest employer of classical musicians, a vast promoter of classical concerts and a pioneer in classical music education for the masses. The Music Department of the BBC only dealt with classical music, and popular music was consigned to the Variety Department. Reith personally promoted initiatives to subsidise classical music, most significantly the annual Proms which the BBC took over from Sir Henry Wood in 1927.[24]

During the war the BBC was forced to radically reconceive its audience. Programming was segmented into the Home Service, which continued Reithian programming, and the Forces Programme targeted specifically at the working classes and transmitting predominantly popular entertainment. After the war radio broadcasting was segmented further into a trinity that broadly represented the class divisions of the nation: the Third Programme which specialised in classical music and art, the Home Service which continued with mixed programming and the Light Programme which continued the popular broadcasting of the Forces Programme. This segmentation was designed as a pyramid of taste which would induce the listener to aspire upwards to the auratic peak of Art.[25]

The early success of the BBC was a crucial inspiration to Grierson as he developed his film unit in the early 1930s. Whilst in America he had been particularly influenced by certain ideas of the proto-fascist theorist Walter Lippman regarding a crisis in democracy.[26] Grierson came to believe that the ideal society was an integrated collective bound together by a consensus of shared assumptions and beliefs and governed by a state which was an amalgamation of semi-autonomous corporations in which power was decentralised and equally distributed.[27] He conceived the role of documentary film as an educational tool in the process of integrating the citizen into corporate society. Without integration there would be social division and conflict. Grierson's ambition for the documentary movement was that it would become a semi-autonomous state corporation similar to the BBC but although the film units were allowed considerable freedom of expression and interpretation, their function as producers of publicity/propaganda was directly regulated by the state.

Grierson theorised documentary as a radical democratic force in opposition to the commercial industry and the avant-garde but he did not conceive the state as a site of conflict.[28] He identified the function of documentary with the function of the bourgeois state; he sought to modernise and so maintain it.[29] The documentary movement's commitment to the study of ordinary people and everyday life was thus not a commitment to cultural democracy; it was a component of a wider state initiative of cultural research and intervention. Grierson did not conceive the education of the citizen as a process of comprehensive intellectual engagement, for that would be counter-productive. The function of the documentary was not to engage the citizen in debate but to dramatise the needs of the state and the duties of the citizen. The art of the documentary was not to provide information but to produce in the citizen patterns of thought and feeling which drew them into the consensus.[30] The vision of Britain dramatised by the movement was of an inter-dependent consensual hierarchy in which social conflict was active but ultimately unnatural and recoverable. It was essentially a bourgeois vision, a modernist folklore which mythologised industrial life to appropriate and control it.[31] The pre-eminent exponent of this mode was Humphrey Jennings.

Jennings went to Cambridge University with Elton, Wright and Legg. In the early 1930s he was a painter involved with the British Surrealist movement and in the late 1930s together with Legg, Tom Harrison and Charles Madge he was a founder member of Mass Observation (M.O.), a group formed with the declared intention of ending the divisions between art, science and the masses.[32]

M.O. was conceived as an anthropological study of everyday British life which would liberate the masses from the oppression of political propaganda, commercial manipulation and advertising; it was to be a new science of ourselves. Clandestine M.O. agents were deployed to penetrate working-class culture, to invisibly probe the night and day of industrial life and to reveal the hidden forces and systems beneath. By 1939 they had gathered a vast amount of documentation, published several reports and recruited a national panel of around four hundred predominantly lower-middle-class observers. When war broke out M.O. was effectively co-opted by the state as an agency to monitor public opinion and negotiate public policy. Jennings left M.O. to concentrate on documentary filmmaking, and his first major film, *Spare Time* (1939), was a direct movement of the M.O. project into cinema. Watching *Spare Time* and Jennings' later poetic montages of war and nationalism it is possible to feel the heart-wrenching poignancy of the distance between the bourgeois and the popular, the nostalgia for the lost Albion, a sublime desire for the common. The emotional intensity of Jennings' films lies in the impossibility of contact – Jennings can only observe in wonder.

The coming of war mobilised the pioneering state institutions of culture; the BBC initiated the Forces Programme and the GPO film unit was co-opted by the Ministry of Information to became the Crown Film Unit which produced wartime propaganda and information films. However the crucial innovation in the state provision of culture was in the funding and management of performance and exhibition. Initially the state was slow to fully realise the importance of culture in the war effort and fearing immediate full-scale bombing prohibited both popular entertainment and art events whether indoor or out. However, by 1940 a cluster of centrally controlled and state financed semi-autonomous agencies had been mobilised and were effectively managing the provision of popular entertainment and art for both the military and civilian populations.[33] The two critical organisations were, respectively, the Entertainments National Service Association (ENSA) and the Council for the Encouragement of Music and the Arts (CEMA).

At the peak of its activity ENSA was effectively the largest coordinated cultural project in British history. It was founded in 1938 by a group of entertainment industry volunteers who initially began to develop coordinated entertainment for the armed forces in national and international installations. As the war progressed the military state increasingly developed ENSA as an integral component of the war effort; entertainment was identified as a means to maintain and improve the morale and fighting spirit of the working class. After Dunkirk in 1940 ENSA extended its provision to civilians and war workers in factories, industrial hostels and air-raid shelters. By 1941 ENSA had been recognised by the state as the vital and predominant provider of live popular entertainment for workers in the war effort and had become a state-funded and controlled agency.[34] Its provision was primarily limited to popular music and drama but it provided a diverse range of entertainment formats, from large-scale plays, musical revues and orchestral concerts staged in permanent camp theatres, to small troupes of touring actors and entertainers, mobile cinemas and popular musicians and dance bands. By 1943 the armed forces were getting over three thousand dramatic performances a week and over two thousand factories were regularly visited with around 1,300 performances a week.[35] By 1944 ENSA had nearly four thousand performers under contract and four out of five professionals worked for it during the war, from relatively unknown performers to stars such as John Gielgud, Vivien Leigh, Gracie Fields, Jack Buchanan, Elizabeth Welch and Noël Coward. The total audience for the duration of the war was around 500 million and the total budget £14 million.[36]

Whilst ENSA was effectively the state conscription of the popular culture industry for war production, the parallel initiatives for the state provision of art were designed to protect, conserve and promote art culture against the dangers and changes of war. CEMA was originally one of a number of organisations set up in the early war years by activists in the cultural establishment who believed there was a crisis in the provision of art. The critical perceptions of the crisis were first that many already struggling artists and art organisations were facing ruin under wartime restrictions and second that neither the BBC nor ENSA were providing art for the nation. CEMA was subsequently established as a joint project between private and state interests; the government matched the private funding and collaborated on the drafting of the initial policy statement.[37] The founding principles of the organisation were to provide art for the people during war and to encourage music-making and play-acting among the people themselves.[38] The crucial unwritten distinction was that whilst ENSA was predominantly targeted at the military, CEMA was designed for the civilian population. The Council began operation by funding key amateur and voluntary organisations, and by giving emergency grants to support vulnerable companies and institutions. However, after around 15 months of operation CEMA responded to a public and internal debate about professional standards by instigating a policy shift which terminated support to amateur activity and targeted funding exclusively at professional artists and art organisations. This shift was consolidated in April 1942 when CEMA was reorganised as a state agency, salaried full-time directors were employed for the departments of music, drama and art, and panels of professional experts were convened to advise the council. The pioneer of state interventionist economics John Maynard Keynes, a founder member of the London Film Society and a member of the Bloomsbury Group who had been involved in various modernist art initiatives before the war, was appointed as the new chairman. In order to function at an integrated national level a network of regional offices and local advisers was set up later that year based on the organisational model of Civil Defence. Under the maxim 'the best for the most', CEMA's activities became structured around the maintenance and expansion of professional art production and national distribution. The core of CEMA's work was the staging and touring of classical music events but this was augmented by theatre events and touring exhibitions of painting and sculpture.

As John Pick has observed, despite its innovatory touring programmes, the trajectory of CEMA was not to increasingly broaden its constituency but to selectively narrow its activity to an elite and inaccessible range of professional excellence.[39] There was within CEMA the aspiration to demonstrably spread the sacred light of art into the darkness of everyday life but this mission was caught in oppositional tension with the aspiration to maintain art as the culture of sublime and unique privilege. Moreover, this contradiction was polarised by the comparatively meagre resources and activities open to the organisation.[40] Ultimately this unresolved conflict led CEMA into a complex and paradoxical strategy which had a fundamental influence on its development as the post-war Arts Council of Great Britain: it increasingly channelled financial support into an exclusive group of prestigious metropolitan institutions and it justified this expenditure by mythologising its success in bringing art to the remotest and most aesthetically deprived geographical and social territories.[41] In this mythological context popular culture counted as an absence of culture.[42] By the end of the war CEMA had established the key elements of the ideological and institutional project which would structure the post-war Arts Council. They had developed a policy of identifying and supporting only elite professional art organisations which were required to be registered limited companies with charitable aims: non-profit-making organisations with educational purposes.[43] They had established the Council as a critical authority which could legitimate the art status of selected cultural activities whilst excluding others as not art. And they had established the myth of their vitality to the nation's culture: they had brought the light of art into the dim lives of the people, they had saved the struggling artists and protected the precious standard of professional excellence. When the war ended ENSA was considered obsolete and was abruptly disbanded, but CEMA made an amicable transition into a permanent state agency. Politicians of both the left and right agreed that art had a vital role to play in the promotion of social harmony, national prestige and aesthetic discrimination, and that this role could no longer be left to private patronage and vulgar trade. CEMA convinced key factions within the bourgeois ruling elite that it was possible for the state to replace feudal, commercial and private institutions as the predominant, legitimate and efficient patron of art. It demonstrated that in exceptional circumstances a sufficient national audience for state art could be generated to legitimise both the art hierarchy and the expenditure of public taxes. In the summer of 1945 the establishment of the Arts Council passed through parliament unopposed and a year later it was granted a Royal Charter which bound it to the dual function of raising the standards of the 'fine arts' whilst also making them more accessible to the public.[44]

As Keynes remarked soon after the Labour victory of 1945, state art patronage had 'crept in'; informal, modest and very English.[45] But it would be a mistake to confuse informality with accident or lack of purpose. As the Council established itself in the following years it promoted an image of arms-length autonomy and independence from government that obscured the subtle but effective control of the state. Moreover, as in the case of many other semi-autonomous cultural agencies, investigation of the relationship between the Council and the state obscures consideration of the Council *as the state* in its implementation of cultural policy. The formation of the Arts Council must be seen as a project within the broader strategy of cultural nationalisation initiated by the bourgeoisie in the nineteenth century and accelerated by the formation of the BBC, the BFI, the Documentary Film Movement and other semi-autonomous state agencies in the interwar period. Crucially the formation of the Arts Council reinforced the legitimacy of art as the official national culture and fused the auratic fetish of art with elements of post-war welfare state socialism to produce the concept of art as a social service.

Meanwhile, the Labour government of 1945 was faced with another crisis in British film production. British cinema was still totally dominated by America. During the war the film industry had achieved popular and critical success but the actual number of films produced had fallen drastically and the exhibitors had effectively abandoned the quota system introduced by the Cinematographic Films Act of 1927. Moreover, it was now generally accepted that the exhibition circuit was controlled by the American industry. On the left a coalition of groups including the Documentary Film Movement, the ACT and the Tribune Group of the Labour Party lobbied for the nationalisation of the British industry. In response to the production crisis and this interventionist lobby the government renewed the quota system and introduced the National Film Finance Corporation (NFFC) and the Eady Levy.[46] Parallel to these developments the Radcliffe Committee (1947–48) was commissioned to consider the future of the BFI. The critical effect of the report was first to persuade the Labour government to augment the income of the BFI with direct grants from the Treasury and second to shift the focus of the Institute from providing educational resources to promoting film as a legitimate culture for academic study and innovation; to encourage the development of the art of the film.[47] Most significantly, production activity for the Festival of Britain in 1951 led to the development of the BFI Experimental Film Fund.[48] Effectively, this was the initiation of the modern independent sector; the BFI became the first semi-autonomous state agency which did not itself make or commission film projects but funded them by selection from applicants.

According to the standard histories of British experimental cinema, between the Documentary Film Movement of the 1930s and the Underground Cinema of the late 1960s the only significant experimental film movement was the celebrated Free Cinema group.[49] Free Cinema was a provisional coalition of films and film-makers identified with a series of six screenings at the National Film Theatre (NFT) in the second half of the 1950s. Three of the screenings were of contemporary international film including work from the Polish and French New Waves and North American independent makers. The other three screenings were of short, low-budget and predominately 16mm British films by directors including Lindsay Anderson, Karel Reisz, Tony Richardson, Lorenza Mazzetti, Alain Tanner, Robert Vas and Michael Grigsby.[50] The principal activists of the group were the directors Lindsay Anderson, Karel Reisz and Tony Richardson, the cinematographer Walter Lasally and the jack of all trades John Fletcher. The relationship between the group members was both coordinated and provisional; it was a movement, a marketing strategy and an act of desire and imagination; Free Cinema was a campaign, and the designer and ideologue of the campaign was Lindsay Anderson.

Like the Documentary Film Movement, Free Cinema had its intellectual roots in the elite culture of the Oxbridge universities. The key members of the group formed around the independent film magazine *Sequence*, which was originally the *Oxford University Film Society Magazine*. *Sequence* ran for 14 issues between 1946 and 1952 and although at its peak distribution was only around four thousand its critical influence was formidable.[51] Most of the articles were written by the editors including Anderson, Penelope Houston, Gavin Lambert and Karel Reisz.[52] Their critical attitude had a number of significant correspondences to Leavisite literary theory; it was characterised by detailed critical observation, liberal humanist ethics, a rejection of theoretical analysis and an ardent belief in a direct and immediate personal, emotional and intellectual response to cinema.[53] They reacted against the bourgeois quality cinema of the older generation of post-war British directors typi-fied by David Lean and Michael Powell, and they also rejected Grierson's model of cinema as propaganda. Crucially they reaffirmed the avant-garde faith: cinema was an art that must be freed from the degradation of commerce and industry. This strategy was nothing new, but what was new in the post-war context was the extent to which Anderson and *Sequence* projected art into a cluster of popular directors including Hitchcock, Preston Sturges, Raoul Walsh, Nicholas Ray and pre-emi-nently the films of John Ford. However, rather than challenging the art/non-art binary, *Sequence* conceptualised Ford and the others as exceptional artists who had fought off the shackles and compromises of the popular industry and achieved the authority of a personal vision: they had transcended the popular and become film poets: authors.[54] In the 1920s Delluc and Canudo had advocated the introduction of authorship into cinema, but the conception of the poet-director in *Sequence* more significantly foreshadows the development of French polemical auteurism in *Cahiers du cinéma* in the mid-1950s.[55]

Parallel to their work for *Sequence* the core writers were also active in the wider film culture and the crucial expansion of activity was linked to the BFI. In 1950 the new chairman, Denis Forman, set out to recruit the *Sequence* group into the Institute. Lambert became the editor of the prestigious BFI periodical *Sight and Sound*, Houston became deputy editor and, subsequently, Reisz and Anderson had regular articles published. In 1952 Houston took over the editorship and Reisz became the programmer for the BFI's newly-opened NFT. A year later Anderson's *O Dreamland* (1953) was the third film to be funded by the BFI Experimental Film Fund and in 1955 he programmed a John Ford season for the NFT.

The Free Cinema campaign was launched on 5 February 1956 as an NFT programme to promote *O Dreamland, Momma Don't Allow* (1956), directed by Karel Reisz and Tony Richardson, and *Together* (1953), directed by Lorenza Mazzetti. Essentially it was Anderson who came up with the idea of the movement and who wrote the manifesto.[56] The screenings were widely covered by national press and television, and the total audience for the three nights was over three thousand, with perhaps thousands more turned away at the door.[57] Encouraged by the success of the first screenings the movement was continued and five more were staged: two in 1956, one in 1957, two in 1958 and the last in 1959. The most influential films to emerge from the later screenings were the documentaries *Nice Time* (Claude Goretta and Alain Tanner, 1957), *Everyday Except Christmas* (Lindsay Anderson, 1957) and *We Are the Lambeth Boys* (Karel Reisz, 1959).

The success of the Free Cinema campaign depended upon a number of interrelated factors: the originality of the work, the stagnation of the post-war British film industry, the co-option of the BFI by both *Sequence* and Free Cinema, the brilliant publicity campaign and the strategic links with the Angry Young Man 'New Wave' in British drama and literature. The trajectory of the campaign was already marked out in *Sequence* in the late 1940s – as early as 1948 Anderson was convinced that the only hope for an artistic renewal of British cinema was small-scale low-budget independent avant-garde production.[58] His industrial model for the new avant-garde was essentially based on a revival of the alternative avant-garde cinema/film society distribution/exhibition network of the 1920s and 1930s. But this proposition took no account of the radical changes in post-war film culture. Since the 1930s the industrial, technological and social division between the commercial cinema and amateur/independent filmmaking had widened and become further institutionalised. The commercial industry had become comprehensively regulated and graded by both managerial and trade union authority, and employment in the film production industry was subject to a 'closed shop' enforced by the ACT. The film societies had effectively given up competing with commercial distribution and converted to 16mm. Meanwhile the pre-war culture of experimental filmmaking had become subsumed in the wider amateur movement, which had effectively become an alternative and autarkic subculture, which had neither the ideological motivation or the industrial means to launch a vanguard offensive for a new art cinema.[59] The problem that Anderson and his contemporaries faced was not how to create an alternative film culture since the amateur movement clearly was an alternative culture. Their ambition was to transform commercial cinema and to do this it was necessary to break out of amateurism and into the industry. In the early

1950s ambitious young filmmakers who were discontented with both the limits of amateurism and the frustrating gradual climb into the commercial ranks had very limited options; they could try to get into the new television industry or they could enter the documentary sector developed by Grierson and the Documentary Film Movement. The Crown Film Unit, the direct link to the pre-war Documentary Film Movement, was disbanded in 1951, but as already noted there was a rapid expansion in the commercial production and distribution of corporate and sponsored 16mm documentaries in the post-war period and this was the professional entry point exploited by most of the Free Cinema makers. But Free Cinema did not chose documentary – it chose them. Anderson considered the Documentary Film Movement and the Griersonian model of semi-autonomous state production compromised and obsolete. As a critic he celebrated the freedom of poetry and personal expression but as a pragmatic filmmaker he drifted into corporate documentary. Karel Reisz began his film career making documentaries for the Ford Motor Company as director of their Television and Films Programme. Grigsby and Vas were members of Unit 5/7, a Manchester-based independent documentary group.[60] However, although they were effectively compelled into documentary, Anderson and his contemporaries were conscious of the tradition of experimental and subjective documentary exemplified by Jean Vigo, Pare Lorentz and most influentially Humphrey Jennings. In Free Cinema they integrated this influence into an exploration of both the limits and the advantages of the new post-war amateur ciné technologies and developed innovative documentary techniques that foreshadowed the *cinéma vérité* style of the 1960s. In comparison with the established, objective and emotionally detached documentaries of the post-war period Free Cinema appeared as a sudden revitalisation of both the documentary form and British film culture.[61] Their work was contemporary and prophetic, they seemed to have broken out of post-war austerity and discovered the real and future life of the people: the working class. The Free Cinema camera seemed a personal participant in the everyday life of its subjects but it was also an unflinching eye that confronted life with love or rage.

The most direct influence of Free Cinema was on the development of television documentary, but the significance of the movement can only be understood as an element of a broader integrated British New Wave in film, literature and drama, which also included the Angry Young Men movement in the theatre and novel and the subsequent Social Realist genre in popular cinema. Moreover, although Free Cinema was successful as a publicity campaign and a critical platform it ultimately lacked the ideological, commercial or institutional support to create or sustain a new art cinema. The eventual breakthrough into the commercial industry was not an avant-garde bridgehead but was facilitated by a complex shift in bourgeois theatrical and literary culture and a major factor in this shift was the incursion of regional/working-class writers into legitimate culture: Stan Barstow, John Braine, Shelagh Delaney, Harold Pinter, Keith Waterhouse, Alan Sillitoe, David Storey and so on.

The New Wave combination of Oxbridge intellectuals, innovative documentary techniques, radical drama and working-class/lower-middle-class writers reinvigorated British cinema and produced many brilliant, highly acclaimed and often commercially successful feature films but the radicalism of the movement must be understood within the bourgeois literary/theatrical tradition of British cinema: the catalyst of British New Wave cinema was not art but a populist challenge to the London-centred bourgeois naturalist theatrical tradition.[62]

The political context of Free Cinema was the radicalisation of the post-war generation of bourgeois intellectuals and the emergence of the New Left and the Campaign for Nuclear Disarmament. But the political ideology of the movement is obscured by its refusal of theoretical analysis and by the vague and poetic character of its declarations. In Anderson's most celebrated manifesto, 'Stand Up! Stand Up!', published in Sight and Sound in Autumn 1956, he argues that cinema is both an art and a powerful form of social propaganda. The film critic, and by extension the filmmaker, cannot escape the responsibility of social engagement and so must commit themselves to upholding the beleaguered values of art and liberal humanism. In this call to commitment, Anderson is desperately seeking contact with a lost truth that will penetrate the phony, bourgeois sentimental stagnation of post-war Britain. This alienation is characteristic of the New Wave generation of intellectuals stranded between post-war austerity and the counter-culture of the 1960s. The defining characteristic of the movement was a reaction against the perceived failure of bourgeois culture and a passionate fascination with the everyday life of ordinary people. But the relationship between everyday life, popular culture and the New Wave was riven with alienation, nostalgia and ambivalence. Although both the makers and the works of the New Wave were widely engaged and in many cases introduced and promoted by the mass popular mediums of television and cinema, the culture was essentially articulated in the bourgeois theatrical and literary tradition, and the audience for the work was predominantly bourgeois. To look back in anger was the gaze of the young alienated intellectual; for the bourgeois intellectual it was to seek authenticity in the lower classes; for the lower-class intellectual it was to gain the authority of bourgeois culture but to become an exile from the people: the Angry generation were always outsiders.[63]

The relationship between the New Wave generation and the commercial popular culture of the 1950s was riven with ambivalent tension. At best it was deemed an exotic underworld, at worst it was the vulgar pseudo-culture invoked by Leavis. The working-class culture sought by Free Cinema and the New Wave was an authentic organic community, a folklore. But the New Wave relocated and updated the folk to a predominantly Northern pre-war urban mythology of smoking factory chimneys, back-to-back houses and sing songs in the Labour club; the realm of Mass Observation and Humphrey Jennings. The clearest theoretical expression of this relocation can be found in one of the most influential books in the history of the development of British cultural studies, The Uses of Literacy by Richard Hoggart, published in 1957. Hoggart came from a working-class background in

Leeds, attended Leeds University and after the war became a Leavisite activist in the Adult Education movement. In 1964 he founded the Birmingham Centre for Contemporary Cultural Studies (BCCCS) as a research group in the English Department of Birmingham University.[64] Under the leadership of Stuart Hall from the late 1960s the BCCCS had a formative international influence on the study of popular culture. *The Uses of Literacy* is a complex series of analytic observations and affectionate reminiscences of pre-war Northern urban working-class culture that Hoggart systematically compares to his perception of the ever-increasing erosion of this culture by the corrupt, immoral, irresponsible and American anti-life of mass/commercial popular entertainment.[65] Hoggart's most damning indictment of the new mass culture is that it exploits the virtues and vitality of the older organic culture but replaces it with alienated spectacle and vacuous sensation, a form of perpetual masturbation.[66] And the most vulnerable are the adolescents lured by thrills and bright lights to the shabby milk bars where they listen to hollow American jukeboxes and stare vacantly at their plastic world. But, he concludes, in spite of the brutal transformations of the industrial revolution, the working classes have developed a resilient and enduring organic culture: popular culture develops in resistance to commercial mass culture.

Hoggart's nightmare vision of the pop anti-life was conceived in film four years earlier by Lindsay Anderson in *O Dreamland*. The film is clearly influenced by Jean Vigo's bourgeois anti-carnival in *À propos de Nice* (1929), but the ideological context is the work of Jennings. Anderson was a passionate admirer of Jennings and in 1954, a year after making *O Dreamland*, he wrote a study of his work for *Sight and Sound* in which he declared him to be the only real poet of the British cinema.[67] A pivotal

Figure 10: Youth seduced by pop in
O Dreamland (Lindsay Anderson, 1953)

film for Anderson was Jennings' *A Diary for Timothy* (1944–45), a brilliant poetic montage that documents the last days of the war and links the post-war hope for a new classless Britain to the fate of a new-born baby.[68] In 'Stand Up! Stand Up!', Anderson refers to *A Diary for Timothy* and suggests that the questions Jennings had asked about post-war Britain had received negative answers. This is the context of *O Dreamland*. Whilst Jennings' fascination with the popular shifts from longing to compassion *O Dreamland* shifts from fascination to repulsion. Using poetic montage, ironic and asynchronous sound and music Anderson transforms the shabby carnival of a Margate amusement park into a kitsch hell where zombie day trippers shuffle to the sounds of Frankie Laine.

Viewed now, the documentary techniques of intimacy and participation deployed by Free Cinema seem patronising and voyeuristic. Despite their fascination with working-class culture they remained bourgeois outsiders who had neither the technology or the radical imagination that would have enabled them to actually understand or participate in that culture. The key films drew their power from an unresolved tension between a longing for social engagement and a conflicting imperative to subjectivise/aesthetise this engagement. The potential of this tension was finally realised not in art but in collaboration with the working-class writers of the New Wave and the breakthrough into popular cinema.

In the programme notes for the final Free Cinema programme of 1959 the group finally admitted they had had enough of independence:

> The strain of making films in this way, outside the system is enormous, and cannot be supported indefinitely. It is not just a question of finding the money. Each time, when the films have been made, there is the same battle to be fought, for the right to show our work.[69]

The development of Free Cinema was an integrated project combining both filmmaking and the critical practice of *Sequence* and subsequently *Sight and Sound*. The inconsistencies between filmmaking and critical practice should not be seen as flaws but as adjustments and negotiations within the project. The crucial element in the formation of the movement was the colonisation of the BFI by the activists of *Sequence* and Free Cinema. Although ultimately unsuccessful, the Free Cinema project within the BFI had the potential to initiate the development of an alternative vertically-integrated state cinema sector which could challenge the commercial distribution monopoly. The majority of the films were either funded or distributed by the BFI, *Sight and Sound* promoted the group and after 1945 the BFI played the central coordinating role in distribution to the film societies through its Central Booking Agency.[70] Ultimately the Free Cinema movement never became an alternative sector because the key activists did not have the ideological base, the desire or the necessity to develop alternative industrial structures.

From the Documentary Film Movement of the 1930s to Free Cinema it is possible to track a number of strategic correspondences into the independent film movement of the 1970s: the interaction of theory and practice, the development of a state-funded sector, the hostility to commercial cinema and the extreme ambivalence to popular culture. However, the Underground Cinema of the 1960s had a different trajectory which did not radiate from the spires of Oxbridge but from the jukebox plastic nightmare of Hoggart and Anderson.

Chapter 7

AMATEUR CINE CULTURE: THE HIDDEN CONTINUITY FROM 1930s EXPERIMENTAL FILM TO 1960s UNDERGROUND CINEMA

Before we redraft the development of Underground Cinema we must first back-track to revise the history of the amateur cine movement which was a vital element of the independent film culture of 1930s and a neglected continuity to the experimental film culture of the 1960s.

The development of relatively inexpensive substandard cine technology in the 1920s was fundamental to the independent film movement of the 1930s. In the early 1920s Pathé introduced the 9.5mm system and Kodak introduced 16mm and non-flammable reversal film stock, which was not only far cheaper than negative stock, but was used to subvert British film censorship. In the early 1930s competition in the market, increasing demand and technical innovation resulted in the production of the first amateur cine equipment within the financial reach of the middle and lower-middle classes. In the mid-1930s Kodak introduced colour reversal film, 16mm sound equipment and the first viable 8mm system. Throughout the 1950s and 1960s a range of sync-sound systems were introduced for the 8mm gauge and finally in the mid-1960s Kodak developed the Super 8 system which increased the relative projected frame size of 8mm film by fifty per cent and was sold in an easy-to-load sealed plastic cartridge. The amateur cine culture which eventually developed around this technology ranged from the predominance of the domestic home movie to a sophisticated national and international autarkic amateur cine movement.[1] The historical development of the movement was an expansion from an elite bourgeois culture at its inception to a mass popular hobby in the 1960s. Moreover, whilst the dynamism of the avant-garde and the Workers' Film movement was effectively dispersed by the onset of World War Two, the expansion of the broader amateur cine movement was only temporarily suspended. The post-war movement proliferated and established itself as a self-sufficient subculture which incorporated key agents and functions of the 1930s independent movement. But this is a crucial point of continuity which is neglected by the key studies of the 1930s movement.[2] What is more remarkable is that none of the standard historical surveys of experimental film since the 1970s, including A. L. Rees's *A History of Experimental Film and Video*, have acknowledged the continuity of British experimental filmmaking from the 1930s through to the post-war amateur movement and the Underground Cinema movement of the 1960s.[3] Almost as a retelling of the immaculate conception of cinema, the creation myth of 1970s independent film and video substantially remains a spontaneous resurrection from a 25-year cultural vacuum, whilst in fact the post-war amateur movement was in many ways more

Figure 11: *Amateur Cine World* Vol. 14, No. 10. February 1951

independent and far more nationally devolved and integrated than the London-centred independent movement of the 1970s.

As amateur cine equipment became increasingly available in the 1930s a national culture of amateur ciné-clubs and specialist amateur cine magazines developed.[4] The clubs made equipment and resources available to members who would otherwise be financially unable to afford them, they offered advice and support to beginners, held screenings and gave lone workers the opportunity to work collectively. A network of interlinked associations was established, principally the Federation of Cinematograph Societies (FCS), which represented the clubs, the Institute of Amateur Cinematographers (IAC), which primarily represented lone workers and the British Amateur Cinematographers' Central Council, which was formed to represent British amateur organisations within the international federation, the Union Internationale du Cinema d'Amateurs (Unica). Amongst the first specialist magazines were *Amateur Film and Home Movies* (exact dates unknown) and *Home Talkies* (1932–40), but the longest running and crucial coordinating publication of the movement was the monthly *Amateur Cine World*, first published in 1934, weekly in the 1960s and now published quarterly as *Amateur Cine Enthusiast*.[5]

The two core overlapping activities of the amateur movement were amateur cinema (exhibition) and amateur filmmaking (production). At its most basic amateur cinema could be limited to a lone enthusiast with a projector giving family screenings of home movies or professional films rented or bought from one of the many cine film libraries.[6] At its most sophisticated it could be a regular club or film society screening in a purpose-designed amateur auditorium. *Amateur Cine World* regularly featured articles on how to stage club screenings, how to build a cinema in your own home or workplace, or how to choose music to play with silent films and so on. Clubs often used local church or civic halls for screenings but a few had permanent premises which doubled as studios and cinemas. During the war there was a vast increase in the use of 16mm film for military/official screenings of instructional, propaganda and entertainment material and this led to a substantial increase in the post-war availability of 16mm films and equipment. After the war the film society movement gradually converted from 35mm to 16mm and the differentiation between a ciné-club and a film society was often blurred; some film societies had production groups and ciné-clubs often held screenings of commercial, classic and foreign films.[7] Many leading ciné-clubs also distributed their own work within the amateur movement, the FCS and the IAC had film libraries and *Amateur Cine World* of December 1956 lists over fifty clubs with films for hire.[8]

Increasingly in the post-war period the state, industry and various national and international institutions and corporations sponsored professional 16mm documentaries and informational films which were distributed free or almost free to the amateur movement. In the early 1950s two 16mm distribution companies were formed with direct links to the 1930s Workers' Film Movement and the British Communist Party: Stanley Forman's Plato Films (1950) and Charles Cooper's Contemporary Films (1951).[9] Founded in 1946, the monthly magazine *Film User* became the standard guide to amateur and institutional 16mm distribution, publishing articles on projection technology and comprehensive reviews of new releases.

The films available to amateurs ranged from substandard versions of new popular feature releases to silent classics, comedy, short documentaries, cartoons, experimental work and prize-winning amateur films. From the late 1950s/early 1960s the back pages of the cine magazines became increasingly peppered with adverts for soft porn marketed as glamour films or later adult films. Many amateur cinema enthusiasts were also collectors; *Amateur Cine World* frequently ran articles on classic cinema and from the middle to the late 1950s the then teenage filmmaker and historian Kevin Brownlow published a series of articles on collecting 9.5mm prints of rare, international and experimental silent films.[10]

The two dominant modes of amateur film production were first by clubs/groups working collectively and sharing resources, and second by self-sufficient lone workers. Both the collective mode of production and the lone worker had the tendency to subvert concepts of 'authorship' since the clubs would frequently share authorship and lone workers would often co-opt friends and family to participate in the collective creation of the film. The primary amateur film form was the home movie which recorded the domestic and festive life of family and friends for their use. Whilst the cine magazines promoted a diversity of filmmaking practices they acknowledged and celebrated the primacy of the home movie in regular editorials, features and reviews. The most basic, cheapest and accessible type of home movie would simply be unedited silent footage of actuality, the filmmaker's equipment would be limited to a wide-angle lens camera and a projector. But there was within the home movie a wide spectrum of varying degrees of sophistication – *Amateur Cine World* often reviewed complex home movies which were planned, scripted and edited, and which used titles, lighting and sound. A constant feature of the cine magazines were articles on how to introduce conventional film techniques into the home movie: how to make holiday films more dramatic, how to script and plan a wedding film, how to structure a work around a theme of childhood or lighting techniques for filming a party and so on.[11] A recurrent variation of the home movie were narratives in which the family/friends would dramatise themselves. In *Amateur Cine World*, October 1955, Peter Bowen described how whilst on holiday with his family he made the prize-winning drama *Low Tide* which features his own son drowning and returning as a ghost:

> The family agreed to co-operate but were not very enthusiastic, because I envisaged all of us appearing in the film – and that meant each being prepared to take a hand with the camera where necessary, they urged the advantages of a restful holiday but were persuaded to capitulate...[12]

The narrative hook of the film is that Bowen, playing himself as the father, dreams the drowning incident after falling asleep reading an article on holiday films in *Amateur Cine World*.

Aside from the many permutations of home movie, amateur makers also developed specifically amateur techniques and practices to produce parallel versions of commercial film forms and genres: comedy, drama, crime thrillers, ghost stories, science fiction, newsreels, documentaries, animation, nature films, historical drama, horror. Most significantly in this context, amateurs also made experimental films.

In the 1930s key activists in the various sectors of the independent movement had hoped that the amateur movement would eventually challenge the cultural dominance of commercial cinema. Throughout the post-war period there were numerous initiatives to institutionalise a relationship between the professional film industry and the amateur movement. Many of these initiatives centred on promoting amateur film into the commercial sector, crucially the winners of the annual *Amateur Cine World* Ten Best Awards.[13] Throughout the period a number of Ten Best films and documentaries about the amateur movement appeared on national television. And yet amateur film never really functioned successfully outside the movement. Certain key amateur activists and makers did move across into the commercial industry, notably the animator Bob Godfrey, the critic and TV presenter Philip Jenkinson and the directors Ken Russell, Peter Watkins and Kevin Brownlow.[14] Nevertheless, interaction between the amateur movement and the commercial sector was always exceptional. As the movement developed from the 1930s into the post-war period the great majority neither challenged nor sought to challenge the dominance of commercial cinema. Instead the amateur movement developed as a discrete autarkic subculture separated from commercial cinema by a complex set of industrial, technological, institutional and ideological factors. Whilst superficially amateur film and commercial cinema seemed to be correspondent sectors of a broad film culture they were at a deeper level divided by irreconcilable differences.

The prohibitive financial expense of amateur filmmaking ensured that up until at least the early 1960s working-class access to the movement was limited. However within a predominant middle-/lower-middle-class context both post-war cinema and the amateur cine industries targeted the leisure interests of the popular market. But whilst the commercial film industry was definitively concerned with the production and promotion of film as theatrical spectacle, the industries competing in the amateur market promoted film as a participant technology. As Michael Chanan observes, the unique characteristic of popular cinema as a commodity is that

> the film does not need to pass physically into the hands of the consumer for its exchange value to be realised. The exchange value of film is realised through its exhibition, which means through the price of admission the viewer pays to see it. This, of course, also allows the film to be consumed collectively, that is, not by the individual but by an audience (whereas the mode of consumption of the gramophone became quickly individual, or at least limited to the household). But if the film does not pass into the ownership of the consumer in order for its exchange value to be realised, nor does it need to pass into the ownership of the exhibitor if the exhibitor is prepared to rent it instead. Thus,

while goods offered on the capitalist market generally pass from the producer (manufacturer) to the wholesaler to the retailer and thence to the consumer, the terms 'producer', 'distributor', 'exhibitor' and 'audience', which apply to the film industry do not signify quite the same set of relationships, because neither legal ownership of the film nor physical possession have to change hands in the same way.[15]

If the development of cinema was driven by the imperative for an integrated form of popular theatrical montage then this must also be understood as the drive for an integrated industrial system for the mass reproduction and distribution of popular theatrical entertainment. The relationship which developed between the popular cinema industry and the audience can be conceptualised as a form of transmission from the various stages of production and distribution to the point of exhibition. Not only is the film never materially exchanged but unlike popular theatre there is relatively no material show at the cinema, no travelling company, no actors' wages, no props, no costumes, no scenery and no scene changes. The show travels in metal cans; the light transmitted from a unique montage constructed somewhere else. Whilst the cost of film production is exorbitant, the cost of mass distribution and exhibition is far cheaper than an equivalent live theatrical performance, and production cost is offset against the profit from mass ticket sales. The economic durability of the film is only limited by audience demand and the material condition of the print. Competition in this economy of scale has historically tended towards the increasing inflation of film production budgets and the dominance of Hollywood, since America has always had a vast domestic market. Commercial film production depends upon a legion of subsidiary trade industries to supply professional technology and resources, but this secondary economy is discrete and internal. The financial investment of the industry is ultimately located in the marketing and publicity surrounding the film. The material commodity of popular cinema is essentially the show and the entire system is governed by its exchange value at the point of exhibition. The leisure of the cinema audience is an active engagement with spectacular and glamorous attractions, allegories and adventure; the show is a convivial utopia, a realm of carnival and justice. The industry has no financial incentive to inform or involve the cinema audience in the industrial and technological production of film, indeed it has every reason to conceal processes which impede the glamour and fluency of the show.

In contrast, the leisure of amateur cine was at every level derived from participation in the process of cinematic production. The expansion of the industry and the movement depended on a reciprocal process of technological innovation and mass marketing which produced relatively cheap and easy-to-use substandard film, cameras, projectors and cine equipment. The industry functioned as a traditional commercial industry supplying this equipment and film from the manufacturer to the wholesaler to the retailer and on to the consumer, but a simple model of consumption is misleading since the leisure activity of the amateur was in itself participation in a form of industrial production. Even amateur cinema enthusiasts who did not make films were not simple consumers, rather they were amateur impresarios and projectionists.

Whilst the commercial cinema industry was organised as a variant of the factory system with a hierarchical division of labour and elements of mass production and standardisation, amateur cine was practised by lone enthusiasts and a range of relatively informal collectives/groups who produced and exhibited film not as work but as leisure or play. The material product of the amateur cine industry was cine technology but whilst technology in the commercial industry was primarily limited to its value as industrial utility, the value of cine technology was articulated in a culture of play, memory and desire. In amateur culture, cine technology and technical procedures took on a sensual and arcane pleasure, the amateur filmmaker was no longer a spectator, they became adept in a magic realm of gadgets, kinks, tips and specifications.[16]

Crucially the amateur cine industry had relatively no direct commercial investment in the production, distribution or exhibition of amateur films. There was limited commercial distribution of prize-winning amateur work but this was exceptional. The growth of the industry depended on the popularity of amateur film production, but the investment of the industry was not in its quality but in its quantity. Indirectly the cine equipment industry guided and responded to the creative practices of amateur makers through design: camera mobility, hand-held shooting, automatic zoom lenses, auto exposure and so on. Many articles and advisers in the cine magazines promoted a variation of Hollywood continuity style and an ideology of professionalism and quality but this was consistently tempered with a pride in self-sufficiency, eccentricity and a commitment to experiment.[17] Whilst competition in commercial cinema tended to drive production costs up, competition in the amateur market drove production costs down. Substandard film, reversal film, fast film for shooting in available light, lightweight fixed focus and auto exposure cameras, all these innovations cut the cost of amateur production but they also produced a cinematography radically different to commercial cinema. Commercial cinematography sought a lucid and fluent transparency, an invisible access to the marvellous space of narrative and spectacle. This is not to say popular cinematography sustained a perpetual naturalistic illusion, but that it was increasingly driven by an aspiration to conventionally simulate the perceptual quality of the human eye: the elimination of photographic grain, controlled exposure, constant focus, smooth movement, stable framing, colour grading and so on. This drive towards clarity eventually produced the modern cinematic attraction which we could term 'hyperlucidity', a form of cinematography which idealises the perception of the human eye: deep focus, increased colour saturation, digital effects and so on. In comparison amateur cinematography, especially 8mm cinematography, is translucent or opaque. It is visible, the screen image does not seem natural or fluent but is composed of photographic grain which in 8mm appears to vibrate and weave. Since the amateur often worked with only one reversal print the final film would also often become scratched and dirty. Moreover, even the best amateur editing equipment tended to make edits visible or projectors jump. The small lightweight cine cameras could be hand-held by a single operator without a crew, technical support or tripods, dollys and other heavy equipment. Amateurs carried their cameras on holiday, to the beach, to festivals and celebrations, in cars, boats, rambling, climbing and so on. The transparency of commercial cinematography is also an objectification, a distance composed in framing and movement. In contrast, the home movie style is physically produced by the subjectivity of the filmmaker and is always a point-of-view shot; in the hands of the filmmaker the camera shakes and jerks, they follow movement, they 'hose pipe pan' along the horizon, their friends make eye contact with them through the lens, and when the filmmaker loses interest they abruptly cut. Add to all these factors occasional mistakes in exposure and focusing, and the experience of watching amateur cinematography alternates between the consciousness of film as an analogue and the impression of gazing through a vibrating mesh into an intangible world. Commercial cinema invokes an immediate and lucid present whilst amateur cine is always an invocation of the past. The irony is that because amateur cinematography cannot hide the marks of its own production and because it was traditionally used to document the everyday life of the home, it came to connote authenticity; popular cinema's realism connotes fiction whilst amateur cine's fabrication connotes the real.

Although sound equipment became available in the mid-1930s amateur cinema was established and expanded on the availability of substandard silent prints.[18] After the war the vast increase in the use of 16mm sound projectors and the mass production of sound prints severely undermined the availability of new silent prints, but many enthusiasts remained committed to silent film and became collectors and advocates. Amateur filmmaking developed a broad range of techniques to produce post-production film soundtracks but the critical obstacle for the amateur movement was developing a cheap and effective synchronised-sound system. The development of the magnetic stripe system for 8mm, and Super 8 in the late 1960s, came very close to solving the problem but there always remained fundamental difficulties with editing striped film. The combined effect of these factors was that amateur cine was always predominantly a visual form which used music, commentary and other unsynchronised sound as post-production augmentation. This visual dominance was fundamental to the home movie which was essentially concerned with perceptible memory and documentation. The audience for the home movie would invariably be the family and friends of the filmmaker, and synchronised sound would have been superfluous to the images of holidays, children, deceased relatives, old houses, beloved pets and so on. Moreover, dialogue would have interfered with the active audience conversation during the film.[19] Amateur cine was also short: most ran for under twenty minutes, few over half an hour and feature-length films were very unusual. The conditions of amateur production imposed both brevity and speed on the amateur maker. Film stock and processing was expensive and so amateurs could not afford long films, long takes and multiple takes, most cine equipment was designed for short film and the vast majority of amateurs had to find time for filmmaking between work and domestic duties. Moreover, since film production in the amateur movement was a leisure activity engaged predominantly with family documentation and social interaction there was a fundamental preference for short films frequently produced and screened as part of a process of continuous social interaction.

Amateur industry and technology was essentially different to commercial cinema. The products were different and the technologies and working practices were incompatible. Furthermore, this dichotomy polarised in the post-war period. From the 1950s onwards amateur technology became increasingly automated and simplified whilst commercial cinema remained the domain of trained technicians and specialists. Amateur film remained predominantly silent whilst commercial cinema became increasingly invested in sync-sound technologies, and commercial silent film was consigned to the archives. Amateur film was short whilst increasingly the supporting programmes of short films at the cinema were phased out until they were effectively eliminated in the 1970s. These factors ensured that amateur work and skills were not directly transferable to the commercial cinema industry. Neither the film industry, television or the unions were actively hostile to the amateur movement but amateurism was absolutely excluded by the industry, which in combination with the unions maintained strict professional standards governing quality of product, hierarchical division of labour, technical specialisation, wage differentials and so on. As it developed, the television industry adopted even more rigid standards but it was also potentially more accessible to amateur filmmaking since it used the 16mm gauge and screened short film. However, the concept of 'broadcast quality' effectively excluded amateur work, specifically 8mm and Super 8 film, from transmission, unless it was clearly framed and identified as an example of amateur filmmaking, an exception to the professional norm.

From the amateur perspective, although there was a controversial borderland between the professional and the amateur, and the amateur aspired to 'professionalism' and 'professional quality', amateur cine was essentially self-selecting. Despite long-running and constant encouragements and admonitions from activists most amateur filmmakers resisted schemes to centralise, aestheticise or industrialise the culture. This resistance was at heart a resistance to professionalisation; most amateurs wanted to be amateur, they worked at other professions and trades; amateur cine was not work, it was freedom from work.

The leisure at the core of the amateur movement was complex for not only was the practice valued as leisure but it was used in home movies to record and store leisure time. Home movies captured the festive life and made it possible to replay that life as a participant spectacle. This had a particular significance for summer and foreign holidays since the expense of the holiday and the fleeting time out of work could be materialised and owned as a form of external memory; the light of summer could be projected into the dark winter nights. Likewise, childhood time and the rituals of family life could be captured and reviewed. Whereas stills photography provided family and friends with documents of the past, home movies invoked the past as a spectacle of recollection.[20] Each film was unique, celebrated in the conversation and recollection of its audience and yet to strangers they all seemed to repeat the same formula: the same babies, couples, grandparents, weddings. For the stranger, the home movie is often meaningless, or worse it is a memory that has lost its home. But home movies also fixed leisure time in the glamour of cinema, they invoked the narrative and attraction of popular cinema, they cinematised the lives of the enthusiasts who became the directors and stars of their own lives and this glamorisation was promoted by the amateur cine industry.[21]

Figure 12: *Amateur Cine World* Vol. 4, No. 21. November 1962

The key issues concerning the amateur movement in a history of Underground cinema are alternativity and experimentalism. If we sidestep the predominance of home movies and focus on the active movement engaged at club and competition level, it must be estimated that the post-war amateur movement achieved a level of organised integrated national production, distribution and exhibition which surpassed the avant-garde and independent film movement of the 1970s and 1980s. And yet, unlike these later formations, the amateur movement remained economically and institutionally autonomous to the commercial film industry, television, state education, academic establishments and the institutions of art. Paradoxically, the obscurity of the movement is the most convincing evidence of its autonomy. Institutionally the amateur movement did not register and it is the institutions which authorise history. The assumption which underlies the omission of the post-war amateur movement from histories of independent film and video is that amateur cine is neither cinema nor art and it is precisely this which makes amateurism a radical alternative.

Two key markers of amateur cine as an alternative film culture were firstly the position of women, and secondly collective production. It is clear from a close reading of the cine magazines that women were intrinsic to the amateur movement; they were members of ciné-clubs, they shared the work with male members and there was a significant percentage of women filmmakers.[22] They frequently featured in club reports, features and correspondence on amateur activity; there were often images of women filmmakers using cameras and projectors and occasionally there were articles opposing the male domination of the amateur movement and encouraging women's involvement at both grass roots and management level.[23]

Collectivity and participation were fundamental to cine culture. Despite many funding initiatives and speculations, amateur production effectively operated outside of both the commercial film industry and the amateur cine industry and so remained overwhelmingly a self-funded voluntary activity which functioned due to the amicable consent and generosity of its participants. This voluntary and collective character also structured amateur cinema screenings and most other club activities since they were effectively non-profit-making organisations which held all resources in common ownership. *Amateur Cine World* functioned as a coordinating centre and clearing house for shared information, debate and collective decision-making and there was a frequent and ongoing series of letters and articles which detailed how to construct cine equipment and so evade and subvert the cine equipment industry. Innovative collective projects frequently appeared in the post-war cine magazines: *Amateur Cine World of* 17 May 1962 has an article on the production and exhibition of a collectively-made two-hour 8mm documentary film called *A River Runs Through Our Town* made by Shoreham Ciné-Club of West Sussex.[24]

The club shows and home screenings of amateur cinema reproduced the attractions of early British cinema but also developed new ones. They were familiar; they allowed their participants to watch themselves and to glamorise and narrate everyday life. And it was alternative – it did not look like commercial cinema, it

looked like someone had made it, like you could make it yourself; for its participants amateur cinema opened up the creative potential of early cinema before the
development of continuity narrative techniques. However, if amateur filmmakers
aspired to the continuity techniques of commercial cinema they also had to learn
them by experiment.

Throughout the post-war decades the amateur movement had both a current
of experimental practice and an awareness of the experimental tradition as a crucial element of amateur film culture. The pages of the cine magazines were full of
experiments, scripts and ideas for films, DIY equipment projects, advice on how to
achieve cinematographic effects and letters from filmmakers detailing their own discoveries. There would frequently be articles on various types of animation: cartoons,
claymation, pixillation and so on. Occasionally, there would be features on how
to achieve abstract animation effects.[25] A direct link between amateur experiment
and the 1930s avant-garde was the filmmaker, novelist and poet Oswell Blakeston
who wrote a standard paperback guide on how to write scripts for amateur films
in 1949, and contributed a series of his own scripts to *Amateur Cine World* in the
early 1950s.[26] These were designed for amateurs to make themselves, and the most
striking is the surreal 'Material for a Poem' which appears in the issue for November
1951. In the brief introduction Blakeston explains that the script is for an 'art' film
and that it takes as its form a dream state which, he observes, is very suitable for
the amateur since it does not require strict continuity. The narrative that follows is
an anguished lament for a bohemian poet, heavily influenced by French Surrealist
film but also integrating post-war atomic bomb anxiety. It would be fascinating to
discover just how many readers of *Amateur Cine World* actually attempted to make
Blakeston's script. There could be a score of amateur Surrealist 'classics' gathering
dust in suburban lofts.[27]

The club news in *Amateur Cine World* regularly noted screenings of experimental
films at various regional centres. Many pre-war silent experimental films were still
available on substandard gauges including work from the French avant-garde, silent
Soviet film and German expressionist cinema, and the work of the British Documentary Film movement, Len Lye and Norman McLaren was known and discussed
in *Amateur Cine World*. From the mid-1950s the amateur filmmaker and activist
Derek Hill and the experimental amateur ciné-club the Grasshopper Group organised screenings and distribution of contemporary American experimental work
including films by Maya Deren, Stan Brakhage, Willard Maas and Marie Menken.[28]
Work by the Grasshopper Group was also distributed in the US by Amos Vogel's
Cinema 16 distribution group. *Amateur Cine World* for December 1956 has a feature
recommending films for public amateur screenings which includes an experimental
section, and the entire selection includes around eight experimental shorts including three films by James Broughton and five by British makers, including Lindsay
Anderson's *O Dreamland*.[29]

In the late 1950s experimental film became a source of intense interest and
controversy in *Amateur Cine World*. For example, in the issue for October 1957 an

editorial article defends the magazine from attacks by both those for and against experimental entries to the Ten Best Awards. In the July 1958 issue there is an editorial report from the Brussels Experimental Film Festival which mentions work by Stan Brakhage, Shirley Clarke, Len Lye, Francis Thompson, John Whitney and Roman Polanski, and in the January 1959 issue there is a two-page review of experimental film at the annual University of London Student Film Festival.[30]

Throughout the 1950s and into the 1960s intriguing references to experimental amateur production frequently appeared in the club pages and articles of *Amateur Cine World*.[31] A series of experimental films won prizes in the Ten Best awards including, in 1953, *Agib and Agab* (Markfilm), *Floral Fantasy* (John Daborn), *Two's Company* (Grasshopper Group), in 1954 *Coming Shortly* (High Wycome Film Society), in 1955 *Doppelgänger* (Solo Films) and in 1956 *Driftwood and Seashell* (Richard H. Jobson) and *Short Spell* (Stuart Wynn Jones). Markfilm, who made *Agib and Agab,* were a group of four artists who produced several experimental amateur films in the early 1950s. The group included Bruce Lacey who later became a key figure in the 1960s counter-culture, as a performer, installation artist and member of the notorious radical jazz combo the Alberts.[32] The most consistent, organised and celebrated amateur experimental filmmakers were the Grasshopper Group founded by John Daborn, which included at various times Derek Hill, Bob Godfrey and Stuart Wynn Jones. They specialised in animation and experiment but otherwise operated as a regular open membership ciné-club holding screenings, training sessions, open nights and so on. Throughout the 1950s and early 1960s the group produced many prize-winning experimental films and organised screenings and distribution of American and continental experimental film. Derek Hill was a filmmaker and journalist who from the early 1950s wrote film reviews and features for *Amateur Cine World*. In the late 1950s he set up the Short Film Service to distribute short films to clubs, societies and the commercial circuit and in the mid-1960s he founded the New Cinema Club, which, along with the London Film-makers' Co-operative and the Electric Cinema Club in Notting Hill Gate, was a key venue for the London Underground Cinema. Another direct link between the amateur movement and the Underground was Jeff Keen, the most influential Underground filmmaker in the British tradition. In 1962 Tony Wigens, the editor of *Cine Camera* magazine, met with Keen and Raymond Barker and viewed some of the 8mm films they had been making around the art college in Brighton.[33] He was so inspired by these films that he organised a programme to tour the ciné-club circuit called the Experimental Film Register, which was launched at the Grasshopper Group in December 1962. Keen was actually working as a Brighton Corporation gardener at the time but was making his work at the college film society. He had made his first film, *Wail,* in 1959, and in 1961 had collaborated on *Autumn Feast* with Piero Heliczer who later became a key filmmaker, performer and poet of the New York Underground.[34] The Experimental Film Register ran for a couple of years and then disappeared when *Cine Camera* magazine ceased publication. Keen was eventually recognised and celebrated by the LFMC activists and attained a unique position of reverence in the 1970s avant-garde, for even at the height of the structuralist dogma when his work was sidelined it still seemed to defy condemnation. Perhaps this was because the structuralists knew that he had been making underground films a decade before the return of the avant-garde, or perhaps it was because they understood that as convincing and esoteric as their theory was, it still stood no chance against the sheer power of Keen's psychedelic barrage of pop montage.

Although there are direct links between the amateur movement and the underground the essential continuity is cultural and comprehensive. Despite its gadget fetish and fascination with arcane technical procedure, the amateur movement consistently sought the democratisation of film culture, popular access to film technology, personal participation and collective production. At a fundamental level it was an experimental culture since every amateur maker was engaged in a personal, playful and inquisitive exploration of the medium. As the cost of amateur cine equipment dropped in the 1950s and early 1960s the movement also became a genuinely popular culture, and at the height of its popularity it was the most successful integrated autonomous film movement in British cinema history. Moreover, the Underground Cinema movement of the late 1950s effectively developed as an amateur movement: the alternativity of the underground was substantially determined by the alternativity of amateur technology and technique.

And yet the 1970s British avant-garde and the independent film and video sector never acknowledged the priority of the amateur movement. The reasons for this are complex: to begin with the key activists of the avant-garde knew very little about amateur cine culture and they despised popular cinema. They were predominantly artists, most of whom had never made a film until joining the LFMC and they were initially engaged with a counter-culture which sought a revolutionary negation of British post-war culture, the square, repressed, suburban world of their bourgeois parents. The overwhelming influence for British underground cinema was American underground film and the American counter-culture. In this context the amateur movement must have seemed a banal and provincial hobby for ageing squares, or worse still an ideological prop for the repressive capitalist patriarchal family. Whilst the amateur movement was diverse and diffuse with no central ideological core or theoretical consciousness, the avant-garde formed around a theoretical praxis essentially hostile to the popular, and in the 1970s the independent film and video sector reinforced this neglect with a state Socialist disdain for leisure and dilettantism.

Nevertheless, the amateur movement was aware of the underground. *Amateur Cine World* of 30 June 1966 carried a four-page feature on American Underground Cinema under the headline 'What are Underground Movies?'. A month later the magazine reported that anyone interested in hiring the films should contact the new London Film-makers' Co-operative.[35]

THE SEARCH FOR THE COOL PLACE:
UNDERGROUND CINEMA
VS. AVANT-GARDE FILM

Chapter 8

ANTI-ART, POP AND BOHEMIA: THE BOHEMIAN CABARET AS PRECURSOR TO THE UNDERGROUND CINEMA

The emergence of Underground Cinema in the second half of the 1950s has its roots in the friction between art and the popular which began with the very advent of art in the early nineteenth century. Whilst the institution of art developed as a means to maintain the reconfigured bourgeois social hierarchy, this does not mean that there were no agents or movements within the realm of art dedicated to radical politics and revolutionary agitation. On the contrary the historical development of art as a repressive institution must be understood as a product of the negation and containment of these radical forces. The three interlinked and initially radical traditions which developed from the formation of art were the avant-garde, anti-art and bohemianism, and the crucial foundation of these traditions was French Romanticism. This chapter will track the development of these currents to the emergence of the bohemian cabaret in the Paris of the 1880s.

ART AGAINST ART

The function of art is to demonstrate, circumscribe and preserve the power and freedom of the bourgeoisie. Romanticism is the primary form of art; it is the shift from feudal prestige to bourgeois aura, the advent of the alienated genius. French Romanticism appears with the restoration of Louis XVIII, it is the revolution invoked and betrayed. The accession of the bourgeoisie at once destroys the feudal hierarchy and then fetishises it as the acquisition of the new ruling class; the feudal king is replaced by the bourgeois king.[1] Romanticism is the sensibility of the new historical time of bourgeois capitalism, of the possibility of an egalitarian democratic utopia and of the betrayal of this possibility by the bourgeoisie. It is a complex system of interdependent cultural formations, tendencies and determinants, it is irrational and progressive; it romanticises the world. At its core is the paradoxical desire for utopia and the fear and suppression of that desire. From Romanticism the avant-garde developed as the pioneers of a utopian realm free from the utility, commodification and alienation of bourgeoisie capitalism. But far from establishing a new alternative realm this trajectory effectively secluded art as an elite fetish and imposed on the avant-garde artist the role of the outcast genius martyr.

By the early twentieth century it had become apparent to politically radical artists that the utopian project of the avant-garde was fatally misconceived and from this recognition a reconfigured utopian art project developed; this was Anti-Art and it was consolidated by the Dadaists.

Figure 13: A night at the Chat Noir, 1889

Anti-Art is a project which becomes possible only when art has become in-stitutionalised as a culture supposedly autonomous to social function, industrial production, capitalist economics and popular culture. After Art for Art's Sake, after Modernism, after the carnage of the Great War of 1914–18, art had developed its institutional autonomy to the degree that its political irrelevance was irrevocably revealed. More than that, the Dadaists realised that this autonomy was in fact the complicity of art with the bourgeois war machine and a means to enervate radi-cal dissent.[2] Before Dada there had been scores of artists (and art movements) who were revolutionary socialists and anarchist activists, but until the Dadaists, revolu-tionary artists had set out to transform art, to create a new art for the people, an art with a social function, an art of liberation.[3] The Dadaists also invoked a new revolutionary culture, but understood that it could not be art, there was only one revolutionary project for the radical artist: self abolition. Art had to be destroyed so that its utopian potential could be released. Anti-Art demands the end of autonomy and the reintegration of art and everyday life: the sublation of art.[4]

Art as an institution consists of production, distribution, exhibition and ideologi-cal apparatus and within these overlapping sectors are the artists, galleries, patrons, the public, the market, the educational sector, museums, state art organisations and so on. The interaction and diversity of art activity prohibits a rigid allocation to agents in the institution; an artist may also be a teacher, a theorist, a curator and a collector. However, art has integrity as a complex functioning institutional system. The production of aura as a commodity, the development of the artist as the pro-ducer of aura and the removal of function from objects is not simply a historical process, it is what art does as an institutional system. The paradox of a feudal handicraft in an industrial society and a mystic ritual in the age of scientific rationalism makes art both mythically fascinating and vulnerable to subversion. Dada realised this and exploited it. In the years between the two world wars art appeared to be most vulnerable to subversion at the point where the aesthetic gaze was summoned, where the ritual took place, the site of exhibition: the gallery, the theatre, the concert hall and so on. Those who attend an exhibition enter into a contract with the exhibitor: the exhibition will provide the auratic objects, the audience will gaze with pure aesthetic disinterest. Bathed in the aura, social being is suspended and the aesthetic gaze interrogates the art object for meaning – the trace of the artist, form, style, connotation, denotation, symbolism, allegory, metaphor. This conversion of social function into meaning renders the art object insignificant; it is a complex

and exclusive game.[5] Dada's most radical strategy was also its fatal flaw: rather than trying to win or refusing to play the game of art, Dada entered the game but broke the rules. The Dadaists subverted the auratic realm of art by inserting objects into it which were not art: popular culture, mechanically-reproduced images, mass-produced objects, anonymous work, mundane functional appliances, found objects. Perhaps the most notorious example was the mass-produced porcelain urinal, *Fountain*, signed by R. Mutt and sent to the hanging committee of the 1917 exhibition of the New York Society of Independent Artists; Marcel Duchamp taking the piss.

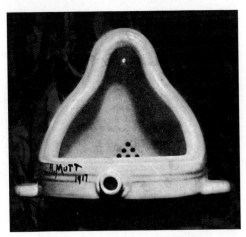

Figure 14: *Fountain* by R. Mutt a.k.a. Marcel Duchamp

This barrage of non-art was designed to expose art as a bourgeois fetish and at first it was very effective, but with each new outrage art did not disintegrate, it actually became more resistant. As Hans Richter recalls:

> The devising and raising of public hell was an essential function of any Dada movement, whether its goal was pro-art, non-art, or anti-art. And when the public, like insects or bacteria, had developed immunity to one kind of poison, we had to think of another.[6]

In its brief and glorious rage the Dada movement developed a repertoire of brilliant subversive techniques, but also initiated a historic dialectic which far from eliminating art effectively vaccinated it against subversion, modernised its technology and expanded and liberated the functionless gaze. How this happened lies in the arcane nature of art as an auratic ritual and the artist as the producer of aura. The function

(-lessness) of art is to maintain the social hierarchy of the bourgeoisie and this maintenance is performed at every level of the art institution from the ritual of exhibition to art education and magazine criticism. The only place where this maintenance does not take place is in the content of the art work, because the aesthetic gaze renders the art work itself insignificant. By opening the rift between signifier and signified, by eliminating representation, the modernists ratified what became apparent to the Dadaists: it does not actually matter what the art work is, because the institution of art is autonomous to the work of art. This is the incredible resilience of art; it cannot be subverted at the level of the artwork. The shock tactics of Dada produced ever-diminishing effects; every attempt to break into the aesthetic gaze of the bourgeois audience simply increased their capacity for disinterest in the face of extreme provocation. The absurd and irrational excesses of the Dadaists may have outraged the bourgeoisie at first, but inevitably such extremism could be contained as the sacred and noble mythology of religious ecstasy and aristocratic eccentricity: aura. Moreover, since the bourgeoisie articulates itself as the ruling elite by the disinterest of its aesthetic gaze, so Dada provided ever more efficient tests of disinterest. The insertion of mass-produced objects, new technology, random products and vulgar humanity into the institution of art did not destroy aura but modernised it. The irony of Dada was that to many of its activists, Anti-Art was just another movement, another avant-garde, so that even as they subverted art they participated in the institutionalisation of that subversion.[7] Ever since the primordial romantic genius emerged out of the bourgeois revolution the life of the artist had become the authority of the aura, but up until Dada the aura was experienced by the viewer as the authenticity of the handmade art work, the fetish of the mystical and noble. The institutionalisation of Dada removed the aura from the art work and projected it back onto the artist and this projection was often encouraged by the Dadaists. A crucial exponent of this appropriation was Duchamp who wrote of his urinal:

> Whether Mr Mutt with his own hands made the fountain or not has no importance, He CHOSE it. He took an ordinary article of life, placed it so that its useful significance disappeared under the new title and point of view – created a new thought for that object.[8]

The revolutionary potential of inserting non-art into the art institution became totally assimilated as the found object and the readymade, and aura could subsequently be experienced no longer as simply the physical trace of the artist but as the mystic projection of the artist's perception. Whereas the artist hitherto had the power to produce aura, after the readymade the artist became living aura, able to transubstantiate the base and vulgar objects of everyday life into art simply by placing them into the art institution.

From Dada an anti-art tradition developed which can be traced through the twentieth century from the Surrealists to the Lettrists, the Situationists, Fluxus, conceptual art, the mail artists and contemporary art hoaxers, pranksters and interventionists. Since Dada, anti-art has been locked into a relentless shadow conflict with the institution of art in which the anti-artists have developed ever more ingenious and resistant subversive strategies and art has proved itself ever more flexible and efficient in its process of enervation and appropriation. This dialectic is inevitable since in the final analysis anti-art as a radical project can only operate within the autonomous institution of art; anti-art is always art. As the Fluxus artist Allan Kaprow observed in 1969,

> Art. There's the catch. At this stage of consciousness, the sociology of Culture emerges as an in-group 'dumb-show'. Its sole audience is a roster of the creative and performing professions watching itself, as if in a mirror, enact a struggle between self-appointed priests and a cadre of self-appointed commandos, jokers, guttersnipes, and triple agents who seem to be attempting to destroy the priests' church. But everybody knows how it all ends: in church, of course, with the whole club bowing their heads and muttering prayers. They pray for themselves and for their religion.[9]

Dada/Surrealism was historically the most radical form of anti-art, after which anti-art effectively became a new avant-garde.[10] Moreover, the anti-art desire for the sublation of art was always and essentially politically equivalent to the avant-garde desire for autonomy. It is the artist's desire for an aesthetic utopia which will bring an end to bourgeois alienation, in the first case by creating the utopian realm of art outside bourgeois society and in the second by eliminating the exclusivity of art and so attempting to extend the utopian realm out to every class and division of society. Although anti-art deployed elements of popular culture as a subversive non-art, both the avant-garde and anti-art projects were ultimately predicated on the negation of the popular. The modernist avant-garde sought to purge art of all trace of the popular whilst the Anti-Art movement transformed the popular into Art. The utopian project of anti-art effectively became the demand for the aestheticisation of popular life, a trajectory which was exemplified by the Situationists active in Paris from the late 1950s and into the late 1960s. In Situationism the ambivalent enmity and desire of the artist for the popular reaches its most fervent and seductive polarity; the popular is conceived as both the totalising hegemonic domain of bourgeois oppression and the base metal for the alchemical transformations of avant-garde liberation.

The avant-garde operates in all its forms as the vanguard of the autonomy of the institution of art. This is an imperative of the ruling culture of the bourgeoisie which represses, appropriates and enervates all radical projects designed to democratise and liberate cultural production. It is a paradox which is infinitely flexible and infinitely transformable. It is a product of the bourgeois fetishisation of both the feudal past and the capitalist future; with progress it makes new cultural developments old. So effective is this arcane enchantment that art has now entered a radical new phase of autonomy in which cultural practices formerly considered as art are now being separated and excluded from art by the creation of ultra-superfluous substitutes: theatre is no longer art since the emergence of performance art and live art, music is replaced by sound art and radio art and so on. (The substitute for cinema we shall come to soon enough.) The last autonomy will be of art from its specialisation as a 'visual art', then perhaps there will be paint art, artists painting and sculpture art.

The avant-garde cannot be simply identified as a specific historical formation, movement or genius, and neither can it be identified by content since the autonomy of art is not a style, form or medium but a social function. Although the purest expression of the avant-garde is modernist abstraction, content is superfluous; even cultural work that was designed as radical anti-art can be appropriated and transformed into avant-garde art; even those who have worked explicitly for the democratisation of culture have had their work appropriated by the avant-garde. The only requirement of content is that it should be new, and since in a society ruled by an elite caste the idea of democracy and liberation is always new, those radical cultural workers who chose to work within the institution of art will always serve the avant-garde; the more they rebel the more they collaborate in their own superfluousness. The Dada liberation of the aura, the transference from the hand to the soul of the artist, enabled the twentieth-century avant-garde to colonise new cultures and technologies without ever risking the reintegration of art and everyday life, because since the art work was no longer defined by its materiality but by inclusion in the institution of art, so aura could be bestowed on anything.

The anti-art separation of the aura from the object accelerated a process of European avant-garde colonial cultural appropriation exemplified by the well documented influence of Japanese woodcuts on the Impressionists and African masks on the Cubists. But the first colony and the primary appropriation was the internal colony of all those in Western society who were excluded from art as it became autonomous: the popular.

BOHEMIA

The avant-garde and anti-art should be understood as historical projects operating within the culture of art; in comparison 'bohemia' should be understood as a broader subculture which contained and produced artists and art movements but which operated at the border of art and the popular.

Bakhtin cites the carnival as a crucial agent in the rise of Renaissance humanism and tracks elements of carnival culture into Romanticism. However, neither the Renaissance or Romanticism were isolated junctures; they were actually critical phases in the gradual ascension of bourgeois culture, and the popular was a vital factor in that ascension. The romantic movement first constituted itself in fascination with the life of the people: the appropriation of popular forms (ballads, melodrama and so on), grotesque carnival imagery, the mythologised feudal countryside, the idealisation of the outlaw and the revolutionary utopian currents of socialism and anarchy.[11] However, the resurgence of carnivalesque themes and forms in Romanticism is not the return of carnival, it is a new element which could only develop because carnival had been excluded from classicism. In the struggle against feudalism the bourgeoisie invoked the utopian power of the carnival, but having finally gained power they set about excluding and controlling it, for in realising the radical potential of the carnival they feared it and understood that it had to be repressed. This fear is also a denial of desire because the bourgeois repression of carnival is not only the repression of carnival amongst the common people, it is the repression of carnival in bourgeois culture. The tension between disgust and desire returns in Romanticism as the romantic grotesque. The grotesque body of Romanticism is the alienated, the living corpse, the bestial, the wanderer, the deformed, it is Frankenstein's monster, the Ancient Mariner, Lautréamont's Maldoror; it is Mr Hyde. The celebration of the cyclical, abundant, collective life of the body in carnival reappears in Romanticism as a delirious horror of, and desire for, degradation and disintegration; to be ravaged by the monster, to be brought low. And this ambivalence is another reason why the shock tactics of the post Dada anti-artists can only maintain the autonomy of art. The use of animal corpses, meat, blood, shit, menstrual fluids, used condoms, self-mutilation and so on may disgust the bourgeois public but this disgust is also a fascination with the means of their own superiority: there is pleasure in alienation, and this pleasure is most profound in the distance between having the aesthetic gaze and losing it. To remove this alienation, to experience the loss of the aesthetic gaze in a moment of ungoverned sensual and emotional pleasure, to be unable to differentiate between the sign, the signified and the referent, to lose your subjectivity in the object … this for the bourgeois is both horrific and seductive.[12] As art developed in the early nineteenth century the bohemian artist became the agent licensed to dramatise the repressed desire of the bourgeoisie.

The development of bohemia can be traced in the culture of the bourgeois revolution. In France between the outbreak of the Revolution of 1789 and the consolidation of the Napoleonic Empire an unprecedented cultural conflict raged concerning the nature of the new revolutionary society and the identity of the new citizen. The revolutionary bourgeoisie collaborated, celebrated and fought with the common people; together they participated in a carnival of riots, marches, executions, the destruction of feudal institutes and monuments, and the euphoria of revolutionary festivals. In the colony of Saint Domingue white bourgeois revolutionaries fought under the command of black officers.[13] In Paris the streets became a theatre for the staging of both radical and reactionary spectacle, and this extravagant conflict found expression in the young bourgeoisie with the adoption of symbolic guises and fashions. The three critical modes of these idealised guises were first the everyday clothing of the common people, second the fashions of the English ruling class, and third the costumes of the ancient classical cultures of Greece and Rome. In the revolutionary struggle for a transformation of society the young bourgeoisie demonstrated their political allegiance by metaphorically transforming themselves and attempting to realise their metaphors. They made themselves political. The radical Sans Culottes adopted the idealised guise of peasants and workers, the reactionary Muscadins and the later Incroyables defied the egalitarian culture of the Revolution by affecting the elegant fashions of the dandies of the English ruling class and a breakaway faction of art students from Jacques-Louis David's studio, known as the Barbus (the Bearded Ones), adopted the cloaks and robes of the classical age and established a utopian vegetarian commune in a suburban district of Paris.[14] However, by the end of the 1790s French society had concluded its experiments with the identity of the citizen, fashion became restrained and standardised, eccentricity condemned. The revolution was postponed, but the bourgeois masque of identity was revived in bohemia.

The bohemian cultural tradition developed parallel to, and engaged with, the utopian socialism, republicanism and emergent anarchism of the years between the fall of Napoleon and the revolutions of 1848. The gypsy realm of Bohemia was founded in the Latin Quarter of Paris, bordered in the East by glamour, fame, heroism, influence, artistic success and bourgeois respectability, and in the West by revolution, poverty, illusion, madness, anonymity, death and oblivion.[15] Though it began in Paris, the culture expanded and shifted internationally throughout the nineteenth century and into the twentieth, from Paris to Barcelona, Vienna, St. Petersburg, Berlin, Amsterdam, Greenwich Village, San Francisco, Soho to Brixton. In the aftermath of the fall of Napoleon young artists were torn by stark and conflicting political tensions. The revolution had been celebrated as the birth of a new society, a new age, a young Republic.[16] The generation of young radical artists born into this zeitgeist anticipated a life of heroic adventure in which they would dedicate themselves to the Republic, to liberty, fraternity and equality. Instead of which, the new bourgeois state replaced the old feudal patronage of the arts with a capitalist market, forcing the artists into trade. The bohemians rebelled against their bourgeois parents, refused trade, embraced voluntary poverty and lived for art.[17]

The national and international popularity of both the myth and the term 'bohemia' dates from the stories and melodramas of bohemian life by Henry Murger in the mid-nineteenth century, but the bohemian realm first coalesced earlier in the century around various groups of radical students and young artists, notably the Jeunes-France, the 'Bousingouts' and the young disciples of Victor Hugo: the poet Gerard de Nerval, the anarchist architect Petrus 'the Werewolf' Borel and Theophile Gautier who was also a central figure in the Art for Art's Sake movement. However, Gautier and his circle were only the stars of a complex subculture which developed an underground network of cafés, cabarets and radical newspapers, a subculture which included both drop-out nobility and beggar prophets selling poems door to door, which at its margins blurred the borders between the artist, the popular entertainer, the criminal and the insane.

At the core of the bohemian mythology is a simultaneous rejection of bourgeois society and the desire for transcendental success and acceptance in that society. This ambivalence has a series of interlocking narrative logics: the young genius artist cannot be constrained by bourgeois normality, normality is rejected because it stifles genius, inevitable success justifies revolt, the suffering of rejection is necessary to produce genius, the tragic death of the genius punishes the philistines, the genius of the artist is revealed in death as a tragic victory and so on. As the mythology developed and spread in the late nineteenth century scores of young, ambitious but often impoverished students, graduates, artists and would-be artists trod the martyrs' road to the Latin Quarter, the Left Bank and Montmartre, the martyrs' mount. In Bohemia, these sons of the provinces and the petit bourgeoisie took working-class lovers and fraternised with cabaret entertainers, circus performers, labourers, paupers, vagrants, transvestites, prostitutes, pimps, frauds and thieves. The secure and earnest path to a career in the bourgeois professions was despised. In the cafés, garrets and studios of Bohemia they wrote, painted, drank, fought, dreamed, devised and expounded their ideas and their poetry. Above all they dedicated themselves to art, for art they rejected their bourgeois destiny and embraced alienation. They Romanticised themselves. As Jerrold Seigel notes, the bohemians

> discovered that elements of their lives could be employed for a novel purpose: acting out the conflict inherent in the bourgeois character … it was the appropriation of marginal life-styles by young and not so young bourgeois, for the dramatisation of ambivalence toward their own social identities and destinies. Many non-bohemians experienced the same ambivalence, but they did not devote their lives to living it out.[18]

The bohemians made their lives into art. Refusing bourgeois identity, the bohemian adopted a guise from the lower classes or from the nobility: in the first case a long-haired gypsy, a dusty peasant, a worker, a street entertainer, a vagabond; in the second, a detached, aristocratic, immaculate and elegant dandy. The gypsy and the dandy stood opposed at the poles of the artist's longing. The gypsy was alien, irresponsible, mystical, passionate, convivial, carnal and savage, whilst the dandy was the autonomous man, emotionless, elite, fantastic, the arbiter of taste, the flâneur, the impassive stroller; the bohemian could switch between poles or hybridise the two. The bohemian life promised all that the Revolution had betrayed: liberty, equality, fraternity. In bohemia it seemed possible to transcend or evade bourgeois alienation, to become other, to become intoxicated, to wander anonymously through the crowd, to sleep in the street, to discover the darkest secrets of the city and the soul, to lose a sense of self, to howl. The grim paradox was that only the rich could afford to live in bohemia. For the young petit bourgeois without family, wealth or connections the bohemian life would often end in hack journalism, the lower ranks of the bureaucracy, poverty, debt, illness, madness or death. The history of bohemia is a slow suicide from Baudelaire to Gerard de Nerval, Verlaine, Alfred Jarry, Jacques Vache, Ivan Chtcheglov, Nina Hamnett, Jackson Pollock and Jean-Michel Basquiat, for example. The artist martyr was born in bohemia, even Murger who celebrated and popularised the bohemian myth died alone in misery and poverty. Actually, Murger always hated the grinding penury and shabby garrets of bohemia;

he developed his definitive bohemian myth because after years of scraping a living as a failed artist and a second-rate journalist he finally found something he could sell, something the bourgeois public wanted to buy: his own misery and alienation Romanticised.

The significance of bohemia for Underground Cinema lies in gauging both its repressive and subversive historical agency. The critical issue is the relationship between bohemia and the autonomisation of art. The formation of bohemia cannot be simply reduced to the development of a new economic sector for the production of autonomous art, even if that is how it ultimately functioned within the art economy. The young bourgeois bohemians rejected commercial utility and bourgeois domesticity; they rejected a function for art and so initiated the inertia of the avant-garde and the misconception of anti-art. But bohemia is also the initiation of a trajectory which culminated in the radical counter-culture of the 1960s. Core factions of the bohemians of the mid-nineteenth century were involved in republican, socialist utopian and anarchist revolutionary activity under the influence of Saint-Simon, Fourier and Pierre-Joseph Proudon; radical factions of bohemia fought alongside the workers on the barricades in the Revolution of 1848 and participated in the organisation of the Commune of 1871.[19] The bohemian Dadaists and Surrealists were actively engaged with revolutionary Marxist politics and the subversive agitation of the Situationists was a crucial factor in the student revolt of May 1968. Refusing the bourgeois life, the radical bohemians lived in working-class districts and socialised with working-class men and women, migrant peasants, immigrants from the colonies, social deviants and the criminal underclass.

The egalitarian and revolutionary desire of the radical bohemian artists led them to construct a utopian culture of masquerade and subversion within the space and logic of capitalism. Whilst their resistance was inevitably franchised and commodified as art, within bohemia it was still possible to lead an experimental life. But the bohemian realm was not simply hollowed out in the dead space of the city's proletarian districts; it was a colony integrated into the subversive underworld of the popular – it was more a discovery than a creation. Whilst the avant-garde dreamt of an autonomous realm of art, bohemia was constructed as a complex integrated culture at the intersection of the bourgeois and the popular: the radical bohemian artists adopted the guise of the common people and discovered the regions of the popular. This masquerade brought them into contact with popular culture, with common people and with the outsiders and deviants of the city, but it was a strategy that in return gave common people, outsiders and deviants access to the bohemian realm. Bohemia developed as a convivial zone of relative transgression beneath the rigid stratification of bourgeois society, a carnival zone in which different classes, genders, sexualities and races could socialise.[20] Whilst art theorists have habitually sought the origins of anti-art and the key formations of the twentieth century avant-garde in the realm of art, the critical inspiration for these projects cannot be found in art, they must be tracked in the mongrel underground of bohemia.

In the second half of the nineteenth century the modernisation and gentrification of Paris led to a shift in the Parisian bohemia from the interior of the city to the then relatively rustic suburb of Montmartre.[21] Urban modernisation made Montmartre more accessible but also reconfigured and characterised the district as a bohemian enclave beyond the margins of bourgeois respectability. This illegitimacy was reinforced by the last stand of the Communards in Montmartre in May 1871.[22] Whilst Paris became increasingly socially stratified and segregated Montmartre developed as a marginal hybrid space where artists, popular entertainers, workers, vagrants, pimps, prostitutes, revolutionaries, transvestites, charlatans, criminals and junkies could fraternise. Inspired by the rise of urban commercial popular culture and consumer capitalism the bohemians of Montmartre produced a new hybrid culture which combined elements of the utopian project of the avant-garde with popular culture. The dynamic motor of this was a fusion of the variety, conviviality and subversion of the popular with the alienation, disillusion and desperation of the romantic bohemian and it produced an underground culture of utopian imagination, ironic festivity, nihilistic black humour, extravagant satire, absurd self-promotion and sensual abandon. The commercial hub of this mutant sphere was the bohemian cabaret and its subsidiary magazines. The characteristic praxis of this culture was 'fumisterie', a subversive and often spectacular form of *blague*, hoax, prank, myth-making and parody.

Paris in the late 1870s had a wide range of popular entertainment with travelling fairs, the circus, dance halls, café-concerts which were comparable to the English song saloons, and increasingly there were more sophisticated music halls which combined the variety of popular forms. Bohemian artists had for many years frequented popular venues and there were numerous bohemian cafés which served as centres for artistic events and groups. However, in the early years of the 1880s there developed in Montmartre a new type of bohemian cabaret which rather than being a refuge for alienated artists was designed to compete and engage with popular entertainment. Perhaps the first and certainly the most influential of these cabarets was the Chat Noir, founded by the writer Emile Goudeau and the one-time painter Rudolphe Salis in 1881.[23] The Chat Noir initially developed as a base for Goudeau's literary group the Hydropathes which operated out of a café theatre in the Latin Quarter and published the weekly magazine *L'Hydropathe* (1879–80). The avowed purpose of this group was to create an arena where young artists, students, poets and musicians could perform for a popular audience and generate publicity for their work. The work produced by the group was diverse but united by the bohemian subculture: young, predominately male, anarchic, anti-bourgeois, hedonistic and hard-drinking.[24] The magazine featured poetry, articles, illustration and caricatures by the Hydropathes and provided reciprocal promotion for the activities at the café. The group proved a prodigious success, attracting audiences of over six hundred to some events, but by 1881 they had split as a result of fumiste provocation, a faction led by Goudeau had dropped out and the remaining membership reconstituted themselves as the short-lived Hirsutes (the Hairy Ones).[25] Several other related groups developed around the Hydropathes in this period, most notably the Zutistes ('zut' meaning, roughly, 'drat') and the Incoherents, who organised a series of fumiste events and exhibitions in which artists entered work under absurd pseudonyms; the entries would include, for instance, a bearded Venus De Milo or sculptures made from bread crumbs.[26] Rudolphe Salis was a failed artist who had renounced painting and opened a small cabaret in Montmartre which he hoped would attract an artistic bohemian clientele. To create a bohemian environment he decorated the interior with rustic and feudal bric-a-brac, copper pots, tapestries, swords, religious statues, antique furniture, diamantine panels, shields, masks, stuffed animals, stained glass and china cats. Not long after the Hydropathe split, Salis invited Goudeau's faction to establish a base at the Chat Noir. At the new venue the student constituent of the group was superseded by a broader range of amateurs, would-be and part-time artists, musicians and poets, and the Chat Noir effectively became a bohemian cultural commercial complex of pub, literary café, music hall, restaurant, art gallery, publishing house and book shop. A month after the move the weekly *Le Chat Noir* magazine was established and continued the reciprocal agency of the defunct *L'Hydropathe*.

In this atmosphere the cabaret reproduced the conviviality, interaction and spontaneity of the popular music hall, the performers mingled with the audience and the audience would often heckle or comment on the performance. Goudeau and later Salis acted as music hall chairmen introducing the acts, which were predominantly poets or *chansonniers* (poet/singers) who would sing, recite or dramatically declaim. The material and style of work at the early Chat Noir ranged from the absurd and provocative songs of Goudeau and Maurice Mac-Nab to the neurotic and macabre songs of Maurice Rollinat, the radical and scathing social protest of Jean Richepin and Jules Jouy, and the urban street songs of Xanrof and Aristide Bruant. Apart from the songs there was also music, storytelling and fumiste comedy. Goudeau was a master of fumiste stunts; most famously he staged the fictitious death and funeral of Salis in 1884. By 1885 the Chat Noir had outgrown its limited premises and the cabaret moved to an expansive venue further from the lawless main drag. On the day of the move, the cabaret mobilised its performers into a well-publicised and outrageous carnival parade which carried all the furniture and fixtures through the streets of Montmartre from the old to the new venue. This form of bohemian carnival procession later became a cabaret tradition known as the *Vachalcade* which was still popular in the 1920s.[27] The new Chat Noir extended the fumiste strategy into the very fabric and life of the cabaret, the decor became an absurd montage which combined the proto-modernist paintings, murals and drawings of the bohemians with Salis's feudal bric-a-brac.[28] The many rooms of the building were given multiple official names such as the Secret Library or the Office of the Archives and Disputed Claims Dept. The waiters were dressed as members of the prestigious Académie Française and the audience was treated with exaggerated and ironic deference. The crucial expansion in the cabaret's entertainment was the construction of a shadow theatre which presented spectacular multi-coloured shadow plays accompanied by spoken narrative, dialogue and improvised or specially-composed music.[29] The key figure in the cabaret revival of the shadow play was Henri Rivière who developed an astonishing repertoire of techniques using magic lanterns, smoke, coloured transparencies, perforations, complex multiple puppets, perspective and montage effects. The shadow play rapidly became an essential element of the bohemian cabaret programme: at the Chat Noir they were presented nightly from around 1887, and as other cabarets proliferated so they also reproduced and developed the form.[30] The phenomenal success of the Chat Noir generated a wave of imitators and breakaway cabarets – most notably Aristide Bruant's Le Mirliton, the Auberge du Clou, the Ane Rouge, Les Quat'z' Arts, the Cabaret des Assassins and the Abbaye de Thélème, named after Rabelais' utopian monastery. These rivals copied and developed the Chat Noir cabaret/magazine formula and gradually the culture expanded nationally and internationally: the Chat Noir and the Mirliton mounted touring shows and derivative cabarets opened in the enclaves of Europe's other bohemian districts. In 1893 the Chat Noir shadow theatre travelled to the World's Columbian Exposition in Chicago, and in 1900 Montmartre shadow theatre and cabaret appeared at the fairgrounds of the Paris World's Fair.[31]

Whilst the artists of the cabarets and magazines held a range of political positions and the most prestigious venues were increasingly invaded by bourgeois interlopers, there was a radical socialist/anarchist allegiance at the core of the culture and many of the founding artists and activists were committed radicals, critically Théodore Steinlen and Adolphe Willette. Perhaps the most integrated expression of cabaret radicalism was the work of the popular actor, writer, music hall performer, cabaret manager and fumiste Maxime Lisbonne who had served as a Colonel in the Commune and was transported to New Caledonia as a convict.[32] In 1881 Lisbonne returned to Paris where he worked as an actor in melodrama and walked the streets in a flamboyant revolutionary uniform. In 1885 he set up the first in a series of cafés and taverns in Montmartre based on his experiences as a revolutionary and a convict: the Taverne du Bagne (Tavern of Convicts), where the walls were adorned with the heroes of the Commune, the waiters were dressed as life prisoners and twice a week Lisbonne would lecture on the Commune and preside over a dramatic shackling of the convicts (waiters). In 1886 Lisbonne followed the success of the Taverne du Bagne with the Taverne de la Révolution Française, and in 1888 he opened the Brasserie de Frites Révolutionaires.

The Chat Noir closed in 1887 and by the turn of the century the spectacular creativity of the Montmartre cabarets had been dissipated by ruthless commercialisation, changes in popular fashion and the advent of new forms of popular entertainment, most significantly music hall, revue, cinema and jazz. Moreover, the commercial success of the bohemian cabaret had encountered a paradox that would later perplex and impede the 1960s counter-culture. The commercial success of the Chat Noir and its most celebrated competitors depended upon creating for their audience a temporary and clandestine zone of bohemian freedom, transgression and conviviality but, paradoxically, commercial success tended to undermine these very qualities: the intimate bohemian diversity and spontaneous interaction of the cabaret became increasingly compromised by a socially conventional and affluent bourgeois audience. This enervation was reinforced by the feuds and schisms within the subculture which were frequently caused by the informal, amateur and collective financial and contractual relations between the venues, managers, writers and performers.[33] Nevertheless, the dynamic fusion of popular culture and bohemian utopianism which coalesced around the Chat Noir continued to expand and mutate.

The development of anti-art and the related avant-garde projects of Futurism and Cubism were driven by a popular renovation of art led by the bohemian cabarets of the late nineteenth century. Key clusters of artists and anti-artists emerged from the cabaret culture, crucially the arch fumiste Alfred Jarry, a seminal influence on Dada and Surrealism, Marcel Duchamp who abandoned painting for fumism and the composer Erik Satie who crossed the intersection of the avant-garde and the popular and influenced a generation of young disciples, including Darius Milhaud and Jean Cocteau.[34] Cabaret and popular culture – montage, music hall revue, graffiti, fumiste comedy, advertising, circus – was a formative influence on the work of Picasso and the development of Cubism.[35] Both the Italian and the Russian Futurists were critically influenced by popular forms; in 1913 Marinetti hailed the variety theatre as the realm of the Futurist marvellous.[36]

In 1922 the Soviet Eccentric group (FEKS) declared that their parents were:

In song – the torch singer, Pinkerton, the cry of the auctioneer, slang.
In painting – the circus poster, the jacket of a cheap pulp thriller.
In music – the jazz band, (black street orchestra), circus marches.
In ballet – American song and dance routines.
In theatre – music hall, cinema, circus, cabaret, boxing.[37]

But the critical and exemplary link between cabaret and the avant-garde is the direct agency of cabaret on the formation of Dada and anti-art. The company, constitution and purpose of Dada was formed at the Cabaret Voltaire founded by the poet Hugo Ball and the cabaret singer Emmy Hennings in the red-light district of Zurich in 1916. The initial discovery made by Ball, Hennings, Richard Huelsenbeck, Tristan Tzara and the Dada gang was not a new art or an anti-art, it was the intoxicating liberation of non-art: the popular, the convivial, montage and the fumiste strategy of bohemia.[38] Although the fumiste/cabaret culture of Montmartre was substantially created by bohemian artists they nonetheless respected and maintained a border between their bohemian lives and the official and autonomous realm of art. The critical transformation of the Dadaists was that they attempted to make bohemia their art. The subsequent development of Paris Dada and Surrealism in the 1920s is not the emergence of a new culture but the return of a culture translated in the East.

Chapter 9

THE ORIGINS OF THE US UNDERGROUND: THE CULTURAL HYBRID OF POPULAR CULTURE, ANTI-ART AND THE COUNTER-CULTURE

Parallel to the development of the European avant-garde of the 1920s and the British independent film movement of the 1930s the US developed an experimental film culture as an integrated component of a national network of amateur ciné-clubs, film societies and specialist Little Cinemas.[1] This chapter will firstly chart the continuities and contrasts between the development of post-war American and European experimental film culture, and secondly contextualise the distinctive development of the American Underground Cinema.

The dynamic hybridisation of Dada was inevitably appropriated by art; nevertheless, the anti-art fusion of pop and utopian experiment entered cinema as the initiation of a new cinematic mode. Dada/Surrealist film is frequently considered an element of the broader avant-garde film movement of the 1920s. However, it must also be understood that Dada/Surrealist film was not conceived as avant-garde by its makers and that the key Dada/Surrealist films mobilised the radical fusion of popular and experimental forms that culminated in Underground Cinema thirty years later.[2] The Surrealist 'classic' *Un Chien Andalou* (Luis Buñuel and Salvador Dali, 1929) has long been subjected to intensive theoretical investigation as a psycho-sexual dream text or a poetic meta-text, but the popular core of the film is routinely neglected: *Un Chien Andalou* is a sophisticated experiment in popular narrative montage, its subversive power is entirely derived from a complex understanding, pastiche and subversion of continuity editing, melodramatic acting, narrative intertitles and so on.[3] If the avant-garde project in cinema was ultimately to free film from the popular then *Un Chien Andalou*, *Entr'acte* (René Clair, 1924), *L'Age d'or* (*The Golden Age*, Luis Buñuel, 1930), *Le Sang d'un poète* (*The Blood of the Poet*, Jean Cocteau, 1930) and a cluster of other Dada/Surrealist films must be understood as the initiation of an experimental cinema project that is not (avant-garde) art but a fusion of the radical elements of anti-art and popular cinema. This is the project that was resumed in the work of the most radical post-war experimental European filmmakers, most significantly the innovative narrative work of Jean-Luc Godard and the subversive montage of the Lettrist/Situationist movement and this pop/anti-art hybrid is a core element of Underground Cinema. However, the development of British Underground Cinema in the late 1950s had few direct links with continental Europe: the dominant influence on Britain was American Underground Cinema, both by example and direct intervention.

In the early 1940s, whilst European experimental cinema was effectively suspended for the duration of the war, America began to supersede Europe as the

Figure 15: Maya Deren in *Meshes of the Afternoon* (Maya Deren and Alexander Hammid, 1943)

international centre of experimental film production. Exemplary agents in this migration were Iris Barry, the original secretary of the London Film Society and an editor of *Close Up* magazine, who became the curator of film at the New York Museum of Modern Art; the German abstract animator Oskar Fischinger, who was a key influence in the development of the West Coast experimental scene; the German Dadaist Hans Richter, who taught filmmaking at City College in New York (1942–56); the Czech filmmaker Alexander Hammid, who co-directed *Meshes of the Afternoon* (1943) with Maya Deren; and the Lithuanian filmmaker, critic, poet and dramatist Jonas Mekas, who became the pivotal advocate and organiser of post-war American experimental film. However, although the ascension of American experimental film was an element of a broader relocation of avant-garde modernist ideology, artists, anti-artists and institutional aesthetic authority from Europe to the new economic and cultural dominance of the US, it would be wrong to suppose that the ascension of US experimental cinema was the seamless transference of European avant-garde film culture to the fertile new colony of America.[4] The cultural context and ultimate trajectory of post-war US experimental film was critically different to European avant-garde film culture. Firstly, the role of art as the official, sacred, elite and autonomous culture of the ruling class was contested in nineteenth-century America and was not secured in the first half of the twentieth century. Consequently, there was no catalyst for a native anti-art movement until after the institutionalisation of American Modernist Abstract Expressionism in the 1950s.[5] Secondly, American popular culture was more socially mobile, traditionally valued and commercially dynamic than in Europe, and the border between the popular and American art was more interactive. Crucially, however, this interaction was tempered by a complex and repressive spectrum of polarity between legitimate and illegitimate culture structured by the colonial hierarchy of race and the radical agency of African-Americans in the popular realm.

The revitalised experimental film culture that developed in the first decades of post-war America was relatively disengaged from the tension of the European avant-garde project – it was loose and dispersed; there was no centralised programme, movement or manifesto. The work produced was diverse, ranging from modernist mystical synaesthetic abstraction to poetic narrative, but a defining feature was an intense and personal exploration of myth, ritual, dream and the psyche. Although an informal framework of public and private sponsorship gradually developed there was no central and systematic institutional state intervention equivalent to Grierson's model or the later BFI sponsorship of the Free Cinema movement. This institutional autonomy was reinforced by an accelerating shift to amateur cine technology which imposed on American experimental film both the liberation and the constraint of amateur cine culture. For the pre-war European avant-garde it had been necessary and desirable to work in the margins of the commercial film industry with access to commercial technology and at least limited access to commercial distribution and exhibition. In post-war America increasing access to cheap and versatile amateur cine technology made it possible for isolated lone filmmakers and small affinity groups to produce experimental films totally independent from the commercial industry, but this amateurism also exiled their work from the commercial realm.[6] In the absence of an effective avant-garde film movement and increasingly excluded from the commercial industry, American experimental film developed as an amateur, illegitimate, diverse, fragmented and hybrid culture. An essential component of this culture was the intimate and complex relationship between experiment and the popular in the work of many of the key makers; Maya Deren was fascinated by voodoo, Kenneth Anger and Jack Smith were obsessed by Hollywood and popular culture, and the abstract animator Harry Smith was a prodigious expert on American popular music and the compiler of the 'Anthology of American Folk Music', a series of recordings which had a seminal influence on the folk music 'revival' of the 1960s.

The emergence of Underground Cinema in the late 1950s was the culmination of the specifically American tendencies in the post-war experimental scene which were condensed and augmented by the Beat movement. The Beat Generation was composed of a cluster of bohemian poets, novelists and filmmakers who extravagantly fostered and sometimes denied their own mythology, but beat culture must also be understood as a broader youth pop subculture centred on New York and the West Coast from the late 1940s to the early 1960s. Beat was nurtured by economic prosperity and ideological, sexual and racial repression. In the decade following the end of the war American corporate capitalism consolidated its triumph, and the Cold War anti-Communist witch-hunts effectively purged the organisations of the left from industry, politics, education and the public sphere. The unprecedented post-war expansion of the American mass media was exploited by the bourgeoisie in a renewed attempt to enforce the legitimate culture of white, bourgeois, Anglo-Saxon, Protestant heterosexual patriarchy: the square world. The young bohemians who rejected the square dream of normal America increasingly recognised that not only were a diversity of popular cultures excluded from the legitimate realm but that these excluded cultures had developed fascinating, vital and effective strategies to resist and subvert bourgeois culture. The exemplary and essential paradigm of this oppositional pop culture was jazz.

Black popular culture was the creative triumph of African-American people over systematic racist oppression and yet it was also a culture formed in that oppression. It was a culture which preserved and developed the suppressed ethnicity of the African-American people and yet it incorporated and hybridised the white European popular tradition and it was appropriated and adopted by white participants. As a component in the development of legitimate white culture, black pop articulated the polarity of the popular vs. legitimate culture binary. Square America projected the carnival onto African-American culture: black pop culture was designated a realm of masquerade, grotesque humour, parody, excess and carnal pleasure. Blackness was conceived as the carnival inversion of official bourgeois culture: irrational, promiscuous, infantile, flamboyant, uninhibited, spontaneous, lazy, brazen, passionate, natural and sensual.[7] This carnivalisation created an ambivalent realm of carnival blackness which although it was racist and restrictive could also be deployed by African-Americans to resist and subvert white bourgeois culture. The most influential form of this radical black pop culture in the first half of the twentieth century was the outlaw jazz music which developed in the dance halls, carnivals, clubs and brothels of New Orleans in the late nineteenth century. Jazz was spontaneous, improvised, illiterate, ambivalent, polyrhythmic, complex, collective and convivial. It was ironic and parodic, it took white music and played with it, broke the musical frame, restructured it, repeated it, scattered its components and miraculously montaged it back together.[8] The double bluff of jazz deflected the racist parody of blackness by parodying its own composition whilst still invoking the freedom of the people. Jazz condensed the radical popular into a means and an end, a method that could be applied not only to music but to poetry, painting and filmmaking; culture could be jazzed up. Moreover, jazz invoked the underground black pop subculture, the cool hipster world which refused and mocked the oppression of the squares. This jazz identity, the masque of blackness, was appropriated by white Beats to masquerade their ambivalence, alienation and resistance to the square world. Beat culture fused European bohemianism and black popular culture and relocated the utopian realm to a mythic liberated America. Whilst the European bohemians dreamt of gypsy travels to ancient exotic lands the Beats sought a contemporary redemption on the endless road from the lofts to the bars, pool rooms, deserts, oceans, cities and canyons, and the forests of America. Like European bohemianism, beat developed as a zone of relative transgression in square society. They shunned the nine-to-five corporate existence and lived desperate lives of voluntary poverty. They experimented with drugs, magic, Zen, popular montage, sex and psychoanalysis. Instead of cabaret they had the jazz club, bebop and poetry readings at the coffee shop. Mostly they were middle-class, male and white but there were working-class Beats, female Beats, black Beats, and the saints of the movement were queer or bisexual: Jack Kerouac, William Burroughs, Allen Ginsberg, Neal Cassady. Bohemianism had always been a culture of sexual freedom, of promiscuity, miscegenation, misalliance, polygamy, of queers, lesbians, bisexuals and transvestites. And the bohemian sensibility had always had an intrinsic camp component which was a definitive element of cabaret culture, fumism and anti-art. What differentiated the sexual character of the Beats from previous bohemian movements was firstly the degree to which they integrated their deviant sexuality into their work and secondly their reconception of camp as a subversive and utopian strategy. This radicalised camp had its most articulate expression in Underground cinema in the work of filmmakers like Kenneth Anger, Jack Smith, the Kuchar Brothers, Andy Warhol, John Waters and Jim Bidgood. The essential shift from European bohemia to American beat culture was that whilst the avant-garde had sought to realise art, and the anti-artists had attempted to make bohemia into art, the writers and filmmakers of the Beat movement formed a hybrid subculture of pop and anti-art which had its most radical agency as a popular form; beat was not art. Beat culture was the initiation of a twentieth-century utopian pop subculture which culminated in the counter-culture of the 1960s.

The two key factors in the development of the counter-culture were the rise of the Anglo-American New Left and the generation of rock music and the axis of both these developments was a complex cultural interaction between America and Britain. The germinal year for the Underground was 1956, a historic convocation of revolutionary events and radical currents.

By the early 1950s the American Left was demoralised by political defeat and suppressed by Cold War witch-hunts and anti-union legislation whilst the British Left had stagnated between the dogmatic poles of Stalinism and the reformist Labour Party.[9] However, in 1956 the inertia of the left was challenged by a series of events which both exposed the tyranny of Stalinist/Soviet rule and the ruthless imperialism of the West: Kruschev's denunciation of Stalin, the Soviet invasion of Hungary, riots and strikes in Poland, the Suez crisis and anti-colonial struggle in the Middle East and Cuba. In Britain a radical New Left movement emerged that rejected both the legacy of Stalin and the reformism of the established Labour movement. The New Left gathered around the development of the journal *New Left Review* (1959), the Campaign for Nuclear Disarmament (CND) and the London New Left Club in Soho. An essential component of the movement was the reciprocal allegiance and involvement of cultural activists from the contiguous Angry Young Man drama/literary movement and the Free Cinema group. The central thematic of the New Left was that socialism had to be radically reconceived if it was to challenge the new forms of post-war corporate and consumer capitalism and that this reconception had to be based on the development of a rigorous intellectual investigation into contemporary society.[10] Structurally the movement reacted against the hierarchical party discipline, dogmatism and anti-intellectualism of the established left by attempting to develop projects which were popular, non-hierarchical, heterogeneous in membership and perspective, and integrated in theory and practice. Crucially, the analysis of popular culture was seen as an integrated component of the New Left revision and a cluster of key New Left theorists subsequently became the founders of British cultural studies: E. P. Thompson, Raymond Williams and Stuart Hall. In the context of the development of the 1960s Underground/counter-culture a crucial factor was that the rapid and phenomenal growth of CND was vitalised by the participation of a bohemian trad jazz youth/student subculture that transformed protest marches and mass sit-down occupations into carnival vachalcades of improvised jazz and laughter.[11] It was from this trad jazz bohemia that the London rhythm and blues scene and the Rolling Stones developed in the early 1960s.[12]

In America the New Left developed from the influence of the British New Left, the rise of the black Civil Rights movement and support for the Cuban Revolution of 1959. Whereas in Britain the New Left developed as a generation disenchanted with the established left, in America the young activists of the New Left emerged from the Cold War suppression of the left and they rediscovered socialism and anarchism as the resurrection of a lost creed.[13]

The development of the revolutionary culture of rock music paralleled the emergence of the New Left. By the late 1950s the beloved bebop jazz of the beat scene was being superseded in Underground culture by hybrid currents of rhythm and blues and revived folk music. The popular form that was to eclipse jazz as the essential music of the Underground began as a hybrid of black rhythm and blues and elements of white hillbilly country and western swing: rock 'n' roll.

White teenage Cold War America encountered rock 'n' roll as the return of the repressed. Rock broke out of the black radio stations and the backwoods white hillbilly circuit into the teenage bedrooms of middle-class America and turned them on. The rockers invoked the carnival blackness of wild subversive and sensual liberation. And the appropriation of this black wildness by white rockers transgressed the legitimate borders of American popular culture and the legitimacy of the white identity. Rock 'n' roll challenged the sedation of bourgeois culture; throughout 1956 America was riven by a wave of teenage rock 'n' roll riots, moral panic and prohibition against the primitive voodoo jungle music. Meanwhile, in New York's Greenwich Village the bohemian subculture developed a radical hybrid of beat poetry, blues and revived folk music. This fusion would become the voice of a generation in the mouth of Robert Zimmerman, the son of a middle-class Jewish family from Minnesota who transformed himself into Bob Dylan, the hobo outlaw protest prince.

In Britain the first incendiary public appearances were not live but cinematic. When *Rock Around the Clock* (Fred F. Sears, 1956), starring Bill Haley and the Comets, was released into British cinemas thousands of teenagers refused the sedation of their cinema seats and danced and sang in the aisles.[14] After 1956, rock 'n' roll developed as a complex of rival subcultures and cultural currents: rockabilly, rhythm and blues, surfing and hot rod pop, the British rockers, the mods, folk rock, the Mersey beat, psychedelic rock.

The counter-culture of the 1960s, although limited and unstable, marked a revolutionary historical nexus, a fusion of pop culture and radical utopian politics convened by a provisional mass confederation of the diversity of Western oppositional subcultures against the square world: radical student activists, working-class youth, feminists, black and Latin American radicals, peace protesters, anarchists, communeists, anti-artists, gay liberationists, ecologists, hippies, heads, freaks, motorcycle gangs and so on. The status of the counter-culture as a radical and lasting political agent is open to dispute but what is certain is the revolutionary effect of it upon popular culture. In the counter-culture the arcane and elite subculture of bohemia was transformed into a radical pop culture which invoked the revolutionary desires of a generation of young people. Whilst it was clearly recognised by contemporary participants and later cultural theorists that the counter-culture was almost immediately appropriated and commodified by the consumer industries and commercial popular media, what is seldom acknowledged is that popular culture was an elementary catalyst of the counter-culture and that the commodification of the counter-culture distributed its radical agency into the domestic heart of the square world. In the counter-culture the bohemian masquerade developed into the hybrid hippie style which combined elements of both the gypsy and dandy with other components of iconic outsiderdom: the cowboy, the comic book hero, the Latin American revolutionary, the native American, the African, the magician, the eastern mystic and so on. This masquerade of dissent was popularised by the mass media and spontaneously understood by a generation of teenagers; all across the West, square parents woke up with bohemian children. Moreover, the popularisation of bohemia by the counter-culture was, crucially, a reclamation of the utopian potential of popular culture. A central element of this was the appropriation and transformation of folklore from repressive bourgeois myth to the subversive and liberating countermyth of nomadic anarchism, neo-paganism, eco-activism and free festival traveller culture. Another essential constituent was drug (ab)use which functioned as a radical catalyst at many social, industrial and aesthetic levels, not least of which was the interaction between drug-altered consciousness and the reception and production of culture.

The term 'Underground' was first deployed by beat and early counter-cultural agents to designate their subculture of resistance beneath the square world: it was a metaphoric invocation of the resistance groups of World War Two who secretly sabotaged the Fascist occupation of Europe. Crucially the Underground understood itself to be a culture; to be not only a community and a way of life but a sensibility that could realise the secret subtext of utopian liberation in popular culture.[15] A pre-eminent exponent and instigator of this subversion was William Burroughs who popularised the experimental, random and ludic montage techniques developed by the Dadaists. Burroughs' novels are cinematic; a montage of hard-boiled crime fiction, pulp science fiction, hard-core porn and utopian satire composed in the cut-up method and spoken in the junkie beat drawl. Burroughs' influence on both the Underground and popular culture is inestimable, his prose style became a characteristic voice of the Underground press, he influenced a new generation of science fiction writers, he inspired countless rock lyrics and band names and his work inspired and consolidated the development of the Underground Cinema movement.

The Underground press developed around the early 1960s as a diverse culture of magazines, fanzines and newspapers produced by and for local or affinity communities within the counter-culture. By the late 1960s there was a national and international Underground press network covering the diversity of the counter-culture: radical politics, feminism, black power, gay liberation, drug culture, ecology, alternative religion, poetry, comic books, rock journalism and Underground news and events.[16] Amongst the most successful and influential imprints were the *Village Voice* and the *East Village Other* (New York), the *Los Angeles Free Press*, the *San Francisco Oracle*, *Rolling Stone* magazine, the *International Times* – *IT* (London) and *OZ* magazine (London and Sydney). Crucially, the development of the Underground press provided the Underground cinema with an effective publicity network and a critical base. Exemplary relationships were between Jonas Mekas and the *Village Voice*, the LFMC and *IT*, and the Australian group UBU films and *OZ*.[17]

Underground cinema first developed around the late 1950s as a component of the emergent counter-culture; a heretical and mercurial combination of experimental film, amateur cine culture, pop, beat, camp, radical agit-prop and anti-art. The shift from experimental film to Underground was a gradual and disparate process; it was the surfacing of a subculture. Nevertheless, the key formative and federate events happened in New York towards the end of 1958 and into 1959.[18] The formation of an Underground coalition began with a phase of activity around the concept of a New American Cinema. In 1949 Jonas Mekas, the pivotal activist in the development of the infrastructure of the New York Underground, left a refugee camp in Germany and arrived in New York. After attending a few of Hans Richter's classes at City College he became increasingly involved in film criticism, independent filmmaking and experimental cinema. In 1955 he founded the highly influential *Film Culture* magazine which initially specialised in European and avant-garde cinema but which also featured the pioneer auteur criticism of Hollywood cinema by Andrew Sarris.[19] In November 1958 Mekas began a long-running polemical cinema column in the prototype New York Underground newspaper the *Village Voice*. That same year the experimental filmmaker Shirley Clarke teamed up with the radical vérité documentary filmmakers Don Pennebaker, Richard Leacock and the Maysles brothers to form a filmmakers' co-operative: Filmmakers Inc. Meanwhile, a number of key low-budget independent films were in production which anticipated the advent of the Underground. The two crucial films were John

Cassavetes' vérité-style narrative feature *Shadows* (1959) and Robert Frank and Alfred Leslie's partially improvised short, *Pull My Daisy* (1959), which featured Kerouac, Ginsberg and Gregory Corso.[20] Both films were premiered at the end of 1959 at Amos Vogel's Cinema 16. Mekas came to believe that these films, his own work and the work of the new vérité documentary filmmakers were the vanguard of a new wave of commercial independent cinema comparable to the European New Wave and the British Free Cinema group, and increasingly he directed *Film Culture*, his criticism and activism towards the development of this New American Cinema. However, it rapidly and brutally became obvious to the makers and advocates of this new wave that low-budget independent film could not break into the American commercial distribution/exhibition industry. In response to this exclusion Mekas, Shirley Clarke, Emile de Antonio and other leading activists organised the New American Cinema Group (NACG), a coalition of low-budget feature directors, vérité documentarists and experimental filmmakers formed to promote an alternative/oppositional film production, distribution and exhibition sector. In the summer of 1961 the group published a manifesto in *Film Culture* which declared their ethical and aesthetic opposition to the commercial film industry, censorship and trade union restrictions, and their commitment to personal filmmaking, freedom of expression, low-budget production and co-operative organisation. Critically the manifesto rejected the classicism and purity of the avant-garde and advocated opposition and engagement:

> We are for art, but not at the expense of life. We don't want false, polished, slick films – we prefer them rough, unpolished, but alive; we don't want rosy films – we want them the colour of blood.[21]

From the founding of the NACG Mekas became the central coordinator, propagandist, publicist and impresario of American experimental cinema; the ringleader of a complex interlinked web of activists, organisations and initiatives. Parallel to the founding of the NACG he set up the first of a series of influential and popular late night screenings of experimental film at various New York theatres and cinemas, which culminated in a screening programme active throughout the 1960s: the Film-Makers' Cinematheque. He organised international touring programmes, he worked with Shirley Clarke to commercially distribute independent feature films and he was a key agent in the founding of the radical agit-prop film collective Newsreel. However, the most influential and effective of the initiatives led by Mekas was the Film-Makers' Co-op (1962), a collective, democratic, non-profit, open access and non-selective distribution group which became the hub of New York Underground activity, the base for international Underground propaganda and the model for Co-op organisations in Britain, Australia and across continental Europe.

The New American Cinema as a concept and a movement was always frustrated by exclusion from the commercial industry and politically compromised by the limited inclusion it did achieve; the hope and desire to compete with the established feature film industry was increasingly abandoned. Instead, Mekas and other experimental activists began to adopt the more radical project of a counter-cultural experimental amateur cinema, an Underground cinema.

The shift from the competitive commercialism of the New American Cinema to the amateur autarky of the Underground should be understood as both the critical and industrial formation of the movement, and as the co-option of an already emergent Underground tendency. Contiguous to the earlier experimental film movement and the beat subculture, the Underground movement developed around and between the two key bohemian zones of New York and the West Coast. In New York the activity centred around the Co-op, the Film-Makers' Cinematheque and later around the Millennium Film Workshop, an open access production/exhibition centre set up by filmmaker Ken Jacobs. In the West the centre was the San Francisco Canyon Cinema Cooperative (1963) founded by filmmaker Bruce Baillie and based on the New York Co-op model. Whereas the New American Cinema campaign had to compete in an industrial context controlled by the commercial industry, Underground cinema operated as an integrated component of the emerging counter-culture. Whilst European avant-garde film had been secluded in the institution of art, the Underground functioned as a new convivial, contingent and radical popular cinema in which audio/visual experiment was an integrated element of a broader subversion of bourgeois authority, a subversion which also cele-brated psychedelic drug use, utopian radicalism, ecstatic mysticism and other forms of altered perception. Underground Cinema developed from the beat bohemia into a counter-cultural cinema of attractions comparable to the bohemian cabaret, the early music hall and fairground booth cinema and the penny gaffs. The venues for the Underground were illegitimate: late night screenings in rundown movie houses, lofts, psychedelic clubs, porn cinemas, bookshops, warehouse parties and rock gigs. The Underground projector would stand amongst the intoxicated audience casting its ray through a fug of dope smoke. The attractions of the Underground Cinema corresponded to the utopian desire of the counter-cultural audience. Against the industrial anonymity of commercial cinema the Underground celebrated the subjective vision of the lone filmmaker. Films marked with amateurism, incompetence and poverty were enjoyed as spontaneous, honest and democratic subversions of the sedated commercial cinema and the repression of legitimate culture. Surreal and fantastic distortions of narrative space and time were perceived as glimpses of alternate, occult and liberated realities. Abstract and experimental cinematic techniques were enjoyed not as art but as psychedelic visual stimulation which promoted or enhanced hallucinogenic intoxication and cosmic fantasy. Taboo images of sex, violence and death were relished for the transgressive thrill of evading the square inertia. The attraction of the Underground was subversion. A defining feature of the movement was the heterogeneity of its production: Underground film included work by lone filmmakers, collective productions, experimental shorts, home movies, low-budget features, agit-prop documentary, psychedelic visuals, the anti-art of the Fluxus group and avant-garde art. The Underground included filmmakers from the earlier post-war experimental scene such as Kenneth Anger and Harry Smith; those who had provisional allegiances with the Underground such as Stan Brakhage and Andy Warhol; and filmmakers who defined the Underground film culture such as Jack Smith, the Kuchar Brothers, Bruce Conner, Ron Rice, Naomi Levine, Barbara Rubin, Bruce Baillie and the Newsreel Collective. This inclusivity was a key strategy of the Underground opposition to the exclusivity of the commercial industry, and to state censorship and control. Against industrial and institutional hierarchical order the Underground deployed chaotic and personal self-selecting participation, bounded and convened by the counter-culture and the radical politic of Underground amateur distribution and exhibition. As the counter-culture blossomed from bohemian enclave to pop culture so amateur experimental film became for a brief and glorious time a popular culture; at the height of its notoriety Underground screenings attracted capacity audiences, national newspapers and magazines ran features on the Underground culture, a series of books were published, film festivals were established all over America, infamous Underground films scandalised the nation and provoked student riots.

Mekas's critical position throughout the 1960s was, like the Underground itself, equivocal. He denounced competitive commercialism and yet he conceived the Underground as an integrated alternative film industry. Moreover, his attitude was at once populist and avant-garde; he simultaneously believed both in the sacred redemptive aura of art and in the potential of cinema to become a truly democratic and convivial popular culture. The reconciliation of this ambivalence was the hope that if only Underground cinema could reach a popular audience it would expose the soulless exploitation of commercial cinema and establish a new 'folk' art of the people.[22] To this end he drove a dynamic, passionate and many-sided populist campaign for a democratic revolution in the cinema. However, by the late 1960s Mekas and his collaborators had reached a crisis and they responded with a fundamental revision of the project. The elements of this crisis were complex and interdependent. To begin with, by the end of the 1960s both the utopian hope of the counter-culture and the popularity of Underground Cinema had begun to wane. Up against the naked aggression of the state and the voracious appetite of consumer capitalism the counter-culture had begun to lose the momentum of its naïve enthusiasm. It soon became apparent that far from succumbing to the revolutionary power of the Underground the commercial cinema would simply appropriate elements of the Underground/amateur cine style and bypass the movement. There would be no spontaneous cinema revolution, only a relentless and formidable conflict. Secondly, the open access/non-selective policy of the Co-op and other Underground organisations promoted more films and filmmakers but did not provide the filmmakers with either competitive box-office success or the authority of institutional taste. Meanwhile, from the mid-1960s a consolidated national framework of state art funding, art centres, museums and academic film study began to assume the authority of taste over experimental film and to institutionalise a canon of art over the movement.[23] Thirdly, the avant-garde tendency within the Underground began to autonomise and institutionalise themselves within art as the new modernist/formalist aesthetic of structural(ist) film, a process legitimated by the avant-garde criticism of P. Adams Sitney and Annette Michelson.[24] Together these factors eventually persuaded Mekas to renounce the Underground and to collaborate with Sitney, Stan Brakhage, Peter Kubelka and other key avant-garde filmmakers and activists in an attempt to legitimise their authority over the experimental movement by founding an institute that would consecrate and maintain a pantheon of film art, a hierarchy of taste and an official history. The discourse used to validate this shift was avant-garde Structural(ism) and the institute was the Anthology Film Archives museum founded in 1970.[25] The foundation marks the eclipse of the first American Underground Cinema. As J. Hoberman observed:

> Opening in December 1970, the Anthology reified the avant-garde tradition, creating a fixed pantheon of filmmakers and a certified canon of masterpieces, drawing heavily upon the late efflorescence of structural film. Avant-garde cinema left the theatres and entered the classrooms. By the early 1970s, almost all of the major filmmakers (and a host of minor ones) had come in from the cold – protected species, like academic poets – to spawn a new generation of university-trained, tenure-seeking filmmakers, film theorists, and film critics.[26]

The Underground project was flawed by cultural misconceptions and unreconciled tensions. Despite their populism and their anti-art rhetoric Mekas and his collaborators never really moved beyond the fetish of an eternal and redemptive art. They failed to understand that art was above all an institution and that the crucial problem facing the Underground was not aesthetic but industrial/economic. This crucial error allowed the art institutions to appropriate the Underground and forced Mekas and his collaborators into the institution of art. As Lauren Rabinovitz has observed:

> Mekas joined with a closed circle of political allies (including Brakhage) to enshrine films in an avowedly apolitical apparatus of formalist ideology. The founding of Anthology may thus be seen as the last ritual of an avant-garde elite in the midst of being threatened and overshadowed by the larger systems of museum and university practices. It represents an attempt to mirror the apparatus of museums and archives as a means for unifying and regulating the avant-garde cinema according to the larger models of structural and ideological relations. At another level, Mekas's move away from the discourse and practice of commercialism may also be seen as an effort to secure for himself and others a toehold of power among shifting institutional and economic bases for avant-garde cinema.[27]

The American Underground film movement of the 1960s was a complex and diffuse culture which involved many activists and filmmakers spread throughout the states. Ironically, it was driven by both the triumphant surfacing of the American amateur experimental tradition and its subsequent professionalisation. In spite of Anthology, Mekas never resolved his ambivalence to the conflicting tendencies of the Underground and the avant-garde, and when the resurgent Underground movement needed a new venue for the fifth annual New York Underground Film Festival in 1998 Mekas and his associates welcomed them into Anthology Film Archives.

Chapter 10

THE LONDON FILM-MAKERS' CO-OPERATIVE AND THE FIRST BRITISH UNDERGROUND CINEMA 1966–70

The 1960s counter-culture was an international movement effectively dominated by American cultural forms, but the reception, appropriation and (re)production of these forms outside the US was subject to complex local and specific cultural contexts. The influence of the American Underground Cinema movement spread throughout the 1960s both as an integrated element of the counter-culture and through a series of international initiatives, tours and festivals. Following the model of the New York Co-op similar but distinctive radical co-operative and collective organisations emerged in the late 1960s in Australia, Austria, Canada, Germany, Holland, Italy, Japan, Sweden and Switzerland. But the first new film co-op formed in London.[1]

The British counter-culture of the 1960s developed from American counter-culture reinterpreted through British bohemianism, and elements of specifically British radical and popular culture. Key currents in this fusion were the peace movement, rock 'n' roll, trad jazz, folk music, beat poetry, European anti-art, British pop art and the eccentric music hall comedy tradition which had been rejuvenated by the cult radio comedy of *The Goon Show* (1951–60), pop performers like Screaming Lord Sutch, the Alberts and, later, the Beatles and the Bonzo Dog Doodah Band.[2] The bohemian costume masquerade of the British counter-culture developed as a complex interaction of various influences including American fashion, the trad jazz beatnik style and elements of continental European student style imported by British groups from Hamburg in the early 1960s. However, the overriding dynamic for British counter-cultural style was the appropriation of bohemian style by British working-class youth. This was explicit in the formation of the Teddy Boy subculture of the early 1950s; the Edwardian dandy fashion of frock coats and fancy waistcoats was first marketed by Saville Row tailors for the young ruling class, but subsequently vulgarised by the Teds.[3] Likewise, the later Mods developed a subversive subculture of dandy style that threatened and parodied the legitimacy of bourgeois taste.

By the spring of 1966 the London counter-culture was gearing up for the revolution. The mods were rioting at the coast, the radical student movement was beginning a cycle of sit-ins and occupations, drug use was becoming a subversive political strategy, there was a steady influx of militant draft dodgers from the US and liberational movements were coalescing around radical feminism, black power, gay liberation, ecology, squatting and the commune movement. Crucially, in a nation rigidly stratified by social class, the British counter-culture was creating limited

Figure 16: Poster for the IRAT Cinema, 1970

and temporary cultural social zones where the hip youth of the working class could fraternise with their bourgeois contemporaries.

The pivotal agent of the British Underground Cinema was the London Film-makers' Co-operative which developed from 1965 into 1966 out of activity around rival counter-cultural book shops: Better Books on Charing Cross Road managed by the poet Bob Cobbing and the Indica book shop/gallery on Southampton Row run by Barry Miles.[4] At Better Books Cobbing had set up Cinema 65, a regular Friday night film club which showed experimental/Underground film as part of a series of events and happenings that included work from the Destruction In Art Symposium and readings by poets including Ginsberg and Alexander Trocchi, the founder of the Situationist-influenced Project Sigma. By the summer of 1966 the programme for Cinema 65 had become predominately open screenings and the interest of the group was expanding into film production and distribution. Meanwhile, Barry Miles was in negotiation with Barbara Rubin and Mekas in New York to develop a London co-operative as a base for European Underground distribution. Out of this rivalry emerged the unified and independent LFMC, officially constituted in October 1966. One of its founding activities was to publish the magazine *Cinim* (1966–69), the first of a series of magazines/journals which emerged from the co-op/Underground movement in the late 1960s/early 1970s, including *Cinemantics*, *Afterimage* and *Cinema Rising*. The first issue of *Cinim* carried a trail-blazing 'Open Letter To Film-Makers of the World' from Jonas Mekas, which claimed that America was on the verge of a financially self-sufficient Underground film industry with a hundred cinemas across the nation, and Underground film widely available in book shops and record stores. From this industrial base Mekas proposed the foundation of an international Underground network based on the model of the New York Co-op:

> The new film-maker … cannot trust any commercial (or state; or one that is based on commercial tradition) film financing, film production, film distribution, film exhibition or film promotion set-ups and organisations. WE HAVE TO START EVERYTHING FROM SCRATCH, FROM THE BEGINNING. NO COMPROMISES, HOWEVER SMALL … I direct this Open Letter to the independent film-makers of the world, to anybody whose life is cinema, who is making and must make films – to create Film-Makers Co-operatives of your own, in your own countries. There is no other visible solution. There is no other way of escaping the grip of the commercial set ups. This net of international co-ops could then exchange among themselves and help each other beyond the boundaries of their own countries. The boundaries are bound to disappear anyway very soon. With the changing times, with the new spirit in the air, with communications and speed increasing…[5]

In its formative stage the LFMC was a coalition of disparate counter-cultural interests including the poet Cobbing, the activist and Underground entrepreneur

Miles, British filmmakers including Jeff Keen and documentarist Peter Whitehead, US filmmakers Stephen Dwoskin and Simon Hartog, experimental theatre impresario Jim Haynes, critic Raymond Durgnat and a number of would-be filmmakers, notably a young artist who was studying painting at the Slade School of Art: David Curtis. A key organiser and publicist during this period was the notorious American triple agent, McCarthy stooge, fixer and stand-up comedian Harvey Matusow.[6] The early LFMC based its organisational structure on the open access New York Co-op, and as it developed it negotiated with Mekas and his colleagues for institutional support and access to the New York distribution catalogue. However, communication between the two organisations was intermittent and often fraught, and this tension was aggravated by the presence of the renegade Matusow who eventually left amid allegations of theft in February 1967. At its formation the LFMC had about fifty members but very few films to distribute and it essentially functioned as an open screening group, and as a distribution/exhibition agency for American Underground cinema. Over the following 18 months the distribution catalogue rapidly expanded to around a hundred films, but these were mostly American imports – British-based Underground filmmaking was limited to a precious few including work from Dwoskin, Keen, Hartog, John Latham, David Larcher, Anthony Scott, the Tattooists and Anthony Balch.

Haynes and Miles were also two of the key founders of London's first weekly Underground newspaper the *International Times* (*IT*) and so, two weeks after its formation, the Co-op staged its first official screening at the *IT* launch party at the Roundhouse in Chalk Farm. This celebrated event was essentially a free gig in a cavernous and derelict Victorian engine house where, amongst the rubble, Soft Machine and Pink Floyd played to the stoned first wave of the London counterculture. Above the rickety stage, the LFMC projected films onto sheets hung on a clothes line.[7] The films screened included work by Keen, Dwoskin and Latham, and the 11-minute *Towers Open Fire*, a collaboration between the British filmmaker and distributor Anthony Balch, William Burroughs and painter Brion Gysin.[8] *Towers Open Fire* was shot between 1961–62 in Paris and Gibraltar; a year later the same team made the 20-minute short *The Cut Ups* in Paris, New York and Tangiers. *The Cut Ups* used a cinematic variant of Burroughs' aleatory montage technique. During 1966 Balch managed to get both films exhibited in commercial, West End London cinemas. Throughout the 1960s and into the early 1970s he developed further projects with Burroughs and directed two low-budget exploitation features which also carry the Burroughs mark: *Secrets of Sex* (1969) and *Horror Hospital* (1973).[9]

From Halloween to Bonfire Night 1966 the LFMC staged the six-day Spontaneous Festival of Underground Film at the Jeanette Cochrane Theatre which screened both American Underground work and films by Keen, Dwoskin and Balch, and which also included six nights of open screenings at Better Books.[10] That summer there had also been a night of Underground film at the first Notting Hill Fayre, a festival organised by the London Free School and coordinated by the counter-cultural impresario John 'Hoppy' Hopkins. From this festival Hopkins and Joe Boyd initiated the UFO or Underground Freak Out Club, an all-night psychedelic acid venue on Tottenham Court Road. Until it closed in October 1967, the UFO served as a rallying point for the expanding counter-culture and a provisional venue for the Underground Cinema movement. Hopkins was also a co-founder of the *International Times*, and so the UFO and the *IT* developed a reciprocal marketing relationship comparable to the bohemian cabaret model. At the UFO, visiting American Underground filmmakers could screen their work. Jack Smith's scandalous *Flaming Creatures* (1963) was first screened in Britain, the first London light shows took place there, and David Curtis and others projected film loops and found footage to the playing of Soft Machine, Pink Floyd, Procol Harum, Tomorrow, and the Crazy World of Arthur Brown. Under the UFO influence two vast all-night happenings were staged fusing live music, light shows, film and thousands of stoned youth: the first was the 14-hour Technicolour Dream which took place at Alexandra Palace, and the second was Christmas on Earth Revisited at Olympia. After the closure of the UFO other psychedelic clubs emerged, crucially the Middle Earth Club in Covent Garden, which took on the pivotal role of the defunct UFO, and which also functioned as a provisional venue for Underground films.[11]

The LFMC continued to hold regular screenings at Better Books until October 1967 when new management sacked Cobbing and kicked out the Co-op. From this displacement onwards the Co-op was increasingly riven with dissent and personality clashes and this conflict eventually began to polarise around a split between two opposing factions. The older Better Books division came from a heterogeneous beat background and believed that the LFMC should primarily promote Underground cinema by developing an Underground film culture through distribution, exhibition and critical publishing. This group included Cobbing, Dwoskin, Hartog and Durgnat. The new younger group were increasingly artists or art students who, although they were active in the radical counter-culture, actually had no interest in popular cinema or positively despised it. This group maintained that the Co-op should shift its primary activity from distribution/exhibition to production and become an organisation exclusively for filmmakers, which could provide production, film processing and post-production equipment and facilities.[12] This new faction was based at the Arts Lab on Drury Lane and it came to include David Curtis, the American filmmaker Peter Gidal, the painter, filmmaker and art lecturer Malcolm Le Grice, and a group of his students from Saint Martins School of Art. The London Arts Lab was set up in September 1967 by Jim Haynes and another American, Jack Henry Moore, as a counter-cultural arts complex housing a theatre, gallery, cinema, restaurant, book shop, studio, workshop space and general crash pad.[13] Haynes had founded the Traverse Theatre and was a crucial figure in the development of the Edinburgh Fringe Festival, and so the Arts Lab became a seminal base for many of the key companies of the British fringe theatre movement, including the People Show, Pip Simmons, Portable and Freehold.[14] Following the example of London and later Brighton, Arts Labs were set up all over the country and by 1969 over 150 were operating. The Drury Lane Arts Lab Cinema, set up by Moore and run by Curtis, held screenings six nights a week, mixing Underground film with avant-garde, cult and European features. With the Better Books division of the Co-op in exile, the Arts Lab became the centre of Underground film activity and this reinforced the ascendance of the new faction, which began to construct printing and processing equipment at the Arts Lab under the direction of Le Grice.

Around this time Anthony 'Scotty' Scott began to splice together *The Longest Most Meaningless Movie in the World*, an always growing, random montage of discarded footage and out-takes, which was eventually screened at the Arts Lab as a continuous loop:

> We moved the projector down into the main gallery and set up a screen so you could see the image backprojected when you went in and could sit and watch it … from the coffee-shop and theatre entrance. One of the reels consisted of about forty identical repetitions of Donald Campbell advertising a boys' adventure magazine with his Bluebird on his desk. After a few times round regular meaningless moviegoers began to learn his script by heart and would snap to from their bored inertia to chant 'Hello fellas, my name's Donald Campbell. Now HERE'S a magazine for everyone who likes advent-CHA' and so forth. Audience participation got quite exciting one night when someone leapt at the screen with a knife, tore a slit in it and leapt through and outside.[15]

Meanwhile, in March 1967, a wave of college occupations began at the London School of Economics and spread rapidly to Leicester, Essex and across the nation. There were Underground film screenings and psychedelic happenings at the Electric Cinema Club on Portobello Road and Derek Hill founded his itinerant New Cinema Club, which moved around a series of venues including the Mermaid Theatre, the Institute of Contemporary Arts (ICA) and The Place (off Euston Road). Under the slogan of 'the Forbidden Film Festival' the club screened uncertificated features, Underground films, agit-prop documentaries, Japanese, continental and Latin American cinema.[16]

In the spring of 1968 the American critic P. Adams Sitney embarked on a highly influential 12-city university tour with a comprehensive retrospective of American Underground cinema organised by Curtis and Hartog. In response to the tour a number of key activists and groups emerged from the universities including filmmakers Tony Rayns, Roger Hammond and John Du Cane at Cambridge, Philip Drummond, Tim Cawkwell and Tim Harding at Oxford and the activists and critics Peter Sainsbury and Simon Field at Essex. Rayns became a leading independent film critic, Hammond and Du Cane later became active in the LFMC avant-garde, and Field and Sainsbury founded the significant independent film journal *Afterimage* (established in 1970).

Contiguous to the development of the LFMC and inspired by revolutionary action in Paris, Derry and Chicago, as well as the radical American Newsreel movement, the Italian Cinegiornale and the French Cinetracts, British filmmakers began to form agit-prop documentary film collectives. These included Cinema Action (1968), Angry Arts Cinema Club (1968), Amber (1968) and later the Berwick Street Collective (1970), the London Women's Film Group (1972), Four Corners (1973) and Newsreel (1974). In May 1968 a debate at the ICA on the possible formation of a 'parallel cinema' distribution network attracted many of the key Underground activists including Hill, the Electric Cinema Club, the Tattooists International, Angry Arts and Marc Karlin of Cinema Action. From this gathering Peter Sainsbury and his colleagues eventually set up the influential Other Cinema distribution group in 1970 which distributed experimental features from filmmakers such as Jean-Luc Godard and Werner Herzog, Latin American and Third Cinema, and Underground and experimental shorts, to film societies, colleges and the growing national network of film workshops and collectives.

Also in May 1968 the students, and a radical faction of the staff, of Hornsey College of Art in North London, began a six-week sit-in occupation.[17] This action began as a protest against the antiquated and bureaucratic conditions at the college but rapidly escalated into a utopian experiment in student autonomy and non-hierarchical education. In their brief liberty, the Hornsey radicals collectively and practically challenged the ideological and institutional legitimacy of art. As one student recounts in the collective narrative of the occupation:

> From the very beginning of my art training I was taught to appreciate that type of art which is recognised by the 'educated' part of our society to be 'good art'. I was taught to revere the old masters and the Impressionists, and gradually, through the process of education, I acquired an admiration for the modern movements in painting and sculpture, which I mistakenly believed to be a form of cultural revolution. For a total of five years, first in grammar school, later in art school, I was made to accept and believe that the standards and criteria of great art were the standards and criteria recognised and accepted by that 'educated' section of society, and that mass culture, if there is such a thing, is something to be scorned as being unrefined, commercialised and base. Simply we have 'good art' and 'bad art'. The good art is the art of an intelligent, enlightened, sensitive minority of the population, and the bad art is the art of the unfortunate, unenlightened working class ... I say shit on their art world, I want nothing of it.[18]

An integrated component of the occupation was subverting cinema and almost every night of the occupation the college canteen became a convivial cinema screening hired features and Underground film until 3am. For variation the films would be shown backwards, sideways or freeze-framed at decisive moments. One fine evening a film was projected out onto trees, houses and inflatable structures.[19] After inconclusive negotiations with the students, the authorities closed the college in early July. When it reopened in November, the students were systematically humbled, the radical staff were sacked and the premises were refurbished with extensive security devices. By spring 1968 both internal and American influence had convinced the rival factions of the LFMC to attempt a reconciliation and Le Grice and Hartog drew up a joint constitution which aimed to unite the two projects.[20]

The fundamental points were:

1 Dedication to the production, distribution and screening of independent film;
2 Open collective democratic membership structure based on General Meetings at which a governing Executive Committee is elected by the membership;
3 The membership would continue to include both filmmakers and non-film-makers ('viewing membership');
4 Non-profit-making/common ownership;
5 Open access distribution;
6 Commitment to promoting all the films in distribution equally and non-selectively.

However, the reconciliation was only partially successful and conflict continued, first over the prospect of state funding for the LFMC and second concerning New York authority over the it.

Throughout 1968 the Arts Lab filmmakers developed primitive printing and processing facilities, motivated firstly by the prohibitive cost of commercial facilities and secondly because the commercial labs would censor by confiscation any material they deemed subversive. However, from a broader perspective, the shift towards the control of printing and processing must be understood as a shift towards the development of a film practice based on an individual, manual and fetishistic relationship between the material of film and the filmmaker: an art of film. Le Grice was at this time teaching art at Goldsmiths College and Saint Martins School of Art and many of his students subsequently joined the LFMC and used the facilities. A group of these were later to form the substantial core of the 1970s avant-garde, including Annabel Nicolson, Gill Eatherley, Mike Dunford, Fred Drummond, Marilyn Halford, David Crosswaite, John Du Cane, Roger Hammond, Stuart Pound and William Raban. Around June 1968 Peter Gidal arrived in London to study at the Royal College of Art. A few weeks later he joined the LFMC and in July he screened his proto-structuralist film *Room* (*Double Take*) (1967) at the Arts Lab; according to Le Grice this screening was a revelation for the British movement.[21]

Initially Curtis and Le Grice were ambivalent to the concept of state funding for Underground cinema. In the first years of the LFMC the only consistent state funding for experimental film came from the BFI Experimental Film Fund. However, in the summer of 1968 the Arts Council began considering a proposal for a film subcommittee of their Arts funding panel. In response to this proposal Curtis wrote a Report on Subsidy to Independent Film-makers which he presented to executives at the Arts Council and the BFI.[22] This report called for an end to state production funding for all non-professional filmmakers:

It is surely impossible to judge which, say out of fifty young people about to make their first serious film, should receive a grant, unless one imposes a set of arbitrary conditions – such as 'scenarios in triplicate should be submitted accompanied by a letter of recommendation from…' and so forth … and then imposing a personal aesthetic decision on written evidence. The sole justification for spending public money on the arts is that it should make possible a wider spectrum of cultural events than private and commercial interests would themselves initiate. While the sources of public money are so few it is difficult for such a spectrum to be adequately represented…[23]

Instead of production funding Curtis proposed that the BFI and the Arts Council embark upon a programme of state funding for independent distribution, exhibition (particularly open screenings) and co-operative/collective production groups such as the LFMC. Subsequently, Curtis and Le Grice approached the BFI to fund production at the Arts Lab, despite strong opposition from Hartog and Dwoskin.

In November the Arts Lab closed amid accusations of financial mismanagement, and the Co-op moved between temporary bases including the offices of the Binary Information Transfer (BIT) in Notting Hill Gate. BIT was a counter-cultural agency which coordinated news and information on agitation, the Arts Lab movement, drug culture, communes and so on.[24] Without a permanent base the LFMC held irregular screenings at the Electric Cinema Club. Meanwhile, the conflict between the two factions broke out again over the appointment of Carla Liss as the paid secretary of the LFMC. Liss was an American artist and friend of Mekas who had met Curtis and become active in the LFMC organisation around the summer of 1968.[25] In November that year she met with Mekas in New York and he agreed to give LFMC distribution the films from the Sitney Underground tour, on condition that Liss would manage them. The Cobbing faction took exception to this intervention and called an Extraordinary General Meeting at which Cobbing, Latham and others resigned. Dwoskin and Hartog stayed on until May 1969; when they left, the Arts Lab faction essentially gained complete control over the LFMC.

In autumn 1969 the LFMC established a permanent base at a new Arts Lab project called the Institute for Research and Technology (IRAT, October 1969–March 1971) in Camden. The IRAT cinema, under the direction of Curtis, seated over a hundred, and had nightly screenings and often two shows a night.[26] The programme was predominately Underground Cinema, but there were also open screenings, independent shorts, student work, classic Hollywood and European avant-garde retrospectives. Although the London Underground scene was still effectively dominated by imported work from America, from the opening of the Arts Lab to the IRAT a new British filmmaking culture developed, the percentage of British work screened amongst the American steadily increased and most of this work was produced on LFMC facilities; by 1970 professional printing and processing equipment was installed at the IRAT.

Amongst the special events at the IRAT cinema were programmes from the Oxford New Cinema Club including films by Tony Rayns, Andrew Barnett and Robert Short, and programmes from Australian, Italian and French film co-ops.[27] The IRAT cinema hosted Derek Hill's New Cinema Club which, amongst its eclectic mix, screened work by Dwoskin and Pat Holland's *The Hornsey Film*, an agit-prop documentary about the occupation of Hornsey College of Art. The IRAT was also the base for John Hopkins' televisionX, the first British public access and community video workshop. Hopkins also organised the first video art festival at the Camden Arts Festival, May 1969.

In September 1970 the LFMC, the IRAT and a group of independent film distributors organised the International Underground Film Festival at the National Film Theatre. The festival was open and included work from Britain, Europe, Australia, Canada and the USA. The British entry included work by David Larcher, Eyeball Films, Mike Leggett, Graeme Ewens, Tim Harding, Tim Cawkwell, Philip Drummond, Al Deval, Letty Naisner, Barbara Schwartz, Tony Rayns, Fred Drummond, Curtis, Dwoskin, Dunford, Le Grice, Hartog, Keen and televisionX.[28] But this was effectively the last year of the Underground – after 1970 the term was resolutely dropped by the movement and replaced with 'avant-garde' and 'independent' by the agencies and the journals of the movement.[29] Moreover, the shift in nomenclature was a component of a deeper ideological and institutional shift away from the popular anarchy of the counter-culture and towards the legitimacy of art and the state.

In January 1971 the IRAT closed and the LFMC sought new premises, eventually moving to an old dairy on Prince of Wales Crescent, Camden. It was here, isolated in its own self-contained institute that the avant-garde production/processing project became completely dominant. Curtis stopped programming and the new co-op cinema was run by Peter Gidal, who was to become the principal theorist of British avant-garde structuralist film. Screenings declined to twice a week and often once a week, seasons and retrospectives were dropped and regular screenings became dominated by the latest work or work in progress.

As the 1970s wore on, the days of the Underground faded into adolescent memory and the LFMC avant-garde assimilated itself into the institutions of art. There were art gallery screenings at the Walker Gallery in Liverpool, in London at the Serpentine Gallery and eventually at the Tate and the Hayward. Art schools introduced filmmaking courses and many LFMC filmmakers became tutors; Ron Haselden at Reading, Mike Leggett at Exeter, Guy Sherwin at the Polytechnic of North East London, David Hall, Tony Sinden and Jeff Keen at Maidstone, Anne Rees-Mogg at Chelsea, Peter Gidal and Stephen Dwoskin at the Royal College of Art.[30] From the mid-1970s the art schools and colleges effectively became the established and sanctioned institutional infrastructure of the LFMC avant-garde; the primary venues for distribution and exhibition, the key source of new membership and the only dependable employment for established members as tutors and lecturers.[31] During this period the BFI and the Arts Council began to recognise the avant-garde and

Figure 17: Filmaktion event at Gallery House, London, 1973. Malcolm Le Grice at a projector top left

fund its filmmakers. Around 1973 the Arts Council Artists' Film Sub-Committee was established, and in 1975 the LFMC received its first major BFI grant for further production facilities. In 1977 David Curtis became the Assistant Film Officer at the Arts Council and he effectively coordinated state funding for avant-garde film and video for the next 25 years. The LFMC proved to be more enduring, and more radical in its organisational structure, than the New York Co-op which inspired its formation.[32] The principles of democracy, common ownership and open access laid out in the constitution of 1968 were extended in the 1970s to film production resources, education and employment of staff. Nevertheless, the institutional history of the LFMC was a process of gradual and intermittent normalisation and professionalisation substantially driven by the requirements of the state-funding agencies on which it became totally dependent. In 1976 it became a registered charity, a public limited company, and it began to employ paid staff. In 1989 it dropped the non-selection equal-distribution policy. In 1991 the constitution was revised to create a binary class membership system of core members with voting rights and 'access' members without votes. Finally, in 1996 the LFMC annulled itself into a normalised hierarchical management structure as a condition of the move to the Lux.

The post-war independent film and video movement was assembled in the early 1970s as a coalition of the LFMC avant-garde, the radical agit-prop collectives, independent distributors such as the Other Cinema and a network of regional film and video workshops, including Amber founded in Newcastle 1968, Chapter Video

Workshop formed in Cardiff 1974, the Sheffield Co-op created in 1975 and the Manchester Film and Video Workshop formed in 1977. A key component of the independent movement was a group of pioneer film theorists who were also writing for the emergent journals of academic film studies, crucially *Screen*, the seminal theoretical journal of the Society for Education in Film and Television (SEFT), which was effectively funded and published by the BFI Education Department. In 1974 the Independent Filmmakers' Association (IFA) was formed to represent the interests of a broad group of filmmakers and by the late 1970s it had become the principal national coordinating and policy-making agency of the movement.[33] The Independent Video Association (IVA) was founded in 1975 and the two organisations were eventually merged in 1983 to become the Independent Film and Video Association (IFVA).

The independent video movement effectively began with televisionX at the IRAT. Although both video practitioners and theorists have tended to emphasise the difference and specificity of the medium, the actual development of independent video had close and reciprocal links with independent film and followed a parallel and contiguous historical development. Like independent film, the independent video sector developed as a coalition of agents structured around an industrial/ideological polarity between agit-prop/community practice and an avant-garde: video art. What is most significant in this context is that whilst the LFMC avant-garde at least bore the shadow of an engagement with the amateur, anarchic and popular counter-culture, avant-garde video art emerged directly from the art institutions as an autonomous art. The key reasons for this immaculate conception are that the LFMC avant-garde had already pioneered the institutionalisation of the moving image as a legitimate art; that unlike avant-garde film, British video art developed before the advent of an equivalent amateur industry or culture, when individual access to video production and exhibition technology was limited to a few legitimate institutions (crucially art schools and notably Maidstone, Coventry, Brighton and St Martin's);[34] and that as a gallery object and auratic commodity, the discrete and luminous video monitor proved far more adaptable to the culture of art than the ephemeral and vulgar projections of the cinema.

The independent movement and its cluster of representative organisations were frequently divided by passionate political debate and dissent; nevertheless, the historical trajectory of the movement was constituted on the absolute assumption that independent cinema was defined by an autonomy from the mainstream commercial industry maintained and legitimised by state funding.[35] This assumption was underpinned and maintained by a complex ideological nexus of state socialism and the historical momentum of the bourgeois nationalisation of art culture. Historical precedents had been set by the Documentary Film Movement, the BBC, the BFI and the Arts Council. Ideologically, the paradox of an autonomous and legitimate state film industry was facilitated by a fusion of Griersonian notions of the social function of cinema and the post-war socialist strategy for a nationalised cinema. Following this trajectory the movement developed as a semi-autonomous industrial sector which was almost totally dependent on state funding and which had key agents and agencies within the authority and institutions of the state. The cardinal strategies of the independent sector as it advanced into the 1980s were to steadily increase the state funding and coordination of independent film and video; to campaign for professional recognition by both the state and the trade unions; and to develop an ideological and industrial stake in the formation of the new state-mandated national television station Channel 4, which began broadcasting in 1982. These strategies of inclusion inevitably and ironically eroded, and finally destroyed, the institutional independence of the movement. Furthermore, this disintegration was compounded by a shift within the sector, from a broad leftist ideology, to a new pluralist politics of identity and difference, which promoted the devolution of the sector into specialised workshops, agencies and initiatives designed to enfranchise social groups excluded from the mainstream media: women's film and video, black film and video, gay and lesbian film and video, Asian film and so forth. Whilst this shift was principally initiated by radical filmmakers, as an element of state film policy it was driven by strategic tokenism, liberal guilt and cultural essentialism, and its crucial institutional effect was to force funding applicants to compete against each other as the delegates of rival marginalised subjectivities.[36] By the late 1980s the independent movement had professionalised and fragmented into freelance commercial television production serving the expanding and deregulated media industries. What survived into the 1990s was the vestigial infrastructure of state film and video funding plus the only component of the independent sector that was ideologically and industrially irreconcilable to commerce: avant-garde film and video art. The disintegration of the independent movement liberated the avant-garde from both the paradox of independence as a political ideology and the conflicting discourses of the diverse independent coalition, but it also threatened the very legitimacy of the avant-garde as a state-sanctioned and -funded culture, since it became increasingly untenable to legitimise the avant-garde as a crucial component of independent film and video culture. The solution to this crisis was to finally relinquish all pretensions to radical opposition and to embrace the terminology first deployed by the Arts Council in the early 1970s: 'artists' film and video'.

Chapter 11

RADICAL THEORY AND ITS PRACTICE: A DEMYSTIFICATION

The development of the British avant-garde of the 1970s depended upon the formation of two discrete but integrated and interdependent sectors of activity: practice (filmmaking/cinema) and theory (education/publishing). Whereas Underground film had been a heterogeneous and vulgar hybrid, the LFMC avant-garde developed a practice which was essentially an art handicraft for the production of film. This practice was broadly theorised as Structural or Structural-Materialist film and its key theorist was the filmmaker Peter Gidal. But before we can address this arcane creed, the development of the avant-garde and avant-garde theory must also be understood as a contiguous and interactive element of the foundation of radical film/cultural theory in the 1970s.

British theory developed from the synthesis of two distinct, apparently conflicting but contiguous critical currents which both had roots in the art/non-art binary, Leavisite literary criticism and Mathew Arnold's conception of the crisis in culture.[1] The first of these currents was the academic discipline of cultural studies, and its development can be traced from Leavis through to Mass Observation, the post-war adult education movement, the work of Richard Hoggart, E. P. Thompson, Raymond Williams, Stuart Hall, the Birmingham Centre for Contemporary Cultural Studies, founded in 1964, and the journal *Working Papers in Cultural Studies*, first published in 1971.[2] Whilst cultural studies was initiated in the context of literary criticism and social history, it developed into the 1970s as a hybrid discipline which combined Marxist politics and sociological research with a detailed theoretical analysis of popular culture. As a radical critique cultural studies commenced from Hoggart's conception of the conflict between the authentic and organic folk culture of the working class, and the repressive pseudo-pop culture of mass production. This conception was then reconfigured and structured by theories of hegemony drawn from the work of Antonio Gramsci and the Frankfurt School.

The second current was Auteur Structuralism which was developed by pioneering Leftist film critics, teachers and activists in the BFI Education Department and the journal *Screen*, principally Peter Wollen, Paul Willemen, Geoffrey Nowell-Smith, Jim Kitses, Ben Brewster and Alan Lovell. As we have seen, the conception of the film director as author can be traced from the avant-garde of the 1920s, through to *Sequence* in the late 1940s. However, the decisive deployment of auteurism was the polemical *politique des auteurs* expounded in the French journal *Cahiers du cinéma* in the mid-1950s. British auteurism was inspired and enhanced by this manifesto and by Andrew Sarris's reformulation of it which first appeared in *Film Culture* in 1962 as the auteur theory. The crucial agent in the development of British auteurism was

Figure 18: THE DRUG COMES INTO YOUR HOME. Anonymous poster from Paris, May 1968

the influential journal *Movie*, first published in 1962. Following the trajectory initiated by *Sequence*, *Movie* synthesised Leavisite literary techniques with auteur film criticism, but it shifted the field of study from predominately European art cinema to Hollywood and popular cinema. Whilst this strategy recognised the critical significance of popular cinema and revitalised British film criticism, in the context of the historical art/non-art binary it should be understood as an initiative to extend the authority of art into the popular: the desire to aestheticise the popular. This paradoxical project inevitably created progressive critical tensions and instabilities.

Following the revolutionary political events of the late 1960s, and radical developments in French critical theory, a new generation of film intellectuals sought new theoretical methods that would reconcile auteurism with radical activism and the collective, multiple and industrial production of popular cinema: the auteur structuralists. The essential core of this revision was first to legitimise auteurism by adopting methodological strategies from the social sciences; second, to recast the auteur from an auratic artist to a theoretical construct; and third, to shift the production of meaning from the auteur to the cinematic text. The critical strategies of Auteur Structuralism were abstracted from the structural anthropology of Lévi-Strauss, the revisionist Marxism of Althusser, the semiotics of Barthes and Metz, and Lacan's revision of Freudian psychoanalysis. However, as structuralist theory developed into the late 1970s and early 1980s, cumulative waves of continental critical thought provided the poststructuralist project with new models: Post-Marxism, Second-Generation Feminism, Postmodernism and so on.

From the BFI Education Department and the influential groundwork of *Screen*, the poststructuralists led the institutionalisation of academic film studies into the universities. In a parallel development, cultural studies expanded into the universities through the social sciences, and notably through the open access/BBC broadcast Open University founded in 1969. Film and cultural theory developed from the historical interaction of these two critical currents and its influence extended from the late 1970s into the academic departments of film studies, communications, media studies, television studies, broadcast media, lens-based media, multimedia, time-based media, visual arts, digital arts and so on. Moreover, this expansion was not only horizontal but also vertical: up into the professional research departments of the universities and down into the colleges of further education and eventually the secondary schools. Internationally, British film and cultural theory served as a pioneering model for the establishment of theoretical movements and institutions in America, Australia and other key Anglophone nations.

The conceptual development of film and cultural theory can be tracked through the ascent of Poststructuralism to its supercession and integration into a broader theory largely informed by contemporary cultural studies.[3] The crucial concern of poststructuralist theory was to analyse the ideological, social and psychic positioning of the subject in popular film. Cinema was theorised as language, a semiotic system, each film a text which used codes and conventions to fabricate a cinematic reality. It was conceived that in mainstream cinema the split and alienated subject of bourgeois capitalist patriarchy was constructed as a unified whole; mainstream popular cinema was conceived as essentially a repressive ideological apparatus. Consequently, oppositional film in the context of Poststructuralism was that which subverted this ideological apparatus.

Throughout the 1970s and early 1980s Poststructuralism dominated film theory but by the late 1980s it had been superseded by the diverse elements of cultural studies. Cultural studies conceived the individual as a far more active social agent than the subject of Poststructuralism. Their subjectivity was not totally locked into a repressive system of representation; they had the ability to make resistant or even subversive readings of the mainstream. Cultural studies shifted the emphasis from the text to the reception of the text, the reader, and the use the reader makes of the text. Instead of the grand narratives of history, cultural studies offered micro-histories and subcultures. This subcultural approach was given a passionate momentum by feminist, working-class, queer, black and Asian theorists who developed radical models of cultural identity and resistance.

Both theoretical traditions considered themselves as radical doctrines engaged in demystifying the repressive mechanisms of popular culture. Moreover, despite the shift from Poststructuralism to cultural studies, elements and agents of both critical currents are active in contemporary theory.

The supposed radicalism and social engagement of theory depends upon the core concept of demystification. Demystification can only be understood in the historical context of the revolutionary activism of the 1960s, specifically in the context of the international student protest and occupation of the colleges and universities in the late 1960s. The impact of this student revolution on leftist intellectuals and academics can hardly be overestimated. In the brief and glorious days of the occupations it seemed that change was irreversible and inevitable; the academy was the vanguard of the revolution and the workers would follow. In the accounts written by activists in the actions at Berkeley, Berlin, Nanterre, Paris and in London at Hornsey College of Art, there is a beatific wonder in the utopian possibilities of the liberated academy. The divisions between students, teachers, non-teaching staff and the wider community would be swept away; decision-making would become open, equal, democratic and collective; the syllabus would be replaced with a new flexible and organic process; education would be revolutionary, it would serve the revolution.

The momentum of the student revolution was provoked, exploited and conceptualised by various groups of ultra left and anarchist activists worldwide (the Provos, the Yippies and so on). The most subversive theorisation was devised by the Anti-Art Situationist International who were directly involved in the agitation and provocation which led to the Paris student revolt of May 1968. Effectively, the Situationists developed a practice of cultural intervention and sabotage based on an inversion of the Marxist doctrine which held that the cultural superstructure of society is determined by its economic base. According to this perception advanced Western capitalism had reached the stage at which social/cultural life had been replaced by the spectacle, the hegemonic realm of mass media, false consciousness, consumption and alienation in which all separation appears as a natural unity. The revolutionary project of the Situationists was not to take control of the means of production; it was to liberate everyday life, beginning with their own lives. To this end they designed cultural techniques, events and products which would subvert the spectacle. This praxis of hegemonic sabotage had a profound influence on French filmmakers and intellectuals during and in the aftermath of May 1968, notably Godard, Baudrilliard, Lyotard and Foucault, who were themselves active in the strikes and occupations.

In Paris the student revolution culminated in attempts to seize control of the production of culture. From the film industry a coalition of critics from *Cahiers du cinéma*, members of trade unions and leading actors and directors attempted to liberate cinema. This coalition constituted itself as the Estates General Du Cinéma (EGC), named after the revolutionary parliament of 1789, and they met in the hall of the occupied Film and Photography School of the Sorbonne.[4] The declared project of the EGC was to destroy the existing structures of the French film industry and to create a new non-capitalist industry: the model proposed for this was state-funded art.

What eventually emerged from the EGC and the radical film culture of May 1968 was a generation of cultural activists who sought to integrate Situationism, Marxism, Structuralism and psychoanalysis in a radical praxis designed to subvert mainstream cinema and create an alternative non-bourgeois cinema. The two key fronts of the project were radical film journals and experimental agit-prop film groups. The key journals were *Cahiers du cinéma*, which in 1969 adopted an explicit Marxist editorial policy, and *Cinethique* which was created in 1969 with the avowed intention of founding an avant-garde Marxist materialist cinema which would free itself from the spectacular and mystic realm of ideology and become scientific; it would become theoretical.[5] The most eminent film groups were the Dziga-Vertov Group, formed by Godard and Jean-Pierre Gorin, and SLON, which included Chris Marker. Vital to the revolutionary intent of the alternative filmmakers was the commitment to eliminating the hierarchical work practices of the mainstream and replacing them with a democratic collective practice; the auteur was now deemed either a capitalist manager or a bourgeois phantom. The pivotal strategy of the post-1968 project was demystification, the development of a diverse set of critical techniques designed to reveal and negate the repressive bourgeois ideology of mainstream cinema. In cinematic practice this meant making films which subverted the ideological realm of the mainstream. In critical theory this meant promoting films which subverted the mainstream and/or interrogating mainstream films to reveal the mechanisms of bourgeois mystification. It is this praxis of demystification, translated from Paris by the auteur structuralists and the LFMC avant-garde, that was to become the rationale of Anglo-American theory, and the theoretical authority of both British avant-garde film and independent film and Counter-Cinema.[6] Although this rationale was to shift and develop from the late 1970s, under the impact of feminism, Third Cinema, Post-Colonial politics, queer politics and so on, there remained at the core of the project the assumption that demystification was the pivotal strategy in the development of a radical independent film and video culture.[7] Sylvia Harvey, the historian and independent film activist, provides a concise articulation of this assumption in her classic study of film culture and May 1968:

If we want cultural production to operate in a different way and to a different sort of purpose, it is not enough simply to place it beneath the control of new masters, we need to understand it in its own way of working in order to change it. What is being proposed here is not the sudden creation of radically new communicative structures but the breaking down of existing popular forms which is made possible through an understanding of the weak points of these forms, an understanding of the points of internal contradiction and tension. When we begin to understand, for example, what a soap opera television serial, or a disaster movie, or a soft-porn sex film, seem to promise but never deliver – the values respectively of community, intense experience and pleasure – then we have discovered the point of entry into the form, the point of ideological tension, which will enable us to take it apart, to destroy it from within, and on this basis to construct new forms.[8]

Harvey's quote raises the crucial reckoning for theory as a politically radical or engaged discipline. According to the logic of demystification it must follow that the most mystified culture is the popular and the most mystified class is the working class. But theoretical demystification cannot be rationalised as a strategy which would *directly* free the proletariat from hegemony, since theory was conceived in/ with generic characteristics which make it inaccessible and incomprehensible to all but the elite academically-educated bourgeoisie. The only possible justification for theoretical demystification as a radical ethic is that it is research aimed at an elite vanguard of academic filmmakers and cinema activists engaged in the development of an autonomous non-bourgeois film industry. It is avant-garde theory: armed with the research of theory, an avant-garde film movement would be able to develop new demystified films and videos for the working class. But most of the avant-garde/independent films and videos produced in the 1970s as an alternative to the mainstream were inscrutable to the mystified proletariat; in fact, since the only effective distribution for the avant-garde was higher education, the proletariat rarely saw them.[9] In their vehement opposition to commodity capitalism and mainstream cinema, the activists of independent cinema rejected box-office success, popularity, entertainment and even pleasure. Instead they chose the independence of state subsidy and the economy of art. But as an art object their ephemeral work was practically unsalable and the state had neither the motivation nor the resources to develop an efficient alternative distribution and exhibition circuit. By the late 1970s it was clear that the revolution had been postponed, avant-garde/independent film was not going to vanquish the mainstream and consequently not going to valorise and vindicate the theoretical project. Theory did not abandon demystification but it increasingly legitimised itself not as a revolutionary project, but as a highly successful and influential academic discipline. Moreover, as the independent film and video project gave way to demands for inclusion into the mainstream the purpose of theoretical demystification became increasingly cut off from independent practice. The conceptual strategies developed by cultural studies in the late 1970s offered a way out of this impasse, for they extended the practice of demystification to the audience. In the cultural studies model audiences are not duped by the mainstream; they can resist or even construct their own subversive readings of the texts. Consequently, a radical alternative cinema was no longer necessary since theoretical demystification was no longer the means, it became the end. Feminism, identity politics and the new pluralism of the 1980s exposed the patriarchal myth of a British monoculture but it also fragmented the revolutionary aspiration of Post-structuralism and replaced it with a reformist agenda of inclusion in the capitalist meritocracy. In the micro-histories and subcultures of cultural studies, theory itself became just another subculture.

Although the historical development of theory has been integral to the develop-ment of independent film and video, it should not be assumed that the practice of theory is filmmaking; the practice of theory is literature. The separation between theory and its practice cloaks the specificity of theory as a genre of academic litera-ture. As David Bordwell has observed, there is no convincing justification for the reduction of cinema to a written language, nor for the consideration of films as texts to be read.[10] The essential explanation of why theorists adopted this analogy, and why it has proved so compelling, is deceptively simple. Structuralism and semiotics notwithstanding, theorists adopted the analogy of literature for cinema because, as academic writers, it was their inveterate and professional medium and the official medium of the academy. The analogy of literature has produced intriguing theo-retical writing about the cinema but the discoveries of grammar, language, codes, syntax, signs and so on are the discoveries that literature is liable to find in cinema, in the way that a musician would discover tempo, harmonics, themes, rhythm, po-lyphony and so on. Thus, if you develop a set of hermeneutic practices for the study of a distinct and primary cultural form, and you then engage these practices in the study of a distinctly different cultural form, you are liable to discover fascinating analogies. However, they will always be analogies. To discover how cinema works as cinema it is necessary to make films. The irony is that in attempting to escape from the signifying practices of the bourgeois mainstream, certain avant-garde/in-dependent films – most significantly the Structural-Materialist work of the 1970s – became impenetrable to the language analogy and so revealed its limits. Moreover, since the pleasure of theory, for theorist and student alike, is to a great extent the startling demystification of the coded ideology and subtext within the text, such films were not attractive propositions for analysis, and so were passed over. Further, and more ironically, when theory passed over the analysis of avant-garde/indepen-dent film, it passed over the only sector of film production in which the filmmaker really was an auteur.[11]

A theoretical education did not teach students how to make popular films, it taught them how to write literature about popular cinema. At its most practical, an understanding of theory could perhaps enable a student to make experimental films encoded as text according to the language analogy. But since by the late 1970s a career as an experimental filmmaker meant consigning yourself to obscurity and penury; becoming a career theorist in the security of the academy was a far safer option. Moreover, once theory was established in the academy it did not need an alternative film and video industry since it could develop an autonomous industry based on education and publishing; a shadow industry which decoded and mapped popular culture but always remained outside its realm. The distance between theory and its practice masks an appropriation by the academy; if theoretical demystification could not participate in the avant-garde transformation of cinema then it would aestheticise the cinema as literature.

As an industry, theory is essentially a sector of post-war education. The educational hierarchy of power and influence, descending from Oxbridge, down to the urban colleges of further education, and the most delinquent state comprehensives, is legitimised by the concept of the meritocracy. Students are tested and graded by meritocratic systems to select who will be granted professional qualifications, who will rise and pass to the higher levels of education or who will be legitimised as a specialist or expert in a given discipline. The meritocratic model replaces the hereditary hierarchy of feudalism with the concept of equality of opportunity in capitalism; it replaces divine inheritance with professional expertise and efficiency. As a political reality the meritocracy may seem immanent, or partial, but it is still only a model. In fact, the economic gap between the working class and the bourgeoisie has widened and polarised in the twenty-first century to an extent not recorded since the late nineteenth century. Academic success is effectively limited to the children of the bourgeoisie. Although a percentage of working-class pupils do go on to higher education, the universities and art schools are effectively dominated by children from fee-paying schools, grammar schools and comprehensives from prosperous middle-class catchment areas. As increasingly both higher education and technology-based industries demand a high level of educational qualification, so the working classes are excluded from managerial and professional positions, and from the financial incomes that would give them class mobility. Moreover, even if the meritocracy were immanent or possible, it would not create an equitable and democratic society; it would consolidate the rule of an elite class of professionals and specialists.

The meritocratic model is the ideological mechanism that allows the modern bourgeoisie to govern as an elite class in the name of liberty and equality. It is the power-sharing compromise that was struck between the aristocracy and the ascendant bourgeoisie; the bourgeoisie in its desire to rule appropriated the culture of the aristocracy and allowed them to abide concealed in the mythical new bourgeois era. As a myth the meritocracy serves as the hope of progress, and as a political project it has the function of channelling radical or revolutionary subversion into reform.

The post-1968 radical film project rejected popular cinema as essentially bourgeois repression and then compounded this misreading by impetuously institutionalising itself into state education and state-funded art. Avant-garde/independent film and video production became dependent on meritocratic selection by state agencies and theory became embedded in the meritocratic structures of the education industry. As revolt gave way to the reformist politics of the late 1970s so the radical agenda shifted from collective and alternative practice to demands for equality of opportunity in the mythic meritocracy.

Ultimately cultural theory must be reckoned both by its actual achievements and by its avowed aspirations. If the crucial achievement of theory has been to establish and legitimise the academic study of popular culture then for what purpose? However distant and compromised, the assumption at the base of contemporary theory is that the theoretical project is an element of a broader Marxist/Socialist transformation of the film and video industry, from apparatus of bourgeois hegemony, to radical agent in the revolutionary class struggle. Whilst this aspiration was initiated in the revolutionary context of the counter-culture and student revolutions of 1968, it has long since lost its radical agency. Theory did not transform the film and video industry and the hope of a revolutionary independent industry was lost. Has theory revealed the secret codes of the popular? Perhaps the demystifying techniques of theory could be vindicated if the results could be successfully deployed by the cultural industries; theory would then be true in cultural practice. Semiotics could be applied to new methods of montage construction, or perhaps psychoanalysis could be used to position the audience into exciting new identities. But the industrial application of theory in popular culture is negligible. The product of theory is not popular: it is a bourgeois culture. Has theory's penetration of the education industry produced a new generation of students immune to bourgeois hegemony or at least with enhanced powers of resistant reading? Such a conclusion rests upon the assumption that popular culture is essentially bourgeois hegemony. But in the context of the historical suppression of the popular by the bourgeoisie and the nationalisation of art as the legitimate culture of the state, it is not the popular which is essentially bourgeois, it is theory.

Cultural theory has become for the British state a crucial bureaucracy for the negotiation and maintenance of the border between art and the popular. The function of theory is to convert the incoherent, chaotic and vulgar collective popular into authorised, academic and legitimate culture. And this is not simply a textual strategy, it is an educational process since state education is the institution developed by the bourgeoisie to convert the illegitimate popular culture of studious working-class youth into art. By which I mean that even if a small percentage of working-class students are able to penetrate into the higher reaches of the academy they can only achieve this by alienating themselves from popular culture.

Chapter 12

THE CONSTITUTION OF THE INDEPENDENT SECTOR: A TRINITY OF TEXTS – CURTIS, GIDAL AND WOLLEN

In the formative years of the first British Underground there had been both the hope and the potential of developing a genuinely anarchic and popular Underground distribution/exhibition network of clubs and counter-cultural venues, perhaps comparable to the amateur ciné-clubs or the fringe theatre movement. But although there were later sporadic distribution/exhibition initiatives, such as the Other Cinema, no effective integrated and anarchic network was ever realised. In the case of the LFMC a key determinant of this limitation can be located as early as the accession of the Curtis/Le Grice production group over the Better Books faction. Whilst the latter camp numbered amongst its membership activists from various cultural, commercial and political backgrounds, the Curtis/Le Grice group were collectively committed both to autonomous art and to the correlated socialist rejection of commercial trade. This effectively meant that the new avant-garde movement was hostile to all commercial frameworks in which it could become financially self-sufficient, and yet, as a culture of mechanical reproduction, neither could it produce the unique auratic objects required by the art market. These factors interlocked to produce a praxis which defined itself as independent and oppositional to mainstream commercial film and television but which increasingly demanded the state subsidy and legitimacy accorded to other art forms. Crucially and specifically, in the case of avant-garde film, the development of the dependency on state subsidy was absolute, since whilst other state-funded art forms had economies and institutions before the development of state art funding, the post-war avant-garde developed as a state-funded institution and it has never, in any of its later incarnations, developed an economy or institution that was not legitimised and funded by the state.

Following the precedents of the Documentary Film Movement, Free Cinema and the BFI Experimental Film Fund, the 1970s avant-garde and the subsequent independent film movement constituted themselves as state agencies with a national state-funded infrastructure of production, distribution and exhibition. Indirect state funding and control developed as the assimilation of the avant-garde/independent sector into the legitimate and academic institutions of the state. Direct state funding and control developed through a web of interlocking initiatives:

1. The development of production funding for individual filmmakers and groups. The primary agencies were the Arts Council of England, the BFI and the Regional Arts Boards. The key client groups were makers from the LFMC,

the IFA, London Video Arts (LVA, later London Electronic Arts), students from the new art school film and video courses and the regional film and video workshops movement. After 1982, Channel 4 became a key funder of avant-garde and independent film and video in collaboration with both the Arts Council and the BFI.

2. The development of funded distribution/exhibition initiatives such as the LFMC, LVA, the network of regional independent film theatres, festivals and national and international touring initiatives. A key distribution agency was the Film and Video Umbrella which was created by the Arts Council in 1983 specifically to distribute avant-garde work. In the 1980s both Channel 4 and later BBC2 began to screen avant-garde and independent material.

3. Funding for key avant-garde/independent agencies such the IFA, the LFMC and the workshop movement. Also, funding for the key journals and publications of the movement including BFI book publishing, and specialist magazines including *Afterimage* in the 1970s, *Undercut* and *Independent Media* in the 1980s, and *Vertigo* and *Coil* in the 1990s. Most recently, *Filmwaves*, which began as a truly independent, low- and no-budget film journal in 1997, has been colonised by artists' film and video in the form of a state-funded supplement magazine *art in-sight*, introduced in 2001.

4. The direct (inter)penetration of theorists, makers and activists into the state agencies. Exemplary agents in this process would be David Curtis at the Arts Council, the appointment of Peter Sainsbury as head of production at the BFI in 1973 and the appointment of IFA delegates to the BFI Production Board in the mid-1970s.

Together these initiatives formed a state industry for the production, distribution and exhibition of avant-garde/independent film and video. The repressive agency of this industry must be understood first as the development of an elite and exclusive bourgeois moving-image culture funded by state taxation levied on all classes of society, and second as a vertical industrial monopoly which effectively stifled and eclipsed the development of a truly anarchic radical, popular and experimental moving-image culture. It could perhaps be argued that most independent organisations were at least semi-autonomous, and many of the leading agents in the sector would deny any direct state control of their agency, or even assert that their work was actually subversive to the state, but such naivety is to misapprehend the complex historical development of art as the legitimate culture of the bourgeois state.

Whilst the independent sector developed as a complex interaction between the major funding agencies, there was also a fundamental binary division within the sector that functioned as a crucial mechanism of selection and exclusion. Although regional funding gradually increased from the 1980s, the two primary state funding agencies from the early 1970s until the creation of the unified Film Council in 2000, remained the Arts Council and the BFI. The BFI Production Board developed from the Experimental Film Fund of the 1950s. In the mid-1970s, under the direction of Peter Sainsbury, the Board effectively adopted a policy of exclusively funding independent film against the mainstream, and this included a broad range of work from low-budget counter-cinema feature films to agit-prop documentary and avant-garde work. However, by the late 1970s the Board had begun to revise this policy, favouring the production of low-budget, but commercially competitive, feature-length narrative and documentary films. In the 1980s this tendency was consolidated under the direction of Colin McCabe and reinforced by a cluster of critically-acclaimed features, crucially Peter Greenaway's *The Draughtman's Contract* (1982) and Derek Jarman's *Caravaggio* (1986). This shift was, in generic, institutional and commercial terms, a move away from the politics of independence and towards the targeting of an educated bourgeoisie minority audience within mainstream feature-film culture; a British art cinema. Concurrent with this shift, BFI short film production was reconfigured as the provision of apprentice funding for first-time potential art cinema directors, and this was formalised in 1987 by the creation of the New Directors scheme.[1] Art cinema or art-house cinema is the aestheticised sector of commercial cinema. It is a specialist cinema which valorizes art, auteurism, experiment, elitism and internationalism, but this specialism functions within the limits of both commercial cinema and bourgeois culture.

Conversely, the Arts Council almost exclusively funded the avant-garde.[2] Essentially, this meant that state funding provision was separated and limited to two broad but clearly prescribed forms of bourgeois cinema: the Arts Council funded art whilst the BFI funded art cinema. The repression of the system functioned by exclusion and deflection; projects deemed by the Arts Council to be mainstream, narrative or popular were rejected or advised to approach the BFI or regional funders; projects deemed by the BFI to be too experimental, abstract or non-commercial were rejected or advised to approach the Arts Council. Projects considered amateur were rejected by all agencies. The crucial exclusion from this binary system was the anarchic, subversive and popular hybridisation of the Underground.

To illuminate the theoretical and institutional development of the avant-garde and the broader independent movement let us take as an exemplary and influential milestone the 1975 special issue of the prestigious contemporary art magazine *Studio International*, which was devoted to 'Avant-Garde Film in England and Europe'. Printed in this edition were three formative texts of the 1970s British avant-garde film movement. The first was David Curtis's 'English Avant-Garde Film: An Early Chronology', a personal history of the London Film-makers' Co-operative; the second was 'Theory and Definition of Structural/Materialist Film', Peter Gidal's first fully developed formulation of his avant-garde practice; and the third was an article by the influential film theorist and filmmaker Peter Wollen, 'The Two Avant-Gardes'. This trinity of texts provided the 1970s avant-garde movement with, respectively, a history, a theory of practice and a historical agenda.

STUDIO
International

Journal of Modern Art   November/December 1975 £1·75 $5

Avant-Garde Film in England & Europe

David Curtis
English Avant-Garde Film

Deke Dusinberre
On Expanding Cinema

Peter Gidal
Structural/Materialist Film

Ron Haselden
MFV Maureen

Birgit Hein
Return to Reason

Malcolm Le Grice
Kurt Kren

Barbara Meter
Film-making in Holland

Annabel Nicolson
Filmy Tales

Alan Sheridan
David Dye

Peter Weibel
Avant-Garde Film in Austria

Peter Wollen
The Two Avant-Gardes

Figure 19: *Studio International,* November/December, 1975.

DAVID CURTIS

A vital historical project of the avant-garde was to develop both an institutional/industrial base and a discourse of validity that would authenticate its aesthetic legitimacy and its claim to state funding; this strategy was at times dynamic and explicit.

Central to this project was the fabrication of a validating history structured around a canon of legitimate work and a pantheon of artist makers.

Curtis's article in *Studio International* is a personal and affectionate reminiscence of the early Underground and the transition to the avant-garde. The narrative is engaging and inclusive, but there is no reference to the early split within the LFMC, or to any conflict or resistance to the avant-garde shift. Nevertheless, it ends with a brief survey of the contemporary advances in state funding and art institutionalisation, which concludes with the speculation:

> These latest moves confirm the avant-garde's complicity in its own institutionalisation, and a further stage in its integration into the English pattern of education and patronage in the arts. To what extent it can survive this orthodoxy, and preserve its radical position in relation to the (equally uncommercial) 'commercial cinema', is a question likely to be answered during the next ten years.[3]

What is remarkable about this foreboding is Curtis's apparent objectivity, since at the time of writing he was already a key agent in the very process he questions, and during the next 25 years he was to become the pivotal agent in the institutionalisation of the post-war British avant-garde.

Prior to his employment by the Arts Council as the Assistant Film Officer in 1977, Curtis was a dynamic activist in the formation of the LFMC, he wrote the classic history *Experimental Cinema* (1971), and he also developed a career as an avant-garde curator organising a series of screenings and festivals at legitimate art institutes, principally the National Film Theatre. In 1973 he was first appointed a member of the Arts Council's production funding selection panel, the Artists' Film Sub-Committee alongside Tony Rayns and Simon Field. Up until its dissolution in the late 1990s the Artists' Film Sub-Committee, which became after 1980 the Artists' Film and Video Sub-Committee, was the most significant and consistent source of production funding for the avant-garde. The membership of the committee was constituted by inviting artists' peers and relevant experts to participate. In practice this meant that the committee was controlled by a shifting elite of LFMC activists and avant-garde filmmakers and academics, including, at various times, Deke Dusinberre, Lis Rhodes, A. L. Rees, Guy Sherwin, Anne Rees-Mogg, Mary Pat Leece, Tina Keane, Malcolm Le Grice, Felicity Sparrow, Michael O'Pray, Alnoor Dewshi, Tony Warcus and others. The production grants awarded to individual filmmakers by the sub-committee were minimal, although the net funding rose from around £12,000 in 1974 to around £50,000 in 1984 and over £100,000 in the 1990s. However, production finance was only an element of the cultural investment made by the Arts Council in individual filmmakers and the net investment must be understood as both institutional and industrial. First, the award of funding would mark and confirm the entry of the filmmaker into the legitimate institution of art. Second, the financial investment in a film and its maker could operate as a multiple investment across the whole range of funded organisations: a film would be first funded, then distributed by funded agencies, exhibited in funded institutions, written about in funded publications and the filmmaker could then use their funded work to secure employment in the independent sector. This integrated cultural and institutional validation was fundamental to the sector since its independence was predicated on the radical negation of popularity and commercial success: the independent sector had relatively no audience or income outside its own institutions.

In 1977, as a member of the Artists' Film Sub-Committee, Curtis was one of the curators of a major Arts Council retrospective of avant-garde film at the Hayward Gallery on the Southbank: Perspectives on British Avant-Garde Film. In the catalogue the purpose of the exhibition was made clear:

> The purpose in showing the series of film programmes titled 'Perspectives on British Avant-Garde Film' is to survey the films funded by the Arts Council through its Artists' Films Committee and to place them in a historical and critical context of avant-garde film practice. The contention is not that the film work funded by the committee is synonymous with the avant-garde in Britain today, but that most film-makers working in this area have been or are currently in receipt of financial support from the committee.[4]

From this assertion it is possible to draw the conclusion that since the Arts Council funded most of the filmmakers working in the area, so those who were not funded were not working in the area; by extension this inference became a self-validating formula which negated the work of all filmmakers rejected by the committee. A year later the Hayward retrospective became a major international touring exhibition curated by Curtis and Deke Dusinberre: A Perspective on English Avant-Garde Film. The comprehensive catalogue for this tour included critical essays and statements from leading avant-garde filmmakers and the first substantial essay in the catalogue was an updated version of Curtis's *Studio International* essay, in which his speculation on the future institutionalisation of the avant-garde was omitted.[5]

In 1979 Curtis was the Exhibition Officer for another avant-garde retrospective at the Hayward which explicitly foregrounded the British structuralist aesthetic: Film as Film. The catalogue for this exhibition is a key document of the structuralist avant-garde; the critical thrust of both the exhibition and the catalogue was to strategically revise the history of experimental film as a teleological progression towards abstract Structuralism. This was also the broad project of Malcolm Le Grice's influential book of 1977, *Abstract Film and Beyond*.[6] In his essay for the Film as Film catalogue, 'The History We Need', Le Grice addresses the role of history and theory in the development of the avant-garde and candidly recognises the purpose of avant-garde film history:

> The underlying thesis of a historical construction not only affects the ordering of facts but also the articulation of what constitutes the facts themselves.

In addition a historical formulation has a different function for the involved practitioner in a field than for the less involved 'general public'. For that nebulous 'general public' (in whose name so many decisions are made) a historical exhibition like 'Film as Film', as well as drawing attention to a particular field of past activity, also validates those current practices which derive from them – providing them with historical credentials. In effect, whilst a current practice is evidently determined by its historical relationship, definition of a structure for this causality is a constructive production very much parallel to the practice itself ... 'The History We Need' implies a recognition that a neutral and inclusive history is broadly impossible and that the historical enterprise should be aimed at aiding the development of contemporary practice.[7]

This is perhaps the clearest acknowledgement of the purpose and trajectory of avant-garde historification from a leading avant-garde activist. As the avant-garde institutionalised itself so it gained control of the means to make its own legitimate history. By careful selection and exclusion it developed a historical canon and a pantheon of elite makers. Moreover, the development of systematic selection and exclusion was not simply an ideological imperative but an industrial necessity, since the institutional finance and employment for the avant-garde remained an elite, exclusive and limited resource.

In 1996 Curtis consolidated his twenty-year avant-garde activism by editing the *Directory of British Film and Video Artists* published by the Arts Council.[8] This book is in effect the published avant-garde pantheon and it resides in practically every British art school, university and college where experimental film and video is studied. Statistical analysis of this directory reveals the complex interrelationships and correspondences of the pantheon. Exemplary instances are that of the 118 filmmakers almost ninety per cent had been funded by the Arts Council, 73 per cent had been funded by the Arts Council at least twice, 21 per cent had served on Arts Council Committees and 38 per cent had been funded by the BFI, Arts Council and Channel 4. Only four filmmakers had received no funding prior to the compilation of the directory, and of these, three had work in the distribution catalogue of the Arts Council-funded London Electronic Arts. More than half the filmmakers had also taught at academic institutes. What must be remembered is that those in the directory represent only a small percentage of the artists selected for production funding between 1973 and 1995. In turn these filmmakers represent only a fraction of the rejected many who applied for funding, and none of the hundreds of amateur and Underground filmmakers active in the period who did not apply for funding. In defence of the avant-garde it must be said that Curtis, Le Grice and other key activists did not believe that they were excluding thousands of artists from the elite avant-garde movement. Because they did not believe that the filmmakers they were excluding were artists.

PETER GIDAL

The concept of a structural avant-garde film first appeared in an article by P. Adams Sitney in *Film Culture* in 1969.[9] Sitney identified, theorised and promoted the structural aesthetic in the work of a cluster of new American filmmakers: Tony Conrad, George Landow, Michael Snow, Hollis Frampton, Joyce Wieland, Ernie Gehr and Paul Sharrits. According to Sitney the structural tendency marked a crucial shift in the American avant-garde away from complex visual lyricism, mythopoeia and abstract animation, and towards a minimalist intellectual aesthetic in which form and process become content; in which the content of the film is subsidiary to the structure. He traced the origins of structural film to the work of Andy Warhol and the Austrian filmmaker Peter Kubelka and he identified four key characteristics of the aesthetic: a fixed/static frame, flicker (strobe) effects, loop printing and rephotography. But the aesthetic crux of Structuralism, Sitney asserted, was the elongation/extension of cinematic experiment into an investigation/defamiliarisation of perception and cognition.

Parallel to the development of American Structuralism the LFMC avant-garde also developed a formal aesthetic led by the work of Le Grice and Peter Gidal.

Gidal was born in America and studied theatre in Massachusetts and Munich. In 1968, at the age of 22, he moved to London to study film at the Royal College of Art and almost immediately became involved with the early LFMC.[10] From his involvement with the co-operative he became a leading activist and filmmaker in the British avant-garde: his films were widely screened both nationally and internationally; he programmed the LFMC cinema 1971–74; he organised screenings of avant-garde film at the NFT; he wrote regular reviews of avant-garde film for *Time Out* magazine from 1972–75; he was on the original organising committee of the IFA in 1974; and he taught filmmaking at the Royal College of Art from 1973–83.[11] Most importantly in this context, he was, in collaboration with Le Grice, the primary theorist of the LFMC avant-garde; Gidal developed an avant-garde aesthetic that inspired a generation of avant-garde filmmakers, and many critical assumptions of contemporary artists' film and video are still underpinned by his theoretical framework.

Gidal's 'Theory and Definition of Structural/Materialist Film' was essentially the answer to a question he had asked five years earlier in the Underground film magazine *Cinemantics*.[12] In that early article, 'Film as Materialist Consumer Product', Gidal ponders how to develop a form of radical avant-garde art (cinema) which would have the power to induce a revolutionary consciousness in the viewer. His eventual theorisation of Structural/Materialist (S/M) film is an attempt to reconcile the work produced by the LFMC avant-garde with his radical aspirations, Sitney's structural film aesthetic and elements of the continental Marxist/poststructuralist philosophy also deployed in British theory.

In his enmity to popular cinema Gidal goes far beyond all other previous cinematic avant-gardes, and his contemporaries in Auteur Structuralism and cultural studies. For theory, the hegemonic mainstream is ironically always the subject of investigation, the code to be broken, the beloved other. But for Gidal the popular is an irredeemable repressive agent which must be totally obliterated. He conceives the key repressive devices of popular film as illusion, narrative and identification; the antidote to this repression is advanced S/M film. If the demystification of theory presumes to reveal the hidden hegemony of the popular, S/M film proposes to confront the viewer with the materiality of film purged of all hegemonic codes and devices:

> Structural/Materialist film attempts to be non-illusionist. The process of the film's making deals with devices that result in demystification or the attempted demystification of the film process. But by 'deals with' I do not mean 'represents'. In other words, such films do not document various film procedures, which would place them in the same category as films which transparently document a narrative, a set of actions, and so forth. Documentation, through usage of the film medium as transparent, invisible, is exactly the same when the object being documented is some 'real event', some 'film procedural event', some 'story', and so forth. An avant-garde film defined by its development towards increased materialism and materialist function does not represent, or document anything. The film produces certain relations between segments, between what the camera is aimed at and the way the image is 'presented'. The dialectic of the film is established in that space of tension between materialist flatness, grain, light, movement, and the supposed real reality that is represented. Thus a consequent attempted destruction of the illusion is a constant necessity.[13]

The imperative of S/M film is to eliminate all bourgeois ideology, all seductive illusion, all identification, narrative, temporal deception, imagism, idealism, all naturalised and obvious meaning and dangerous mystification. Free from the web of illusion, S/M film is a record of its own production, a generative system that creates a radical dialectic between viewer and film; it confronts the viewer with the material production of consciousness.

> Attempted in structural/materialist film is a non-hierarchical, cool, separate unfolding of a perceptual activity … Through the attempted non-hierarchical, cool, separate unfolding a distance(ing) is sought. This distance reinforces (rather than denying) the dialectic interaction of viewer with each film moment, necessary if it is not to pass into passiveness and needlessness.[14]

Ultimately S/M is the final demystification, it is the stripping away of all illusion and ideology to reveal the materiality of film; it is a theoretical practice:

> The structural/materialist film and production of meaning in film is the

production of film itself, in its (thought or 'unthought') theoreticalness, and (thought or 'unthought') ideological intervention. To crucially intervene in film practice, the unthought must be brought to knowledge, thought. The set of relations between film practice and film as theory, can then be brought forth to operate in clarity.[15]

Implicit throughout is the assumption that S/M film is a necessary element of an advanced revolutionary Marxist struggle, but the question that Gidal neglects is just how S/M film will function in this struggle: who is to be demystified? After *Studio International* in 1975, Gidal continued to refine and expand his theoretic and produced a series of influential articles and collections culminating in the book *Materialist Film* (1989).[16] His film work also expanded in duration and ambition but still remained committed to materialising the S/M aesthetic.

However, the theory of S/M was contested from almost the moment of its formulation. In a special independent cinema edition of *Afterimage* in the summer of 1976 Anne Cottringer opened a poststructuralist critique of Gidal's essay. A year later Constance Penley launched a controversial feminist/psychoanalytic attack on S/M and a series of evaluations and disputes followed into the 1980s.[17] But the most damaging, incisive critique appeared alongside Cottringer's article in *Afterimage*: 'Experimental/Avant-Garde/Revolutionary Film Practice', by Mike Dunford.

Dunford's concise critique is a direct and polemical Marxist/Leninist attack on the theory and practice of S/M film, the radical aspirations of the avant-garde and the constitution of the LFMC. It is all the more damning since it is a renunciation by a leading filmmaker of the structuralist avant-garde. The key point of Dunford's attack is that S/M theory was not based on an objective analysis of its own social, historical and material conditions and its role in the production of bourgeois ideology. Instead it had developed a theory derived from and validating its own art practice:

It has evolved a particular form of practice stemming from the material nature of the medium, and from a rejection and exposure of the practices, codes and forms of naturalistic industrial/commercial film practice. The theory of this work has been a form of technical theory, deriving from the methodology of its practice, and that of other practices within the fine arts, and it is therefore unconscious of its aim within ideology.[18]

Although he does not refer to it as Underground Cinema, Dunford recognises that the counter-cultural phase of experimental film in the 1960s was a radical democratic/anarchic project that was finally repressed by avant-garde art. The shift in the LFMC from the counter-culture to the aesthetics of Structuralism was a shift towards a professionalised art (handicraft) practice that fetishised the production process: printing, processing, editing, rephotography, projection and so on. This aesthetic fetishisation was theorised/valorised as Materialism. But whilst the LFMC theorised against the bourgeois hegemony of the mainstream they were actually developing the avant-garde as an elite and autonomous institution under the direct control of the bourgeois state.

> A theory is much more than a simple rationalisation of procedure and process, but, denied access to any understanding of the ideological role that experimental film plays as part of the avant-garde, and participating so closely in the reproduction of that ideological function, the theories of experimental film practice have been unable, and will be continuously unable to do more than be an apologetics, and the more invested and committed the film-makers become, the more implicated in the reproduction of that ideology, the more they will be unable to perceive their position within it.[19]

Dunford asserts that far from negating or transcending the mainstream, the avant-garde locked itself into an antithetical dependency on the mainstream which obscured its actual ideological function; the conflict between the mainstream and the avant-garde is no more than a disagreement between bourgeois experts. Moreover, the anti-illusionism of the avant-garde is no more free from ideology than the illusionism of the mainstream; both serve to hide the social, historical and material conditions of their production. Finally, Dunford insists that experimental film is still a potentially radical project but that this potential will never be realised in art.

Dunford's renunciation is convincing within the bounds of its context. However, his revision still falls within the broad assumptions of film/cultural theory: he still believes that demystification should be the primary technique for a radical film practice and he still conceives the popular as a mainstream of bourgeois hegemony. To gain a complete historical overview of Gidal's theory of Structural/Materialist film it is necessary to revise Dunford's renunciation in the context of the historical conflict between art and the popular.

The structural shift at the LFMC was the aggregate of a cluster of determining factors which included a change in membership and ideology towards art, artists and art students, the increasing access and ownership of artisanal production equipment and an aesthetic minimalism reinforced by relative poverty and isolation in an autonomous institute. The opposition to popular cinema was not based on analysis or engagement; the avant-garde simply assumed that the mainstream was repressive.[20] Gidal's anti-illusionism was not conceived against the truly popular diversity of the marvellous narrative of attractions, it was conceived against an untheorised and mostly imaginary mainstream cinema of bourgeois Naturalism. Reinforcing their hostility to the mainstream, the S/M avant-garde had no training, experience or interest in the basic techniques of popular cinema: narrative construction, working with actors, continuity editing and so on. Combined, all these factors drove the LFMC filmmakers towards abstract Structuralism. Nevertheless, it must also be understood that within the historical trajectory of the autonomisation and nationalisation of British art, and within that sector of this process which is the development of a film art, Gidal's theory of Structural/Materialist film is the definitive theorisation for the modernist autonomisation of the content of film. S/M eliminates all trace of the vulgar popular from film and renders its meaning superfluous. Far from being an antidote to bourgeois hegemony, S/M is the method that would finally sedate and gentrify cinema. The idea that working-class audiences or even non-avant-garde filmmakers would be demystified by Structural/Materialist film is clearly absurd. After the populism of the Underground, the shift to structural film in both Europe and America effectively reduced the audience for experimental film to an institutional bourgeois elite. Moreover, the shift to the aesthetics of art reinforced by the devout and ascetic dogma of Structuralism effectively purged the convivial and interactive popular from the auditorium. In the cool detached unfolding of Structural/Materialist film the elite audience experienced the dialectic of their own perception, the distance from themselves to the work of art: aura.

Gidal's films over the next 28 years more or less succeeded to materialise his increasingly mystic theories. Against the spectacular illusion of the mainstream and the seductive pleasure of entertainment he produced a series of films funded by the Arts Council that must be amongst the most radically tedious work ever produced.[21]

As the 1970s progressed the structuralist aesthetic at the LFMC was gradually fragmented and the avant-garde began to develop new genres and projects; the Landscape films of the late 1970s, feminist initiatives, the New Romanticism and New Pluralism of the 1980s, video art, digital art and so on. Moreover, as the avant-garde established new agencies and expanded into the national network of academic institutions so there was also a relative decentralisation of the avant-garde project from London. Nevertheless, the fundamental aestheticisation and institutionalisation of the avant-garde had been effected through the theory and practice of Structural/Materialism and this conceptual substructure was incorporated and maintained by Gidal, Le Grice and their collaborators from their respective academic bases: Gidal at the RCA and Le Grice at Central Saint Martin's and so on.[22] This institutional hegemony was reinforced by the development of the vertical monopoly of the independent (state-funded) sector. Consequently, the successive movements and projects that emerged after the 1970s may have diverged from the avant-garde structuralist aesthetic or even subverted the aesthetic, but this subversion always remained an Oedipal bid for power within the avant-garde and never challenged the aesthetic legitimacy of film and video art or the supposed autonomy of the independent sector. To actually develop work which subverted art and the state control of the independent sector would mean to deny and exclude yourself from the vertical monopoly of the independent sector and to work underground. In this way, film and video art eventually developed an elegant and highly effective strategy to defend its legitimacy.

PETER WOLLEN

Peter Wollen emerged as the pre-eminent auteur structuralist of the late 1960s and early 1970s. He was educated at Oxford and subsequently wrote for *New Left Review*, worked in the Education Department of the BFI and was a key contributor to the relaunched journal *Screen* in 1969. That same year the BFI published his seminal book *Signs and Meaning in the Cinema*. Over the next thirty years he became one of the leading film theorists and academics in both Britain and America. But Wollen was not only a theorist, he was also a pivotal filmmaker in the independent movement. Working in the 1970s and early 1980s with his wife, and fellow ex-Oxford theorist, Laura Mulvey, Wollen also co-wrote and directed a controversial series of state-funded, feature-length films.[23]

Of the three articles which appeared in *Studio International* in 1975, Peter Wollen's 'The Two Avant-Gardes' is the text that has become the most established, respected and readily available – in fact it has become perhaps the most ubiquitous and influential text in the history of Anglo-American experimental film and video. Its trajectory winds through the work of the leading theorists of the avant-garde over three decades. It has been interpreted by Deke Dusinberre, Anne Cottringer, Laura Mulvey, Philip Drummond, Sylvia Harvey, Paul Willemen, J. Hoberman, Anne Friedberg and Juan A. Suárez amongst others.[24] It has provided the basis for debate in numerous journals and it has appeared in many critical anthologies and bibliographies.[25] And it is still used as a key document in art schools, colleges, universities and academic institutions where film and video is studied.[26]

The attraction of Wollen's article as an educational tool is that (i) it can be photocopied on five easily-assembled A4 pages; (ii) its brevity makes it easy to read, explain and discuss in a class; (iii) it is both a condensed history, a typology and a theoretical model; it is a beginner's guide and a means to generate discussion. For many film and media students 'The Two Avant-Gardes' may be the only theoretical work on the avant-garde they ever read or at least the only work they remember. Although it was written during the heroic phase of the avant-garde/independent sector (1971–1980), and in spite of shifts in theory and practice, Wollen's article is still widely believed to be relevant.[27] A. L. Rees in his *History of Experimental Film and Video* refers to the article and claims that 'the dilemmas Wollen adduces still remain, adapted to new social pressures'.[28]

In 'The Two Avant-Gardes' Wollen employs concepts and terms from structural linguistics and Althusserian Marxism to construct a binary dialectic between two European avant-gardes; first the Co-op movement (the LFMC and related groups in Austria, Holland and Germany), and second, the work of continental directors exemplified by Jean Luc-Godard and Jean-Marie Straub and Danièle Huillet, what can be termed the Straub/Godard avant-garde.[29] At the extreme, each faction would exclude the other from theoretical and radical legitimacy: they each claim to be the real vanguard. America is effectively relegated from the dialectic since, because although it is the hub of the Co-op movement, it has no equivalent to the Straub/Godard avant-garde.

Next, Wollen compares the split in the 1975 avant-garde with a split in the European avant-garde of the 1920s; between the movement that sought to extend the scope of painting into cinema (the French avant-garde, Eggeling, Richter, Man Ray and so on) and the Soviet avant-garde (Eisenstein, Dovzhenko and Vertov), which developed from theatre and poetry. Wollen aligns the painters' group with the Co-op movement, and the Soviet avant-garde with the Straub/Godard faction. However, by the end of the article this comparison has become a single historic division of two separate developing traditions: it is the split of the 1920s which caused the split in 1975. The origin of the split can be located at the modernist breakthrough in painting, the advent of Cubism, which had a radical effect on all the arts.

> The innovations of Picasso and Braque were seen as having an implication beyond the history of painting itself. They were intuitively felt, I think, very early on, to represent a critical semiotic shift, a changed concept and practice of sign and signification, which we now can see to have been the opening-up of a space, a disjunction between signifier and signified and a change of emphasis from the problem of signified and reference, the classic problem of realism, to that of signifier and signified within the sign itself. When we look at the development of painting after the cubist breakthrough, however, we see a constant trend towards an apparently even more radical development: the suppression of the signified altogether, an art of pure signifiers detached from meaning as much as reference…[30]

The abstract trend of the suppression of the signified in painting produced the avant-garde tradition that culminated in the Co-op movement,[31] whilst the earlier disjunction between signifier and signified produced the Straub/Godard avant-garde by way of literature and theatre. The key figure in the Straub/Godard avant-garde is Godard:

> In a sense, Godard's work goes back to the original breaking point at which the modern avant-garde began – neither realist or expressionist, on the one hand, nor abstractionist, on the other.[32]

Whilst Wollen's model is provisional and paradoxical, and whilst he allows for exceptions to the binary classification, the oppositions and membership of the groups can be systematically laid out:

The Co-op avant-garde		Straub/Godard avant-garde
FORM	VS.	CONTENT
painters		dramatists/writers
sound		poetry
pure signifiers		the signified
abstraction		realist
non-narrative		narrative

anti-illusionist	naturalist
film as material	cinema as expression
self-reflexive	intertextual
visual	verbal
filmmakers	directors
artisanal	commercial
reconciled to minority	uneasy about minority
audience	audience/aimed at mass audience
implicitly political	consciously political/ political subject matter

1920s filmmakers

Leger-Murphy	
Picabia-Clair	
Eggeling	
Richter	Eisenstein
Man Ray	Dovzhenko
Moholy-Nagy	Vertov
Van Doesburg	
Lizitzky	
Duchamp	

1975 filmmakers

The Co-op movement, including:	Godard
Malcolm Le Grice	Straub and Huillet
Peter Gidal	Hanoun
Steven Dwoskin	Jancso
Kurt Kren	Godard and Gorin
Annabel Nicolson	Dziga Vertov Group
Birgit Hein	

But Wollen's text is not a simple binary dialectic: it is, on close analysis, the invocation of two separate historical traditions that have developed different practices in different historical phases but always within a dialectic determined by the modernist (semiotic) shift of Cubism. It is a teleological history, it is an avant-garde history. And the assumption of ascendant progress can be discerned in certain key phrases used in the article. The model is fixed with the opening line: 'Film history has developed unevenly…'[33] From this it must be assumed that film history could, or rather should, develop evenly. What would an even film history be like? At the end of the article Wollen tentatively suggests:

…in a way, the cinema offers more opportunities than any other art – the cross fertilisation which was so striking a feature of those early decades, the reciprocal interlocking and input between painting, writing, music, theatre ... could take place within the field of cinema itself. This is not a plea for a great harmony, a synaesthetic *gesamtkunstwerk* in the Wagnerian sense. But cinema, because it is a multiple system, could develop and elaborate the semiotic shifts which marked the origins of the avant-garde in a uniquely complex way, a dialectical montage within and between a complex of codes. At least writing now as a film-maker, that is the fantasy I like to entertain.[34]

Despite his doubts and protestations to the contrary, the convergence of the two avant-gardes is exactly what Wollen desires and believes is necessary. This is the synthesis of the dialectic, a single modernist avant-garde which would combine the formal experiments (painting) of the Co-op movement with the semiotic strategies and political radicalism (literature/drama) of the Straub/Godard avant-garde. This would be the evening of film history as the two parallel avant-gardes meet at the cusp of the present to form a dialectical cutting edge. Wollen's language of ascendant progress suggests that this convergence is possible and even immanent, but it has been delayed:

> During the first decade of this century, when the historic avant-garde embarked on its own path ... the cinema was still in its infancy, scarcely out of the fairground and the nickelodeon, certainly not yet the Seventh Art. For this reason – and for others, including economic reasons – the avant-garde made itself felt late in the cinema and it is still very marginal, in comparison with painting or music or even writing.[35]

But this lateness and the vague 'economic reasons' are not the principal causes for the marginality of the avant-garde. It is implicit in Wollen's model that the progress of the avant-garde has been blocked by the historical split, the distinct traditions are polarised around mutually exclusive practices and ideologies. The Co-op movement has become increasingly entrenched in positions of extreme, essential and pure visuality, abstraction and anti–illusionism, whilst the Straub/Godard avant-garde has lost the radical collective and experimental dynamism of May 1968. The dialectic of the two avant-gardes condemns both to isolation; only a synthesis can revitalise the avant-garde project. Writing in 1975 Wollen believed there was going to be a synthesis, and as a filmmaker and a radical theorist his work could help bring this about.[36]

Wollen's dialectic is informed by debates surrounding the mutual hostility between two factions of the avant-garde and his purpose is to bring coherence to this conflict and to reconcile these factions in theory and practice. But his brief exposition does not reveal the political and industrial context of the divided avant-garde. Moreover, notwithstanding the international scope of Wollen's model, its real significance must be understood in the context of the development of British independent cinema.

The post-war dispute concerning the true path of the avant-garde can be traced back to a critical interchange in the mid-1950s between Hans Richter in *Film Culture* (New York) and André Bazin in *Cahiers du cinéma* (Paris): Richter advocated non-representational film art and Bazin proposed a new avant-garde working within the popular cinema industry.[37] The advent of the French New Wave, the New American Cinema and Underground Cinema problematised and suspended these contesting theoretical claims. However, after the utopian passion of May 1968 the dispute was again polarised into a division between the Marxist adherents of *Cahiers du cinéma, Cinethique* and the agit-prop collectives, and the theorists and filmmakers of the nascent structural avant-garde. In Britain a crucial and exemplary confrontation between the factions was the publication of the first *Afterimage* special issue on the avant-garde in 1970.[38] The issue opens with a scathing editorial by Peter Sainsbury in which he accuses the American Underground of bourgeois mysticism and potential fascism. This invective is later followed by a more measured, but equally caustic article, 'Which Avant-Garde' by Graeme Farnell, that indicts not only the American Underground, but also Gidal and the British movement, as hopelessly bourgeois, compromised and reactionary. After a series of quotes from the Dziga Vertov Group, *Cinethique* and allied radicals, Farnell invokes the creation of a new scientific Marxist-Leninist dialectical materialist avant-garde.[39] Significantly, it is this same issue of *Afterimage* that decisively drops the term and the model of Underground Cinema and adopts the logic of the avant-garde; by which I mean to suggest that this contest for the vanguard of radical art necessitated and reinforced the shift to the avant-garde. Farnell's article can in part be read as a response to Gidal's early structural theorisations and attacks on Godard in *Cinemantics* that same year,[40] whilst Gidal's eventual theorisation of S/M film can be read as a refutation of the *Afterimage* critique of 1970. Both the S/M avant-garde and the disciples of Godard claimed to be developing the true Marxist dialectical materialist cinema.

In 1975 the British Straub/Godard tendency effectively consisted of a coalition of radical independent film theorists, filmmakers and activists which included the core faction of the IFA, Wollen, Mulvey and other *Screen* theorists, the key agit-prop collectives and the Other Cinema distribution group. This coalition can be broadly identified as the Counter-Cinema tendency. In institutional and industrial terms the historical context of Wollen's conceptual split was the development of two competing industrial sectors within the independent movement. The LFMC (Co-op movement) was developing a power base at the Arts Council and an infrastructure within art education. Meanwhile, the filmmakers and theorists of the Counter-Cinema tendency were developing an institutional base at the BFI which was both practical and theoretical: Peter Sainsbury had been appointed head of BFI production, and *Screen* and the BFI Education Department effectively functioned as the demystifying theoretical wing of Counter-Cinema.

Wollen's attempt to reconcile the conflicting factions of the avant-garde is essentially theoretical; it is the substitution of a complex social, industrial and political separation with a semiotic and textual separation – an attempt to transpose practice into theory. The power and charm of 'The Two Avant-Gardes' is its analogous correspondence to its actual historical context, its utopian promise of synthesis and the determining effect it subsequently had on the culture it theorised. Certainly Wollen identified two avant-garde traditions, but they were not determined by an epic semiotic shift. In the context of the British independent cinema, the destiny of the LFMC avant-garde was to create an autonomous film art, whilst the destiny of the independent Counter-Cinema was to aestheticise popular cinema. This is to say that both factions served the Seventh Art: bourgeois cinema. Whereas Wollen's argument seems to be grounded in the formal criteria of experimental film, his dialectic actually depends upon the exclusion of not only all popular forms, but all anti-art forms, notably Underground cinema, Dada and Surrealist film, the popular experiments of Soviet film and pre-1968 Godard.[41] Of course this exclusion can be rationalised and maintained through the logic of the avant-garde; Wollen understands that only art can be avant-garde. He is also right in identifying a modernist shift in Cubism, but he fails to recognise the decisive agency of the conflict between art and popular culture in the modernist shift. The discoveries of Cubism were not scientific explorations into the space between the signs, they were cultural strategies developed at the border of the popular. The development of avant-garde cinema was not the late flowering of a retarded aesthetic, it was essentially a bourgeois strategy to legitimise, gentrify, sedate and appropriate a threat to the hierarchy of art.

The repressive agency of Wollen's model is exclusion. By invoking two apparently antithetical practices and the possibility of a utopian synthesis, his brief article seems to open up a critical space for cultural debate, experimentation and hybridisation. But in fact the exclusivity of Wollen's dialectic effectively precluded the consideration of alternate models of experimental film: the Underground, the popular and the amateur. Moreover, as the independent sector developed into the 1970s the model of 'The Two Avant-Gardes' became a legitimising discourse for key agencies of the independent sector, most significantly it was the keynote document for the Edinburgh Film Festival in 1976; it initiated a long-running debate in *Afterimage* and crucially it was integrated into the ideological constitution of the BFI.

Wollen's avant-garde project was not only conceptual: in collaboration with Laura Mulvey he also attempted to synthesise the divided avant-garde in Counter-Cinema practice. The two films which exemplify and document this endeavour are *Pentheselia* (1974) and *Riddles of the Sphinx* (1976). Both films are essentially attempts to politicise the aesthetic; to structure experimental formal techniques with theory: radical feminism, Marxism, semiotics and Lacanian psychoanalysis.[42] Wollen and Mulvey believed that theory had to be central to Counter-Cinema, that demystification without theory would be simply reactionary. The Counter-Cinema they offered was neither Godard nor Le Grice, nor was it the epic synthesis of both. Against the hegemonic pleasure of popular mainstream cinema, Wollen and Mulvey constructed a theoretical cinema: apart from sporadic sequences of fragmented and mostly tedious audio/visual experiment, the overall effect of both films is of an illustrated lecture on film theory and Greek mythology delivered direct to camera, by emotionless and classically educated bourgeois academics. Whilst Gidal and the Structural Materialists developed a theory to legitimise their practice, Wollen and Mulvey literally made their theory into a practice; they actually became the authors of cinematic texts.

In 1984 Paul Willemen revised Wollen's model in his influential essay 'An Avant-Garde for the '80s', which appeared in the journal of new cinema *Framework*. The editor at this time was Don Ranvaud, the associate editors were Willemen, Wollen and Mulvey. Willemen's revision was that the binary model still worked except that it misidentified the two traditions. Drawing on the work of Brecht, Benjamin and Andreas Huyssen, Willemen reformulated the binary division into that most avant-garde of oppositions, the revolutionary artist vs. the reactionary artist; in Willemen's model the Straub/Godard tradition is the radical socialist avant-garde and the Co-op movement is actually reactionary bourgeois Modernism.[43] As key instances of the new radical avant-garde Willemen cites two contemporary productions from the BFI.[44]

In rationalising this desperate repair Willemen comes close to acknowledging the instability in his argument:

> In the light of the historical emergence of Modernism, the split between Modernism and the avant-garde cannot be mapped simply onto the bourgeois/working class distinction. Both artistic practices are firmly middle class, as all professional art practices are. As far as class positions are concerned, artists must be seen as middle-class intellectuals, and the divergence between avant-garde and Modernism as opposing tendencies within the middle-class intelligentsia, each tendency engaging in politics for social change. One, as its name indicates, is a politics of modernisation, i.e. a bringing up to date of values and procedures in order to establish, maintain or preserve a bourgeois hegemony. The other is a politics of negation and transformation aligned with a process of change in a socialist direction, i.e. transformation instead of modernisation.[45]

Of course, what Willemen does not acknowledge is that since the rage of Dada, to negate and transform art is also to modernise art. The dead end finally reached in the mid-1980s by both the debate and the project of 'The Two Avant-Gardes', can be gauged by the fact that Willemen republished his revision virtually intact ten years later in his book *Looks and Frictions* (1994) under the title 'An Avant-Garde for the 1990s'.[46]

Chapter 13

THE UNDERGROUND CINEMA RESURGENCE: FROM THE NEW YORK CINEMA OF TRANSGRESSION TO THE NEW LONDON UNDERGROUND 1991–2006

The dynamism and popularity of the inaugural Underground Cinema movement was due first to its status as an integrated element of the 1960s counter-culture and second to its radical initiative in popularising experimental film culture. As the 1970s progressed, the counter-culture in Europe and America lost its radical momentum whilst the avant-garde effectively institutionalised itself as the legitimate, dominant form of experimental film (art). However, this was not the end of either the counter-culture, or Underground Cinema. In the face of a reactionary political backlash, comprehensive bourgeois appropriation, commodification, disenchantment and compromise, the counter-culture abandoned the naïve optimism of the 'hippie love generation' and traced a darker subterranean course which retrenched counter-cultural opposition as an ironic celebration of disillusion and negation: punk rock. Although punk rock was vitalised by a new generation of disaffected youth, it was also the first rock subculture which had an intellectual grasp of its own historical context, and which used this consciousness to mythologise and sensationalise itself; punk rock was characteristically fumiste. Further, the formation of punk rock in the late 1970s had direct links to the most radical factions of the 1960s counter-culture through key agents and influences. Notable amongst these was Malcolm McLaren, who had been involved with the English Situationist group King Mob, and the influence of the MC5 rock band who had worked with the New York counter-cultural anarchist affinity group the Motherfuckers.

Most significantly, the punk rock movement's core radical strategy was to eschew the realm of activity deemed political by the bourgeois state and to instead politicise culture. Learning from the vulnerabilities of the 1960s counter-culture, punk rock specifically valorised the radical democratic and egalitarian aspects of popular culture: amateurism, conviviality, improvisation, illegitimacy, profanity, transgression and collectivity. Beyond music, punk rock generated an eclectic and comprehensive recuperation of popular culture, anti-art, bohemianism, beat and the counter-culture. This process was incorporated into a further series of interlinked post-punk rock subcultures that emerged in the early 1980s, most notably the fan culture surrounding cult and trash cinema and the prodigious expansion of fanzines and DIY publishing. Although there were sporadic and fragmented instances of a British punk rock cinema, the decisive and conscious renewal of (punk rock) Underground Cinema developed in New York around the end of the 1970s.[1]

Despite the institutionalisation of the avant-garde in the early 1970s, the New York Underground persisted through the activities of a cluster of influential filmmakers including Jack Smith, John Waters and Mike and George Kuchar. The advent of punk rock in the late 1970s opened up both a critical alternative to the structuralist avant-garde aesthetic and a renewed allegiance between rock subculture and experimental film. Moreover, a crucial technological and industrial catalyst for the punk rock Underground was the accelerating availability of cheap, efficient and automatic Super 8 equipment, and the introduction of integrated sync-sound Super 8 in 1974; the amateur, illegitimate status of Super 8, and the immediacy and degradation of the home movie image, provided a dynamic visual correlative to punk rock music.

The first cycle of the New York Underground renewal formed around the No Wave punk rock scene of the Lower East Side, around bands that played at CBGBs, the Mudd Club and Max's Kansas City: Richard Hell, Teenage Jesus and the Jerks, the Lounge Lizards, DNA, the Contortions, Mars and others. The key filmmakers were Vivienne Dick, Amos Poe, Eric Mitchell, James Nares, Becky Johnston and Beth and Scott B.[2] Against the sedate minimalism and modernism of the avant-garde, the No Wave makers produced no-budget Super 8 documentaries and ironic spectacles which parodied and celebrated 1960s Underground cinema, *film noir*, European art cinema and trash exploitation movies. The subjects of these films were mostly musicians and activists from the No Wave scene and many of the films were premiered at punk rock clubs; Beth and Scott B.'s *The Offenders* (1979) was first screened as a serial, with weekly segments shown between bands at Max's Kansas City.[3] Nevertheless, the No Wave eventually sought its own venue, and in the winter of 1979 the group set up the New Cinema in a rented storefront on St. Marks Place, where they began regular screenings advertised by neighbourhood flyposting. However, the financial burden of running a permanent Underground venue closed the New Cinema after only a few months, and after this setback the group gradually fragmented into more established commercial and artistic projects.

Whilst the No Wave group operated outside the established avant-garde institutions, they did not deliberately develop this alternativity as an organised subversion of legitimate experimental film culture. However, around the early 1980s, a second Underground wave developed from the Lower East Side punk rock scene which not only shunned the venues and institutions of art, but which launched a subversive campaign against the avant-garde and academic film theory. The Cinema of Transgression movement formed around the activities of a group of young filmmakers and performers who shared and expanded the Lower East Side club scene initiated by the No Wave group. The leading filmmakers included Nick Zedd, Richard Kern, Lydia Lunch, Tommy Turner, Cassandra Stark, Ela Troyano and Tessa Hughes-Freeland. Like the No Wave group, the Cinema of Transgression formed strategic links with the punk rock music scene but followed that culture into the wilder post-punk rock of Sonic Youth, Foetus, Swans, Killdozer and G. G. Allin and so on. Following the post-punk rock trajectory, the filmmakers of the group deliberately and ironically sought to outrage and incite their audiences by enacting spectacles of lurid violence, sex, drug use, blasphemy, obscenity and perversion.

Figure 20: Nick Zedd in his film *Police State,* 1987

Crucially, the movement developed across the axis of film and performance: they played in bands, they staged performances and plays, they made Super 8 films, they projected multiple expanded cinema work, and they hybridised all these modes, live and in film. The live performances were characterised by improvisation and audience participation, which was often involuntary and messy: Kern was infamous for attacking audience members and simulating injuries with fake blood.

The coordinating activist and polemicist of the Cinema of Transgression was Nick Zedd, who first started making and performing in punk rock clubs in the late 1970s. However, by the mid-1980s he had become totally frustrated by the exclusion of transgressive work from the venues and publications of the legitimate experimental film culture and so he initiated a deliberate strategy to promote and mythologise transgression as a coherent movement.[4] In 1984 he started publishing the fanzine *Underground Film Bulletin* and in issue four he launched the manifesto of the Cinema of Transgression, written under the alias Orion Jeriko:

> We who have violated the laws, commands and duties of the avant-garde; i.e.,
> to bore, tranquillise and obfuscate through a fluke process dictated by practi-
> cal convenience, stand guilty as charged. We openly renounce and reject the
> entrenched academic snobbery which erected a monument to laziness known
> as Structuralism and proceeded to lock out those filmmakers who possessed

the vision to see through this charade. We refuse to take their easy approach to cinematic creativity; an approach which ruined the underground of the 1960s when the scourge of the film school took over. Legitimising every mindless manifestation of sloppy movie-making undertaken by a generation of misled film students emulating the failures of profoundly undeserving non-talents like Brakhage, Snow, Frampton, Gehr, Breer, and so forth; the dreary media arts centres and geriatric cinema critics have totally ignored the exhilarating accomplishments of … a new generation of filmmakers daring to rip out of the stifling straight jackets of film theory in a direct attack on every value system known to man. We propose that all film schools be blown up and all boring films never be made again. We propose that a sense of humour is an essential element discarded by the doddering academics and further, that any film that doesn't shock isn't worth looking at.[5]

At their best the Cinema of Transgression movement produced visceral and compulsive films which celebrated the dangerous borderland of grotesque comedy, sexual liberation and vertiginous horror; at their worst they were incompetent adolescent pretension; often they were an uncanny combination of both extremes. In fact, despite their street outlaw stance, most of the movement's filmmakers had academic training: Nick Zedd had dropped out of art school, Kern studied philosophy and art at the University of North Carolina, Tessa Hughes-Freeland was taking a Masters Program in Cinema Studies. But it was this ambivalent disillusion and interaction with the academy that fuelled their strategy; they sought an alternative to both sedate commercial cinema and the avant-garde. The overriding significance of the group was that they promulgated and rejuvenated the Underground as a radical pop culture and consequently reactivated the potential for a national Underground network in the 1990s.

Three crucial interlinked factors in the development and expansion of the new American Underground movement were video distribution, fanzines and the development of Underground festivals. The New York Film Festival Downtown was organised by Tessa Hughes-Freeland and Ela Troyano, and ran annually from 1984 to 1990. Screenings at the Downtown festival were convivial hybrids of film and video, performance, expanded cinema and music, compered by local celebrity MCs. The festival proved a dynamic showcase for both the established Underground movement and new makers such as John Moritsugu, Todd Haynes and Kembra Pfahler. Parallel to the festival Nick Zedd and others began to develop mail order video distribution for Underground film and promote this initiative through the growing cluster of fanzines which combined a fascination for cult/trash popular film with coverage of the Underground. (The most influential and widely distributed of these was *Film Threat*, founded by Chris Gore in 1985.) Although the Downtown festival lapsed in 1990 the American Underground scene continued to develop through the 1990s and gradually across the nation a network of Micro-Cinema screening clubs emerged. As the Internet became widely available Underground/Micro-Cinema websites proliferated and a potential national distribution and exhibition network began to develop. In 1993 the Chicago Underground Film Festival was founded, followed by the New York Underground Film festival in 1994 and Underground festivals in Seattle, Baltimore, Boston, Las Vegas, San Francisco and Washington DC. Festivals were also founded in Canada which had developed its own punk rock Underground scene in the late 1980s, the most celebrated maker being Bruce LaBruce.

Although New York was a key influence and an industrial centre, the American Underground resurgence should be understood as a resurfacing rather than a spontaneous generation; many of the clubs and filmmakers that emerged in the early 1990s had actually developed in relative seclusion. The determining factors are more complex, but the priority must be given to punk rock DIY culture, accelerating access to cheap film and video equipment and increasing opposition to the avant-garde. Meanwhile, parallel to the New York Underground resurgence a similar culture was emerging in London, but whilst the New York experimental film scene had never completely lost its Underground potential, London had become the dead heart of the independent sector.

The institutionalisation of the avant-garde, and the development of the independent sector, effectively annexed and suppressed the anarchic potential of the British Underground. But this repression was not total, for the fragmented Underground still surfaced sporadically, almost unconscious of its own tradition. In the late 1970s there was a brief punk rock film movement and in the 1980s there was the community video movement (Sheffield Video Workshop, Community Video Workshop Cardiff and so on), the Super 8 New Romantics (Ceryth Wynn Evans, John Maybury), the scratch video makers (George Barber, Gorilla Tapes) and the DIY activism of the Build Hollywood group. But the eventual resurgence of the London Underground cinema in the early 1990s can be traced to the point where the counter-culture resurfaced and the last vestiges of alternativity were dropped by the independent sector.

Whilst the anti-politics of British punk rock was an effective strategy against the logic of bourgeois annexation, it also tended to frustrate the formation of organised counter-cultural protest and projects. Nevertheless there were a series of radical currents which intertwined into the late 1980s: the radical feminist peace movement, the free festival/traveller subculture, the urban squatters network, the anarcho-populist Class War group, the fanzine/mailart network and the post-Situationist provocations of groups such as Karen Eliot and *Smile* magazine. The eventual coalition of these currents was activated by the campaign against the poll tax in the late 1980s which culminated in the exultant riot of 1990. However, this carnival of dissent was soon eclipsed by the inevitable build up to the first Gulf War.

Parallel to these developments, no-budget/amateur filmmaking was transformed by a rapid expansion in home video technology, availability and ownership. This had three key effects: first, cheap user-friendly video camcorders fostered a wave of amateur activity, home-made and screened on domestic televisions; second, as thousands of households bought into video they disposed of their amateur cine equipment which became available at incredibly low prices at the car boot sales which swept the country from the late 1980s; third, with the advent of Home Cinema video systems manufacturers brought the first cheap domestic video projectors onto the market, making video cinema screening a possibility for the no-budget maker. The significance of the no-budget economy for the new Underground should not be underestimated. Many of the activists and filmmakers involved were part of a London bohemian subculture which subsists on welfare, part-time work, fraud and general dodginess, a sort of suburban hunter-gatherer culture which has totally abandoned the official *brand new* consumer economy and exists on the cast-off commodities from car boot sales, jumble sales, skips and market stalls. Moreover, some of the Underground filmmakers were so socially dysfunctional that they effectively disbarred themselves from the career structures of the professional media industry. This creates an interesting paradox, for whilst the media establishment perceives the postmodernist cutting edge to be at the frontiers of digital technology, the new Underground, which is certainly the most adept cultural producer of radical montage, collage, detournment, intertextuality and self-referentiality, often still works with the outmoded detritus of the industrial age.

Increased access to projection technology was also a crucial factor in the development of London rave culture in the late 1980s. The advent of techno, Ecstasy, mass illegal raves and psychedelic retro styling created a new demand for club visuals. Filmmakers collaborated with promoters, dance clubs and DJs to produce spectacular multiple projections using film, 35 mm slides and ultimately video projection. By the early 1990s a group of video jockeys (VJs) had emerged: armed with cheap video projectors and vision mixers they could mix moving images live to music. A complementary development was the 'chill out room' where the frazzled intoxicated dancers could relax for a while and watch cool visuals.

The final factor in the renovation of the Underground was the emergence of a British trash/Underground film fanzine subculture. A critical influence on this subculture was the import of American fanzines, notably *Film Threat* and the 'Incredibly Strange Films' issue of *(Re)search*. Leading British imprints and fanzines that emerged in the early 1990s were Creation Books, Headpress, *Samhain* and *Rapid Eye*. Allied to the fanzines was the development of a nascent British video distribution network, significantly from Visionary Communications (formerly Jettisoundz) and Ikon which both primarily distributed post-punk rock music videos but also Underground film including work by Anger and Burroughs/Balch. Together these diverse elements formed the context for the return of the London Underground Cinema.

THE EXPLODING CINEMA

About nine o'clock you find the doorway which leads to a dirty alley which then opens on to a shabby courtyard that smells of burnt plastic, crushed nettles and piss.

There is a hand-drawn arrow scrawled on the dusty door of the high dark factory opposite. Through the door you climb a musty staircase, six flights to another door, where there waits a big broken television converted into an illuminated sign. Through the last door and you emerge onto a vast whitewashed roof high above the lights of Peckham, South London. At a makeshift table you pay £4, your hand is ink-stamped with a baby skull and you are given a programme. Next you wander out under the stars onto the wide open roof. Around the parapet ghostly banners flutter, people alone or in clusters are talking, smoking, drinking beer or peering over the edge down to the ivy and broken glass far below. On a concrete tower at the far end of the roof a rank of spectral blue video monitors are showing *Godzilla versus Mothra* and the *Bitter Tea of General Yen*. You make for the tower. As you walk, lucid elongated projections flicker and stretch beneath your feet. You enter the sudden darkness of the tower and then ascend onto another broader rooftop where a vast cinema screen has been set up. Around you on the walls projections glow against the dark violet sky ... a giant dog with a green concertina body ... a grainy monochrome car crash looped endlessly ... a vast magnification of a pink-fringed plankton. Music

Figure 21: An *Exploding Cinema* poster

is playing, some kind of lounge moog giving way to digital hardcore. The audience gathers on the makeshift benches and the MC starts the show. This is the EXPLODING CINEMA, eight in the evening until two in the morning, twenty no-budget underground films and videos, performances and live music.

On the screen is the slogan:

NO STARS NO FUNDING NO TASTE

In February 1991 London was snowbound while the Gulf War raged. At the height of the air strikes a desperate séance was held at the Riverside Studios in the Hammersmith slush, and this was called the BP EXPO, a festival of British and International Student Film and Video. Amongst those linking hands were artists, independent filmmakers and delegates from the BFI, the Arts Council and Greater London Arts (replaced by the LFVDA in 1992). They were trying to raise the spirit of independence. Debate was minimal; the fact that the event was sponsored by a multinational oil company during an oil war caused only slight ironic embarrassment.

Meanwhile, in Camden, the LFMC was locked into an endless series of bitter feuds, schisms and scandals, mostly concerning money, power and the possibility of a move to new premises (The Lux Centre); its screenings were sparse and often deserted. Actually, the social ambience at the LFMC had been tense and inhospitable since the mid-1980s, and even if not by design, this tended to alienate all but the most assertive and compatible candidates.

What remained of the avant-garde and the independent film and video sector had become a closed circuit of state agencies, desperately underfunded workshops and an elite circle of established artists and production companies locked into mutual self-legitimisation. Unfunded experimental filmmakers were effectively excluded from all the established routes to distribution and exhibition, and those who did not desist were forced to spend their time and energy competing against each other for funding from agencies who had become so disengaged from economic and public accountability that they were both the critics and the audience of their own product. By creating a vertical state monopoly the independent sector had at last become truly autonomous. What got funded was good, what was good got funded and what did not get funded remained invisible.

The only glimmer of hope against this incestuous network was a cluster of sporadic and fragmented Underground activities around South London, notably the work of the filmmakers at Ken McDonald's Reel Love Super 8 screenings, David Leister's fabulous Kino Club, the Strand Super 8 Workshop in Brixton and Lepke B.'s incredible low-fi club visuals. Ken Mcdonald had run a screening club on the New York Underground scene of the early 1980s. The Kino Club was a one-man cinema cabaret held mostly in the back rooms of pubs which featured David Leister's films, weird found footage, competitions and musicians playing live improvised film soundtracks.

That summer a group called Pullit squatted in a derelict suntan oil factory on Effra Road in Brixton. This was the Cooltan and it soon became an Underground cultural centre housing a gallery, theatre, performance space, rave venue, café and office for the Brixton Green Party. At the very back of the ground floor, a cinema was built into what was once a cold storage room with a sliding steel door. On the door in red wooden letters was spelt out 'The Regal'. Around June, McDonald, filmmaker and impresario, moved his Reel Love show to the Regal. Reel Love was a regular open screening of Super 8 films punctuated by technical breakdowns and drinking to excess. Around the same time the Australian filmmaker Stephen Houston began to organise weekly open meetings of people interested in getting involved with film and video at the Cooltan. Out of this activity a group of no-budget film- and video-makers emerged with the idea of forming a South London-based media collective and there the weekly meetings developed into open screenings where anyone and everyone could show their work. Slowly a hardcore membership developed which included Stephen Houston, Kathy Gibbs, Jenny Marr, Danny Holman, Laura Hudson, Suzanne Currid, Jennet Thomas, Anthony Kopiecki, Lorelei Hawkins, Lepke B., William Thomas and myself.

From the very beginning we decided to be totally open and democratic: anyone could show their work, anyone could join the group, all you had to do was come to a meeting and get involved. We drew up a loose constitution: the group was to be non-profit-making, all work would be voluntary, no wages would be paid, all the money we made would be used to run our screenings and to buy equipment to be collectively owned. I drafted the constitution and based it on the radical democratic model of the LFMC, but I tried to incorporate safeguards against the careerist manipulations, factionalism and bureaucracy that dogged that particular collective.

As winter approached the Pullit group and Reel Love left the Cooltan and the organisation was taken over by a council of representatives from the various activity groups who were working at the building. The film and video group took over the Regal and we held public screenings of no-budget film and video, but it was freezing cold, damp and it stank. Even with their coats on the audience froze, so we moved the cinema to the Cooltan café and began to hold fortnightly open screenings called Cinema Café.

The Café was housed in the old factory canteen. The far wall held a sweeping wooden counter behind which lay a vast iron stove. For tables there were several giant industrial cable spools laid horizontally and the place could hold about 75 at a push. We held our bi-weekly screenings on Friday nights, showing Super 8, Standard 8 and 16mm on a screen above the counter and VHS video on a television in the opposite corner; most of the equipment was lent by members or their friends. The Café had a sound system so we borrowed a microphone and took it in turns to MC the show. We cooked and sold hot food and cheap beer. One night a projector broke down and so to fill the gap Jenny Marr sang a couple of songs. After that we introduced regular performance work, live music, live dialogue with film, shadow puppets and 35mm slide shows. In the early days most of the work and performances came from members of the group, which meant that we had to constantly produce new work, but through publicity and word of mouth non-members' work began to fill the programmes. After a few shows we gave up previewing the work and just showed whatever filmmakers wanted to screen and let the audience judge for themselves. Danny Holman had made a film about the LA Underground scene and I had researched the 1960s London Underground Film movement, but essentially we developed the shows not from historical precedent but from material necessity, process, experiment and audience interaction. Bored by the sedate and puritan format of established independent film and video screenings we began to develop techniques of combination and mutation, and to create a hybrid fusion of projection, performance and convivial interaction. We projected slides and Super 8 loops on the walls and windows of the Café, we screened home movies, splatter horror, experimental video, drama, porn, documentaries, scratch Super 8, rave visuals, kitsch melodrama, animation and found footage back to back. We introduced the filmmakers and encouraged them to debate their work with the audience, we produced a programme/fanzine for each show and we distributed leaflets and propaganda all over London. If the audience found the work 'boring' or 'bad' we encouraged them to make better work themselves; if our equipment broke down we asked the audience to help us fix it and we discovered that if you created a space where anything could happen, and if you included the audience into the action, then it did not really matter what went wrong.

As our events evolved and mutated we named ourselves the Exploding Cinema and began a cycle of venue changes, moving on whenever things got too predictable. After the eviction from Cooltan we first moved to a vegetarian café in Clapham in June 1992 and then to an immense hall at the back of an old pub in Borough in March 1993. The earliest shows had consisted of about ten films with an audience of around thirty; within a year we were showing over twenty films per show to an average audience of two hundred a night. With the money we began to make on the door we were able to buy our own projection and sound equipment and become self-sufficient without state intervention or funding of any kind.

As the collective expanded and developed a group of members/filmmakers formed whose work was regularly screened, including me, Jennet Thomas, Lepke B., Colette Rouhier, Paul Tarrago, Donal Rouane, Caroline Kennedy, Andre Stitt, Susanne Currid, Katia Rossini and Antony Kopiecki. As word spread about the screenings a hidden Underground subculture contacted us, many who had been making films in relative seclusion for years, including Arthur Lager, Andrew Coram, Rob Ryan, Victoria Kirkwood, the Lovely Movies group, Mix Up, Vito Rocco, Dick Jewel, Mark Video, Mark Conway and Alan Dein. Moreover, the DIY and convivial spirit of the Exploding Cinema meant that some filmmakers actually began to make work specifically to be screened at our shows, and some audience members began to experiment with film and video for the first time.

With only a vague knowledge of the historic precedent of the Cinema of Transgression, the Exploding Cinema constituted itself as a project against the repression of the avant-garde and the independent sector. This radicalism was both intrinsic and active. From the early years we published and distributed polemical pamphlets and flyers against the vertical monopoly of the independent sector and distributed these leaflets at our shows, and at independent screenings and events. Perhaps the most celebrated and enduring was the rant 'Fuck off avant-gardist' which I wrote around July 1992:

For how much longer must the underground tolerate your elite nepotistic enclave, your sacred art object economy, your white male liberal

Figure 22: A still from *Naked Double Bill* by the London underground filmmaker Arthur Lager.

guilt complex, your public school Masonic fraternity, your fish fetish, your shaved heads, your artist anal craft professionalism, your adolescent narcissism, your psycho linguistic gobbledygook, your cottage in Provence, your rabid careerism, your bogus radicalism, your half naked relatives, your intellectual bankruptcy, your art school tutorials, your intoxicated brown nosing, your catholic opera cult, your international bourgeois tourism, your water rituals, your meaningful silence, your state-funded cynicism, your sado-masochistic posturing, your inability to comprehend film as anything other than your archaic fine arts mysticism, your fashion victims, your fields of wheat, your church based installation worship, your desperate search for marginality, your corrupt non-industry, your contempt for anyone outside of your pathetic clique, your boring, lazy, unwatchable films, your computer video masturbation, your insatiable egomania.

It was you who consigned the underground to twenty years of drivel, we've had enough so fuck off.

Aside from the regular bi-weekly shows we began to organise special one-off shows, and one of the first of these was an event which got us national press coverage and a cult reputation.[6] In the summer of 1993 we were contacted by a group of squatters who had taken over the Lido in Brockwell Park, between Brixton and Herne Hill. The Lido was a derelict, 1950s pop-modernist municipal outdoor swimming pool surrounded by a high wall and a series of buildings, formerly offices, a café, changing rooms and showers. The squatters had been holding parties and raves and they offered us the space for an Exploding Cinema event. In turn we contacted filmmakers and performers and organised a series of meetings to plan the event. The more we planned the more ambitious the event became; finally it developed into an anarchic all-night spectacular with a cinema installed in the empty pool, a video/performance show in the offices, a chill out space in the café and installations in the showers and changing rooms. As the audience entered into the flickering celestial glow of the Lido they were welcomed with a vast banner across the poolside which read 'Welcome to hell'. We showed over seventy films and videos including feature films and performance/expanded cinema work. There was also food and drink, live music, a counter-cultural bookstall, a teepee, a wandering hairdresser, pyrotechnics and a dazzling rooftop performance from the Loophole Cinema group. For publicity we sent out a press release and some photos of the pool: *Time Out* magazine ran a feature and we got on local radio. When we opened the doors there was a queue round the block: we were expecting an audience of around six hundred – nearly two thousand came.

Contiguous to the resurgence of the London Underground was the renewal of an organised counter-culture. In the early 1990s a network of eco-activists and anti-road protesters (re)invented and deployed a dynamic repertoire of direct action/performance protest techniques against a range of state/commercial aggression: the destruction of ancient woodland, the Criminal Justice Bill, anti-squatting legislation, the Arms Industry and so on.[7] One of the seminal formations of this movement was the Dongas Tribe, a group that coalesced around the Twyford Down protest camp in 1992, and hybridised new age mysticism, eco-activism and the free festival/traveller subculture. This hybrid developed through the 1990s by way of the temporary autonomous zones of Wanstonia and Claremont Road in the anti-M11 struggle. The build up to the Criminal Justice Bill around 1994 further radicalised and united the diverse currents of the counter-culture, since it specifically targeted counter-cultural activity: protest, illegal raves, squatting and hunt sabotage.

Figure 23: Eco protesters vs. security guards in *Undercurrents 5: Celtic Enemy* (Eric Evans, 1995).

This renewed counter-cultural activism eventually became known as the DIY movement and it culminated in the formation of the Reclaim the Streets group in 1995 and the anti-capitalist demonstrations of the late 1990s.

Participant in this counter-cultural renewal was the development of an Underground agit-prop video movement comparable to the agit-prop collectives of the 1960s. This movement developed as video activism, and the key agents were the Oxford-based Undercurrents group, the Conscious Cinema group of Brighton and the older Despite Television group. *Undercurrents* was a biannual two-hour video compilation of news and documentary made by, for and about activists involved in road protest, green politics, rave culture, animal liberation, squatting and anarcho-liberation. The most striking development in the Video Activist movement was the use of the video camcorder as a media weapon documenting police violence and exposing illegal state and corporate activity; most significantly the presence of a camcorder at the site of protest was used by the activists as a defence against such violence and as a threat of its exposure. Although the video activists were not directly involved in exhibition there was a motivated and effective informal Underground network of screenings often at raves, festivals and the growing number of Underground cinema clubs.

Inspired by the Exploding Cinema, filmmakers Philip Ilson and Tim Harding set up the Halloween Society cinema club in 1993. A year later Steven Eastwood initiated OMSK, an Underground cinema/performance club. From the mid-1990s a subculture of clubs developed including My Eyes My Eyes, Films That Make You Go Hmmmmm, Renegade Arts, Kinokulture, Cinergy, Shaolin and iconscious in London, Vision Collision in Manchester, Head Cleaner in Coventry, Junk Television in Brighton, and Dazzle! in Plymouth. Other groups have also formed under the name Exploding Cinema, in Amsterdam, Frankfurt and most recently in Los Angeles.

Since 1991 the Exploding Cinema has screened more than fifteen hundred un-funded no-budget films and videos in squats, pubs, clubs, cafés and church halls; we have staged one-off shows in disused factories, a church, a circus tent, on rooftops and an old Victorian school. Internationally we have toured Germany with the German Underground Kaos Film Gruppe (1994) and Belgium and Holland with Kino Trotter, a Brussels-based Underground film collective (1995), staged shows in Dublin, New York and Prague (1997), and in Cologne and Frankfurt (1998). Most recently we showed a programme of work at the fabulous Cinema Nova in Brussels (2003) and at the 6th Annual New York Underground Film Festival (10–14 March 1999). The Exploding Cinema was also a core organiser of the VOLCANO!!! Un-derground Film Festival (1996–2000), an annual event in which most of the Lon-don Underground film groups came together for two weeks to stage a city-wide multi-venue collective celebration of low- and no-budget Underground film and video. Aside from exhibition we have distributed a video compilation of British Underground work, *Vacuum*, and we have an influential website which includes an update on our shows, advice on setting up your own Underground club and an archive of rants and propaganda: www.explodingcinema.org.

Nevertheless, despite the success and rapid expansion of the new British Un-derground, and after more than a decade of activism, it has become clear that there are limits to the movement's development. For Underground cinema to become a practice in which filmmakers could at least recover their production costs or even earn enough to make a living, it would be necessary to develop a popular, com-mercial and national distribution and exhibition industry.

Internationally the Underground is still expanding. On the Internet there is now an established culture of underground webcast/download video sites and co-ordinated video and DVD distribution; independent video shops are beginning to stock short film compilations and Underground festivals now get some degree of sponsorship from major commercial companies. Perhaps the most radical develop-ment has been the emergence of a cluster of coordinated international networks, most significantly the production and exhibition group Kino founded in Montreal in 1998, the commercial distribution network Future Shorts founded in London 2003, the network of independent film labs which met in 2005 at Cinema Nova, Brussels, and the 'Indymedia' movement: a global network of radical DIY news col-lectives that originated in the protests against the World Trade Organisation meeting in Seattle 1999.[8]

But in Britain the struggle to develop an integrated Underground industry has reached an invisible perimeter, and a critical element of this complex limit is the ideology and institutions of art and the independent sector. The Underground still has to compete, both industrially and ideologically, with the financial and institu-tional power of state art.

Resolution
STATE OF THE ART

The Lux Centre for Film, Video and New Media failed because the project was riddled with the unreconciled tensions of the Art/non-Art binary and betrayed by the agencies of the state. Whilst the new London Underground developed a broad popular and commercial audience for experimental film, the Lux lay fatally stranded in its modernist institute, captive to the elite sedation and bogus radicalism of the avant-garde. But the fall of the Lux was far from the end of British film and video art. As the 1990s progressed, the historic process of cultural nationalisation was reinvigorated by unprecedented state investment and coordinated initiatives to popularise Art. The crucial acceleration in this process was the founding of the National Lottery in the winter of 1994.

Art was defined as one of the original five good causes to be supported by the National Lottery Act of 1993. The others were sport, heritage, charities and Millennium projects: each cause was to get twenty per cent of the revenue raised. But from its inception the Lottery was conceived and marketed as an event in popular culture; the axis of the Lottery was the live televised draw which was an integrated element of a longer popular variety show. Moreover, the Lottery was not marketed primarily as a means to raise funding for good causes but as the random possibility of fabulous wealth, and so targeted the working class and the poorest and most desperate sectors of society. Since the first ball rolled in 1994 the Arts Council of England has invested over £2 billion in art. The audacity of this initiative is staggering – effectively the British state has developed a method to mobilise popular culture to harvest cash from the masses to fund bourgeois culture.

A culminating and exemplary event in this process was the opening of the vast new Tate Modern museum in London in May 2000. This museum is the latest addition to the extensive South Bank complex of national state culture which began with the Festival of Britain in 1951, and which now includes the BFI Southbank (formerly the National Film Theatre), the Imax Cinema, the Hayward Gallery, the Royal National Theatre, the Queen Elizabeth Hall and the Royal Festival Hall. Converted from a former power station, the Tate Modern cost over £134 million of public and private money, £56 million from the Lottery. It is a lasting monument to the modern state and to the public and private partnership. Gazing from its vast tower, north across the Millennium bridge, the visitor can contemplate St Paul's Cathedral, an earlier national shrine. In the Tate Modern vaults, famous and infamous work has been assembled and preserved. Duchamp's urinal has been restored to its original finish by dedicated conservationists who for many hours, in rubber gloves, have dabbed its mottled surface with tiny cotton buds. And the Tate Modern is a culminating triumph in the rebirth of British Art, Young British Art, which, salted amongst the modern masterpieces, gives a reciprocal new context and continuity. Whilst artists' film and video was an integrated element from the opening of the Tate Modern, in the wake of the failed Lux closer vital links were forged by the key agents of the avant-garde; crucially Shoot, Shoot, Shoot!, a major Lux retrospective of work from the first decade of the LFMC, was transferred from the defunct Lux to the Tate Modern in May 2002.[1]

Once, obscured by fog, its great turbines sparking and droning, the Bankside power station provided light, heat and power for thousands of homes. Now by electronic and digital media a new power is transmitted, the power of the postmodern rehabilitation of Art. In the mythic postmodern, the other, the marginalised and the excluded are gathered into an exciting heterogeneous spectrum of culture. Old enmities are reconciled, past fallibilities forgiven. British culture once riven by a terrible polarity between the high and the low now becomes a dynamic melting pot where all culture is equivalent and available. In the galleries of the Tate Modern monitors and projections flicker, in the bookshop you can buy Dada T-shirts and Situationist manifestos, and at the lavish openings artists, media executives and corporate sponsors mingle in their evening wear.

Art was not the only cultural project funded by the Lottery: from 1995 onwards hundreds of millions of pounds was invested in the British film industry. The first phase of this investment was administrated by the Arts Council of England, but after five years of notorious incompetence a new centralised state agency, the Film Council, was launched to replace all other state film funding, including the Arts Council, the BFI and the regional film-funding agencies. By this time the Arts Council Film, Video and Broadcasting Department had been closed, and film and video art had been subsumed into the broader Visual Art Department. After another five years of investment it is now becoming clear that the Film Council has not lived up to its commercial ambitions. Figures relating to the total Lottery investment in British film over the last decade are difficult to discover, but it is at least £250 million.[2] The total recoupment (not profit but net return) is suspected to be currently running at around twenty per cent. Now this loss would be defensible if the investment had at least funded a sustainable infrastructure for a future industry, but it has not. The British film industry is still in perpetual crisis, and the cause of the crisis is still the failure to depose the cartels that control distribution and exhibition.

The grass roots DIY exhibition model of the Underground offers a radical alternative to the monopolies of both the British film industry and state Art. But the Underground movement is caught in a paradox: so long as the ideology, institutions and financial power of state Art can co-opt the key agents and cultural products of the Underground it will be almost impossible to develop a popular experimental industry, but only a popular experimental industry will free the Underground from the repression of state Art. Moreover, most Underground activists have no understanding of this paradox, or of the historical struggle in which they have become involved. The official history of experimental cinema is still controlled and maintained by the academics of state Art, and this control has not been diminished by the rise of the Underground and the fall of the Lux. On the contrary, the spectre of the Underground has galvanised the complacent agents of the avant-garde into renewed projects to secure their authority.[3] The consecration of the term 'film and video art' in the mid-1990s should be seen as a strategy in this process, and the founding of the Film Council has further institutionalised this category shift by effectively making art the only form of state-funded filmmaking exempt from its control. A more concrete strategy was the founding in 2002 of the British Artists' Film and Video Study Collection as part of the Arts and Humanities Research Board (AHRB): Centre for British Film and Television Studies, at Central Saint Martins School of Art and Design. This centre is a major research project which was directed by Laura Mulvey (2000–2003); the Artists' Study Collection is essentially an audio/visual, textual and on-line archive of the avant-garde devised by Curtis and LeGrice. Predictably, the core critical activity of the study centre has been to develop research and debate around the history of state funding for experimental film.[4]

A POETICS FOR THE SUBVERSIVE ELEMENTS OF POP: STRATEGIES FOR THE NEW UNDERGROUND

Following the trajectory of the post-war nationalisation of British culture, the independent/avant-garde film and video sector developed an ideological and institutional tendency towards the aestheticisation, regulation, centralisation and gentrification of amateur experimental and Underground film culture. Film and video art was conceived as both an elite and specialised profession and a vital component of the state provision of culture for the nation. Whilst it is true that independent film- and video-makers developed radical initiatives for public access, training and regional diversification, these initiatives never effectively challenged either the commercial imperative of the popular industry or the deepening institutionalisation of independence. The critical role of the popular audience was not as a vast source of potential film and video artists but as a deprived and mystified mass who had both the need and the right to state Art. The assumption at the core of the independent model is that Art is a social service which can and should be provided by the state in the same way as healthcare or city planning. This superficially socialist but fundamentally bourgeois assumption is underpinned first by the supposition that Art cannot be produced in the commercial market, popular culture is not Art, and second by the supposition that the mystified popular audience cannot produce Art; they only consume. Moreover, their consumption is indiscriminate, since because they are mystified they have no taste. Consequently it is the responsibility of the state agencies to arbitrate, authorise and deliver Art to the masses. It is supposed that if the masses ignore or reject state Art it is not because it is bad or unsuccessful, it is because they do not understand it, because they are mystified; a fortunate situation which has consistently exempted the independent avant-garde film and video sector from accusations of incompetence and elitism. For thirty years this knot of assumptions has underpinned the independent/avant-garde sector and it is now informing the shift to the new legitimacy of artists' film and video. To flourish, or to even abide, the contemporary Underground movement must become aware of itself as a radical project subversive to the institution of state Art and to the cultural hierarchy that it legitimises. The new Underground must have at its heart the principles of the anarchist counter-culture: total democracy, liberty, equality, anti-authority, common ownership, decentralisation, conviviality, imagination and experiment.

BEFORE POSTMODERNISM

In her engaging and irreverent re-evaluation of postmodern culture, *Window Shopping* (1993), Anne Friedberg draws on the work of Peter Bürger, Richard Abel, Frederic Jameson, Peter Wollen and others in an attempt to answer a crucial problem afflicting postmodern theory: why the concept of the postmodern does not work for cinema.[5] Leaving aside Friedberg's conclusions, the problem can be formulated like this: if we take the decisive shift from the modern to the postmodern as dating from a cluster of formations beginning around the late 1950s (Pop Art, John Cage, Warhol and so on) and if we sidestep the euphoric 'schizophrenia' invoked by postmodern theory, and take a broad definition of postmodern aesthetics as a tendency against the pure abstraction of Modernism, and towards eclecticism, inter-textuality, self-referentiality and the playful, then it would seem that the postmodern happened in cinema before the modern. The entry of Art into the field of cinema pioneered by the French avant-garde of the 1920s, was simultaneously the entry of Modernism, but the culmination of cinematic Modernism actually developed in Structuralism, twenty years after the postmodern shift. Moreover, popular cinema seemed to have had postmodern aesthetics from its very inception, or to be more precise popular cinema seems to have been a product of postmodern aesthetics. The aesthetics discovered by the postmodern theorists can clearly be seen operating in popular culture long before the postmodern juncture, in pantomime, melodrama, music hall, serial fiction, comic books, cinema and so on. Which is to say that the postmodern shift only has conceptual integrity as a shift in bourgeois culture; the vertigo of Postmodernism is the realisation by the bourgeoisie that Art is not the only culture, and nor is it eternal or sacred.[7] Postmodernism is actually no more than the latest and most systematic attempt by the institution of Art to appropriate, sedate and gentrify the radical popular. It is essentially a rationalisation in which the forms and strategies of the radical popular, Anti-Art and commercial mass media are aestheticised into insignificance.

The conflict between Underground Cinema and the avant-garde is a component of the historical conflict between the radical popular and Art. And this conflict is no less than a struggle for the control and purpose of culture. So long as Art is able to maintain its institutional hierarchy, legitimate cultural expression will be the privilege of an elite caste of bourgeois professionals. The incredible speed of technological development has initiated the potential for an anarchic international digital cinema network, and yet experimental film and video is still held in thrall to the aura of feudal power: Art. The Dadaists knew in 1916 that the only radical art project is the destruction of Art. But the Oedipal struggle of Anti-Art will always lead back to the pantheon. The agents and institutions of film and video art control an extensive educational and industrial network legitimised by their exclusive and specialised aesthetic expertise. The Underground is a threat to this expertise and so the state sector has attempted to both negate and appropriate it. Against this repression the mere existence and continuity of the new Underground is a startling achievement since it involves constant resistance to normalised elitism, cynicism, co-option and nepotism. Nevertheless, the dilemma now facing many of the film-makers and activists of the new Underground is to either dedicate themselves to years more amateurism in the uncertain hope of eventually constructing a viable industrial network, or simply drift into cynical pragmatism and join the state sec-tor. The only alternative for the Underground is to develop a radical praxis, which would not only positively motivate and radicalise Underground activists, but which would also be ideologically and industrially toxic to the state sector. To do this the Underground must finally relinquish the utopian myths of Art and actuate the radi-cal strategies of the popular.

Following the historical trajectory from carnival to the counter-culture a mani-festo can be composed for the radical elements of popular culture. You will re-member that Bahktin identified in carnival a combination of essential interlock-ing factors: it is alternative, participatory, ambivalent, material, utopian, anarchic, transgressive and unfinished. Tracing the shifts of these factors as they run through illegitimate cultural history into the twentieth century, it is possible to identify a repertoire of radical subversions against the bourgeois state in both its official cul-tural sphere (Art) and its industrial structures:

Convivial – radical pop-culture promotes interactive participation between the work and the audience; the work is a product of this interaction; the play is charac-terised by an equality between performers and spectators which acknowledges the presence and unity of a shared humanity.

Consensual – whilst Naturalism/Realism seeks to subject its characters to scien-tific objective scrutiny without seeking consent, pop narrative seeks a convention between audience and performer; pop is consensual, Naturalism is coercive and colonial.

Illegitimate – pop-culture developed outside and between the gaps of official cul-ture; state prohibition, suppression, fear and disgust were key factors in the develop-ment of pop and have made it flexible, evasive and resistant to repression.

Profane – against the sacred aura of Art, pop-culture is irreverent, shoddy, provi-sional, temporary and human.

Subversive – pop-culture refuses to take Art seriously; pop is not auratic, it is amiable, chaotic and confrontational.

Resilient – in spite of prohibition and repression pop can abide, function underground without resources, lie dormant for many years and still return triumphant; pop is a celebration, its meaning cannot be understood from the origin or occasion of the celebration but only as the action of the celebration.

Montage – pop culture negates aura and Author/ity by materialising its collective origin; it assembles and combines work from the diversity of culture using techniques of collage, quotation, compendium, pastiche, parody and plagiarism; it is a tradition which syncretically incorporates its own history.

Variation – a key formal technique of pop-culture is that work proceeds by the repetition and variation of a repertoire of standard conventional elements; innovation takes place not by reaction and rejection, but by prototype, variation and transformation.

Improvisation – the structure of prototype and variation allows makers to take a conventional form and play with the possibility of its variants, for example the comedy sketch, the western, be-bop jazz and so on.

Anonymity – pop-culture negates Author/ity and this anonymity is reinforced by industrial organisation and mechanical reproduction; pop-culture is a network of anonymous makers, collective production, intertextuality, plagiarism, pseudonyms and disguise.

Indiscretion – without Author/ity pop is free to blur and transcend the discrete borders between works, genres, media, activities; pop-culture is intertextual and self-reflexive, it plays between the concrete and the mythic; narratives are episodic/serialised variants; fictional characters transcend mediums and can even enter pop-culture as collective identities; pop-culture is never finished; it can always be changed, updated, remade.

Mongrel – the combination and transgression of pop-culture constantly creates new variant and hybrid cultural forms.

Marvellous – the shift towards realism/anti-illusionism which characterises the modernist art of the late nineteenth and early twentieth century is essentially meaningless to the pop tradition since figurative/narrative pop-culture is not based on mimetic illusion but convention; in dramatic terms the fundamental imperative of pop-culture is the spectacular and material enactment of the allegorical, it is fabulous and material – for example, pantomime, melodrama, crime thrillers and so on;

pop-culture is not bound to the either/or realist vs. fantastic binary of Art, pop-culture plays between planes of performance, narrative and actuality.

Simultaneous – pop-culture has no progress, it does not improve and it does not decline; moreover, all historical pop culture is becoming available simultaneously; changes in the fashion of pop-culture are not legitimised by concepts of perfectibility or utility, but by desire.

Collective – the creative montage of pop culture tends towards collective creation by multiple agents; improvisation tends to negate centralised and hierarchical control.

Illiterate – historically pop culture has both developed for an audience with no formal education and has been prohibited from using spoken dialogue – consequently it has developed in primarily audio-visual forms.

Commercial – as an unofficial/illegitimate culture pop has rarely received institutional or state finance and has therefore developed as a commercial enterprise – however, this commercialism has often taken the subversive forms of profit sharing, plagiarism, piracy and bootlegging.

The new Underground Cinema already deploys most of these cultural strategies but now it must understand their meaning and begin to dedicate them to a revolutionary experimental purpose. The post-war avant-garde/independent movement sought an autonomous cinema free from the repression of bourgeois capitalism. The fatal and inherent flaw in this endeavour was the utopian assumption that autonomy is possible within capitalism, and it was this that doomed them to the fetishised and bogus realm of state Art. Whilst counter-cultural movements have developed radical strategies of resistance and alternativity to capitalism, they have only done so through active engagement, subversion and imaginative innovation. Underground Cinema is chaotic and indiscrete, and it still rages with the unresolved tensions of its hybrid development. Against the factory production of mass popular cinema the Underground empowers and celebrates the lone worker, against the myth of the genius artist it deploys collective and convivial production.

To subvert the assumption that commerce is incompatible with radical cultural production other successful radical and illegitimate commercial pop cultures must be analysed and analogised. This would include fringe theatre, comedy clubs, fanzines, street fashion, car boot sales, pornography and street sports. But the most productive and dynamic analogy for Underground Cinema is independent pop music. Whilst media theorists have long been fascinated with modern pop music as a mass industry, its true significance as a radical culture lies in its localised diversity and diffusion as a national network of independents, amateurs, semi-professionals and specialist audiences. This culture is fragmented by the shifting diversity of subcultures: punk, drum and dass, death metal, country, techno, dancehall, garage, emo,

Figure 24: The Exploding Cinema Collective circa 1994

grime, psychobilly, ska, jazz, folk, skiffle and so on. But it is unified by a convivial and anarchic passion which subverts the hierarchic structures of both legitimate culture and the commodification of mass production. Whilst at the international mass level pop music is controlled and commodified like any other industrial product, and whilst myths of international stardom permeate the culture at every level, it is also true that at the grass roots, pop is a democratic and equitable participant culture. Moreover, against the regimentation and discipline of factory and office life, or the synthetic individualism of Art, the pop group provides both a model and a functioning prototype of utopian collective cultural production. Most significantly through its network of venues, festivals, independent record labels, fanzines, websites and pirate radio stations, independent pop music culture has effectively developed an autarkic commercial industry which not only provides the primary or supplementary income for its activists, but which has repeatedly challenged the cultural control of the mass industry. The historical development, technology and cultural practice of pop music and popular cinema/television are clearly disparate, and yet the two forms developed interactively and the analogy is both revealing and productive. Moreover, innovations in cheap video projection and domestic digital editing, coupled with the widespread development of sophisticated audio-visual systems in pubs, bars and clubs now make the comparison a potential industrial model for Underground Cinema. There is now no technical reason why every provincial city or urban district should not have weekly cabaret screenings of Underground film in the same way that every district has a range of weekly live music. Further, like pop music, Underground film and video is predominately a short form which can be assembled into programmes and compilations, sold on DVD like the music CD, downloaded from the web, distributed to Underground clubs or broadcast through the new digital mediums. Of course there are many key distinctions and incompatibilities between the two models which must be worked out for an equivalent national Underground industry to develop; however, the experimental struggle to synthesise these differences could in itself be a valuable source of creative energy.

The crucial barriers and limits to the development of an autarkic Underground are now not technological and logistical, they are ideological and institutional. The movement for a New Underground must have a dual agency, it must seek to develop a national network of Underground screening clubs and it must simultaneously subvert state control of experimental film. The hope of the Underground lies in the subversive strategies of the radical popular; the hope of radical experimental cinema lies in the anarchy of the Underground.

NOTES

FOREWORD

1   See, for instance, Xavier Mendik and Steven Jay Schneider (eds) (2002) *Underground USA: Filmmaking Beyond the Hollywood Canon*. London: Wallflower Press.

INTRODUCTION

1   Most recently the term has been deployed by Wheeler Winston Dixon and Gwendolyn Audrey Foster (eds) (2002) *Experimental Cinema: The Film Reader*. London: Routledge. Significantly the term was also recently applied as a broad category by the British Artists' Film and Video Study Collection at Central Saint Martins College of Art and Design which is part of the Arts and Humanities Research Board (AHRB) Cente for British Film and Television Studies. See Artists' Film and Experimental Film in Britain 1915–99 available at http://www.studycollection.co.uk.
2   For the paradoxical concept of 'Independent' film see the Organising Committee for the IFA Conference (Simon Hartog, Marc Karlin, Claire Johnston, Paul Willemen and Stephen Dwoskin), 'Independent Film-Making in the '70s', compiled in Margaret Dickinson (1999a) *Rogue Reels: Oppositional Film in Britain 1945–90*, London: British Film Institute, 126–37.
3   Deke Dusinberre, a leading critic of the 1970s avant-garde, writing in *Afterimage* in 1981, admitted: 'It's true, too true, that everyone here in England is bored by the avant-garde. Everyone – truly everyone – will acknowledge the importance of its role in nurturing that new champion dubbed 'British Independent film culture', but most of those (the politicos especially, and also the closet Hollywood-Mosfilm apologists) remain bored by the films, frustrated by their esoteric appeal, and seeking – no, demanding – a way out of the obligation to like them. For the rest (the Fine Art crowd), uneasiness surrounds the stale smell which, it is feared, belongs to the carcass of Modernism, which someone claims to have seen lifelessly nudging the muddy edge of the lake in St James's.' Deke Dusinberre (1981) 'See Real Images!', *Afterimage* 8/9 (Spring), 88. At the muddy edge of St James's Park lies the Institute of Contemporary Arts (ICA).
4   In 1995 the selector of the third ICA Biennial of Independent Film and Video, John Wyver, stated in the catalogue essay: 'In the mid-1990s in Britain there is no independent film and video culture. None – at least none of the kind so clearly identifiable fifteen years ago, and none with any significant presence. No independent film avant-garde, no independent video art production ... this is a state which we might – cautiously – celebrate.' Wyver was the influential director of Illuminations, the production company responsible for the first broadcast television compilations of independent film and video in the 1980s. His contention in this essay for the Biennial was that the independent sector was now totally *dependent* on television. From 'What You See Is What You Get', catalogue essay for the 3rd ICA Biennial of Independent Film and Video, 1995. At the fourth and last ICA Biennial in 1997, the selection included five major broadcast television commercials: Adidas, Polaroid, Capital Radio,

AT&T and Guinness. See 'The Raw and the Cooked', catalogue essay for the 4th ICA Biennial of Independent Film and Video, 1997, written by Chris Darke and B. Ruby Rich.

5   In the autumn of 1996 Steve McIntyre, then Chief Executive of the London Film and Video Development Agency (LFVDA), the state funding body for the capital, commented in an article on the future for film funding:'Unlike traditional funders … the LFVDA undertakes activity itself … it could be argued that this approach is setting the LFVDA in competition with the independent sector it is there to fund. The problem with this argument is that it assumes there is still such a thing as a coherent "independent sector", with its own agenda and plans. There isn't. Perhaps there never was.' Steve McIntyre (1996) 'The Very Model of a Modern Funding Agency', *Vertigo*, 1, 5, 50–1.

6   Lux programme, March/April 1999.

7   The LFMC was perhaps the last of the democratic/common-ownership media collectives to submit to a historical process of state-induced industrial normalisation which was initiated in the mid-1970s. This process was accelerated in the mid-1980s by the codes of practice developed by state funding agencies and the Association of Cinematographic and Television Technicians (ACTT) in the Grant-Aided Workshop Production Declaration. See Margaret Dickinson (1999b) 'Assault on the Mainstream (1974–80)', 58–9. Exemplary groups affected by this process would include Four Corners and Liberation Films.

8   See the minutes of the Emergency Meeting of Film/Video-Makers Artists with Work In Distribution held by the former Lux Centre - and All Former Members of the LMFC and London Electronic Arts which was held on 20 October 2001 at the Delegates Centre, National Film Theatre (now BFI Southbank), London SE1.

9   Originally this information came from Mark Shehan who was an active member of the LFMC executive during the move to the Lux. The figure was later confirmed by Dr Peter Thomas, Postdoctoral Research Fellow, University of Sunderland and the British Artists' Film and Video Study Collection at the University of the Arts, London.

10   The new Lux organisation is a normalised state agency, the distribution catalogue is curated – there is no open access. The film production and processing equipment was subsequently salvaged by the artist filmmaker group no.w.here lab which is not a co-op but which does have a relatively open membership structure. See www.no-where-lab.org.

11   For the debate surrounding the fall of the Lux see Benedict Seymour (2002a) 'The Last Picture Show', *Mute Magazine*, 22 (January) and also the Letters Page, *Mute Magazine*, 23 (March) (2002b).

12   A. L. Rees (1999) *A History of Experimental Film and Video*. London: British Film Institute (back cover).

13   Laura Mulvey (1975) 'Visual Pleasure and Narrative Cinema', *Screen*, 3,16.

14   The compromised objectivity and male dominance of American avant-garde film history has been challenged by incisive feminist critiques. See Constance Penley (1989) *The Future of an Illusion: Film, Feminism, and Psychoanalysis*. London: Routledge; Constance Penley and Janet Bergstrom (1978) 'The Avant-Garde: Histories and Theories', *Screen*, 19, 113–27; Patricia Mellancamp (1990) *Indiscretions: Avant-Garde Film, Video and Feminism*. Bloomington: Indiana University Press; and Lauren Rabinowitz (1991) *Points of Resistance: Women, Power and Politics in the New York Avant-Garde Cinema 1943–71*. Chicago: University of Illinois Press.

15 '…other younger film and video artists were to be seen en masse at the "Pandae-monium" ICA festival. But for some, programmes such as these, however diverse, are limited by jury selection and official imprimatur. In response groups like the Exploding Cinema and festivals such as "Volcano" in London continue to promote the classic underground principles of non-selected, open screenings and avoid the more high-profile venues. The current organ of this movement, *Filmwaves*, is dedicated simply to 'low-budget filmmakers and audiences' (1999: 119). *Exploding Cinema* is also mentioned in footnote 170 (1999: 145).

16 This would include, amongst many others, BBC Radio Four, 4 April 1995; BBC Radio Three, 28 October 1995; *Guardian*, 9 July 1993, 6; *The Face*, September 1993, 144–5; *Time Out*, 23–30 October 1996, 28–9; and *Time Out*, 16–23 June 1999, 26.

17 The television compilations included *Midnight Underground* (Illuminations for Channel 4) and *Expanding Pictures* (Arts Council/BBC 2). The events included Dirty and Dangerous, at the ICA 1997, Underground America, at the Barbican, London, 1999, and Mark Weber's Little Stabs at Happiness at the ICA in the late 1990s.

CHAPTER 1

1 For a fascinating insight into this cross-border transaction see Jim Collins (ed.) (2002) *High-Pop: Making Culture into Popular Entertainment*. Malden, MA: Blackwell.

2 Mikhail Bakhtin (1984 [1965]) *Rabelais and His World*, trans. Helene Iswolsky. Bloomington: Indiana University Press. François Rabelais was an ex-Franciscan and Benedictine monk who, between 1532 and 1564, wrote the satiric, bawdy and fabulous history of Gargantua and Pantagruel in which there appears the hedonistic proto-anarchist utopia of the Abbey of Theleme, governed by a single law: 'Do what you will'. See also Peter Marshall (1992) *Demanding the Impossible: A History of Anarchism*. London: Fontana Press, 108–9.

3 Bakhtin 1984: 20.

4 Ibid., 39–40.

5 Ibid., 273–5.

6 For a survey of refutations of the 'safety valve' theory see John Docker (1995) *Postmodernism and Popular Culture*. Cambridge: Cambridge University Press, 192–7.

7 See Ronald Hutton (1996) *The Stations of the Sun*. Oxford: Oxford University Press; and also Barbara A. Hanawalt (1993) *Growing Up in Mediaeval London*. Oxford: Oxford University Press.

8 See Peter Stallybrass and Allon White (1986) *The Politics and Poetics of Transgression*. London: Methuen, 14.

9 See Norman Cohn (1993) *The Pursuit of the Millennium*. London: Random House.

10 For an overview of the 1990s' protest movement see George McKay (1996) *Senseless Acts of Beauty*. London: Verso.

11 See Peter Burke (1978) *Popular Culture in Early Modern Europe*. Aldershot: Wildwood House, 208–86.

12 See Arnold Hauser (1951) *The Social History of Art. Vol 2*. New York: Vintage Books, 131–58.

13 Burke 1978: 272.

14 Ibid., 244–86.

15 Hutton 1996: 408–27.

16 See Ian Starsmore (1975) *English Fairs*. London: Thames and Hudson, 12.

17 Bakhtin 1984: 29.

18 Although the common people were mostly illiterate at this time, the ability amongst the population to read (though they were unable to write) is often underestimated. See Victor E. Neuburg (1977) *Popular Literature*. Harmondsworth: Penguin, 53–5.

19 See Leslie Shepherd (1973) *The History of Street Literature*. Newton Abbott, Devon: David and Charles, 16–17.

20 See Burke 1978: 263.

21 See David Kunzle (1973) *The Early Comic Strip: Narrative Strips and Picture Stories in the European Broadsides from c. 1450–1825*. Berkeley: University of California Press.

22 Burke 1978: 95.

23 Neuburg 1977: 102–8.

24 See Michael D. Bristol (1985) *Carnival and Theatre*. London and New York: Methuen, 116–17.

25 Ibid., 123.

26 Shakespeare was played with great success to both upper-class and popular audiences throughout the eighteenth and into the mid-nineteenth century, but there was no single authentic version, the text was often abridged and adapted, and the convivial audience would often interrupt or contribute to the performance. However, by the mid-nineteenth century a new bourgeois theatre audience was rejecting popular Shakespeare and demanding an authentic text. In New York on 10 May 1849 the conflict between the popular and the authentic exploded into mass protest: the Astor Place Riot. When, despite long-running popular opposition, an authentic English *Macbeth* was performed at the Astor Place Opera House, ten thousand rioters lay siege to the building showering the elegant windows with stones to cries of 'Burn the damned den of the aristocracy!' Overwhelmed, the police called in the armed militia who fired point blank into the crowds: 31 people were killed and 150 wounded. See James B. Twitchell (1992) *Carnival Culture*. New York: Columbia University Press, 28–31; and also Richard Moody (1958) *The Astor Place Riot*. Bloomington: Indiana University Press, 1–12.

27 See Keir Elam (1980) *The Semiotics of Theatre and Drama*. London: Methuen, 87–97.

28 Ibid., 90.

29 See Andrew Hopton's (1989) 'Introduction', in *Digger Tracts 1649–50*. London: Aporia Press, 3; also Cohn 1993: 290.

30 Christopher Hill (1993) *The World Turned Upside Down*. Harmondsworth: Penguin, 341–2.

31 See Richard Courtney (1982) *Outline History of British Drama*. Totowa, NJ: Littlefield, Adams and Company, 115.

32 See Vincent J. Leisenfeld (1984) *The Licensing Act of 1737*. Madison, WI: University of Wisconsin Press, 3.

33 See Gerald Frow (1985) *'Oh, Yes It Is!' A History of Pantomime*. London: BBC.

34 Frow 1985: 34.

35 See Michael R. Booth (1981) *Victorian Spectacular Theatre 1850–1910*. Boston, London and Henley: Routledge and Kegan Paul, 75.

36 See Michael R. Booth (1965) *English Melodrama*. London: Herbert Jenkins, 53.

37 These statistics are taken respectively from John Springhall (1998) *Youth, Popular Culture and Moral Panics*. Hampshire: Macmillan Press, 15; and from James Grant (1838) *Sketches in London*, quoted in Paul Sheridan (1981) *Penny Theatres of Victorian London*. London: Dennis Dobson, 11.

38 Most of the information on penny gaffs and penny dreadfuls which follows is drawn from the excellent study by Springhall (1998).

39 See Louis James (1974) *Fiction for the Working Man*. Harmondsworth: Penguin, 175–6.

40 Ibid., 172–5.

41 Springhall 1998: 42.

42 See John L. Fell (1974) *Film and the Narrative Tradition*. Oklahoma: University of Oklahoma Press, 37–53.

43 Booth 1965: 46–51.

44 See Robert Malcolmson (1982) 'Popular Recreations Under Attack', in Tony Bennett, Graham Martin and Bernard Waites (eds) *Popular Culture Past and Present*. London: Croom Helm, 20.

45 Ibid., 38–41.

46 Ibid.

47 Stallybrass & White 1986: 14.

48 See Michael Chanan (1980) *The Dream That Kicks*. London: Routledge and Kegan Paul, 157.

49 See Hugh Cunningham in Bennett *et al.* 1982: 66–7.

50 Ibid., 83.

51 Ibid., 73.

52 Springhall 1998: 28–33.

53 Ibid., 11–71.

54 See Penelope Summerfield (1981) 'The Effingham Arms and the Empire: Deliberate Selection in the Evolution of the Music Hall in London', in Eileen Yeo and Stephen Yeo (eds) *Popular Culture and Class Conflict: 1590–1914*. Sussex: Harvester Press, 209–40.

55 See Dagmar Kift (1996) *The Victorian Music Hall: Culture, Class and Conflict*. Cambridge: Cambridge University Press, 53.

56 Ibid., 51–2.

57 Summerfield 1981: 220.

58 See Summerfield 1981; and Gareth Steadman Jones (1974) 'Working Class Culture and Working Class Politics in London, 1870–1900: Notes on the Remaking of a Working Class', *Journal of Social History*, 7 (Summer), 460–508.

59 Notwithstanding the innate subversion of music hall culture, the industrialisation of the halls activated trade union militancy which led to the formation of the Variety Artists' Federation and the music hall strike of 1907. See Chanan 1980: 165–9.

CHAPTER 2

1 This argument was principally devised as a revision of the influential essay, written in 1974, by Peter Bürger, 'Theory of the Avant-Garde' (1984 [1974]), trans. by Michael Shaw. Minneapolis, MN: University of Minnesota Press.

2 Victor Burgin (1986) *The End of Art Theory*. London: Macmillan, 143.

3 The fine arts were formulated as the 'beaux arts' by the Abbe Charles Batteaux in *Les Beaux Reduits a Un Meme Principe* (1747), cited in Burgin 1986: 144. See also Mary Anne Staniszewski (1995) *Believing is Seeing: Creating the Culture of Art*. New York: Penguin, 111–19.

4 Bürger 1984 [1974]: 46.

5 'The emergence of an abstract, capitalised Art, with its own internal but general principles, is difficult to localise. There are several plausible C18 uses, but it was in C19 that the concept became general'. Raymond Williams (1983) *Keywords*. London:

Fontana Press, 42.

6 Roger Taylor (1978) *Art, An Enemy of the People*. Sussex: Harvester Press, 48.

7 See Guy Debord (1987) *The Society of the Spectacle*. Exeter: Rebel Press, Aim Publications (Clause 140) (unpaginated).

8 For the romantic character of the avant-garde see Renato Poggioli (1968) *The Theory of the Avant-Garde*. Cambridge, MA: The Belknap Press of Harvard University Press, 52.

9 See Peter Marshall (1993) *Demanding the Impossible: A History of Anarchism*. London: Fontana Press, 108–39.

10 See Donald D. Egbert (1970) *Social Radicalism and the Arts: Western Europe*. London: Duckworth, 122: According to Egbert, Saint-Simon's formulation of the artist as the political vanguard predates the use of 'Avant-Guard' as a solely political term.

11 Henri de Saint-Simon and Leon Halevy (1825) *Opinions Litteraires, Philosophiques et Industrielles*, quoted in Egbert 1970: 121.

12 See Henri de Saint-Simon (1814) 'The Reorganisation of the European Community', quoted in Carl Cohen (ed.) (1962) *Communism, Fascism and Democracy*, trans. F. H. M. Markham. New York: Random House, 25–6. The term 'meritocracy' was first used by Michael Young (1958) in his historical speculation *The Rise of the Meritocracy 1870–2033*. Harmondsworth: Penguin.

13 Egbert 1970: 134.

14 Theophile Gautier (1834) *Mademoiselle de Maupin*, quoted in Jean Gimpel (1991) *Against Art and Artists*. Edinburgh: Polygon, 93.

15 Taylor 1978: 43.

16 For example the Gothic Revival, Morris and the Arts and Crafts Movement and so forth.

17 Bürger 1984 [1974]: 36.

18 Walter Benjamin (1979 [1936]) 'The Work of Art in the Age of Mechanical Reproduction', in *Illuminations*. Glasgow: Fontana/Collins, 223.

19 Ibid., 225–6.

20 Ibid., 245.

21 John Ruskin (1907) 'The Unity of Art', *Sesame & Lilies, The Two Paths & The King of the Golden River*. London and Toronto: J. M. Dent & Sons, 120.

22 Bürger 1984: 48.

23 See Burgin 1986: 154; and also Hauser 1968: 70.

24 Bürger 1984: 48.

25 This semiotic interpretation of the Modernist 'breakthrough' is drawn from Peter Wollen's celebrated essay on avant-garde cinema, 'The Two Avant-Gardes', to be considered in detail towards the end of this text. See Wollen (1975) 'The Two Avant-Gardes', *Studio International* (Nov./Dec.), 190, 978, 172.

26 Wollen 1975: 172.

27 See for instance the influential study by Nikolaus Pevsner (1974 [1936]) *Pioneers of Modern Design*. Harmondsworth: Penguin.

28 The search for pure aura was explicit in the work of a faction of the leading pioneers of abstract art who were influenced by occult philosophy, notably Mondrian and Kandinsky. Kandinsky was fascinated by the occult concept of spiritual aura and collected and studied photographs which appeared to reveal aura, ectoplasm and phantom images. For the search for aura in abstract film see William Moritz (1986) 'Abstract Film and Colour Music', in Maurice Tuchman (ed.), *The Spiritual in Art: Abstract Painting 1890–1985*. New York: Abbeville Press, 297–311.

29 Pierre Bourdieu (1986) *Distinction: A Social Critique of the Judgment of Taste*. London: Routledge and Kegan Paul, 4.

30 Bourdieu 1986: 31–2.

31 Eric J. Hobsbawm (1973) *The Age of Revolution*. London: Weidenfield and Nicholson, 312–33.

32 Burgin 1986: 188.

CHAPTER 3

1 A comprehensive and engaging attempt to unravel the theoretical fragmentation of popular culture and to map the historical continuities from carnival to contemporary pop culture is John Docker (1996) *Postmodernism and Popular Culture: A Cultural History*. Cambridge: Cambridge University Press, pp. 192–7.

2 Arnold was the son of the influential headmaster of Rugby public school, Dr Thomas Arnold. He served as an Inspector of Schools and later held the Chair of Poetry at Oxford University (1857–67).

3 Matthew Arnold, 'Culture and Anarchy' [1869] in P. J. Keating (ed.) (1970) *Matthew Arnold, Selected Prose*. Harmondsworth: Penguin, 205.

4 Roger Fry, 'Art and Socialism' [1912] reprinted with alterations in *Roger Fry (1961), Vision and Design*. Harmondsworth: Penguin, 51–69.

5 See Iain Wright (1979) 'F. R. Leavis, The Scrutiny Movement and the Crisis', in Jon Clark, Margot Heinemann, David Margolies and Carol Snee (eds) *Culture and Crisis in Britain in the 1930s*. London: Lawrence and Wishart, 37–67.

6 See Pamela McCallum (1983) *Literature and Method: Towards a Critique of I.A. Richards, T.S. Eliot and F.R. Leavis*. Dublin: Gill and Macmillan/Humanities Press, 178–203.

7 F. R. Leavis and Denys Thompson (1962 [1933]) *Culture and Environment*. London: Chatto and Windus, 96–7.

8 Clement Greenburg (1939) 'Avant-Garde and Kitsch', *Partisan Review*, VI, 5, Fall, 34–9. Reprinted in Charles Harrison and Paul Wood (eds) (1992) *Art in Theory*. Oxford: Blackwell Publishers, 529–41.

9 Theodor Adorno and Max Horkheimer (1947), 'The Culture Industry: Enlightenment As Mass Deception', extracted from *Dialectic of Enlightenment*. New York: Herder and Herder. Reprinted in Simon During (ed.) (1993) *The Cultural Studies Reader*. London and New York: Routledge, 29–43.

10 Adorno & Horkheimer (1993: 33–4).

11 Notably E. P. Thomson, Robert Malcolmson and Peter Burke. See Ronald Hutton (1994) *The Rise and Fall of Merry England*. Oxford: Oxford University Press; and idem (1996) *The Stations of the Sun*. Oxford: Oxford University Press.

12 The term was first introduced by the writer and editor W. J. Thoms as part of a wider trend of Anglo-Saxon semantic revivalism. Thoms became a director of the Folk-Lore Society in 1878. The term Folk Song dates from around the 1870s. See Williams 1983: 136.

13 Notably James Frazer, author of the highly influential *The Golden Bough* (pub. 1890–1915), Sir Edmund Chambers, Charlotte Burne, Margaret Murray, Violet Alford, Mary Macleod Banks, and Cecil Sharp. See Hutton 1996: 408–27.

14 Hutton 1996: 299.

15 Hutton 1994: 50–1.

16 See Peter Marshall 1993:108–39.

17 The Societe Des Observateurs de l'Homme. See George W. Stocking Jr (1968) *Race,*

Culture and Evolution. Chicago: University of Chicago Press, 13–41.

18 See Jacques Revel (1984) 'Forms of Expertise: Intellectuals and "Popular" Culture in France (1650–1800)', in Steven L. Kaplan (ed.) *Understanding Popular Culture*. New York: Moulton, 269.

19 Marshall 1993: 108–39.

20 See Jean-Jacques Rousseau (1751) 'A Critique of Progress', reprinted in Isaac Kramnick (1995) *The Portable Enlightenment Reader*. New York: Penguin, 363–8.

21 See Stocking Jr 1982.

22 See Joanna Banham and Jennifer Harris (eds) (1984) *William Morris and the Middle Ages*. Manchester: Manchester University Press.

23 Morris' attitude to the working class is explored in Stefan Szczelkun (1993) *The Conspiracy of Good Taste*. London: Working Press, 13–38. See also Morris' lecture, Art and Socialism, given to the Secular Society of Leicester of 1884, extracted in Christopher Harvie, Graham Martin and Aaron Scharf (eds) (1970) *Industrialisation and Culture 1830–1914*. London: Macmillan for Open University Press, 339–45.

24 See his writing on the future of May Day celebrations in William Morris (1995 [1891]) *News From Nowhere*. Cambridge: Cambridge University Press, 69.

25 See Szczelkun (1993). The key figures he considers are Morris, Clough, Williams-Ellis the architect and writer, and the folklorist Cecil Sharpe.

26 The contemporary continuity of the folklore myth can be gauged in the cult surrounding Tolkein's *The Lord of the Rings*, an alliance of humans and aristocratic elves against the dark industry of the underworld.

CHAPTER 4

1   The modern circus developed principally from spectacular exhibitions of athletic and trick horse riding by teachers who turned to entertainment as the spread of private carriages undermined the riding schools. Astley was the son of a cabinet maker who had joined the dragoons and become an accomplished and renowned horseman and trainer. On leaving the army he originally founded a riding school in Lambeth but soon discovered that there was more money to be made in show business. See Rupert Croft-Cooke and Peter Cotes (1976) *Circus: A World History*. London: Elek, 39–50.

2   Chanan 1980: 175.

3   See Chanan (on Noel Burch) 1980: 290–91.

4   This would include Edison and Armat in America, the Lumières and Reynaud in France, Skladanowsky in Germany, Friese-Green and Paul in England.

5   Montage as linkage was a concept Eisenstein attributes to his contemporary filmmaker/theorist V. I. Pudovkin. See Sergei Eisenstein (1951a) *Film Form*, trans. and ed. Jay Leyda. London: Dennis Dobson, 36–7.

6   Eisenstein 1951a: 76–80.

7   Eisenstein 1951a: 24–5.

8   See, for instance, Eisenstein 1951a: 57.

9   The complete article is reprinted in Richard Taylor and Ian Christie (eds) (1988) *The Film Factory*. London: Routledge and Kegan Paul, 87–9.

10 See Segei Iosipovich Yutkevitch (1973) *Teenage Artists of the Revolution in Cinema in Revolution,* trans. and ed. David Robinson. London: Secker and Warburg.

11 Yutkevitch 1973: 31–2.

12 Eisenstein 1951b: 12.

13 See Richard Balzer (1998) *Peep Shows: A Visual History*. New York: Harry N.

Abrams.

14 Quoted in Samuel Mckechnie (1932) *Popular Entertainments Through the Ages*. London: Sampson, Low, Marston & Co., 41.

15 Martin Quigley, Jr (1948) *Magic Shadows: The Story of the Origin of Motion Pictures*. Washington, DC: Georgetown University Press, 71–3.

16 Ian Christie (1994) *The Last Machine*. London: British Film Institute, 111–112.

17 Quoted in Mckechnie 1932: 50–1.

18 Chanan 1980: 114.

19 Starsmore 1975: 16.

20 A direct link between the fairground ride and early cinema was the series of 'phantom ride' films which were shot from the front of moving railway locomotives, and the chain of Hales Tours cinemas which were designed and furnished as simulated railway carriages in which the audience would sit in passenger seats and watch a phantom ride film.

21 C. W. Ceram (1965) *Archeology of the Cinema*. London: Thames and Hudson, 73.

22 See Vanessa R. Schwartz (1998) *Spectacular Realities: Early Mass Culture in Fin-De-Siecle Paris*. Berkeley: University of California Press, 177–99.

23 Christie 1994: 65.

24 Chanan 1980: 141.

25 Noël Burch (1981) 'How We Got Into Pictures', *Afterimage*, 8, 9, Spring, 26.

26 See André Gaudreault (1990) 'Showing and Telling: Image and Word in Early Cinema', in Thomas Elsaesser (ed.) *Early Cinema: Space-Frame-Narrative*. London: British Film Institute, 275; also Charles Musser (1990) 'The Nickelodeon Era Begins: Establishing the Framework for Hollywood's Mode of Representation', in Elsaesser (ed.), 264.

27 The revision of early cinema history is widely held to begin with the Congress of the International Federation of Film Archives in Brighton 1978. See Thomas Elsaesser (ed.) (1990) *Early Cinema: Space-Frame-Narrative*. London: British Film Institute, 5–7.

28 Tom Gunning (1996 [1993]) '"Now You See It, Now You Don't": The Temporality of the Cinema of Attractions', in Richard Abel (ed.), *Silent Film*. London: Athlone, 71–85.

29 Burch 1981: 24.

30 Gunning 1996: 73.

31 See Tom Gunning (1990 [1986]) 'The Cinema of Attractions, Early Film, its Spectators and the Avant-Garde', in Elsaesser (ed.) 1990: 58–9.

32 Gunning 1990: 80–1.

33 See ibid., 61.

34 A. Nicholas Vardac (1987 [1949]) *Stage To Screen: Theatrical Origins of Early Film: David Garrick to D. W. Griffith*. New York: Da Capo Press.

35 Vardac 1987: 26.

36 Griffith's film *Intolerance* (1916) was a spectacular combination of theatrical melodrama, innovative parallel editing and multiple narrative which had a profound international influence.

37 Vardac 1987: 235–6.

38 Several key documents including texts by Zola, Shaw and Otto Brahm are compiled in Eric Bentley (ed.) *The Theory of the Modern Stage*. Harmondsworth: Penguin.

39 See Raymond Williams (1980) *Problems in Materialism and Culture, Selected Essays*. London: Verso, 127.

40 Williams 1980: 132–3.

41   Ibid.
42   M. Thomas Inge (1990) *Comics As Culture*. Jackson and London: University of Mississippi Press, xx and 143–4.
43   Gunning 1990: 60.
44   Chanan 1980: 252–63.
45   Richard Gray (1996) *Cinemas in Britain. One Hundred Years of Cinema Architecture*. London: Lund Humphries, 22.
46   Springhall 1998: 103.
47   This would include Walter Haggar, R. W. Paul, G. A. Smith and James Williamson.
48   Margaret Dickinson and Sarah Street (1985) *Cinema and State: the Film Industry and the British Government 1927–84*. London: British Film Institute, 9–11.
49   In 1909–10 British production accounted for only 15 per cent of domestic cinema programmes. The rest were imports: forty per cent French, thirty per cent North American and ten per cent Italian. By 1914 the North American share had increased to sixty per cent nationally, or 75 per cent in London, whilst the British share of the market was estimated at around two per cent. See Michael Chanan 1980: 244–5.
50   The trend for theatrical adaptation became dominant around 1910 when Will Barker persuaded Sir Herbert Beerbohm Tree to star in a film version of his celebrated stage production of Shakespeare's *Henry VIII* (1911). This was followed by a score of Shakespeare adaptations including Frank Benson's *Richard III* (1911) and Sir Johnston Forbes-Robertson in *Hamlet* (1913) directed by the prolific Cecil Hepworth. See Geoff Brown (1986) 'Sister of the Stage: British Film and the British Stage', in Charles Barr (ed.) *All Our Yesterdays: 90 Years of British Cinema*. London: British Film Institute, 143–55; see also Geoffrey MacNab (2000) *Searching for Stars*. London: Cassell, 1–33.
51   Brown 1986: 145.
52   See Rachael Low (1971) *The History of British Film 1918–29*. London: George Allen and Unwin, 305–6; and also Don Macpherson (ed.) (1980) *Traditions of Independence*. London: British Film Institute, 103–7.
53   John Carey (1992) *The Intellectuals and the Masses*. London: Faber and Faber, 80–2.
54   See Low 1971: 305–6.

CHAPTER 5

1   Fernand Léger, 'Ballet Mécanique' (unpublished c. 1924), in Fernand Léger, *Functions of Painting (1973)*, ed. E. F. Fry. London: Thames and Hudson, 49.
2   My outline history of this movement is principally derived from Richard Abel (1984) *French Cinema: The First Wave 1915–29*. Princeton, NJ: Princeton University Press.
3   Most significantly Canudo was preceded by the Futurists. See F. T. Marinetti, Bruno Corra, Emilio Setimelli, Arnaldo Ginna, Giacomo Balla and Remo Chiti (1916), 'The Futurist Cinema', reprinted in the catalogue *Film As Film: Formal Experiment in Film 1910–1975*. London: Hayward Gallery, Arts Council of Great Britain, 79.
4   These were published first as *The Birth of the Sixth Art* (1911), and later as the *Manifesto of the Seventh Art* (1923) in Canudo's own magazine *Gazette Des Sept Arts* (No. 2). From notes accompanying Ricciotto Canudo (1911) 'The Birth of the Sixth Art', trans. Ben Gibson, Don Ranvaud, Sergio Sokota and Deborah Young, *Framework* 13, 1980, 3–7.
5   Ricciotto Canudo (1988 [1923]) 'Reflections on The Seventh Art', trans. Claudia Gorbman, in Richard Abel (ed.) *French Film Theory and Criticism Vol. 1. 1915–29*.

Princeton, NJ: Princeton, 293.

6   Abel 1984: 248–9.
7   Jan-Christopher Horak (1995) 'The First American Film Avant-garde, 1919–1945', in Jan-Christopher Horak (ed.) *Lovers of the Cinema*. Madison, WI: University of Wisconsin Press, 17–20.
8   Germaine Dulac, 'Visual and Anti-Visual Films', from an excerpt of an article published in *Les Cahiers du Mois*, No. 16/17 (1925), trans. Robert Lamberton, in P. Adams Sitney (ed.) (1978) *The Avant-Garde Film. A Reader of Theory and Criticism*. New York: New York University Press, 42.
9   See Ian Christie (1979) 'French Avant-Garde Film in the 1920s', in the catalogue *Film As Film: Formal Experiment in Film 1910–1975*. London: Hayward Gallery, Arts Council of Great Britain, 38.
10 Wollen 1975: 172.
11 Léger 1973: 49.
12 See Siegfried Kracauer (1961) *The Nature of Film*. London: Dennis Dobson, 178–9.
13 Abel 1984: 243.
14 Abel 1984: 252.
15 Abel 1984: 245.
16 Abel 1984: 253.
17 Abel 1984: 264–7.
18 Dusinberre 1980: 34.
19 Abel 1984: 274.
20 Bürger 1984: 22–58.

CHAPTER 6

1   Montagu was editor on Hitchcock's *The Lodger* (1926), *Downhill* (1927) and *Easy Virtue* (1927) and producer on *The Man Who Knew Too Much* (1934), *The 39 Steps* (1935), *Sabotage* (1935) and *The Secret Agent* (1936).
2   James Park (1990) *British Cinema: The Lights That Failed*. London: B. T. Batsford, 38.
3   Dusinberre 1980: 46.
4   Although *Close Up* followed a characteristically British critical trajectory it was actually published in Switzerland and had numerous continental contributors and correspondents. For instance in Vol. I, No. 3 (1927), a Paris correspondent is first credited, and Vol. III, No. 3 (1928) was billed as a special Russian edition. See also Dusinberre 1980: 34–51.
5   A key venue for continental avant-garde cinema was the Academy on Oxford Street, London, which was founded and run by Elsie Cohen. See E. Coxhead (1933) 'Towards A Co-Operative Cinema', *Close Up*, X, 2, 133–7.
6   Quoted in Trevor Ryan (1980) 'Film and Political Organisations in Britain 1929–39', in Macpherson (ed.) 1980: 56.
7   All figures from Ryan 1980: 65.
8   See 'Film in the Streets', *Daily Worker*, 3 August 1933, in Macpherson (ed.) 1980: 146.
9   For example see Benn in 'The Cinema: An Instrument of Class Rule', *The Plebs*, April 1931, reprinted in Macpherson (ed.) 1980: 138–9.
10 See the selection of articles in Macpherson (ed.) 1980.
11 See Ryan 1980: 57.
12 Dickinson 1999a: 24–31.

13 Ibid.

14 The IFA was a short-lived initiative formed to co-ordinate the various factions of the independent movement including the Workers' Film Movement and the amateur ciné-clubs. Its board of advisors included Grierson, Legg, Rotha, Wright and Anthony Asquith. See Annette Kuhn, 'Recontextualising A Film Movement', in Macpherson (ed.) 1980: 28.

15 See John Grierson (1979) *Grierson on Documentary*. London: Faber and Faber, 11–17.

16 See Forsyth Hardy (1979) *John Grierson: A Documentary Biography*. London: Faber and Faber, 31–43.

17 See Paul Rotha (1936) *Documentary Film*. London: Faber and Faber, 49.

18 Matthew Arnold, 'The Popular Education of France' (1861), in Arnold 1970: 121–2.

19 Arnold 1970: 256–73.

20 See John Pick (1988) *The Arts in a State*. Bristol: Bristol Classical Press, 35.

21 Paddy Scannell and David Cardiff (1991) *A Social History of Broadcasting Volume One 1922–1939*. Oxford: Basil Blackwell, 16.

22 See Andrew Crisell (1997) *An Introductory History of British Broadcasting*. London: Routledge, 29–35.

23 See also Tom Burns (1977) *The BBC: Public Institution and Private World*. Oxford: Macmillan Press, 38–40.

24 See Crisell 1997: 30–1.

25 Sir William Haley (1974 [1948]) 'The Pyramid of Taste', in Anthony Smith (ed.) *British Broadcasting*. Newton Abbott: David and Charles, 83–4.

26 See Ian Aitken (1989) 'John Grierson, Idealism and the Inter-war Period', *The Historical Journal of Film, Radio and Television*, 9, 3, 247–57.

27 Aitken 1989: 254.

28 Kuhn 1980: 29.

29 Aitken 1989: 256.

30 John Grierson (1979 [1941]) 'Education and Total Effort', in Forsyth Hardy (ed.) Grierson on Documentary: London: Faber and Faber, 139.

31 See also the justly celebrated *Nightmail* directed by Wright and Watt with poetry by W. H. Auden and music by Benjamin Britten.

32 See Tom Jeffrey (1978) *Mass Observation: A Short History*. Birmingham: University of Birmingham.

33 See John Pick (1984) *Managing the Arts?: The British Experience*. London: Rhinegold, 35–73; John S. Harris (1970) *Government Patronage of the Arts in Great Britain*. Chicago: University of Chicago Press, 19–36; and Janet Minihan (1977) *The Nationalisation of Culture*. London: Hamish Hamilton, 215–49.

34 Harris 1970: 21.

35 Ibid., 23.

36 See Pick 1984: 37.

37 CEMA was first formed as a committee of the Pilgrim Trust founded by the American millionaire philanthropist Edward S. Harkness, whose father had been a major stockholder in Rockefeller's Standard Oil Company. See Dr Thomas Jones quoted in Harris 1970: 26.

38 Quoted in Pick 1984: 38.

39 Pick 1984: 40.

40 CEMA received only 5 per cent of the grant given to ENSA and staged less events a year than ENSA did in a week. This estimate is based on statistics for 1943 from Minihan 1977: 220 and Harris 1970: 23.

41 Pick 1984: 40.

42 In 1949 Mary Glasgow, the first post-war Secretary General of the Arts Council, wrote of her wartime experience in staging CEMA events in factory hostels that the audiences actually had to learn how to behave with live performers since they seemed to mistake live shows for cinema and would continue to talk, drink and move around. Glasgow misinterprets the convivial culture of the popular for an ignorance of culture and commends the gradual sedation of the audience as they submitted to the naturalist conventions of bourgeois theatre and the etiquette of the classical concert. This is quoted from 'The Arts in England', in Harris 1970: 23.

43 Pick 1984: 44.

44 Quoted in Harris 1970: 41.

45 Quoted in Harris 1970: 39.

46 The NFFC was a credit organisation authorised to give loans to British film production and distribution companies. Under the control of the Board of Trade it had an initial total resource of five million pounds and as early as 1950 it participated in half the British films in production. The first chairman of the NFFC was Reith. The Eady Levy was charged as a percentage of every cinema ticket sold and half of the money raised was returned to British film producers according to their takings at the box office: popular films received a higher percentage and made more money.

47 See the Radcliffe Report (1948) *Report of the Committee of Enquiry into the Future of the British Film Institute*. London: Her Majesty's Stationery Office.

48 The fund was launched with £12,500 from the Eady Levy and over the following six years 15 short films were funded out of the initial investment.

49 The standard histories allow for only a few isolated experimental makers in this period. The key example is Margaret Tait. See David Curtis (1999) 'Britain's Oldest Experimentalist ... Margaret Tait', *Vertigo*, 1, 9, Summer, 62–3.

50 Alan Lovell and Jim Hillier (1972) *Studies in Documentary*. London: Secker and Warburg, 135.

51 See Erik Hedling (1997) 'Lindsay Anderson and the Development of British Art Cinema', in Robert Murphy (ed.) *The British Cinema Book*. London: British Film Institute, 178–9.

52 Elizabeth Sussex (1969) *Lindsay Anderson*. London: Studio Vista, 9.

53 Lovell & Hillier 1972: 133–75.

54 This argument is implicit in Anderson's work for *Sequence*, but see in particular Lindsay Anderson (1950) 'The Director's Cinema', *Sequence*, 12, Autumn, 6–11 and 37.

55 See John Caughie (ed) (1999) *Theories of Authorship*. London: Routledge, 15.

56 See the transcript of a Panel Discussion with Kevin MacDonald, David Robinson, Walter Lassally, Karel Reisz and Lorenza Mazzetti at the NFT, 22 March 2001, from the BFI website: www.bfi.org.uk.

57 See Anon. (1956a) 'Exciting Evening of Amateur Films', *Amateur Cine World*, 19, 12, April, 1229–31 and 1270.

58 See Lindsay Anderson (1948) 'A Possible Solution', *Sequence*, 3, Spring, 9.

59 I use the term 'autarkic' in this context to denote self-sufficiency in distinction to 'autonomy' which denotes self-governing.

60 See Lovell & Hillier 1972: 151.

61 See, for instance, Anon. 1956: 1229–31 and 1270; and John Berger (1957) 'Look at Britain', *Sight and Sound*, 27, 1, Summer, 12–14.

62 See Raymond Durgnat (1970) *A Mirror for England: British Movies from Austerity to Affluence*. London: Faber and Faber, 129.

63   This crisis of class identity is a crucial theme of the New Wave culture exemplified in John Osbourne and Harold Pinter but also in cinema with films such as *Room At the Top* (directed by Jack Clayton and written by Neil Paterson from the novel by John Braine, 1958), *A Kind of Loving* (Schlesinger, 1962), *Billy Liar* (Schlesinger, 1963), *Morgan – A Suitable Case for Treatment* (directed by Reisz and written by David Mercer, 1966) and so forth. The most intriguing and passionate expression was Anderson's *If* (1968).

64   Victor Burgin (1996) *In/different Spaces*. Berkeley: University of California Press, 2–5.

65   Richard Hoggart (1968 [1957]) *The Uses of Literacy*. Harmondsworth: Penguin, 340.

66   Hoggart 1968: 246–7.

67   Lindsay Anderson (1954) 'Only Connect', *Sight and Sound*, April–June, 23, 4, Spring, 181.

68   Anderson considered Jennings' post-war work to lack the passion and contemporaneity of his earlier work; Jennings was lost without the certainty and patriotic determination of the war. In 1950, aged 43, he fell fatally from a cliff in Greece. Not long before he died he was in Battersea with the poet Kathleen Raine. He surveyed the urban landscape and remarked: 'This has all grown up within less than two hundred years. Has anyone ever suggested that this is the way in which human beings ought to live? It will all have to go, it has been a terrible mistake!' Quoted in Lovell & Hillier 1972: 120.

69   Quoted in Lovell & Hillier 1972: 156.

70   See the British Federation of Film Societies website: www. bffs.org.uk.

CHAPTER 7

1   I use *autarkic* here to denote self-sufficiency.

2   A significant example of this neglect is Macpherson 1980: 191–8.

3   The works of the Free Cinema movement and the Scottish maker Margaret Tait have been acknowledged as exceptional and most recently Margaret Dickinson has briefly outlined certain key continuities from the 1930s' independent movement into the post-war period in her collection *Rogue Reels: Oppositional Film in Britain, 1945–90*, London: British Film Institute.

4   As early as 1932 there was a national network of at least ninety public ciné-clubs including twenty clubs in London. See Marjorie A. Lovell Burgess (1932) *A Popular Account of the Development of the Amateur Ciné Movement in Great Britain*. London: Sampson Low, Marston & Co.

5   The outline of the post-war Amateur Film Movement which follows is based on a broad reading of *Amateur Cine World* and similar publications including *Amateur Movie-Maker, Cine Camera* and *8mm Magazine*, and it concentrates on the heyday of the movement, from the end of the war to the mid-1960s. Despite the advent of video and the venerable age of most of its participants, the movement still exists, but in the context of this history the crucial issue is the significance of the movement as an unofficial culture prior to the advent of the Underground Cinema of the 1960s.

6   *ACW March–May 1946* carries adverts for around a dozen regional cine libraries with catalogues of 16mm, 9.5mm and 8mm films for hire.

7   The society movement thrived after the war increasing from around 50 in 1945 to around 250 in 1954 and 500 in the early 1960s. See the British Federation of Film Societies website: www. bffs.org.uk. These figures are probably underestimates since

there were many clubs and societies not affiliated to the BBFS. According to Charles Cooper there were around 700 film societies in the early 1950s. See interview in Dickinson 1999a: 211.

8   Anon. (1956b) 'A Catalogue of Amateur Films for Club and Home Showing', *Amateur Cine World*, 20, 8, December, 841–6.

9   Cooper had been involved in the Workers' Film Movement as secretary of the Kino group in the mid-1930s. Contemporary Films began as a 16mm distributor for film societies and clubs specialising in foreign/radical features, but it eventually became a leading art cinema distributor/exhibitor of both 35mm and 16mm films and ran three major art cinemas between the mid-1960s and the mid-1980s: the Paris Pullman and the Phoenix in London and another Phoenix in Oxford. See Dickinson 1999a: 31–2 and also the interview with Cooper in ibid., 210–15. Contemporary Films is also listed in *Amateur Cine World* as the distributor of a selection of experimental student films. For links to student film see the review: Anon. (1959) 'University Students Film', *Amateur Cine World*, 22, 9, 946–7.

10 Despite, but also because of, the advent of video technology, there is still a thriving subculture of film collecting. In Britain an annual convention was founded in 1977 as the British Film Collectors Convention http://www.bfcc.biz/index. The Internet has further opened up international contact and trade between collectors. See the US-based efilmforum at http://www.film-center.com/.

11 A key subsector of the cine industry was titling equipment and titling services; apart from various lettering systems and special lighting rostrums there were also companies who would shoot film titles to order. It was also possible to buy ready-made all-purpose title footage which could be cut into a home movie with titles such as 'Our Holiday', 'Our Family' and 'THE END'. Occasionally the cine magazines would also print home movie titles to cut out and film. See for example Stuart Wynn Jones (1958) 'Summer Summary', *Amateur Cine World*, 22, 1, 53–7.

12 Peter Bowen (1955) 'Putting Drama into the Holiday Film', *Amateur Cine World*, 19, 6, 554.

13 In 1950 a 35mm compilation film of four of the Ten Best with documentary material about the amateur movement was released on the commercial cinema circuit as *Filming for Fun*, directed by Harold Baim. From 1956, screenings of the awards were held at the National Film Theatre and substandard prints of the winning films were distributed variously by Adventure Films Ltd, Wallace Heaton Ltd, the IAC and the BFI. See Anon. (1958a) 'Personal Choice', *Amateur Movie-Maker*, 4, January, 24–5.

14 Kevin Brownlow is now best known as a film historian and restorer but was first celebrated for his amateur feature film *It Happened Here* (1964), a speculative history of a Nazi invasion of Britain. Brownlow began work on the film when he was 18, it took him and his co-director Andrew Mollo seven years to make and it was eventually released for a limited art-house run in 1963. Brownlow and Mollo went on to make a second feature, *Winstanley* (1975), a historical drama based on the life of Gerrard Winstanley and the Diggers.

15 Chanan 1980: 229.

16 This fascination tended towards an ardent loyalty to particular film gauges and techniques which was often disputed in the pages of *ACW*. Conflict often took the form of a complex class struggle; the more money you spent on your technology the closer you could get to the 'professional' standards of the commercial cinema. Accordingly, advocates of 16mm spurned 8mm as primitive, whilst 8mm advocates accused the 16mm users of elitism. Throughout the 1950s the percentage of 8mm entries to the

ACW Ten Best rose steadily and yet this increase was not represented in the overall winners which were consistently dominated by 16mm, and this under-representation aroused an ongoing controversy in the *ACW* about aesthetics, technology and the nature of amateurism. See, for example, Anon. (1957b) 'A Special Class for 8mm?', *Amateur Cine World*, 21, 4, August, 329.

17   For a defence of experimental film see Anon. (1957d) 'Comment on Competitions', *Amateur Cine World*, 21, 6, November, 563.

18   See Anon. (1955) 'Equipment, Materials, Technical Developments, Services', *Amateur Cine World*, 19, 1, May, 40.

19   See for instance H .A. Postlethwaite (1956) 'What's the Date?', *Amateur Cine World*, 20, 1, May, 43.

20   This argument draws on Don Macpherson's paraphrasing of Stephen Heath in Macpherson (ed.) 1980: 194–5.

21   For a remarkable example see Anon. (1946) 'A Novel Idea From America', *Amateur Cine World*, 10, 9, Autumn, 437, which comments on the production of professionally shot holiday footage which the amateur maker could edit into their own footage to create a glamorous virtual holiday.

22   A particular celebrity maker who frequently featured in the cine magazines in the late 1950s was the popular black boogie-woogie pianist Winifred Atwell who, together with her husband, specialised in 16mm travel and wildlife films. See D. M. Phythian (1958) 'Round-the-World Record', *Amateur Movie-Maker*, 4 January 1958, 33–4. The black tennis star Althea Gibson was also noted as an amateur maker in *Amateur Cine World*, 21, 4, August 1957, 329.

23   See, for instance, Leslie Wood (1951) 'Wanted: Cine Suffragettes', *Amateur Cine World*, 14, 10, February, 993–7; Iris Fayde (1952) 'Woman's Viewpoint', *Amateur Cine World*, 15, 10, February, 1019–20 and 1039–40.

24   Alan Gill (1962) 'The Longest Little Show on Earth', *Amateur Cine World*, 27, 20, 776–7.

25   For instance, in *Amateur Cine World*, February 1952, there is an article detailing how to construct a rostrum-mounted kaleidoscope for the creation of infinite symmetrical patterning and in *Amateur Cine World*, December 1957, the animator Stuart Wynn Jones details techniques for drawing images directly onto 16mm film and how to compose music by drawing directly onto the optical soundtrack. See respectively Anon. (1952) 'Soundtrack, Running Commentary: *Kaleidoscope*', *Amateur Cine World*, 15, 10, February, 1005; and Stuart Wynn Jones (1957) 'Cartooning Without A Camera', *Amateur Cine World*, 21, 8, December, 782–5 and 826.

26   See Oswell Blakeston (1949) *How To Script Amateur Films*. London: Focal Press.

27   See Oswell Blakeston (1951) 'Material for A Poem', *Amateur Cine World*, 14, 10, February, 997–1001.

28   See Anon. (1957a) 'Controversy Corner', *Amateur Cine World*, 21, 2, June, 171.

29   Anon. (1956c) 'Programme Building for Public Shows', *Amateur Cine World*, 20, 8, December, 840 and 856. The attitude of *ACW* to Free Cinema was almost entirely enthusiastic: the six programmes of films held at the NFT between 1956 and 1959 were extensively featured and discussed. What is most significant is that *ACW* initially celebrated Free Cinema as a vindication and outstanding example of amateur film-making despite the fact that all of the films in the first programme were produced by the BFI Experimental Film Fund.

30   See respectively Anon. 1957b: 563; Anon. (1958b) 'What Does It All Mean?', *Amateur Cine World*, 22, 3, October, 245–7; Anon. 1959: 946–7.

31 A long-running series of items followed the making of the abstract film ballet, *Between Two Worlds*, by the Oxford Experimental Film Group in the early 1950s. See, for example, Derrick Knight (1952) 'We Found A New Idea', *Amateur Cine World*, 15, 10, February, 991–4 and 1018. In August 1957 a short item referred to a group called Camera Obscura Experimental Films working in Blackheath, SE3, who were experimenting with double exposure of film to create 'a kind of cinematic spirit writing'. See Anon. (1957c) 'Experimental', *Amateur Cine World*, 21, 4, August, 367. In November 1958 a full page article reviews the work of two obscure experimental makers and laments that it is very unlikely that anyone will ever see their work. Jack Smith, 'Flights of Fancy', *Amateur Cine World*, 22, 7, November, 671.

32 See, for instance, Jeff Nuttall (1970) *Bomb Culture*. London: Paladin, 117.

33 Tony Wigens (1968) 'Not To Be Shown in Public', *8mm Magazine*, 7, 7, 50–1.

34 Heliczer also organised happenings with the Velvet Underground and ran the Dead Language Press which published the limited edition *Beautiful Book* (1962), a collection of photographs by the definitive Underground star, Jack Smith.

35 See Camille Cook (1966) 'What are Underground Movies?', *Amateur Cine World*, 11, 26, June, 876–9; and also the advert in *Amateur Cine World*, 1966: 11, 28, August, 149.

CHAPTER 8

1 See Henri Saint-Simon (1975 [1823]) 'On the Intermediate (Bourgeois) Class', in *Selected Writings on Science, Industry and Social Organisation*, ed. Keith Taylor. London: Croom Helm, 250–1.

2 See for instance Richard Huelsenbeck (1922) 'En Avant Dada', in Robert Motherwell (ed.) (1951) *The Dada Painters and Poets*. New York: George Wittenborn, 44.

3 For example, the contemporaneous Italian Futurist movement had amongst its number the anarchists Russolo and Boccioni, whilst amongst the Russian Futurists Mayakovsky's involvement in revolutionary communism began at the age of 14. See also Egbert 1970: 274–5.

4 Bürger 1984: 22–58.

5 Bourdieu 1986: 54–5.

6 Hans Richter (1966) *Dada: Art and Anti-Art*. New York: McGraw-Hill, 35.

7 This is specifically the charge that the radical Huelsenbeck levels at Tzara in his 1936 essay, 'Dada Lives', quoted in Stewart Home (1988) *The Assault on Culture*. London: Aporia Press, 5.

8 Quoted in Calvin Tomkins (1968) *Ahead of the Game*. London: Penguin, 42–3.

9 Allan Kaprow, 'Education of the Un-Artist', in Allan Kaprow (1993) *Essays on the Blurring of Life and Art*. Berkeley: University of California Press, 103.

10 Key points of my argument in this section were conceived in opposition to the work of Andreas Huyssen in his collection of essays *After the Great Divide* (1988a). See specifically Andreas Huyssen (1988b) 'The Hidden Dialectic', in Andreas Huyssen *After the Great Divide*. London: Macmillan, 3–15.

11 In early nineteenth-century England the revolutionary utopian writings of William Godwin, Mary Wollstonecraft and Robert Owen had a profound influence on Mary and Percy Shelley, Blake, Coleridge, Landseer and others.

12 See first Bourdieu 1986: 488; and also Peter Stallybrass and Allon White (1986) *The Politics and Poetics of Transgression*. London: Methuen, 5.

13 The classic account of the black revolution of Saint Domingue is from C.L.R. James

(1994) *The Black Jacobins*. London: Allison and Busby.

14 The Barbus were perhaps the first movement that sought an autonomous Art based on the fetish of a pre-industrial feudalism. They began the tradition that runs through the Nazarenes, the Pre-Raphaelites, the Arts and Crafts Movement, the Symbolists and into the Hippie communes of the 1960s. In England this tradition can first be identified in the Ancients, the youthful circle that gathered around William Blake in the 1820s. See George Levitine (1978) *The Dawn of Bohemianism: The Barbu Rebellion and Primitivism in Neoclassical France*. University Park: Pennsylvania State University Press. For the Ancients see Laurence Binyon (1968) *The Followers of Blake*. London: Benjamin Bloom.

15 See Jerrold Seigel (1986) *Bohemian Paris: Culture, Politics and the Boundaries of Bourgeois Life*. New York: Viking.

16 See Seigel 1986: 20.

17 Hauser 1968: 195.

18 Seigel 1986: 11.

19 Seigel 1986: 181–215.

20 As Griselda Pollock has observed, this bohemian (in her terms modernist) zone operated within the spatial confines and power relations of patriarchy and so excluded women artists and feminine art. See Griselda Pollock (1988) 'Modernity and the Spaces of Femininity', in her *Vision and Difference*. London: Routledge, 69–70. However, Pollock's argument effectively denies creative agency to working class bohemian women and entertainers since their popular culture is not identified as Art but as merely the expression of a male economy. Moreover, since Art is the nineteenth-century fetish of sacred feudal power, which is to say patriarchal power, it is hardly surprising that few women could participate in its formation.

21 Seigel 1986: 224–6.

22 Philippe Jullian (1977) *Montmartre*, trans. Anne Carter. Oxford: Phaidon Press, 44–50.

23 See Charles Rearick (1985) *Pleasures of the Belle Epoque: Entertainment and Festivity in Turn of the Century France*. New Haven, CT: Yale University Press, 55–73.

24 Harold B. Segel (1987) *Turn of the Century Cabaret*. New York: Columbia University Press, 7–8.

25 Segel 1987: 19.

26 Rearick 1985: 61.

27 Nancy Perloff (1991) *Art and the Everyday: Popular Entertainment and the Circle of Erik Satie*. Oxford: Clarendon, 12.

28 Rearick 1985: 58–9.

29 Segel 1987: 1.

30 Perloff 1991: 23.

31 See also Phillip Dennis Cate and Mary Shaw (eds) (1996) *The Spirit of Montmartre: Cabarets, Humor and the Avant-Garde, 1875–1905*. New Brunswick, NJ: Jane Voorhees Zimmerli Art Museum and Rutgers.

32 Daniel Gerould (1994) 'Melodrama and Revolution', in Jacky Bratton, Jim Cook and Christine Gledhill (eds) *Melodrama, Stage, Picture, Screen*. London: British Film Institute, 190–1.

33 Rearick 1985: 71–9.

34 For Duchamp's deployment of fumism, see Jeffrey Weiss (1994) *The Popular Culture of Modern Art*. New Haven, CT: Yale University Press, 109–45.

35 See Jeffrey Weiss (1990) 'Picasso, Collage and the Music Hall', in Adam Gopnick

and Kirk Varnedoe (eds) *Modern Art and Popular Culture: Readings in High and Low.* New York: Museum of Modern Art, 82–115; and also the excellent survey by Adam Gopnick and Kirk Varnedoe (1990a) *High and Low: Modern Art and Pop Culture.* New York: Museum of Modern Art.

36   Filippo Tommaso Marinetti, 'The Variety Theatre' (1913), reprinted in Filippo Tommaso Marinetti, *Selected Writings,* ed. R. W. Flint. London: Secker and Warburg, 117.

37   See Grigori *Kozintsev, Georgii Kryzhitskii, Leonid* Trauberg and Sergei Yutkevich (1992) *The Eccentric Manifesto.* London: Eccentric Press, 14.

38   The context of Dada, Anti-Art and the popular is documented in the captivating study by Greil Marcus (1990) *Lipstick Traces: A Secret History of the Twentieth Century.* London: Secker and Warburg.

CHAPTER 9

1   Horak 1995: 14–66.

2   For the Surrealist rejection of avant-garde cinema see Robert Desnos (1978 [1929] 'Avant-Garde Cinema', in Paul Hammond (ed.) *The Shadow and its Shadow.* London: British Film Institute, 36.

3   For a characteristic psychoanalytic reading of *Un Chien Andalou* see Linda Williams (1992) *Figures of Desire: A Theory and Analysis of Surrealist Film.* Berkeley: University of California Press, 56–79.

4   See also Lauren Rabinovitz (1992) 'Wearing the Critic's Hat: History, Critical Discourses, and the American Avant-Garde Cinema', in David E. James (ed.) *To Free the Cinema: Jonas Mekas and the New York Underground. Princeton, NJ: Princeton University Press,* 271–4.

5   Huyssen 1988; see especially page 168.

6   This is a point partially suggested by Juan A. Suárez (1996) *Bike Boys, Drag Queens and Superstars: Avant-Garde, Mass Culture, and Gay Identities in the 1960s' Underground Cinema.* Bloomington, IN: Indiana University Press, 59–60. The potential of amateur cine as a radical experimental sector was actually recognised by the American amateur cine movement before the war. See Patricia R. Zimmermann (1995) 'Startling Angles, Amateur Film and the Early Avant-Garde', in Horak (ed.) 1995: 137–55.

7   The carnivalisation of blackness can be clearly illustrated by the history of the development of black face minstrelsy both in the US and Europe. See, for instance, Michael Pickering (1986), 'White Skin, Black Masks: "Nigger" Minstrelsy in Victorian England', in Jacqueline S. Bratton (ed.) *Music Hall Performance and Style.* Milton Keynes: Open University Press, 70–91.

8   See Taylor 1978: 89–155.

9   The most audacious account of the birth of the New Left in America is by David Zane Mairowitz (1976) *The Radical Soap Opera.* Harmondsworth: Penguin. For the British New Left see the Oxford University Socialist Discussion Group (eds) (1989) *Out of Apathy.* London: Verso.

10   See Stuart Hall (1989) 'The "First" New Left: Life and Times', in the Oxford University Socialist Discussion Group (eds) 1989: 11–39.

11   Nuttall 1970: 42–52.

12   Ibid., 34–9.

13   See Paul Jacobs and Saul Landau (1967) *The New Radicals.* Harmondsworth: Penguin Books, 20–1; also Roger Lewis (1972) *Outlaws of America.* Harmondsworth: Penguin Books, 154–9.

14 John Swenson (1982) *Bill Haley*. London: W. H. Allen, 86–7.
15 The subversive underground of Hollywood pulp action movies was first explored by the critic Manny Farber in 1957 in the article 'Underground Films', later compiled in Manny Farber (1998) *Negative Space*. New York: De Capo Press, 12–24.
16 See Lewis 1972.
17 For Ubu Films see Peter Mudie (1997) *UBU FILMS: Sydney Underground Movies 1965–1970*. Sydney: University of South Wales Press Ltd.
18 The dating of the first wave of the American Underground is difficult since the movement must be understood as a complex combination of production, distribution and exhibition factors. Various historians have made inclusive and exclusive periodisations. Whilst many have blurred the distinction between the avant-garde and the Underground recently Juan A. Suárez has localised the Underground to five years: 1961–66. See Suárez 1996: 55.
19 See P. Adams Sitney (1971) *Film Culture: An Anthology*. London: Secker and Warburg, 13.
20 The contemporary filmmaker and writer Stephen Dwoskin cites *Pull My Daisy* as the first Underground film. See Stephen Dwoskin (1975) *Film Is*. New York: The Overlook Press, 50.
21 Jonas Mekas (1971) 'The First Statement of the New American Cinema Group', in P. Adams Sitney (ed.) *Film Culture: An Anthology*. London: Secker and Warburg, 79–84.
22 For Mekas on populism see Jonas Mekas (1972) 'On "People's Movies", or the Difference Between Melodrama and Art', in Jonas Mekas *Movie Journal*. New York: Collier Books, 155–6.
23 See Rabinovitz 1992: 279–80.
24 Ibid., 272–3.
25 See ibid., 280–81.
26 J. Hoberman (1984) 'After Avant-Garde Film', in Brian Wallis (ed.) *Art After Modernism*. New York: New Museum of Contemporary Art, 65.
27 Rabinovitz 1992: 280.

CHAPTER 10

1 Dwoskin 1985: 61.
2 Nuttall 1970: 115–18.
3 Tony Jefferson (1978) 'Cultural Responses of the Teds', *Cultural Studies*, 7, 8, 81–6.
4 See David Curtis (1975) 'English Avant-Garde Film: An Early Chronology', *Studio International*, Nov./Dec., 176–82; also Deke Dusinberre's unpublished thesis, *The History of English Avant-Garde Film* (1974) available at the BFI Library; and Mark Webber (2002) 'Chronology of Events and Developments 1966–76', in *Shoot, Shoot, Shoot* catalogue, London: Tate Modern, 6–7.
5 Jonas Mekas (1966) 'Open Letter To Film-Makers of the World', *Cinim*, 1, 5–8.
6 See Mairowitz 1976: 137–41.
7 See Mick Farren (2001) *Give The Anarchist A Cigarette*. London: Jonathon Cape, 70–6.
8 See Jack Sargeant (1997) *The Naked Lens: An Illustrated History of Beat Cinema*. London: Creation Books, 169–83; also Rob Bridgett (2001) *An Appraisal of the Films of William Burroughs, Brion Gysin and Anthony Balch in Terms of Recent Avant-Garde Theory and History*. Available at: www.sound.design.org.uk/burroughs [accessed 19 December 2001].

9　Sargeant 1997: 174–5.

10　Webber 2002: 6; see also Elizabeth Nelson (1989) *The British Counter-Culture 1966–73*. London: Macmillan.

11　For a description of the psychedelic subculture see, for instance, Richard Neville (1971) *Playpower*. London: Paladin, 24–31.

12　See Dusinberre 1974: 40–2.

13　See Farren 2001: 119–21.

14　See Sandy N. Craig (1980) 'Reflexes of the Future: the Beginnings of the Fringe', in Sandy N. Craig (ed.) *Dreams and Deconstructions: Alternative Theatre in Britain*. London: Amber Lane Press, 15–16.

15　Anthony Scott (1969) 'The Longest Most Meaningless Movie in the World', *Cinema*, October, 32.

16　For Derek Hill and the New Cinema see David Prothero (2000) 'Interview with Derek Hill', *The Journal of Popular British Cinema*, 3, 32; also 'Independent Film-Making in the '70s' by the Organising Committee for the I.F.A. Conference May 1976', in Dickinson 1999a: 130–1; also Albie Thoms (1978) *Polemics for A New Cinema*. Sydney: Wild and Woolley, 30.

17　Students and Staff of Hornsey College of Art (1969) *The Hornsey Affair*. Harmondsworth: Penguin.

18　Ibid., 70–1.

19　Ibid., 66–7.

20　See Malcolm Le Grice (1993) 'A Reflection on the History of the London Filmmakers' Co-op', *LFMC Catalogue*, London, 163.

21　Malcolm Le Grice (1978 [1969]) '*Room (Double Take)*', in the *LFMC Catalogue*, 21.

22　See Dusinberre 1974: 229–35.

23　Included as Appendix IV in Deke Dusinberre's unpublished thesis, *The History of English Avant-Garde Film*.

24　Curtis 1975: 180.

25　Webber 2002: 6.

26　Unpublished programme of the New Arts Lab cinema prepared by Mark Webber (2002).

27　Rees 1999: 88.

28　See Anon. (1970) 'Festival programme', *Time Out*, 46, September, 26–35.

29　A key example of this shift is the rejection of 'Underground' as a term in the avant-garde issue of *Afterimage*, 2, Autumn 1970.

30　Curtis 1975: 182.

31　See the revised version of David Curtis, 'English Avant-Garde Film: An Early Chronology', in the catalogue *A Perspective on English Avant-Garde Film*. London: The Arts Council of Great Britain/British Council, 17.

32　See David Curtis (1992) 'A Tale Of Two Co-Ops', in David E. James (ed.) *To Free the Cinema*. Princeton, NJ: Princeton University Press, 253–65.

33　Dickinson 1999b: 48–50.

34　Julia Knight (1996) 'A Chronological Guide to British Video Art', in Julia Knight (ed.) *Diverse Practices*. Luton: University of Luton Press, 351–8.

35　The first IFA annual general meeting was actually funded by the BFI and the Association eventually folded in 1990 when its BFI funding was withdrawn. See Jonathon Curling and Fran McLean (1977) 'The Independent Film-makers' Association – Annual General Meeting and Conference', *Screen*, 18, 1, 107–117.
　　See also the founding document of the IFA: the Organising Committee for the IFA

Conference May 1976 (Simon Hartog, Marc Karlin, Claire Johnston, Paul Willemen and Stephen Dwoskin), 'Independent Film-Making in the '70s', compiled in Margaret Dickinson (1999a) *Rogue Reels: Oppositional Film in Britain 1945–90*, London: British Film Institute, 126–137.

36 Dickinson 1999a: 72–3.

CHAPTER 11

1 A critical intersection of the two currents was the *New Left Review* since it served as a key agent in the development of both. Moreover, the internal editorial coup of 1962 can be conceived as the temporary eclipse of the Cultural Studies tendency by the new structuralist faction.

2 For the roots of Cultural Studies in the post-war adult education movement see Tom Steele (1997) *The Emergence of Cultural Studies 1945–65*. London: Lawrence and Wishart.

3 This brief conceptual outline is drawn from David Bordwell's incisive critique of the irrationality of theory. David Bordwell (1996) 'Contemporary Film Theory and the Vicissitudes of Grand Theory', in David Bordwell and Noël Carroll (eds) *Post-Theory: Reconstructing Film Studies*. Madison, WI: The University of Wisconsin Press, 3–37.

4 Historical references here are taken from Sylvia Harvey (1978b) *May '68 and Film Culture*. London: British Film Institute.

5 Harvey 1978b: 36–8.

6 Counter-Cinema was the term first devised by Peter Wollen in the early 1970s to describe Godard's oppositional film practice. It was subsequently taken up as a term and a model by various radical factions of the independent sector. See Peter Wollen (1982b) 'Godard and Counter Cinema: *Vent d'Est*', in Peter Wollen (1982a) *Readings and Writings: Semiotic Counter Strategies*. London: Verso, 79–91.

7 This assumption had different functions and inflections for the diverse elements of the British independent film and video sector; the agit-prop collectives sought to subvert the mainstream with alternative ideology, independent makers such as Wollen and Mulvey, John Davies and Pat Murphy or the Sankofa group, foregrounded and exposed the construction of meaning in the mainstream text, the LFMC avant-garde sought to purge their films of every element, code and convention of mainstream cinema.

8 Harvey 1978b., 72.

9 Notable exceptions to this exclusivity were the agit-prop groups such as Cinema Action and Angry Arts/Liberation Films and the later community video movement of the early 1980s. However, these groups were not avant-gardist and theoretical demystification was not their core radical ethic.

10 See Bordwell 1996: 17–18.

11 For an examination of the problem of authorship in avant-garde film see Rabinowitz 1991: 12–36.

CHAPTER 12

1 Throughout the 1990s the New Directors scheme annually selected around seven projects from the many hundreds of submissions: in 1993 there were five hundred applications for funding; by 1998 this had risen to 1,772. Source: *BFI Yearbook 1987–1998*. London: British Film Institute.

2   The BFI New Directors scheme did fund a number of avant-garde makers, but according to Ben Gibson, the head of BFI production between 1989–97, they were selected on the personal recommendation of David Curtis at the Arts Council. Consequently, there was no actual avant-garde access to the New Directors initiative except through the primary avant-garde funding agency. (Gibson was speaking at a Study Day on Institutional Support for British Experimental Film and Video organised by the British Artists' Film and Video Study Collection, 13 December 2002.)

3   Curtis 1975: 182.

4   Arts Council of Great Britain catalogue (1977) *Perspectives on British Avant-Garde Film*. London: Hayward Gallery, 2 March–24 April (unpaginated).

5   This was the version included in the major compendium of writing on the British avant-garde which was co-published by the Arts Council in 1995: Michael O'Pray (ed.) *The British Avant-Garde Film 1926–1995*. Luton: University of Luton Press.

6   Malcolm Le Grice (1977) *Abstract Film and Beyond*. London: Studio Vista.

7   Malcolm Le Grice (1979) 'The History We Need', from the catalogue for *Film As Film: the Formal Experiment in Film 1910–1975*. London: Hayward Gallery, 3 May–17 June, Arts Council of Great Britain, 113.

8   David Curtis (ed.) (1996) *Directory of British Film and Video Artists*. Luton: John Libbey/Arts Council.

9   Sitney's definition and history of structural film was, however, contested by the filmmaker Peter Kubelka and the Fluxus ideologue George Maciunas. See P. Adams Sitney (1969) 'Structural Film', *Film Culture*, 47; revised Winter 1969 and compiled in P. Adams Sitney (ed.) (1971) *Film Culture: An Anthology*. London: Secker and Warburg, 326–349. See P. Adams Sitney (1979) *Visionary Film: The American Avant-Garde 1943–1978*. Oxford: Oxford University Press, 369–446.

10   See Peter Gidal (1999) 'Flashbacks: Peter Gidal', *Filmwaves*, 7, Spring, 16–20.

11   Webber 2002.

12   Peter Gidal (1970a) 'Film As Materialist Consumer Product', *Cinemantics*, 2, 14.

13   Peter Gidal (1975) 'Theory and Definition of Structural/Materialist Film', *Studio International*, Nov./Dec., 190, 978, 189.

14   Gidal 1975: 192.

15   Ibid., 194.

16   Peter Gidal (1989) *Materialist Film*. London: Routledge.

17   Anne Cottringer (1976) 'On Peter Gidal's Theory and Definition of Structural/Materialist Film', *Afterimage*, 6, Summer, 86–95; also Constance Penley (1977) 'The Avant-Garde and its Imaginary', *Camera Obscura*, 2, Fall, 24–5.

18   Mike Dunford (1976) 'Experimental/Avant-Garde/Revolutionary Film Practice', *Afterimage*, 6, Summer, 107.

19   Ibid., 106.

20   In the case of Gidal, this assumption was almost pathological, since he considers himself to be specifically vulnerable to the seductive narcotic of narrative. This was clear in comments made by Gidal about being 'hooked' on narrative at the panel discussion of *Shoot Shoot Shoot: The First Decade of the London Film-Makers' Co-Operative and British Avant-Garde Film 1966–76*, 4 May 2002. See also Peter Gidal 1999: 20.

21   Of Gidal's 11 major films between 1974–1996, at least seven were funded by the Arts Council. See Curtis (ed.) (1996), 66–7. From personal experience I have seen Gidal's 40-minute film *Guilt* (1988) vanquish a committed audience in about 15 minutes. Of the three people who remained to the end of the film one eventually began to cast hand shadow puppets on the screen, whilst the other two giggled. This was at a

public screening at the ICA Biennial of Independent Film and Video 1989 (October 1989).

22 Students taught by either Le Grice or Gidal would include Cerith Wyn Evans, Steve Chivers, John Smith, Michael Mazière, Lucy Panteli, Nino Danino, Sandra Lahire, Kobena Mercer, Isaac Julien *inter alia*.

23 Wollen and Mulvey's feature films included *Riddles of the Sphinx* (Funded: Arts Council, 1977), *Crystal Gazing* (Funded: BFI/Channel Four, 1981) and *The Bad Sister* (Funded: Channel Four, 1983). In 1975 Wollen co-wrote the script for Michelangelo Antonioni's *The Passenger* with Mark Peploe and Antonioni. In 1987 he wrote and directed the feature *Friendship's Death* (Funded: BFI, 1987).

24 The references are respectively: Deke Dusinberre (1976) 'St George in the Forest: the English Avant-Garde', *Afterimage*, 6, 4–20; Anne Cottringer (1976) 'On Peter Gidal's Theory and Definition of Structural/Materialist Film', *Afterimage*, 6, 86–96; Laura Mulvey (1989) 'Film, Feminism and the Avant-Garde', in Laura Mulvey *Visual and Other Pleasures*. London: Macmillan Press, 111–27; Philip Drummond (1979) 'Notions of Avant-Garde Cinema', in *Film as Film*. London: Arts Council of Great Britain, 9–16; Sylvia Harvey (1978a) *Independent Cinema?* Stratford: West Midlands Arts; Paul Willemen (1984) 'An Avant-Garde for the 1980s', *Framework*, 24, 53–74; J. Hoberman (1984) 'After Avant-Garde Film', in *Art After Modernism*. New York: New Museum of Contemporary Art, 59–73; Anne Friedberg (1993) *Window Shopping*. Berkeley: University of California Press, 157–77 and Juan A. Suárez (1996) *Bike Boys, Drag Queens and Superstars*. Bloomington, IN: Indiana University Press, xxii–xxviii.

25 Most recently all three *Studio International* texts were anthologised in Michael O'Pray (ed.) (1997) *Avant-Garde Film*. Luton: University of Luton Press. Significantly *The Two Avant-Gardes* was substantially reproduced by Julian Petley in his introduction to the 'Avant-Garde(s)' section of the BFI Distribution Library Catalogue 1978.

26 In *The Cinema Book*, the British Film Institute's '*definitive introduction to Film Studies for students of all levels*', Alison Butler uses *The Two Avant-Gardes* to map out the history of avant-garde film. Alison Butler (1999) 'Avant-Garde and Counter Cinema', in Pam Cook and Mieke Bernink (eds) *The Cinema Book,* 2nd Edn. London: British Film Institute, 114–19.

27 I date this period from the move to its first autonomous premises at Prince of Wales Crescent (1971), to the establishment of the Association of Cinematographic, Television and allied Technicians (ACTT) Committee for Independent Grant Aided Film (1980). For an overview of this period see Simon Blanchard and Sylvia Harvey, 'The Post-War Independent Cinema – Structure and Organisation', in James Curran and Vincent Porter (eds) *British Cinema History*. London: Weidenfield and Nicholson, 227–41.

28 Rees 1999: 93.

29 'Film history has developed unevenly, so that in Europe today there are two distinct avant-gardes. The first can be identified loosely with the Co-op movement and includes most of the film-makers written about in this number of Studio International. The second would include film-makers such as Godard, Straub and Huillet, Hanoun, Jancso. Naturally there are points of contact between these two groups and common characteristics, but they also differ quite sharply in many respects: aesthetic assumptions, institutional framework, type of financial support, type of critical backing, historical and cultural origin.' Peter Wollen (1975) 'The Two Avant-Gardes', *Studio International*, Nov./Dec., 190, 978, 171. When it was republished in Wollen's own anthology *Readings and Writings: Semiotic Counter Strategies* in 1982, the line: ' …and

includes most of the film-makers written about in this number of Studio International' was omitted from the text. This republished version, by virtue of its wide availability, rapidly replaced the Studio International version, and so isolated the text from its original intertextual context. Peter Wollen (1982a) *Readings and Writings: Semiotic Counter Strategies*. London: Verso, 77.

30 Wollen 1975: 172.

31 'One powerful influence has come from painting, bringing with it a tendency to abstraction – pure light or colour; and non-figurative design – or deformation of conventional photographic imagery, involving prismatic fragmentation and splintering, the use of filters or stippled glass, mirror shots, extreme and microscopic close ups, bizarre angles, negative images etc. All of these are to be found in 1920s films' (Wollen 1975: 2).

32 Wollen 1975: 174.

33 Ibid.: 171.

34 Ibid.: 175.

35 Ibid.: 175.

36 In Wollen's 1993 essay 'The Last New Wave' he seems to suggest that the synthesis of the two Avant-Gardes was finally accomplished in the films of Derek Jarman and Peter Greenaway. Peter Wollen (1995) 'The Last New Wave', in O'Pray (ed.) 1995: 239–56.

37 See Annette Michelson in the Introduction to Noël Burch (1969) *Theory of Film Practice*. London: Secker and Warburg, v–vi.

38 *Afterimage*, 2, Autumn 1970.

39 Graeme Farnell (1970) 'Which Avant-Garde?, *Afterimage*, 2, Autumn, 65–71.

40 See Gidal 1970a: 2. Also Gidal 1970b 'Film As Materialist Consumer Product II', *Cinemantics*, 3, 5.

41 Of course another crucial exclusion is non-European experimental film. The American avant-garde is briefly considered but only to except it from the equation. Nevertheless, Lauren Rabinowitz extends and critiques Wollen's binary in an American context in Rabinowitz 1991: 17–19.

42 Laura Mulvey and Peter Wollen (1976) 'Written Discussion', *Afterimage*, 6, Summer, 30–40.

43 Willemen 1984.

44 *Maeve* (John Davies and Pat Murphy, 1981) and *So That You Can Live* (Cinema Action, 1981).

45 Willemen 1984: 58.

46 Willemen (1994) *Looks and Frictions*. London: British Film Institute, 141–61.

CHAPTER 13

1 The most prominent example of British punk film was Don Letts' *The Punk Rock Movie* (1978), a Super 8 documentary shot around the seminal Covent Garden Punk venue, the Roxy.

2 My principal source for this brief historical outline of the new American Underground Cinema is Jack Sargeant (1995) *Deathtripping: The Cinema of Transgression*. London: Creation Books.

3 Sargeant 1995: 16.

4 The term 'transgressive' was first coined by *Soho Weekly News* critic Amy Taubin in 1979 about Zedd's film *They Eat Scum*. See Sargeant 1995: 25.

5   Compiled in Sargeant 1995: 76–7.

6   See for instance the untitled article on the Lido event by David Eimer (1993) *The Face*, 60, September, 144–5; and also Sean O'Hagan (1993) 'Against the Tide', *Guardian*, 9 August, 7.

7   For an overview of the 1990s' protest movement see: George McKay (1996) *Senseless Acts of Beauty*. London: Verso. See also the collection of essays: George McKay (ed.) (1998) *DIY Culture*. London: Verso.

8   See the Indymedia UK website at www.indymedia.org.uk

RESOLUTION

1   See 'Shoot Shoot Shoot: the First decade of the London Film-Makers Co-Operative and British Underground Film 1966–76' at the Tate Modern, 3 May–28 May 2002. Remarkably at the conference Experimental Film Today (Preston: University of Central Lancashire, 4 July–6 July 2003), Julia Knight gave a paper – 'Reaching Audiences – the Role of a Distributor', which attempted to mythologise *Shoot Shoot Shoot* as the rediscovery of an obscure, neglected and underprivileged cause.

2   Figures estimated from the House of Commons, Culture, Media and Sport Commitee (2003), *Sixth Report*, British Film Industry, London: The Stationery Office, and from correspondence with the UK Film Council, 28 June 2005, courtesy of Ian Thomson, Press and PR, UK Film Council.

3   Ironically, the renewed repression by the avant-garde/independent sector has actually been augmented by the trash/cult film fanzine subculture, which although it promotes American Underground cinema, has resolutely failed to recognise and promote the British Underground. As I have noted, this exoticism has always been a feature of British cinema intellectuals, but in the case of the trash/cult subculture it appears as an irrational ambivalence to the legitimacy of culture; the trash/cult fans have fetishised the visceral thrills of subversion but only if that subversion is legitimised and objectified in the authenticity of America. This fan fetish also makes trash/cult subculture amenable to co-option by the avant-garde/independent sector since they can appropriate the products of the American Underground without risk to their native power base. For instance, in the late 1990s, the BFI launched a new series of video compilations, the *History of the Avant-Garde*, with the compilation *Cinema of Transgression*. The tape included work by Zedd, Kern and Tessa Hughes-Freeland.

4   The Junior Research fellow 2002–2003 was Michael Mazière, who in November 2000 suddenly lost his job as Director of the Lux, shortly before the true depth of the financial crisis was discovered. The circumstances of his departure remain obscure. See also Benedict Seymour (2002a) 'The Last Picture Show', *Mute*, 22 Jan. On-line version at http://www.metamute.com.

5   Anne Friedberg (1993) *Window Shopping*. Berkeley: University of California Press, 157–77.

6   Frederic Jameson (1985 [1982]) 'Postmodernism and Consumer Society', in Hal Foster (ed.) *Postmodern Culture*. London: Pluto Press, 111.

7   See for instance the formative essay by Susan Sontag (1968 [1965]) 'One Culture and the New Sensibility', in Susan Sontag *Against Interpretation and Other Essays*. London: Eyre and Spottiswoode, 293–304.

BIBLIOGRAPHY

Abel, Richard (1984) *French Cinema: The First Wave 1915–29*. Princeton, NJ: Princeton University Press.

_____ (1988) *French Film Theory and Criticism 1. 1915–29*. Princeton, NJ: Princeton University Press.

Abel, Richard (ed.) (1996) *Silent Film*. London: Athlone.

Adorno, Theodor and Max Horkheimer (1993 [1947]) 'The Culture Industry: Enlightenment as Mass Deception', in Simon During (ed.) *The Cultural Studies Reader*. London and New York: Routledge, 29–43.

Altick, Richard D. (1978) *The Shows of London*. Cambridge, MA: Belknap Press, Harvard University.

Arnold, Matthew (1970 [1869]) 'Culture and Anarchy', in *Matthew Arnold: Selected Prose*, ed. P. J. Keating. Harmondsworth: Penguin, 202–300.

Bailey, Peter (1998) *Popular Culture and Performance in the Victorian City*. Cambridge: Cambridge University Press.

Bakhtin, Mikhail (1981) *The Dialogic Imagination*. Austin, Texas: University of Texas Press.

_____ (1984 [1965]) *Rabelais and His World*, trans. Helene Iswolsky. Bloomington: Indiana University Press.

Balzer, Richard (1998) *Peep Shows: A Visual History*. New York: Harry N. Abrams.

Banham, Joanna and Jennifer Harris (eds) *William Morris and the Middle Ages*. Manchester: Manchester University Press.

Barr, Charles (ed.) (1986) *All Our Yesterdays: 90 Years of British Cinema*. London: British Film Institute.

Battcock, Gregory (ed.) (1967) *The New American Cinema*. New York: E. P. Dutton.

Benjamin, Walter (1979) *Illuminations*. Glasgow: Fontana/Collins.

Benn (1980 [1931]) 'The Cinema: An Instrument of Class Rule' in Don Macpherson (ed.) *Traditions of Independence*. London: British Film Institute, 138–9.

Bennett, Tony, Graham Martin and Bernard Waites (eds) (1982) *Popular Culture Past and Present*. London: Croom Helm.

Bentley, Eric (ed.) (1980) *The Theory of the Modern Stage*. Harmondsworth: Penguin.

Bey, Hakim (1994) *Immediatism*. Edinburgh: Ak Press.

_____ (1996) *Temporary Autonomous Zone*. Brooklyn, New York: Autonomedia.

Binyon, Laurence (1968) *The Followers of Blake*. London: Benjamin Bloom.

Blakeston, Oswell (1949) *How to Script Amateur Films*. London: Focal Press.

Blanchard, Simon and Sylvia Harvey (1983) 'The Post-War Independent Cinema – Structure and Organisation', in James Curran and Vincent Porter (eds) *British Cinema History*. London: Weidenfield and Nicholson, 227–41.

Blanchard, Simon and David Morley (eds) (1982) *What's This Channel For?* London: Comedia Publishing Group.

Booth, Michael R. (1965) *English Melodrama*. London: Herbert Jenkins.

_____ (1981) *Victorian Spectacular Theatre 1850–1910*. Boston, London and Henley: Routledge and Kegan Paul.

Booth, Michael R. (ed.) (1976) *English Plays of the Nineteenth Century, V. Pantomimes, Extravaganzas and Burlesques*. Oxford: Clarendon Press.

Bordwell, David (1996) 'Contemporary Film Theory and the Vicissitudes of Grand Theory', in David Bordwell and Noël Carroll (eds) *Post-Theory: Reconstructing Film Studies*. Madison: University of Wisconsin Press, 3–37.

Bordwell, David and Noël Carroll (eds) (1996) *Post-Theory: Reconstructing Film Studies*. Madison: University of Wisconsin Press.

Bourdieu, Pierre (1986) *Distinction: A Social Critique of the Judgment of Taste*. London: Routledge and Kegan Paul.

Bratton, Jacky, Jim Cook and Christine Gledhill (eds) (1994) *Melodrama, Stage, Picture, Screen*. London: British Film Institute.

Brewer, John (1997) *The Pleasures of the Imagination*. London: HarperCollins.

Bridgett, Rob (2001) *An Appraisal of the Films of William Burroughs, Brion Gysin and Anthony Balch in Terms of Recent Avant-Garde Theory and History*. Available at: http://www.sound.design.org.uk/burroughs [accessed 19 December 2001]

Briggs, Asa (1979) *The History of Broadcasting in the UK, vol. 4*. Oxford: Oxford University Press.

Bristol, Michael D. (1985) *Carnival and Theatre*. London and New York: Methuen.

Brooks, Peter (1995) *The Melodramatic Imagination*. New Haven, CT. and London: Yale University Press.

Brown, Geoff (1986) 'Sister of the Stage: British Film and the British Stage', in Charles Barr (ed.) *All Our Yesterdays: 90 Years of British Cinema*. London: British Film Institute, 143–67.

Bruner, Jerome (1996) *The Culture of Education*. Cambridge, MA: Harvard University Press.

Bucknell, Peter A. (1979) *Entertainment and Ritual 600–1600*. London: Stainer and Bell.

Burch, Noël (1969) *Theory of Film Practice*. London: Secker and Warburg.

Bürger, Peter (1984 [1974]) *Theory of the Avant-Garde*, trans. Michael Shaw. Minneapolis: University of Minnesota Press.

Burgin, Victor (1986) *The End of Art Theory*. London: Macmillan.

_____ (1996) *In/different Spaces*. Berkeley: University of California Press.

Burke, Peter (1978) *Popular Culture in Early Modern Europe*. Aldershot: Wildwood House.

Burns, Tom (1997) *The BBC: Public Institution and Private World*. London: Macmillan Press.

Burroughs, William (1982) *A William Burroughs Reader*, ed. John Calder. London: Picador.

Butler, Alison (1999) 'Avant-Garde and Counter Cinema', in Pam Cook and Mieke Bernink (eds) *The Cinema Book*, 2nd Edn. London: British Film Institute, 114–19.

Canudo, Ricciotto (1988 [1923]) 'Reflections on The Seventh Art', trans. Claudia Gorbman, in Richard Abel (ed.) *French Film Theory and Criticism Vol. 1. 1915–29*. Princeton, NJ: Princeton, 291–302.

Carey, John (1992) *The Intellectuals and the Masses*. London: Faber and Faber.

Carpenter, Kevin (1983) *Penny Dreadfuls and Comics*. London: Victoria and Albert Museum.

Carroll, Noël (1998) *A Philosophy of Mass Art*. Oxford: Oxford University Press.

Cate, Phillip Dennis and Mary Shaw (eds) (1996) *The Spirit of Montmartre: Cabarets, Humor and the Avant-Garde, 1875–1905*, New Brunswick, NJ: Jane Voorhees Zimmerli Art Museum and Rutgers.

Caughie, John (ed.) (1999) *Theories of Authorship*. London: Routledge.

Ceram, C. W. (1965) *Archeology of the Cinema*. London: Thames and Hudson.

Chanan, Michael (1975) *The Dream That Kicks*. London: Routledge and Kegan Paul.

Chesire, D. F. (1974) *Music Hall in Britain: Illustrated Sources in History*. Newton Abbot: David and Charles.

Christie, Ian (1979) 'French Avant-Garde Film in the 1920s', in *Film as Film: Formal Experiment in Film 1910–1975*. London: Arts Council of Great Britain, 37–46.

———— (1994) *The Last Machine*. London: British Film Institute.

Clark, Jon, Margot Heinemann, David Margolies and Carol Snee (eds) (1979) *Culture and Crisis in Britain in the 1930s*. London: Lawrence and Wishart.

Clarke, Tim, Christopher Gray, Donald Nicholson-Smith and Charles Radcliffe (1994) *The English Section of the Situationist International: The Revolution of Modern Art and the Modern Art of Revolution*. London: Chronos.

Cohen, David and Ben Greenwood (1981) *The Buskers: A History of Street Entertainment*. Devon: David and Charles.

Cohn, Norman (1993) *The Pursuit of the Millennium*. London: Random House.

Collin, Mathew (1996) *Altered State*. London: Serpent's Tail.

Collins, Jim (ed.) (2002) *High-Pop: Making Culture into Popular Entertainment*. Malden, MA.: Blackwell.

Cook, Pam and Mieke Bernink (eds) (1999) *The Cinema Book,* 2nd Edition. London: British Film Institute.

Corbin, Alain (1995) *Time, Desire and Horror*. Cambridge: Polity Press.

Courtney, Richard (1982) *Outline History of British Drama*. Totowa, NJ: Littlefield, Adams.

Cox, Jeffrey N. (ed.) (1992) *Seven Gothic Dramas*. Athens: Ohio University Press.

Craig, Sandy N. (1980) 'Reflexes of the Future: the Beginnings of the Fringe', in Sandy N. Craig (ed.) *Dreams and Deconstructions: Alternative Theatre in Britain*. London: Amber Lane Press, 8–29.

Crisell, Andrew (1997) *An Introductory History of British Broadcasting*. London: Routledge.

Croft-Cooke, Rupert and Peter Cotes (1976) *Circus: A World History*. London: Elek.

Crossley, Ceri and Ian Small (eds) (1989) *The French Revolution and British Culture*. Oxford: Oxford University Press.

Cubitt, Sean (1993) *Videography*. London: Macmillan.

Curtis, David (1971) *Experimental Cinema*. New York: Delta.

———— (1992) 'A Tale of Two Co-Ops', in David E. James (ed.) *To Free the Cinema*. Princeton, NJ: Princeton University Press, 253–65.

—— (ed.) (1996) *Directory of British Film and Video Artists*. Luton: John Libbey/Arts Council.

Davis, Douglas and Allison Simmons (1977) *The New Television: A Public/Private Art*. Cambridge: MIT Press.

Debord, Guy (1987) *The Society of the Spectacle*. Exeter: Rebel Press, Aim Publications.

———— (1992) *Society of the Spectacle and Other Films*. London: Rebel Press.

Deleuze, Gilles and Felix Guattari (1987) *A Thousand Plateaus*. Minneapolis: University of Minnesota Press.

Desnos, Robert (1978 [1929]) 'Avant-Garde Cinema', in Paul Hammond (ed.) *The Shadow and its Shadow*. London: British Film Institute, 36–8.

Dickinson, Margaret and Sarah Street (1985) *Cinema and State: The Film Industry and the British Government 1927–84*. London: British Film Institute.

Dickinson, Margaret (ed.) (1999a) *Rogue Reels: Oppositional Film in Britain 1945–90*. London: British Film Institute.

———— (1999b) 'Assault on the Mainstream (1974–80)' in Margaret Dickinson (ed.) *Rogue*

Reels: Oppositional Film in Britain 1945–90. London: British Film Institute, 46–61.

Disher, Maurice Willson (1949) *Blood and Thunder: Mid-Victorian Melodrama and its Origins*. London: Frederick Muller.

Dixon, Wheeler Winston (1997) *The Exploding Eye: A Revisionary History of 1960s American Experimental Cinema*. Albany: State University of New York.

Dixon, Wheeler Winston and Gwendolyn Audrey Foster (eds) (2002) *Experimental Cinema: The Film Reader*. London: Routledge.

Docker, John (1995) *Postmodernism and Popular Culture: A Cultural History*. Cambridge: Cambridge University Press.

Dowmunt, Tony (ed.) (1993) *Channels of Resistance*. London: British Film Institute.

Drummond, Philip (1979) 'Notions of Avant-Garde Cinema', in *Film as Film: Formal Experiment in Film 1910–1975*. London: Arts Council of Great Britain, 9–16.

Dulac, Germaine (1978 [1925]) 'Visual and Anti-Visual Films', trans. Robert Lamberton, in P. Adams Sitney (ed.) *The Avant-Garde Film. A Reader of Theory and Criticism*. New York: New York University Press, 31–48.

Durgnat, Raymond (1970) *A Mirror for England: British Movies from Austerity to Affluence*. London: Faber and Faber.

Dwoskin, Stephen (1985) *Film Is*. New York: The Overlook Press.

Easton, Sue (1988) *Disorder and Discipline*. Temple Smith: Gower.

Egbert, Donald D. (1970) *Social Radicalism and the Arts: Western Europe*. London: Duckworth.

Eisenstein, Sergei (1943) *The Film Sense*, trans. and ed. Jay Leyda. London: Faber and Faber.

_____ (1951a) *Film Form*, trans. and ed. Jay Leyda. London: Dennis Dobson.

_____ (1951b) 'Through Theatre to Cinema', in Sergei Eisenstein *Film Form*, trans. and ed. Jay Leyda. London: Dennis Dobson, 3–17.

_____ (1988a [1923]) 'The Montage of Attractions', in Richard Taylor and Ian Christie (eds) *The Film Factory*. London: Routledge and Kegan Paul, 87–9.

_____ (1988b) *The Film Factory*. London: Routledge and Kegan Paul, 87–9.

_____ (1998) *The Eisenstein Reader*, ed. Richard Taylor. London: British Film Institute.

Elliot, Bridget and Jo Anne Wallace (1994) *Women Artists and Writers*. London: Routledge.

Elam, Keir (1980) *The Semiotics of Theatre and Drama*. London: Methuen.

Elsaesser, Thomas (1990) 'Early Cinema: From Linear History to Mass Media Archaeology' in Thomas Elsaesser (ed.) *Early Cinema: Space-Frame-Narrative*. London: British Film Institute, 1–8.

Farber, Manny (1998) *Negative Space*. New York: De Capo Press.

Farren, Mick (2001) *Give the Anarchist a Cigarette*. London: Jonathan Cape.

Farson, Daniel (1972) *Marie Lloyd and the Music Hall*. London: Tom Stacey.

Feldman, Gene and Max Gartenberg (eds) (1987) *Protest: The Beat Generation and the Angry Young Men*. London: Souvenir Press.

Fell, John L. (1974) *Film and the Narrative Tradition*. Oklahoma: University of Oklahoma Press.

Foster, Hal (ed.) (1985) *Postmodern Culture*. London: Pluto Press.

Frayling, Christopher (1991) *Vampyres: Lord Byron to Count Dracula*. London: Faber and Faber.

Friedberg, Anne (1993) *Window Shopping*. Berkeley: University of California Press.

Frow, Gerald (1985) *'Oh, Yes It Is!': A History of Pantomime*. London: BBC.

Fry, Roger (1961) *Vision and Design*. Harmondsworth: Penguin.

Furst, Lillian R. (ed.) (1980) *European Romanticism*. London: Methuen.

Gablik, Suzi (1984) *Has Modernism Failed?* London: Thames and Hudson.

Garland Thomson, Rosemarie (ed.) (1996) *Freakery: Cultural Spectacles of the Extraordinary Body*. New York: New York University Press.

Gaudreault, André (1990) 'Showing and Telling: Image and Word in Early Cinema', in Thomas Elsaesser (ed.) *Early Cinema: Space-Frame-Narrative*. London: British Film Institute, 274–81.

Gerould, Daniel (1994) 'Melodrama and Revolution', in Jacky Bratton, Jim Cook and Christine Gledhill (eds) *Melodrama, Stage, Picture, Screen*. London: British Film Institute, 185–98.

Gidal, Peter (ed.) (1976) *Structural Film Anthology*. London: British Film Institute.

_____ (1989) *Materialist Film*. London: Routledge.

_____ (1991) *Andy Warhol Films and Paintings: The Factory Years*. New York: Da Capo.

Gimpel, Jean (1991) *Against Art and Artists*. Edinburgh: Polygon.

Gopnick, Adam and Kirk Varnedoe (1990a) *High and Low: Modern Art and Pop Culture*. New York: Museum of Modern Art.

_____ (eds) (1990b) *Modern Art and Popular Culture: Readings in High and Low*. New York: Museum of Modern Art.

Gray, Richard (1996) *Cinemas in Britain: One Hundred Years of Cinema Architecture*. London: Lund Humphries.

Greenburg, Clement (1939) 'Avant-Garde and Kitsch', *Partisan Review*, 6, 5, Fall, 34–9.

Grierson, John (1979 [1941]) 'Education and Total Effort', in Forsyth Hardy (ed.) *Grierson on Documentary*. London: Faber and Faber, 133–41.

Guerin, Daniel (ed.) (1997) *No Gods No Masters 1*. Edinburgh: AK Press.

_____ (ed.) (1998) *No Gods No Masters 2*. Edinburgh: AK Press.

Gunning, Tom (1990 [1986]) 'The Cinema of Attractions, Early Film, its Spectators and the Avant-Garde', in Thomas Elsaesser (ed.) *Early Cinema: Space-Frame-Narrative*. London: British Film Institute, 56–62.

_____ (1996 [1993]) '"Now You See It, Now You Don't": The Temporality of the Cinema of Attractions', in Richard Abel (ed.) *Silent Film*. London: Athlone, 71–85.

Haining, Peter (ed.) (1976) *The Penny Dreadful*. London: Victor Gollancz.

Haley, Sir William (1974 [1948]) 'The Pyramid of Taste', in Anthony Smith (ed.) *British Broadcasting*. Newton Abbott: David and Charles, 83–4.

Hall, Doug and Sally Jo Fifer (1990) *Illuminating Video*. New York: Aperture.

Hall, Stuart (1989) 'The "First" New Left: Life and Times', in Oxford University Socialist Discussion Group (eds) *Out of Apathy*. London: Verso, 11–39.

Hammond, Paul (ed.) (1978) *The Shadow and its Shadow*. London: British Film Institute.

Hanawalt, Barbara A. (1993) *Growing Up in Mediaeval London*. Oxford: Oxford University Press.

Harding, Thomas (1997) *The Video Activist Handbook*. London: Pluto Press.

Hardy, Dennis (1979) *Alternative Communities in Nineteenth-Century England*. London and New York: Longman.

Hardy, Forsyth (1979) *John Grierson: A Documentary Biography*. London: Faber and Faber.

Harrison, Charles and Paul Wood (eds) (1992) *Art in Theory*. Oxford: Blackwell.

Harris, John S. (1970) *Government Patronage of the Arts in Great Britain*. Chicago: University of Chicago Press.

Harvey, Sylvia (1978a) *Independent Cinema?* Stratford: West Midlands Arts.

_____ (1978b) *May '68 and Film Culture*. London: British Film Institute.

Hauser, Arnold (1951) *The Social History of Art 1–4*. New York: Vintage Books.

Hawkins, Joan (2000) *The Cutting Edge, Art-Horror and the Horrific Avant-Garde*. Minneapolis: University of Minnesota Press.

Hebdige, Dick (1979) *Subculture*. London: Methuen.

Hedling, Erik (1997) 'Lindsay Anderson and the Development of British Art Cinema', in Robert Murphy (ed.) *The British Cinema Book*. London: British Film Institute, 241–7.

Heiferman, Marvin, Carole Kismaric and Edward Leffingwell. (1997) *Flaming Creature: Jack Smith, His Amazing Life and Times*. London: Serpent's Tail.

Heisner, Beverly (1990) *Hollywood Art: Art Direction in the Days of the Great Studios*. Chicago and London: St. James Press.

Hill, Christopher (1993) *The World Turned Upside Down*. Harmondsworth: Penguin Books.

Hillier, Jim (ed.) (1986) *Cahiers du Cinéma: The 1950s: Neo-Realism, Hollywood, New Wave*. London: Routledge and Kegan Paul.

Hoberman, J. (1984) 'After Avant-Garde Film', in Brian Wallis (ed.) *Art After Modernism*. New York: New Museum of Contemporary Art, 59–73.

Hobsbawm, Eric (1973) *The Age of Revolution*. London: Weidenfield and Nicholson.

Hoggart, Richard (1968 [1957]) *The Uses of Literacy*. Harmondsworth: Penguin Books.

Home, Stewart (1988) *The Assault on Culture*. London: Aporia Press.

Hopton, Andrew (1989) 'Introduction', in *Digger Tracts 1649–50*. London: Aporia Press, 3–8.

Horak, Jan-Christopher (1995) 'The First American Film Avant-Garde, 1919–1945', in Jan-Christopher Horak (ed.) *Lovers of the Cinema*. Madison: University of Wisconsin Press, 14–66.

Huelsenbeck, Richard (1951 [1922]) 'En Avant Dada', in Robert Motherwell (ed.) *The Dada Painters and Poets*. New York: George Wittenborn.

_____ (1991) *Memoirs of a Dada Drummer*, ed. Hans J. Kleinschmidt. Berkeley: University of California Press.

Hutton, Ronald (1994) *The Rise and Fall of Merry England*. Oxford: Oxford University Press.

_____ (1996) *The Stations of the Sun*. Oxford: Oxford University Press.

Huyssen, Andreas (1988a) *After the Great Divide*. London: Macmillan.

_____ (1988b) 'The Hidden Dialectic', in Andreas Huyssen, *After the Great Divide*. London: Macmillan, 3–15.

Inge, M. Thomas (1990) *Comics as Culture*. Jackson, MI: University of Mississippi Press.

Jacobs, Paul and Saul Landau (1967) *The New Radicals*. Harmondsworth: Penguin.

James, C. L. R. (1994) *The Black Jacobins*. London: Allison and Busby.

James, David E. (1989) *Allegories of Cinema: American Cinema in the 1960s*. Princeton, NJ: Princeton University Press.

—— (ed.) (1992) *To Free the Cinema*. Princeton, NJ: Princeton University Press.

James, Louis (1974) *Fiction for the Working Man*. Harmondsworth: Penguin.

Jameson, Frederic (1985 [1982]) 'Postmodernism and Consumer Society', in Hal Foster (ed.) *Postmodern Culture*. London: Pluto Press, 111.

Jeffrey, Tom (1978) *Mass Observation: A Short History*. Birmingham: University of Birmingham.

Jullian, Philippe J. (1977) *Montmartre*, trans. Anne Carter. Oxford: Phaidon Press.

Kandinsky, Wassily (1994) *Kandinsky: Complete Writings on Art*. New York: Da Capo Press.

Kaplan, Steven (1984) *Understanding Popular Culture*. New York: Moulton.

Kaprow, Allan (1993) 'Education of the Un-Artist', in Allan Kaprow *Essays on the Blurring of Life and Art*. Berkeley: University of California Press, 125.

Kellein, Thomas (1995) *Fluxus*. London: Thames and Hudson.

Kift, Dagmar (1996) *The Victorian Music Hall: Culture, Class and Conflict*. Cambridge: Cambridge University Press.

Knabb, Ken (ed.) (1981) *Situationist International Anthology*. Berkeley: Bureau of Public Secrets.

Knight, Julia (1996) 'A Chronological Guide to British Video Art', in Julia Knight (ed.) *Diverse Practices*. Luton: University of Luton Press, 351–8.

Kozintsev, Grigori, Georgii Kryzhitskii, Leonid Trauberg and Sergei Yutkevich (1992) *The Eccentric Manifesto*. London: Eccentric Press.

Kracauer, Siegfried (1961) *The Nature of Film*. London: Dennis Dobson.

Kuhn, Annette (1980) 'Recontextualising A Film Movement', in Don Macpherson (ed.) *Traditions of Independence*. London: British Film Institute, 24–33.

Kunzle, David (1973) *The Early Comic Strip: Narrative Strips and Picture Stories in the European Broadsides from c. 1450–1825*. Berkeley: University of California Press.

Kuspit, Donald (1995) *The Cult of the Avant-Garde Artist*. Cambridge: Cambridge University Press.

Laing, Stuart (1986) *Representations of Working Class Life*. London: Macmillan.

Lawdor, Standish (1975) *The Cubist Cinema*. New York: New York University Press.

Leavis F. R. and Denys Thompson (1962 [1933]) *Culture and Environment*. London: Chatto and Windus.

Le Bourhis, Katell (ed.) (1989) *The Age of Napoleon: Costume From Revolution to Empire 1789–1815*. New York: Metropolitan Museum of Art/Harry N. Abrams.

Lefebvre, Henri Francois (1971) *Everyday Life in the Modern World*. London: Penguin.

Léger, Fernand (1973 [c.1924]) 'Ballet Mécanique', in *Functions of Painting*, ed. E. F. Fry. London: Thames and Hudson, 48–9.

Le Grice, Malcolm (1977) *Abstract Film and Beyond*. London: Studio Vista.

_____ (2001) *Experimental Film in the Digital Age*. London: British Film Institute.

Leisenfeld, Vincent J. (1984) *The Licensing Act of 1737*. Madison: University of Wisconsin Press.

Le Roy, George (1952) *Music Hall Stars of the 1990s*. London: British Technical and General Press.

Levitine, George (1978) *The Dawn of Bohemianism: The Barbu Rebellion and Primitivism in Neoclassical France*. University Park and London: Pennsylvania State University Press.

Lewis, Helena (1988) *Dada Turns Red*. Edinburgh: Edinburgh University Press.

Lewis, Roger (1972) *Outlaws of America*. Harmondsworth: Penguin.

Lipton, Lenny (1974) *Independent Filmmaking*. London: Studio Vista.

Lovell, Alan (1976) *The BFI Production Board*. London: British Film Institute.

Lovell, Alan and Jim Hillier (1972) *Studies in Documentary*. London: Secker and Warburg.

Lovell Burgess, Marjorie A. (1932) *A Popular Account of the Development of the Amateur Ciné Movement in Great Britain*. London: Sampson, Low, Marston.

Low, Rachael (1971) *The History of British Film 1918–29*. London: George Allen and Unwin.

Macdonald, Scott (1988) *A Critical Cinema – Interviews with Independent Filmmakers*. Berkeley: University of California Press.

_____ (1992a) *A Critical Cinema 2*. Berkeley: University of California Press.

_____ (1992b) *A Critical Cinema 3*. Berkeley: University of California Press.

_____ (1993) *Avant Garde Film: Motion Studies*. Cambridge: Cambridge University Press.

MacNab, Geoffrey (2000) *Searching for Stars*. London: Cassell.

Macpherson, Don (ed.) (1980) *Traditions of Independence*. London: British Film Institute.

Madge, Charles and Tom Harrison (2002) *Britain By Mass Observation*. Harmondsworth: Penguin.

Malcolmson, Robert W. (1973) *Popular Recreations in English Society 1700–1850*. Cambridge: Cambridge University Press.

_____ (1982) 'Popular Recreations Under Attack', in Tony Bennett, Graham Martin and Bernard Waites (eds) *Popular Culture Past and Present*. London: Croom Helm, 20–46.

Manvell, Roger (ed.) (1949) *Experiment in the Film*. London: Grey Walls.

Marcus, Greil (1990) *Lipstick Traces: A Secret History of the Twentieth Century*. London: Secker and Warburg.

Marinetti, Filippo Tommaso (1972 [1913]), 'The Variety Theatre', in Filippo Tommaso Marinetti: *Selected Writings*, ed. R. W. Flint. London: Secker and Warburg, 116–22.

Marinetti, Filippo Tommaso, Bruno Corra, Emilio Setimelli, Arnaldo Ginna, Giacomo Balla and Remo Chiti, 'The Futurist Cinema', in *Film As Film: Formal Experiment in Film 1910–1975*. London: Arts Council of Great Britain, 79–80.

Marshall, Peter (1993) *Demanding the Impossible: A History of Anarchism*. London: Fontana Press.

Mayer III, David (1969) *Harlequin in His Element: The English Pantomime 1806–1836*. Cambridge, MA: Harvard University Press.

McCallum, Pamela (1983) *Literature and Method: Towards a Critique of I. A. Richards, T. S. Eliot and F. R. Leavis*. Dublin: Gill and Macmillan/Humanities Press.

McKay, George (1996) *Senseless Acts of Beauty*. London: Verso.

_____ (ed.) (1998) *DIY Culture*. London: Verso.

Mckechnie, Samuel (1932) *Popular Entertainments Through the Ages*. London: Sampson, Low, Marston & Co.

Mekas, Jonas (1971 [1962]) 'The First Statement of the New American Cinema Group', in P. Adams Sitney (ed.) *Film Culture: An Anthology*. London: Secker and Warburg, 79–84.

_____ (1972) 'On "People's Movies", or the Difference Between Melodrama and Art', in Jonas Mekas, *Movie Journal*. New York: Collier Books, 155–6.

Mellancamp, Patricia (1990) *Indiscretions: Avant-Garde Film, Video and Feminism*. Bloomington: Indiana University Press.

Mendik, Xavier and Steven Jay Schneider (eds) (2002) *Underground USA: Filmmaking Beyond the Hollywood Canon*. London: Wallflower Press.

Michelson, Annette (1969) 'Introduction', in Noël Burch *Theory of Film Practice*. London: Secker and Warburg, v–vi.

_____ (1985) *Kino Eye*. Berkeley: University of California Press.

Minihan, Janet (1977) *The Nationalisation of Culture*. London: Hamish Hamilton.

Montagu, Ivor (1929) *The Political Censorship of Films*. London: Victor Gollancz.

Moody, Richard (1958) *The Astor Place Riot*. Bloomington: Indiana University Press.

Moritz, William (1986) 'Abstract Film and Colour Music', in Maurice Tuchman (ed.) *The Spiritual in Art: Abstract Painting 1890–1985*. New York: Abbeville Press, 297–311.

Morris, William (1995 [1891]) *News From Nowhere*. Cambridge: Cambridge University Press.

Motherwell, Robert (ed.) (1995) *The Dada Painters and Poets*. New York: Wittenborn.

Mudie, Peter (1997) *UBU FILMS: Sydney Underground Movies 1965–1970*. Sydney: University of South Wales Press.

Mulvey, Laura (1989) 'Film, Feminism and the Avant-Garde', in Laura Mulvey, *Visual and Other Pleasures*. London: Macmillan, 111–27.

Murphy, Robert (ed.) (1997) *The British Cinema Book*. London: British Film Institute.

Musser, Charles (1990) 'The Nickelodeon Era Begins: Establishing the Framework for Hollywood's Mode of Representation', in Thomas Elsaesser (ed.) *Early Cinema: Space-Frame-Narrative*. London: British Film Institute, 256–73.

Nadeau, Maurice (1978) *The History of Surrealism*. Harmondsworth: Penguin.

Nehring, Neil (1993) *Flowers in the Dustbin*. Ann Arbor: University of Michigan Press.

Nelson, Elizabeth (1989) *The British Counter-Culture 1966–73*. London: Macmillan.

Neuburg, Victor E. (1977) *Popular Literature*. Harmondsworth: Penguin.

Neville, Richard (1971) *Playpower*. London: Paladin.

Newsome, David (1997) *The Victorian World Picture*. London: John Murray.

Nigg, Heinz and Graham Wade (1980) *Community Media*. Zurich: Regenbogen-Verlag.

Nochlin, Linda (1989) *The Politics of Vision: Essays on Nineteenth Century Art and Society*. New York: Harper and Row.

Nuttall, Jeff (1970) *Bomb Culture*. London: Paladin.

O'Pray, Michael (ed.) (1996) *The British Avant-Garde Film 1926–1995*. Luton: University of Luton Press.

____ (ed.) (1997) *Avant-Garde Film*. Luton: University of Luton Press.

Oxford University Socialist Discussion Group (1989) (eds) *Out of Apathy*. London: Verso.

Park, James (1990) *British Cinema: The Lights That Failed*. London: B. T. Batsford.

Penley, Constance (1989) *The Future of an Illusion: Film, Feminism, and Psychoanalysis*. London: Routledge.

Perloff, Nancy (1991) *Art and the Everyday: Popular Entertainment and the Circle of Erik Satie*. Oxford: Clarendon.

Perry, Paul (1990) *On the Bus*. London: Plexus.

Pertwee, Bill (1979) *Pertwee's Promenades and Pierrots*. Newton Abbot: Westbridge Books.

Peterson, James (1994) *Dreams of Chaos, Visions of Order: Understanding the American Avant-Garde Cinema*. Detroit: Wayne State University Press.

Pevsner, Nikolaus (1974 [1936]) *Pioneers of Modern Design*. Harmondsworth: Penguin.

Pick, John (1984) *Managing the Arts?: The British Experience*. London: Rhinegold.

____ (1988) *The Arts in a State*. Bristol: Bristol Classical Press.

Pickering, Michael (1986) 'White Skin, Black Masks: "Nigger" Minstrelsy in Victorian England', in Jacqueline S. Bratton (ed.) *Music Hall Performance and Style*. Milton Keynes: Open University Press, 70–91.

Pines, Jim and Paul Willemen (1989) *Questions of Third Cinema*. London: British Film Institute.

Plant, Sadie (1992) *The Most Radical Gesture*. London: Routledge.

____ (1999) *Writing on Drugs*. London: Faber and Faber.

Pleij, Herman (2001) *Dreaming of Cockaigne: Medieval Fantasies of the Perfect Life*. New York: Columbia University Press.

Poggioli, Renato (1968) *The Theory of the Avant-Garde*. Cambridge, MA: The Belknap Press of Harvard University Press.

Polan, Dana (1985) *The Political Language of Film and the Avant-Garde*. Ann Arbor: Research Press.

Pollock, Griselda (1988) 'Modernity and the Spaces of Femininity', in *Vision and Difference*. London: Routledge, 50–90.

Polsky, Ned (1971) *Hustlers, Beats and Others*. Harmondsworth: Penguin.

Quigley, Jr., Martin (1948) *Magic Shadows: The Story of the Origin of Motion Pictures*. Washington, DC: Georgetown University Press.

Rabinowitz, Lauren (1991) *Points of Resistance: Women, Power and Politics in the New York Avant-Garde Cinema 1943–71*. Chicago: University of Illinois Press.

_____ (1992) 'Wearing the Critic's Hat: History, Critical Discourses, and the American Avant-Garde Cinema', in David E. James (ed.) *To Free the Cinema: Jonas Mekas and the New York Underground*. Princeton, NJ: Princeton University Press, 268–84.

Rearick, Charles (1985) *Pleasures of the Belle Epoque: Entertainment and Festivity in Turn of the Century France*. New Haven, CT: Yale University Press.

Rees, A. L. (1999) *A History of Experimental Film and Video*. London: British Film Institute.

Renan, Sheldon (1968) *The Underground Film*. London: Studio Vista.

Revel, Jacques (1984) 'Forms of Expertise: Intellectuals and "Popular" Culture in France (1650–1800)', in Steven L. Kaplan (ed.) *Understanding Popular Culture*. New York: Moulton, 255–73.

Richards, Jeffrey and Dorothy Sheridan (1987) *Mass Observation at the Movies*. London: Routledge and Kegan Paul.

Richter, Hans (1966) *Dada: Art and Anti-Art*. New York: McGraw-Hill.

Rosenfield, Sybil (1960) *The Theatre of the London Fairs*. Cambridge: Cambridge University Press.

Roszak, Theodore (1970) *The Making of a Counter Culture*. London: Faber and Faber.

Rotha, Paul (1936) *Documentary Film*. London: Faber and Faber.

Rousseau, Jean-Jacques (1995 [1751]) 'A Critique of Progress', in Isaac Kramnick (ed.) *The Portable Enlightenment Reader*. New York: Penguin, 363–8.

Rubin, Jerry (1970) *Do It*. London: Jonathon Cape.

_____ (1971) *We Are Everywhere*. New York: Harper and Row.

Ruskin, John (1907) 'The Unity of Art', *Sesame & Lilies, The Two Paths & The King of the Golden River*. London and Toronto: J.M. Dent & Sons.

Ryan, Trevor (1980) 'Film and Political Organisations in Britain 1929–39', in Don Macpherson (ed.) *Traditions of Independence*. London: British Film Institute, 51–69.

Saint-Simon, Henri (1975 [1823]) *Selected Writings on Science, Industry and Social Organisation*, ed. Keith Taylor. London: Croom Helm.

Samson, Anne (1992) *F. R. Leavis*. Hemel Hempstead: Harvester Wheatsheaf.

Sargeant, Jack (1995) *Deathtripping: The Cinema of Transgression*. London: Creation Books.

_____ (1997) *The Naked Lens: An Illustrated History of Beat Cinema*. London: Creation Books.

Scannell, Paddy and David Cardiff (1991) *A Social History of Broadcasting Volume One 1922–1939*. Oxford: Basil Blackwell.

Schnitzer, Luda and Jean & Marcel Martin (eds) (1973) *Cinema in Revolution*, trans. David Robinson. London: Secker and Warburg.

Schwartz, Vanessa R. (1998) *Spectacular Realities: Early Mass Culture in Fin-De-Siecle Paris*. Berkeley: University of California Press.

Segel, Harold B. (1987) *Turn of the Century Cabaret*. New York: Columbia University Press.

Seigel, Jerrold (1986) *Bohemian Paris: Culture, Politics and the Boundaries of Bourgeois Life*. New York: Viking.

Shapiro, Nat and Nat Hentoff (1971) *Hear Me Talkin' To Ya*. Harmondsworth: Penguin.

Shepherd, Leslie (1973) *The History of Street Literature*. Newton Abbott: David and Charles.

Sheridan, Paul (1981) *Penny Theatres of Victorian London*. London: Dennis Dobson.

Sinclair, Andrew (1995) *Arts and Cultures: the History of the 50 Years of the Arts Council of Great Britain*. London: Sinclair-Stevenson.

Sitney, P. Adams (1971 [1969]) 'Structural Film', in P. Adams Sitney (ed.) *Film Culture: An*

Anthology. London: Secker and Warburg, 326–349.

_____ (1975) *The Essential Cinema*. New York: New York University Press/Anthology.

_____ (ed.) (1978) *The Avant-Garde Film. A Reader of Theory and Criticism*. New York: New York University Press.

_____ (1979) *Visionary Film: The American Avant-Garde 1943–1978*. Oxford: Oxford University Press.

Small, Edward S. (1994) *Direct Theory: Experimental Film as a Major Genre*. Carbondale, IL: Southern Illinois University Press.

Small, Ian (ed.) (1979) *The Aesthetes*. London: Routledge and Kegan Paul.

Smith, Jack (1997) *Wait for Me at the Bottom of the Pool: The Writings of Jack Smith*, eds J. Hoberman and J. Leffingwell. London: Serpent's Tail.

Smith, Anthony (ed.) (1974) *British Broadcasting*. Newton Abbot: David and Charles.

Sontag, Susan (1968 [1965]) 'One Culture and the New Sensibility', in *Against Interpretation and Other Essays*. London: Eyre and Spottiswoode, 293–304.

Southern, Richard (1970) *The Victorian Theatre*. Newton Abbot: David and Charles.

Speaight, George (1990) *The History of the English Puppet Theatre*. London: Robert Hale.

Springhall, John (1998) *Youth, Popular Culture and Moral Panics*. Hampshire: Macmillan Press.

Stallybrass, Peter and Allon White (1986) *The Politics and Poetics of Transgression*. London: Methuen.

Staniszewski, Mary Anne (1995) *Believing is Seeing: Creating the Culture of Art*. New York: Penguin.

Stansill, Peter and David Zane Mairowitz (eds) (1971) *BAMN (By Any Means Necessary): Outlaw Manifestos and Ephemera 1965–70*. Harmondsworth: Penguin.

Starsmore, Ian (1975) *English Fairs*. London: Thames and Hudson.

Staveacre, Tony (1987) *Slapstick!* London: Angus and Robertson.

Steele, Tom (1997) *The Emergence of Cultural Studies 1945–65*. London: Lawrence and Wishart.

Sterritt, David (1998) *Mad To Be Saved: The Beats, the 50s and Film*. Carbondale, Il: Southern Illinois University Press.

Stevenson, Jack (1996) *Desparate Visions 1: Camp America*. London: Creation Books.

Stocking Jr., George W. (1968) *Race, Culture and Evolution*. Chicago: University of Chicago Press.

Storey, John (ed.) (1996) *What is Cultural Studies?: A Reader*. London: Edward Arnold.

_____ (ed.) (1998) *Cultural Theory and Popular Culture: A Reader*. London: Prentice Hall.

Students and Staff of Hornsey College of Art (1969) *The Hornsey Affair*. Harmondsworth: Penguin.

Suárez, Juan A. (1996) *Bike Boys, Drag Queens and Superstars: Avant-Garde, Mass Culture, and Gay Identities in the 1960s Underground Cinema*. Bloomington: Indiana University Press.

Summerfield, Penelope (1981) 'The Effingham Arms and the Empire: Deliberate Selection in the Evolution of the Music Hall in London', in Eileen Yeo and Stephen Yeo (eds) *Popular Culture and Class Conflict: 1590–1914*. Sussex: Harvester Press, 209–40.

Sussex, Elizabeth (1969) *Lindsay Anderson*. London: Studio Vista.

Swenson, John (1982) *Bill Haley*. London: W. H. Allen.

Szczelkun, Stefan (1993) *The Conspiracy of Good Taste*. London: Working Press.

Taylor, Richard and Ian Christie (eds) (1988) *The Film Factory*. London: Routledge and Kegan Paul.

Taylor, Roger (1978) *Art: An Enemy of the People*. Sussex: Harvester Press.

Thompson, E.P. (1978) *The Poverty of Theory and Other Essays*. London: Merlin.

_____ (1984) *The Making of the English Working Class*. Harmondsworth: Penguin.

_____ (1991) *Customs in Common: Studies in Traditional Popular Culture*. London: Merlin Press.

Thoms, Albie (1978) *Polemics for a New Cinema*. Sydney: Wild and Woolley.

Tomkins, Calvin (1968) *Ahead of the Game*. London: Penguin

Traies, Jane (1980) *Fairbooths and Fit-Ups*. Cambridge: Chadwyck-Healey.

Tuchman, Maurice (ed.) Edward (1986) *The Spiritual in Art: Abstract Painting 1890–1985*. New York: Abbeville Press.

Twitchell, James B. (1992) *Carnival Culture*. New York: Columbia University Press.

Tyler, Parker (1974) *Underground Film: A Critical History*. Harmondsworth: Penguin.

Vardac, A. Nicholas (1987 [1949]) *Stage to Screen: Theatrical Origins of Early Film: David Garrick to D. W. Griffith*. New York: Da Capo Press.

Virilio, Paul (1994) *The Vision Machine*. London: British Film Institute.

Vogel, Amos (1974) *Film as a Subversive Art*. New York: Random House.

Wade, Graham (1980) *Street Video*. Leicester: Blackthorn Press.

Wallis, Brian (1984) *Art After Modernism*. New York: New Museum of Contemporary Art.

Walsh, Martin (1981) *The Brechtian Aspects of Radical Cinema*. London: British Film Institute.

Walton, John K. and James Walvin (eds) (1983) *Leisure in Britain 1780–1939*. Manchester: Manchester University Press,.

Watt, Ian (1987) *The Rise of the Novel*. London: The Hogarth Press.

Wayne, Mike (1997) *Theorising Video Practice*. London: Lawrence and Wishart.

Webster, Richard (1996) *Why Freud Was Wrong*. London: HarperCollins.

Wees, C. William (1992) *Light Moving in Time: Studies in the Visual Aesthetics of Avant-Garde Film*. Berkeley: University of California Press.

Weiss, Jeffrey (1990) 'Picasso, Collage and the Music Hall', in Adam Gopnick and Kirk Varnedoe (eds) *Modern Art and Popular Culture: Readings in High and Low*. New York: Museum of Modern Art, 82–115.

_____ (1994) *The Popular Culture of Modern Art*. New Haven, CT: Yale University Press.

White, Allon (1993) *Carnival, Hysteria and Writing*. Oxford: Clarendon Press.

Willemen, Paul (1994) *Looks and Frictions*. London: British Film Institute.

Williams, Linda (1992) *Figures of Desire: A Theory and Analysis of Surrealist Film*. Berkeley: University of California Press.

Williams, Raymond (1980) *Problems in Materialism and Culture, Selected Essays*. London: Verso.

_____ (1983) *Keywords*. London: Fontana Press.

Wolfe, Tom (1998) *The Electric Kool-Aid Acid Test*. London: Black Swan.

Wollen, Peter (1982a) *Readings and Writings: Semiotic Counter Strategies*. London: Verso.

_____ (1982b) 'Godard and Counter Cinema: *Vent d'Est*', in Peter Wollen *Readings and Writings: Semiotic Counter Strategies*. London: Verso, 79–91.

_____ (1993) *Raiding the Icebox*. London: Verso.

_____ (1995) 'The Last New Wave', in Michael O'Pray (ed.) *The British Avant-Garde Film 1926–1995*. Luton: University of Luton Press, 239–56.

_____ (1998 [1972]) *Signs and Meaning in the Cinema*. London: British Film Institute.

Wright, Iain (1979) 'F. R. Leavis, The Scrutiny Movement and the Crisis', in Jon Clark, Margot Heinemann, David Margolies and Carol Snee (eds) *Culture and Crisis in Britain in the 1930s*. London: Lawrence and Wishart, 37–67.

Yeo, Eileen (ed.) (1981) *Popular Culture and Class Conflict: 1590–1914*. Sussex: Harvester Press.

Young, Michael (1958) *The Rise of the Meritocracy 1870–2033*. Harmondsworth: Penguin.

Youngblood, Gene (1970) *Expanded Cinema*. London: Studio Vista.

Yutkevitch, Segei Iosipovich (1973) 'Teenage Artists of the Revolution', in Luda Schnitzer and Jean & Marcel Martin (eds) *Cinema in Revolution*, trans. David Robinson. London: Secker and Warburg, 13–41.

Zane Mairowitz, David (1976) *The Radical Soap Opera*. Harmondsworth: Penguin.

Zimmermann, Patricia R. (1995) 'Startling Angles, Amateur Film and the Early Avant-Garde', in Jan-Christopher Horak (ed.) *Lovers of the Cinema*. Madison: University of Wisconsin Press, 137–55.

ARTICLES/JOURNALS

Abiezer the Ranting Geezer (1999) 'Brechgardism: An Unfair Amalgam', 'Cinema at the Bottom of a Swamp', *Melancholic Troglodytes*, 2+1/2, Autumn, 29–44.

Aitken, Ian (1989) 'John Grierson, Idealism and the Inter-war Period', *The Historical Journal of Film, Radio and Television*, 9, 3, 247–57.

Anderson, Lindsay (1948) 'A Possible Solution', *Sequence*, 3, Spring, 7–10.

____ (1950) 'The Director's Cinema', *Sequence*, 12, Autumn, 7–11.

____ (1954) 'Only Connect', *Sight and Sound*, April–June, 23, 4, Spring, 181–6.

Anon. (1946) 'A Novel Idea From America', *Amateur Cine World*, 10, 9, Autumn, 437.

____ (1952) 'Soundtrack, Running Commentary: *Kaleidoscope*', *Amateur Cine World*, 15, 10, February, 1005.

____ (1955) 'Equipment, Materials, Technical Developments, Services', *Amateur Cine World*, 19, 1, May, 40.

____ (1956a) 'Exciting Evening of Amateur Films', *Amateur Cine World*, 19, 12, April, 1229–31, 1270.

____ (1956b) 'A Catalogue of Amateur Films for Club and Home Showing', *Amateur Cine World*, 20, 8, December, 841–6.

____ (1956c) 'Programme Building for Public Shows', *Amateur Cine World*, 20, 8, December, 840, 856.

____ (1957a) 'Controversy Corner', *Amateur Cine World*, 21, 2, June, 171.

____ (1957b) 'A Special Class for 8mm?', *Amateur Cine World*, 21, 4, August, 329.

____ (1957c) 'Experimental', *Amateur Cine World*, 21, 4, August, 367.

____ (1957d) 'Comment on Competitions', *Amateur Cine World*, 21, 6, October, 563.

____ (1958a) 'Personal Choice', *Amateur Movie-Maker*, 4, January, 24–5.

____ (1958b) 'What Does It All Mean?', *Amateur Cine World*, 22, 3, October, 245–7.

____ (1959) 'University Students Film', *Amateur Cine World*, 22, 9, January, 946–7.

____ (1970) 'Festival programme', *Time Out*, 46, September, 26–35.

Arpad, Joseph J. (1975) 'Between Folklore and Literature: Popular Culture as Anomaly', *Journal of Popular Culture*, 9, 403–22.

Ashman, Gordon (1994) 'West Gallery Music'. Available at http://www.westgallerymusic.co.uk/articles/Ashman94.html [accessed 7 September 2007].

Bayuk Rosenman, Ellen (1996) 'Spectacular Women: The Mysteries of London and the Female Body', *Victorian Studies*, 40, 1, Autumn, 31–64.

Berger, John (1957) 'Look at Britain', *Sight and Sound*, 27, 1, Summer, 12–14.

Blakeston, Oswell (1951) 'Material for A Poem', *Amateur Cine World*, 14, 10, February, 997–1001.

Bowen, Peter (1955) 'Putting Drama into the Holiday Film', *Amateur Cine World*, 19, 6, October, 554–5.

Burch, Noël (1981) 'How We Got Into Pictures', *Afterimage*, 8, 9, Spring, 22–38.

Canudo, Ricciotto (1980 [1911]) 'The Birth of the Sixth Art', trans. Ben Gibson, Don Ranvaud, Sergio Sokota and Deborah Young, *Framework*, 13, 3–7.

Cayford, Joel (1990) 'Workshops: Workhorse or Workhouse?', *Independent Media*, 100, June, 11.

Clarke, J. and R. Elliot (1978) 'The Other Cinema: Screen Memory', *Wedge*, 2, 3–11.

Claypole, Jonty (1999) 'The Underground', *Filmwaves*, 7, Spring, 12–14.

Cook, Camille (1966) 'What are Underground Movies?', *Amateur Cine World*, 11, 26, 876–9.

Corbett, Andrea (1999) 'The State of Independence', *Vertigo*, 1, 9, Summer, 16–18.

Cottringer, Anne (1976) 'On Peter Gidal's Theory and Definition of Structural/Materialist Film', *Afterimage*, 6, Summer, 86–95.

Coxhead, E. (1933) 'Towards A Co-Operative Cinema', *Close Up*, X, 2, 133–7.

Curling, Jonathon and Fran McLean (1977) 'The Independent Film-makers' Association – Annual General Meeting and Conference', *Screen*, 18, 1, 107–117.

Curtis, David (1975) 'English Avant-Garde Film: An Early Chronology', *Studio International*, Nov./Dec., 190, 978, 176–82.

_____ (1978) 'English Avant-Garde Film: An Early Chronology', revised edition, in *A Perspective on English Avant-Garde Film*. London: The Arts Council of Great Britain/British Council, 9–18.

_____ (1999) 'Britain's Oldest Experimentalist … Margaret Tait', *Vertigo*, 1, 9, Summer, 62–3.

Dunford, Mike (1976) 'Experimental/Avant-Garde/Revolutionary Film Practice', *Afterimage*, 6, Summer, 96–112.

_____ (1981) 'The History of English Avant-Garde Film' (unpublished thesis) 1974.

Dusinberre, Deke (1974) *The History of English Avant-Garde Film* (unpublished thesis). London University College.

_____ (1976) 'St George in the Forest: the English Avant-Garde', *Afterimage*, 6, 4–20.

_____ (1981) 'See Real Images!', *Afterimage* 8/9 (Spring), 86–111.

Dwoskin, Stephen (1998) 'A Little Bit of Then', *Filmwaves*, 3, February, 10–12.

Eastwood, Steven (1999) 'The Screen Into the Space and the Space Into the Screen: A Brief Overview of OMSK', *Filmwaves*, 9, Autumn, 14–16.

Eimer, David (1993) 'Films', *The Face*, 60, September, 144–5.

Farnell, Graeme (1970) 'Which Avant-Garde?', *Afterimage*, 2, Autumn, 65–71.

Fayde, Iris (1952) 'Woman's Viewpoint', *Amateur Cine World*, 15, 10, February, 1019–20; 1039–40.

Fell, Nolan (1995) 'The Independence of the Moving Image', *Rushes*, 19, Summer, 14–17.

Garratt, Chris (1994) 'L'Avant Garde et Apres Parts 1–4', *Vivid: The Moving Image Newsletter of the South West*, Spring, 3.

Gawthrop, Rob (1990) 'The 1990s – Taking Control', *Undercut*, 19, Autumn, 23–4.

Gidal, Peter (1970a) 'Film as Materialist Consumer Product', *Cinemantics*, 2, 14.

_____ (1970b) 'Film as Materialist Consumer Product II', *Cinemantics*, 3, 5.

_____ (1975) 'Theory and Definition of Structural/Materialist Film', *Studio International*, Nov./Dec., 190, 978, 189–96.

_____ (1999) 'Flashbacks: Peter Gidal', *Filmwaves*, 7, Spring, 16–20.

Gill, Alan (1962) 'The Longest Little Show on Earth', *Amateur Cine World*, 27, 20, May,

776–7.

Goaman, Karen (1989) 'Marx, Christ and Satan United in Struggle: Stewart Home Interviewed by Karen Goaman', *Variant*, 7, 19–23.

Grieveson, Lee (2001) 'A Kind of Recreative School for the Whole Family': Making Cinema Respectable, 1907–09', *Screen*, 42, 1, 64–76.

Harvey, Sylvia (2001) 'Smoke Signals: The 1970s: Or Whatever Happened To Independent Film?', *Vertigo*, 2, 1, 39.

Hogenkamp, Bert (1976) 'Film and the Workers' Movement in Britain 1929–39', *Sight and Sound*, 45, 2, Spring, 68–76.

Hopkins, John (1990) 'That Was the 1980s That Was', *Independent Media*, 100, June, 6–7.

Ilson, Philip (1999) 'The Halloween: Five Years On!', *Filmwaves*, 8, Summer, 12–14.

Jefferson, Tony (1978) 'Cultural Responses of the Teds', *Cultural Studies*, 7, 8, 81–6.

Keighron, Peter (1990) 'Questions of Independence', *Independent Media*, 99, May, 14–15.

Kinokaze (1993–97) *Report the Underground*, 1–4.

Knight, Derrick (1952) 'We Found A New Idea', *Amateur Cine World*, 15, 10, February, 991–4, 1018.

Le Grice, Malcolm (1978 [1969]) '*Room (Double Take)*', in the *LFMC Catalogue*, 21.

_____ (1979) 'The History We Need', in the catalogue for *Film As Film: Formal Experiment in Film 1910–1975*. London: Arts Council of Great Britain, 113.

_____ (1993 [1986]) 'A Reflection on the History of the London Filmmakers' Co-op', in the *LFMC Catalogue*, London, 161–2.

_____ 2001 'Improvising Time and Image', *Filmwaves*, 14, Winter/Spring, 14–19.

Mazière, Michael (1999) 'Michael Mazière', *Filmwaves*, 9, Autumn, 18–22.

McIntyre, Steve (1996) 'The Very Model of a Modern Funding Agency', *Vertigo*, 1, 5, 50–1.

Mekas, Jonas (1966) 'Open Letter To Film-Makers of the World', *Cinim*, 1, 5–8.

Mitchell, Carla (1998) 'How Not To Disappear From That Choice: Four Corners 1972–1985', *Filmwaves*, 4, Spring, 10–13.

Monk, Catherine (1997) 'The Volcano Is Erupting Again', *Filmwaves*, 2, November, 7–9.

Moran, Joe (1998) 'Cultural Studies and Academic Stardom', *International Cultural Studies*, 1, 1, 67–82.

Mulvey, Laura (1975) 'Visual Pleasure and Narrative Cinema', *Screen*, 3, 6–18.

Mulvey, Laura and Peter Wollen (1976) 'Written Discussion', *Afterimage*, 6, Summer, 30–40.

O'Hagan, Sean (1993) 'Against the Tide', *Guardian*, 9 August, 7.

Parsons, David (1997) 'Picture Planes', *Filmwaves*, 2, November, 10–11.

Pawson, Mark (1989) 'Mail Art: the Eternal Network', *Variant*, 7.

Penley, Constance (1977) 'The Avant-Garde and its Imaginary', *Camera Obscura*, 2, Fall, 3–33.

Penley, Constance and Janet Bergstrom (1978) 'The Avant-Garde: Histories and Theories', *Screen*, 19, 113–27.

Phythian, D. M.(1958) 'Round-the-World Record', *Amateur Movie-Maker*, 4 January 1958, 33–4.

Postlethwaite, H. A. (1956) 'What's the Date?', *Amateur Cine World*, 20, 1, May, 43.

Prothero, David (2000) 'Interview with Derek Hill', *Journal of Popular British Cinema*, 21, 133–4.

Raban, William (1998a) 'Expanded Practice in Television, Defending the Right to Difference', *Vertigo*, 1, 8, 42–4.

_____ (1998b) 'Lifting Traces', *Filmwaves*, 4, Spring, 14–16.

Szczelkun, Stefan (1999), 'Volcano !', *Variant*, 2, 7, 1.

Scott, Anthony (1969) 'The Longest Most Meaningless Movie in the World', *Cinema*, October, 32.

Seymour, Benedict (2002a) 'The Last Picture Show', *Mute Magazine*, 22, January.

_____ (2002b) Letters Page, *Mute Magazine*, 23, March.

Smith, Jack (1958) 'Flights of Fancy', *Amateur Cine World*, 22, 7, November, 671.

Smith, Karen and Tom Heslop (1990) 'Behaving Badly in Public', *Undercut*, 19, Autumn, 32–3.

Spartan, Molly (2000) 'No Stars, No Funding, No Taste: Molly Spartan Interviews the Exploding Cinema', *Filmwaves*, 11, Spring, 24–7.

Steadman Jones, Gareth (1974) 'Working Class Culture and Working Class Politics in London, 1870–1900: Notes on the Remaking of a Working Class', *Journal of Social History*, 7, Summer, 460–508.

Taylor, Mel (1999a) 'To Whom it May Concern. Please Note: Cinenova', *Filmwaves*, 8, Summer, 16–19.

_____ (1999b) 'Thinking About Experimental Film and Video: Interview with A. L. Rees', *Filmwaves*, 8, Summer, 20–22.

Thew, Anna (2001) 'Cultural Imperialism or Vibrant Moving Image?', *Vertigo*, 2, 1, 28–9.

Wayne, Mike (2002) 'A Cultural Film Policy: Who Needs It?', *Filmwaves*, 18, Spring, 44–7.

Wallace, Paul (2003 [1986]) 'Media Production in Higher Education: the Problem of Theory and Practice', in Nina Danino and Michael Mazière (eds) *The Undercut Reader: Critical Writings on Artists' Film and Video*. London: Wallflower Press, 55–62.

Walsh, Jez (1989) '20 Questions, or: Leaving the Twentieth Century (again, at last)', *Variant*, 7, 46–9.

Webber, Mark (2002) 'Chronology of Events and Developments 1966–76', in *Shoot, Shoot, Shoot: The First Decade of the London Film-makers' Co-operative and British Avant-Garde Film 1966–76*. London: Tate Modern, 6–7.

Wigens, Tony (1968) 'Not To Be Shown in Public', *8mm Magazine*, 7, 7, 50–1.

Willemen, Paul (1984) 'An Avant-Garde for the 1980s', *Framework*, 24, 53–74.

Wollen, Peter (1975) 'The Two Avant-Gardes', *Studio International*, Nov./Dec., 190, 978, 171–5.

Wood, Leslie (1951) 'Wanted: Cine Suffragettes', *Amateur Cine World*, 14, 10, February, 993–7.

Wynn Jones, Stuart (1957) 'Cartooning Without A Camera', *Amateur Cine World*, 21, 8, December, 782–5, 826.

_____ (1958) 'Summer Summary', *Amateur Cine World*, 22, 1, June, 53–7.

INDEX